Introduction to Programming:
A BASIC Approach

Introduction to Programming: A BASIC Approach

VAN COURT HARE, JR.
University of Massachusetts

HARCOURT BRACE JOVANOVICH, INC.
New York / Chicago / San Francisco / Atlanta

ISBN: 0-15-543600-7

Library of Congress Catalog Card Number: 73-115864
Printed in the United States of America

Cover design based on frames from a film by John Whitney, produced under a research grant from IBM.

Preface

This book is an introduction to the use of electronic computers. It describes the current computer scene and speculates on future trends. Moreover, it encourages the reader to move beyond what he has learned about elementary computer use and to undertake more advanced applications.

The book is divided into three parts. Chapters 1 through 5 cover the history and economics of computer development, the parts of a computer system, and the way in which computers handle data. These chapters also present some informative detail about computer input/output devices and memory units as they affect the user. Chapters 6 through 14 provide an introduction to computer programming by means of BASIC, a simple computer language developed at Dartmouth College and consisting of only a few rules of grammar and a vocabulary of fewer than twenty words. Extensions of BASIC and selected advanced illustrations complete this part. Chapters 15 through 18 demonstrate how BASIC and the programming principles that have been discussed can be used in handling the more difficult, but more powerful, FORTRAN IV language. Here the BASIC examples of Chapter 13 are translated into FORTRAN IV, and the differences between the two forms of computer instruction are explained. Chapters 17 and 18 assume that the reader has access to a FORTRAN IV manufacturer's manual appropriate to the computer being used. Appendix A compares the BASIC and FORTRAN languages by command and topics. Appendixes B, C, and D offer notes on operating detail. The Glossary summarizes and defines terms used in the text and the computer literature.

Since the best way to learn about a computer is to use one, the book urges the reader to use the machine as soon as possible. The illustrative device used is the familiar typewriter keyboard, in particular the Model 33 "Teletype" of the Teletype Corporation and its electric typewriter cousins. A Teletype connected to a computer by a telephone line in what is known as a "time-sharing" service permits the immediate confirmation of results and the diagnosis of difficulties. This immediacy, together with the student's familiarity with the keyboard, enable the student to progress rapidly in his use of the computer.

The contents of the book have been tested with more than 5,000 students from high school to graduate school as well as in industrial courses. In response to that testing, special attention is given to the difficulty beginning students often have in moving from a problem statement to the formalization required to solve the problem. A six-step method for making this transition is proposed and is illustrated repeatedly. A wide range of subjects are used as examples, and the examples are reinforced by end-of-chapter questions and problems.

The author is indebted to Courtney Brown, former Dean, Graduate School of Business, Columbia University, for his financial support of mass computer instruction using remote terminals. In this effort a number of vendors of time-sharing services provided advice and counsel as well as services: General Electric, Call-A-Computer, Rapidata, Inc., IBM, and Control Data Corporation's CEIR, Inc. Wendell Smith, Dean, School of Business Administration, and George Simmons, Head, Department of Management, University of Massachusetts at Amherst provided the time required to prepare the manuscript. The Research Computing Center of the latter institution, under Conrad Wogrin's direction, provided continuing time-sharing facilities to the author and to students using these materials. Other organizations, as indicated in the book, have aided through the provision of illustrative materials. And, finally, the author's students, both academic and industrial, have provided or suggested many of the examples shown here. To Alan Parker, John Stewart, Dick Munklewitz, and John Carrara, who prepared and checked many of the programs herein, special thanks are due.

Van Court Hare, Jr.

Contents

Introduction

Unlike James Watt's steam engine, the modern electronic computer does not belch fumes, nor was it designed for physical labor. The steam engine harnessed energy for the alleviation of physical drudgery. The other energy machines of the Industrial Revolution accomplished similar ends, and, of course, had an effect upon society and our everyday lives. Although the computer is a completely deterministic physical device which uses energy in small amounts to do its work, its output is not primarily physical. The computer processes symbols and produces symbolic results. The computer, in short, is an information machine and its primary purpose is the alleviation of mental drudgery.

The same computer can take on many different jobs because it *is* a symbolic machine: its physical parts need not be rewired each time a new task confronts it. The logical construction of the user's instructions makes the machine specific for a given job. And, since symbols are easy to change, so are the jobs themselves.

You may think of a computing system as having two parts: the physical apparatus which you see when you walk into a computing center, and the sets of instructions which the machine processes, which are not so visually evident. The first part is called hardware, the second, software.

Hardware

The physical components of the computing system consist of (1) an arithmetic and control unit, to perform the arithmetic, data manipulation, and direction of work; (2) one or more memory devices to store the results of intermediate computations, data to be used, and instructions to be processed; (3) an input unit to receive user data and instructions, or programs; and (4) an output unit to display results. The latter two functions are often combined into one device, such as a Teletype machine (a kind of electric typewriter), or other forms of user-oriented units. In many cases, the user need only concentrate upon his problems as they may be communicated to his input/output device without regard to the details of the hardware he will use, or to the demands of other users, who may be employing the same equipment.

The remote terminal

In addition to combining input and output functions in one unit, modern practice permits the user input/output unit to be located at some distance from the main computing machine. In such applications the user remote terminal is usually connected to the computer by a standard telephone line, so the computer may be dialed, just as you would call your friend. Thereafter, when you type on your keyboard, you are in direct communication with the computer and may have a two-way "conversation" with it, following the rules discussed in the text.

When users are supplied with remote terminals, many individuals may have the services of a computer on demand at low cost. By time sharing the facilities, even though a number of users are simultaneously requesting results, each user appears to be getting individual service. This is made possible by the computer's high speeds in comparison to the needs of the individual. This same speed also permits the computer to interact or converse with the user on an almost instantaneous, or real-time, basis, so that it can aid the user in the preparation and the perfection of instructions for the machine. As you will shortly see, the computer will literally talk back to you, help you find mistakes in the way you use its service, and often turn out to be an electronic friend. It is not unusual to find students who first encounter the conversational computer remark, "Look, now he's answering back!"

The computer memory

From your viewpoint, the computer's memory devices will seem the most important of the machine's components. (Once you get to know the use of the input/output device, you will probably forget about the details.) You will store your data, your programs for the machine to execute, and your files for later recall in the memory. You will find that the computer vendor or computer center has also stored other information—data and instructions for many different jobs—that you may call upon at will. And, finally, encyclopedias and dictionaries are available which will permit you to talk to the computer in a familiar language with the computer translating your instructions into something that it can understand.

This vast storehouse of information differs from the computer's hardware in that it is readily altered by you or by experts at your computing center. It is often possible to use hardware or software to accomplish the same end, a fact which will be evident from the examples that follow.

You will encounter two fundamental types of computer memory: fast and slow. The time-sharing user will use the slow memory for long-term storage of data and programs, the fast for creation of new jobs and the execution of either old or new jobs. In most current installations, the fast memory is called "core" and the slow memory "disk." The terms "fast" and "slow" as used above are really computer terms; the user will not distinguish any time difference in their use because both work thousands or millions of times faster than human response capability. The terms are helpful in later descriptions of some forms of information processing, and therefore are mentioned here. A better distinction, or pair of synonyms, might be "working memory" and "file memory" as we shall see.

Software

You may not, of course, usually talk to a computer directly in its own language, since that language will be totally foreign to you. (The computer does its work entirely with numbers—in fact with numbers or codes made up entirely of 0's and 1's. To handle such detail is not something humans like to do, or can do well.) Thus, by special tricks of the trade, the computer's manufacturer usually causes the machine to provide an automatic conversion between symbols you can understand, such as those on your keyboard, and those the computer needs for its work. Further, by appropriate translation procedures, described in Chapter 6 and summarized below, the computer may be made to recognize groups of characters, like READ, WRITE, etc., or the meaning of special symbols, such as "+" or "−" so you can put together meaningful sentences if you observe the grammar necessary for a given "user" language.

There are, in fact, many "user" languages available:

If you are a banker, you can have a language appropriate for financial transactions and banking needs. If you are an engineer, you can have a specialized engineering language. The range of possibilities is endless, since the translation from a specific vocabulary to that of the computer is handled by the machine itself using its stored reserves of terms, words, and actions. The process of going from your language to the machine's language is called *compilation*, and the *software* which performs this—literally a combination of dictionaries and encyclopedias committed to the computer's memory—is supplied by the vendor or computing center. The automated translating package is your *compiler.*

We are concerned here, however, with languages which may be generally applied, not with those in specialized fields. In particular we first study BASIC, the language originally developed at Dartmouth College for undergraduate use in the mid-1960's. Then we extend the general programming and language rules learned from BASIC to a more difficult, but more powerful language, FORTRAN.

FORTRAN introduces a number of additional rules so you can control data formats yourself, easily place library programs into your own, and process data more flexible on alternate computer devices.

A technical note

The first four chapters of this edition present background material. A brief history of computer development, some economics, and a summary description of computer hardware parts and how they work usually provide a deeper understanding of programming rules and processing methods. The introductory material also builds the vocabulary helpful in your understanding of computer literature. An extensive glossary has been provided for reference to unfamiliar terms which arise in the text, although they will usually be defined as they first appear.

One point, further explained in Chapter 1, should be noted here: We are concerned hereafter with general purpose *digital* computers as opposed to *analog* machines, which are usually more specialized and limited in their use. The term analog implies a method of producing numbers, or of computation, by means of a measurement process, rather than by counting. To illustrate, you could add 2 + 2 using a 12-inch ruler by first laying out a line two inches long, then another adjacent two-inch segment, and finally measuring the total length along the straight line drawn. The result would be *approximately* four, depending upon your drafting accuracy, the quality of your ruler, and your visual acuity. Compare this analog computation to the same operation performed with poker chips. To add 2 + 2 using the chips, make two piles of two, then combine or add the stacks together, then count the result. The count will be four *precisely*. Our digital computers work in the latter manner, although in many applications conversions between one form of processing and the other may be desirable, or necessary.

The information revolution

The age of the computer has often been called the Information Revolution. It is a good bit more than that. If you can appreciate the steam engine and its effect upon industry and society, and if you can appreciate the revolution that is now occurring in information handling as a consequence of the electronic computer, you may well also ponder the future combinations of the two. As computers extend human problem-solving into the areas of management, organization, and policy formulation and control—with the obvious links to the energy machines—the outlook is startling. For those who understand this text it will be less so.

ONE

From loom to electron

Charles Babbage, a contemporary of Darwin, gave us the essential logical designs for today's modern electronic computers. He also developed many of the approaches to business analysis now called operations research, or management science.

While specializing in mathematics and logic at Cambridge, Babbage founded a student group known as the Analytical Society, and vowed as his life work first to analyze, then to cure the "stupidities" of his time—a phrase typical of his temperament. Infuriated with the persistent errors found in mathematical tables, he set out to design an "Analytical Engine" to mechanize their production and improve their reliability. In this effort, he became greatly impressed with the designs used by Frenchman Joseph Jacquard, who in 1801 perfected a loom controlled by punched cardboard cards.[1] The desired design for one line of the woven fabric was punched into one card. Mechanical fingers in the loom's control mechanism, actuated by the presence or absence and location of holes in the card, trans-

[1] Much of the material in this chapter has been adapted from Jeremy Bernstein, *The Analytical Engine* (New York: Vintage Books, 1966) and Philip and Emily Morrison, eds., *Charles Babbage and His Calculating Engines* (New York: Dover, 1961). The latter work contains selected reprints of Babbage's works, together with a number of his drawings. The reader may also enjoy B. V. Bowden, *Faster Than Thought* (London: Sir Isaac Pitman & Sons, 1953), which contains many historical essays and Babbage anecdotes. The 1968 edition of the *Encyclopaedia Britannica* includes many articles on Computing and Information Handling as well as Weaving. The original Jacquard loom, which had been displayed at the Industrial Exhibition at Paris in 1801, was declared public property in 1806, and Jacquard was given a pension and a royalty on each machine sold. So successful was the invention that by 1811 there were 11,000 Jacquard looms in France alone.

ferred the design to the cloth by raising selected threads in the background, or warp, before the loom's shuttle laid down the fill, or weft (see Figure 1.1). By varying the number and location of the holes in the Jacquard card, a great variety of weft and warp interweavings could be achieved. The process was entirely mechanical, eliminating the "pullboys" who with former looms had to adjust the thread interweaving manually.

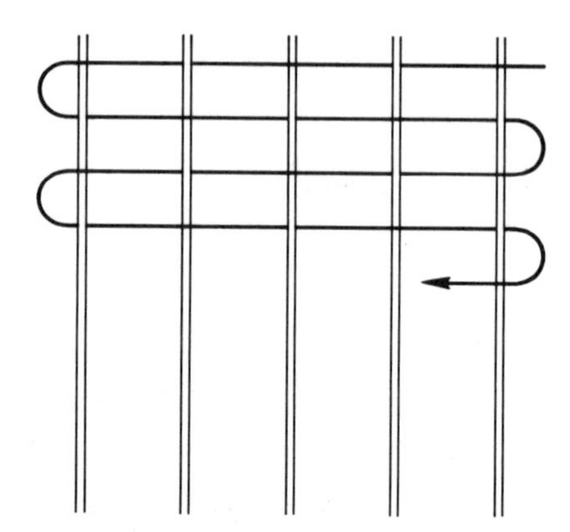

1.1. The warp and weft of a fabric. The warp shown as double lines forms the base for weaving. The weft, shown as a single line, is supplied by a horizontal movement of the shuttle and provides the structure and pattern. Jacquard's invention permitted automatic raising and lowering of the warp threads in selected combinations so intricately patterned cloth could be produced.

By repeating the one-line control process, using a *sequence* of differently punched control cards, Jacquard's loom could generate intricate patterns in the cloth; flowers, birds, tapestries, even portraits, could be produced automatically. Moreover, if the cards from such a *program* were made into a *loop*, the design could be repeated automatically to weave yards and yards of perfect cloth without human intervention.

Babbage realized the power of this concept in computation. By stating the computing steps to be performed in advance of computation and storing this sequence as a computing program with the data to be used, the machine operations could proceed unaided to a correct conclusion. Thus, he developed the concept of the *stored program*, the feature that separates computers from calculators, machines which require human intervention at each step of a problem's solution.[2]

---

[2] We have omitted discussion of the history of calculator development, which began before the time of Babbage. Both Pascal and Leibnitz, famous seventeenth-century mathematicians, had proposed and constructed working models of mechanical adding machines, multipliers, and the like, and many of their ideas were used by Babbage as well as later inventors. Since these mechanical developments are not directly related to today's computers, however, we need not go into their development.

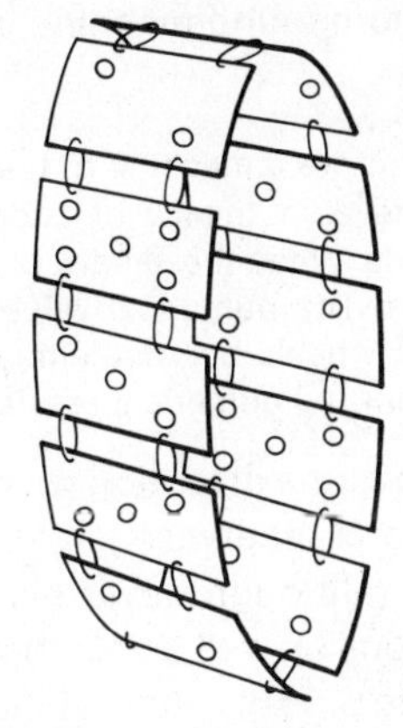

1.2. A loop of jacquard cards. This schematic diagram shows how a loop, or set, of Jacquard cards were connected to perform many repetitive operations. Babbage proposed the same idea, which he called making the machine "eat its own tail," for his Analytical Engine. Both conditional and unconditional looping are major components of modern computer programs.

That Babbage understood the import of his design is clear, for his own words in describing his proposed machine sound modern. First, Babbage describes the concept of Jacquard's loom and what it could do:

> It is well known that the Jacquard loom is capable of weaving any design which the imagination of man may conceive. It is also the constant practice for skilled artists to be employed by manufacturers in designing patterns. These patterns are then sent to a peculiar artist, who, by means of a certain machine, punches holes in a set of pasteboard cards in such a manner that when those cards are placed in a Jacquard loom, it will then weave upon its product the exact pattern designed by the artist.
>
> Now the manufacturer may use, for the warp and weft of his work, threads which are all of the same colour; let us suppose them to be unbleached or white threads. In this case the cloth will be woven all of one colour; but there will be a damask pattern upon it such as the artist designed.
>
> But the manufacturer might use the same cards, and put into the warp threads of any other colour. Every thread might even be of a different colour, or of a different shade of colour; but in all cases the *form* of the pattern will be precisely the same—the colours only will differ.[3]

Then Babbage goes on to describe the two kinds of information to be fed to his proposed computer: the *program* consisting of the steps to be performed (corresponding to the program for a Jacquard loom) and the *data* (corresponding to the manufacturer's selection of threads and colors in the warp and weft). The ability to control the machine by a program which is separate from the data to be employed, of course, is one essential fea-

[3] Morrison and Morrison, *op. cit.*, p. 54. One of Babbage's prized possessions was a portrait of Jacquard, woven in tapestry of many colors, an effort that demanded over 24,000 punched cards for its execution. Jacquard was a good promoter of his own work.

ture of a general purpose computing machine, as Babbage noted for machines of his own design:

> The Analytical Engine is therefore a machine of the most general nature. Whatever formula it is required to develop, the law of its development must be communicated to it by two sets of cards. When these have been placed, the engine is special for that particular formula. The numerical value of the constants must then be put on the columns of the wheels below them, and on setting the Engine in motion it will calculate and print the numerical results of that formula.[4]

A more poetic description of the invention was supplied by Augusta Ada, Lord Byron's daughter, who is otherwise known as Lady Lovelace. A lifelong friend of the inventor (although never his wife), Lady Lovelace understood Babbage's ambitions as well as his thoughts. "We may say most aptly," she wrote in a note to a description of the Babbage machine, "that the Analytical Engine *weaves algebraical patterns* just as the Jacquard loom weaves flowers and leaves."[5]

Thus, the history of early information-processing efforts is of interest not only for its colorful figures but also for the initial ideas about computer design and information handling that have persisted to this day. For this reason, we may study more of the events of the nineteenth century with benefit—such a study will help us to understand the mysteries of modern, high-speed computation and cause us to realize that today's success in information handling has been largely a triumph of materials and manufacturing technology. The important concepts are often those of yesteryear.

Babbage, for example, knew what a modern computing machine should do, and he in effect wrote its functional specifications. Yet he never succeeded in making a satisfactory model, largely because he worked with mechanical components which could not be made to the required precision (backlash in gears was a major problem) and also because of his irascible nature (his workers often quit in pique and removed his tools and drawings). Thus, we have only a legacy of ideas from the 1800s. Only when electrical components were substituted for mechanical ones did the modern computer become a feasible device. But that final success gets ahead of our story.

The Babbage machine

Babbage had in mind a machine consisting of four major parts:

1. An *input* device to receive the data and the program steps to be executed;

---

[4] *Ibid.*, p. 56.
[5] *Ibid.*, p. 252.

2. An *output* device to print the answers desired;
3. An *arithmetic and control* unit to perform the computations and direct the flow of work (Babbage called this unit the *mill*);
4. A *repository* within the machine to hold intermediate answers so that long computations could be performed (Babbage called this unit the *store* and we call it the computer *memory* device).[6]

As shown in Figure 1.3, modern computers, with a few elaborations, are similarly organized. Babbage also introduced a number of schemes for computing the solutions to problems. In this respect, he was greatly influenced by the "division of labor" of Adam Smith[7] and in particular by a large-scale effort made in France to produce 14-place logarithm tables by hand.

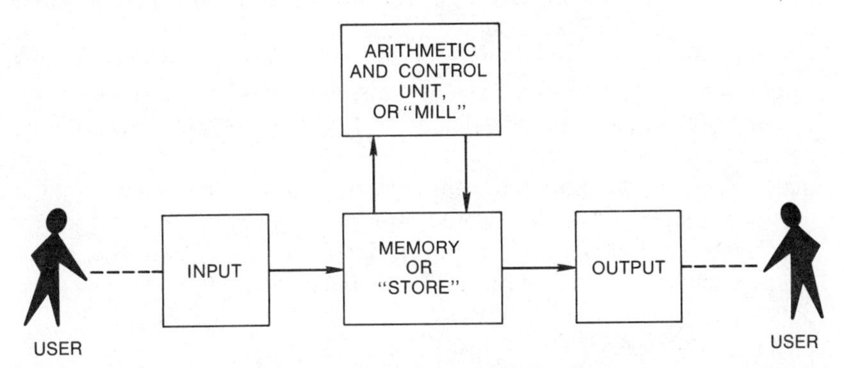

1.3. Major functional units of Babbage's analytical engine and modern computers. Users communicate with the machine via input and output devices. Computations and control are exercised by the "mill." And, the memory, or "store," holds data and program steps needed for operation, as well as intermediate answers for long computations. Note that the user is part of the overall system. For a variety of reasons, the weakest link in the system is often that shown as a dashed line: the interface between man and the machine.

Started in 1784 under the direction of G. F. Prony, director of the Ecole des Ponts et Chaussées, the logarithm project is notable not so much for its result, which would be trivial using modern computers, but rather for its organization. Prony, realizing that his proposed tabulation for all the

[6] Babbage's storage of intermediate information was by means of the position of mechanical wheels. In today's computers, the memory device is usually constructed of magnetic materials, which store information in the form of magnetized spots. The form of memory device used is often critical to the computer application, and several modern forms will be discussed in Chapter 4. We assume no further knowledge of memory devices in this chapter, except that they can be made to work at speeds nearly comparable to those of the arithmetic and control unit. *Read* and *write* speeds of modern memories can be as fast as a few millionths or a few billionths of a second, yet such memories can also be made to hold information in essentially permanent form for later reference.

[7] The eighteenth-century Scotch economist who proposed labor specialization for greater production efficiency.

natural numbers to 200,000 was a superhuman task for one individual, decided to organize a group effort. At the apex of Prony's hierarchy were outstanding mathematicians of the stature of Legendre, who selected the best formulas to be used for computation. Selected formulas were passed on to eight well-trained numerical analysts, who put them into numerical form, devised a procedure for computation, and produced check computations at wide intervals. Finally, the work was passed to a group of from 60 to 80 unskilled workers. It was their task to do no more than addition and subtraction, according to the rules specified, interpolating between the check results provided by the masters. "It seems that nine tenths of them literally knew no more than addition and subtraction, and these turned out to be the best computers."[8] The work was completed in two years and was thereafter used by other mathematical workers as a standard of comparison for accuracy.

In this scheme of computation, it was the 60 to 80 unskilled workers whom Babbage hoped to replace with his Analytical Engine in future tabulations. The expert mathematicians and skilled analysts would still be needed—as they are today—to formulate the problem to be solved and then reduce the solution to a step-by-step procedure that the computing machine could handle. (We would refer to the problem and procedure specialists as systems analysts and programmers.) So, Babbage left us not only the architecture of his hardware, but also the methods of its computational use.

Early data processing developments

Babbage was mostly interested in scientific computation. Others, however, directed their efforts toward data processing (e.g., order processing, inventory control, payroll computation).

In the 1870s a young U.S. Army officer, Lt. Henry Metcalfe, was assigned to the Frankford Arsenal to reorganize the cost system there.[9] The Civil War had left operations in a turmoil; the rapid increase in personnel levels, the proliferation of products, and the general scale of operations had outstripped suitable control procedures, and costs had risen as a consequence.

Metcalfe found that he could not trace the flow of a product through the arsenal, either for summarizing costs or for expediting. Many of the rec-

---

[8] Morrison and Morrison, *op. cit.*, p. xxvii. Babbage described this example in "On the Division of Mental Labor," in Chapter XIX of his *Economy of Manufactures and Machinery*, reprinted by the Morrisons, pp. 315–321. His *Economy* was the forerunner of today's studies in operations research and management science.

[9] The Army's famous Frankford Arsenal, located in what is now northeast Philadelphia, produced ordnance for Federal forces during the Civil War. In line with modern trends, it now serves as an electronic procurement and distribution center.

ords were kept only by department, in leatherbound ledgers. To trace a product's flow each of these ledgers had to be consulted in turn, and little if any control could be exercised in detail.

Again, cards came into the picture. Metcalfe was inspired by the librarian's practice of indexing books on 3 x 5 inch cards. He saw the "unit record" as the secret to manufacturing control, and began to convert the arsenal's system of record keeping from ledgers to decks of cards, which could be manipulated, sorted, arranged, and summarized at will.

In setting up his new system, Metcalfe expounded three principles of information system design:

1. The initiation and completion of each order, or process step, should be indicated by a unit record.
2. Control should be central, so that the records can be collected, compared, and analyzed for action.
3. The vocabulary, nomenclature, or coding scheme for products, tools, departments, and other statistical categories must be standardized so that comparisons and checks can be made.[10]

Although the computing machine of today mechanizes the manipulation and comparison of records as proposed by Metcalfe, the segmented, well-coded, well-defined record and the system design required to assure a smooth flow of this data to the computing machine are human feats.

Meanwhile at the U.S. Census Bureau, the volume of statistical tabulation required for taking the census every ten years had, with manual methods, reached staggering proportions.

The census of 1880 had taken seven years to tabulate, and estimates for that of 1890 ran to over twelve years: the results of the 1890 census would not be available until after the 1900 census had been taken! Faced with this prospect, the Census Bureau decided to automate. Professor Herman Hollerith was retained as a consultant to devise mechanical methods of tabulation and summary. This inventive statistician from upstate New York set to work at once. Like his predecessors, he turned to cards punched with coded holes similar to those of Babbage and Jacquard.[11] The modern key punch machine, card sorter, tabulating machine, and other unit-record equipment are all derivatives of his early work. One measure of Hollerith's success was that the census tabulation of 1890 was completed in two years instead of 12, and an almost immediate acceptance of the new equipment ensued. By 1910 commercial organizations, such as public utilities, were using punched cards and the new machines for accounting purposes.

---

[10] Henry Metcalfe, *The Cost of Manufactures and the Administration of Work Shops Public and Private* (New York: John Wiley & Sons, 1885).

[11] Hollerith was said to have arrived at his punched card idea while watching a streetcar conductor punch tickets. In any case, the idea provided a natural extension to Metcalfe's work.

The outgrowth of the Hollerith machines, which combined mechanical and rudimentary electrical components, have been the Electric Accounting Machines (EAM equipment), which are still used for business applications as well as for the preparation of data input for modern electronic computers. It is beyond the scope of our history to trace the detail of punched card development (which is well documented elsewhere[12]), but it is interesting to note that Hollerith's inventions later became the backbone of the tabulating services offered by the International Business Machines Corporation (IBM) and that the work of Hollerith's associate James Powers led to a competitive, but purely mechanical, group of tabulating machines marketed by the Remington Rand Corporation. These firms, of course, are well known today in the field of electronic computer manufacture.

Although no other major advances occurred in the mechanization of computation for several decades, the first decades of the twentieth century were devoted to a series of improvements in the mechanics of tabulation, the development of electromechanical devices for the reproduction and transmisssion of information (e.g., the electric typewriter, teletyper, printing tabulator), and, most important, to the emergence of the new field of electronics and electrical communication.

By the mid 1930's the vacuum tube had been perfected, the components necessary for telephone switching and distant communication had been developed, and a wide range of mechanical calculators were in operation.

The beginning of the modern era

Although historians generally agree that the era of modern computation began about 1925 at the Massachusetts Institute of Technology when Dr. Vannevar Bush and his associates began work on a large-scale mechanical computer of the analog type—a machine which was perfected in 1935 and served well for wartime computation of artillery firing tables—the first digital machine that worked was developed a few years later.

In 1937, at Harvard, Howard H. Aiken needed to make numerous repetitive computations in order to solve problems that involved what are known as nonlinear ordinary differential equations. Since the solution of these equations by hand was tedious and time-consuming, Aiken began to develop a number of special-purpose machines to solve his problems. In his initial designs, which were to use electromechanical telephone components, he noted a certain similarity of architecture.

---

[12] R. S. Casey *et al., Punched Cards: Their Applications to Science and Industry*, 2d ed. (New York: Reinhold Publishing Corp., 1958), (all forms of punched cards illustrated with applications), and Leon E. Truesdell, *The Development of Punched Card Tabulation in the Bureau of the Census 1890–1940* (Washington, D.C.; Department of Commerce, Bureau of the Census, U.S. Government Printing Office, 1965).

All the special purpose machines seemed to require the same functional parts. Thus Aiken proposed to make a general purpose computer which could perform the operations of all his special purpose units. In a remarkable historical document, later retrieved by his secretary from a musty file and published for the record,[13] Aiken in 1937 sought financial support from International Business Machines for his brainchild. He received the support and had a mass of telephone relays, rotating mechanical wheels, and associated tabulating equipment working by 1943. Data input was provided at first by punched paper tape, later by punched cards. The machine was called the Automatic Sequence Controlled Calculator, Mark I. From 1943 to 1948 Mark I was pressed into military service, producing mathematical tables day and night.

A few years after Aiken began work on his general purpose machine, a colleague confronted him with the Babbage papers, which appeared to Aiken to be the work of a modern associate. "If Babbage had lived seventy-five years later," Aiken remarked, "I would have been out of a job."[14] It was surprising how many of Babbage's principles had been incorporated into the new machine—and even more startling that they continued to be applied more widely in the machines to come.

Because of its partially mechanical construction the Aiken machine was by modern standards relatively slow: the time required to open or close one of its relays was a few hundredths of a second. The machine was also subject to the usual mechanical breakdowns associated with moving parts. It was a decimal machine, that is, it worked with numbers to the base 10, a design choice later found to be undesirable for reliability and speed (see Chapter 2). Nevertheless, the Mark I was heralded as a prime success in making a true Analytical Engine work, and for that reason Howard Aiken is often called the grandfather of today's computer industry.

The first electronic computer

It was not long after Aiken's success, however, that the first electronic machine, composed of radio vacuum tubes rather than telephone relays, was made to work.

Motivated by a desperate wartime need for faster computation to pro-

---

[13] Howard H. Aiken, "Proposed Automatic Calculating Machine," *IEEE Spectrum*, August, 1964, pp. 62–69. The original document was dated November 4, 1937, by an unknown recipient, and was discovered in Professor Aiken's files in early 1964. See also Howard H. Aiken and G. M. Hopper, "The Automatic Sequence Controlled Calculator," *Electrical Engineering*, August-September, 1946, pp. 384–391; October, 1946, pp. 449–454; November, 1946, pp. 522–528. A comprehensive survey of computing machine development to 1962 may be found in R. Serrell *et al.*, "The Evolution of Computing Machines and Systems," *Proc. IRE*, May, 1962, pp. 1040–1058. The latter article contains photographs of most of the machines described, their technical specifications, and a 142-item historical bibliography.

[14] Bernstein, *op. cit.*, p. 52.

duce artillery firing tables, the Moore School of the University of Pennsylvania and the Army's Aberdeen Proving Ground cooperated to support the ideas of Professors J. Presper Eckert and John Mauchly in the construction of a large-scale electronic machine. The project, begun in 1943, produced a working machine called the ENIAC (Electronic Numerical Integrator and Calculator) by 1946. It was at the time the most complex electronic device in the world with over 18,000 vacuum tubes and operated 180 times faster than the Mark I. The ENIAC was a decimal machine, and the frequency of its breakdowns would be by today's standards intolerable. Yet when ENIAC was computing, it was the most powerful device of its kind available and converted a desperate impasse in military computation to a tolerable state.

In 1944 the famous Princeton mathematician John von Neumann, in the company of Lt. Herman H. Goldstein, the Army's liaison with the Moore School, improved ENIAC designs with Eckert and Mauchly. There were a number of intermediate results of the team effort, including the construction of several improved machines. (Similar work was going on in England as well as at the Bell Labs in the United States.) However, the main improvements that resulted were (1) the conversion from decimal to binary computation,[15] and (2) the elimination of the plug-board program in favor of storage of program steps within the main memory of the computer.[16] Both steps had a profound effect upon computer reliability and speed as well as its generality of use, and since ENIAC all electronic computers have been constructed to use some form of binary manipulation (as illustrated in Chapter 2) and some degree of internally stored programming (further detailed in Chapter 6).

The commercial result of this effort was UNIVAC I (Universal Automatic Computer), designed by Eckert and Mauchly and produced in 1951 for data processing applications. The first of the UNIVACs went to the Census Bureau—for statistical processing of the mass data Herman Hollerith had first encountered!

Ironically, IBM turned down the Eckert and Mauchly patents and the

---

[15] Binary computation is to the base 2 and is not familiar to the average reader. Fundamentally this method counts using only "0" and "1," thus greatly simplifying the computing mechanism.

[16] The change was to place the stored program, not on an external electromechanical device which could only be sequenced slowly and changed with difficulty, but in the main memory of the machine as a sequence of stored symbols. This change permitted the program to be sequenced at approximately the same speeds as the arithmetic computations were performed, so that the machine was no longer program-limited in its execution speeds. Further, since a program's symbols can easily be changed and manipulated, the variety of jobs that could be processed in a given time was greatly increased. In fact, internally stored instructions can be made to change themselves! The internally stored program, of course, was a modern extension of the original Babbage idea, but its actual implementation in working electronic hardware was a major conceptual and engineering achievement.

UNIVAC line became the property of Remington Rand.[17] Regrettably, John von Neumann's premature death cut short his contribution to the computer field (as well to mathematics). Dr. Mauchly returned to private life as did Dr. Eckert and Dr. Aiken in his later years. Thus, most of the men who developed modern computers lived to see their success, or are still living—a remarkable example of the rapidity with which modern technology advances.

The commercial parade

The 1950s brought commercial production of electronic computers. Remington Rand was producing improved UNIVACs, although at a modest rate. (Only 20 computers of all types including experimental units were built between 1946 and 1951.) And, based on its start with the Mark I, IBM was organizing to produce a commercially marketable machine.

In the mid-50s, IBM took charge of the market. The firm held dominating leadership in the tabulating machine field and adroitly exploited this natural entry into the electronic computer field. A historical error also helped Thomas Watson, Jr., IBM's president, recently recalled that "when IBM announced its first computer, some people estimated there would be no more than 50 likely customers."[18] That this initial estimate was wide of the mark is evidenced by the 2,000 machines that were sold in the mid-50s. An economist or accountant might gather that IBM's error was eventually of great financial advantage: it appears that the company maintained the short production-run prices—even when run lengths tripled and more than quadrupled. The extra dollar margin so produced made computer production profitable for IBM at the outset (not so in the early years for IBM's competitors), and no computer manufacturer has yet approached IBM's dominance of the field. IBM now has 70 to 80% of the market in a field which is growing at a compound rate of 15 to 25% annually on an international basis and which, it is estimated by *Fortune*, will reach $30 billion annually by 1972.[19]

IBM's Model 650 computer made commercial use of the electronic machines feasible, and it became the workhorse of the business as well as

---

[17] See "Where IBM Looks for New Growth," *Business Week*, June 15, 1968, pp. 88–91. In a later management error, IBM also turned down the Xerox patents as well as the original patents on the core memory which is now used in most machines (see Chapter 4). However, management mistakes are sometimes beneficial, as the subsequent history of IBM indicates. Its erroneous marketing estimates for its Model 650 were a blessing in disguise.

[18] *Ibid.*, p. 88.

[19] Gilbert Burck, "The Computer Industry's Great Expectations," *Fortune*, August, 1968, pp. 93–146 (see chart, p. 97). Competing firms in order of market share are IBM, Sperry Rand (formerly Remington Rand), Honeywell, Control Data, General Electric, RCA, Burroughs, NCR, Scientific Data Systems, and Digital Equipment Corporation.

the scientific world (in partnership with its larger cousins, as indicated in Table 1.1).

Many observers have wondered why Remington Rand, with its initial lead in the manufacture of large-scale machines, lost to its competitor. Computer experts generally agree that the early UNIVACs and their successors were generally electronically superior to the machines initially offered by IBM. But superior electronics is not necessarily the secret in making a computer installation work in practice—as even present users often discover. An essential complement is programming support, reliable service, and competent supplier organization. Many observers allege that Remington Rand's failure was due to the lack of these latter abilities, which were critical for the general user introducing a costly innovation. The management reorganizations that occurred at Remington Rand during its early computer marketing experiences are testimony to this fact, and only recently has the firm overcome its preliminary difficulties. UNIVAC models are now in worldwide use, particularly in the military services, and so are those of the smaller-volume suppliers. Control Data Corporation (CDC), for example, an offshoot of Remington Rand's early operations, is now a major challenger to IBM in the specialty of very large-scale machines.

The transistor

The true age of the computer in business and industry, however, began with the 1948 development of the transistor, that small semiconductor device which is a component of the pocket radio, as well as the late 1950s generation of electronic computers.

The transistor, which in the computer acts as a small switching device, has many virtues not found in the vacuum tubes used in the UNIVACs and the IBM 650s of the early 1950s. The transistor, unlike the vacuum tube, does not depend upon a heated filament and so does not require an elaborately air-conditioned environment. Moreover, the transistor is many times smaller than the vacuum tube and is constructed as a solid mass. Thus, it is more reliable, not as subject to vibrational stress, and can be compactly wired into complex circuits. Even more important to the computer designer is the fact that the transistor is faster as a switching device than the vacuum tube it replaced. So, by the late 1950s and early 1960s the transistor had replaced the vacuum tube not only in small radios but also in the computer.

By far the largest sales of a transistorized computer were those made of the IBM Model 1401. Well over 10,000 of these units and their family were installed within less than a decade, and the increased reliability, lowered cost per computation, and decreased physical size made commercial use of data processing a widespread phenomenon.

TABLE 1.1

A Picture of Historical Trends

		First Generation		Second Generation		Third Generation	Fourth Generation
	MARK I	ENIAC	IBM MODELS	IBM MODELS		IBM MODELS	FUTURE DESIGNS
1.	(Harvard–IBM)	(Univ. of Penna. –UNIVAC)	650 707 704 709 705	1620 1401 1410	7080 7040 7044	System 360	(To be announced)
2.	Relay	Vacuum Tube		Transistor		Hybrid	Monolithic Chip
3.	Hundredths of a second	Milliseconds (Thousandths)		Microseconds (Millionths)		Several Nanoseconds (Billionths)	1 Nanosecond
4.	1940–1946	1945–1950	1952–1957	1959–1963		1965–1966	1972
5.	(Installed Systems) 3	25	2,000	10,000		40,000	70,000
6.	$450/100 *K* (By Hand)	$25/100 *K*	$2.50/100 *K*	$0.25/100 *K*		2.5¢/100 *K*	0.9–0.7¢/100 *K*

Although the figures shown in this table are approximate, they do provide general guides to the development of computer technology and application. In row (1), reading to the right, we have typical computers. Row (2) shows the basic components used in their manufacture. Row (3) roughly estimates the time required to perform an elemental switching operation. Row (4) gives approximate dates of these developments. Row (5) shows estimates of the number of individual computer installations in the United States. Finally, Row (6) gives rough estimates of the cost per 100,000 computations, using the cost by hand (on a desk-top mechanical calculator as a base). Such figures vary widely with the problem computed, but again show the trend. In row (6) the letter *K* stands for 1,000, a usual abbreviation in computer work. The figures in row (6) are also the most striking statistics in the table: They show the trend to currently minute costs per computation. Relatively speaking, human costs now dominate the computing scene.

In this table and in general literature the term *generation* is used to denote major historical changes in electronic technology.

1. First generation machines were made with vacuum tubes;
2. Second generation machines were made with individual transistors, usually wired on printed circuit boards in modular construction;
3. Third generation machines are made of clusters of transistors, either mechanically affixed to small ceramic chips or photochemically deposited on small chips of rare materials. The latter are called integrated circuits.
4. Fourth generation machines, in addition to the employment of more advanced circuit and system design principles, are usually made of large-scale integrated circuits (LSI), in which 40 to 400 transistors are photochemically deposited on one chip of rare material. The LSI approach speeds up the machine, increases reliability, and under extended mass production methods will simultaneously decrease the cost per computation as well as the absolute cost of a given computing installation.

Enter the microcircuit

By the mid-1960s, acceptance of electronic computation in business, industry, and science had been assured not only for exotic applications—such as those of the military—but also for the everyday order processing, inventory control, and accounting operations that constitute most business procedures.

In the laboratory, new developments were still in the making.[20] It seemed possible that if transistors could be made individually of small globs of rare materials such as germanium it might also be possible to construct groups of transistors or their equivalent by a similar process and to link them not with hand-wired or even machine-wired connections, but with optically printed threads of silver, gold, or another good conductor. Such a marriage of the graphic arts with electronic and chemical technology produced another improvement in computer technology.

By the mid-1960s computer designers disagreed about the approaches to follow in furthering the miniaturization of computer components in order to achieve further increases in machine reliability and speed. One approach was to assemble the existing transistors without their usual metal casings by applying them to a small chip of ceramic on which the appropriate wiring had been etched or printed photographically. The second approach, which might lead to even greater reductions in circuit size and thus to greater computer speeds, was to form the transistors chemically (by means of a combined graphic arts and vacuum-depositing process) into one self-contained chip, known as a monolithic circuit.

At this stage of development, the fundamental switching speeds of the transistor (which determine to a large extent the computational speed of the modern electronic computer) had been reduced to a few millionths of a second. The proposed developments would reduce that time to a few billionths of a second, thereby improving performance. Such electronic switching speeds present certain interesting design problems because it does no good to increase the speed of the components if the time required to send an electronic impulse from one place to another is large (in a billionth of a second, light travels less than one foot). Thus packing the computer's components as tightly as possible should be a concomitant requirement of increasing speeds of the components themselves. For this reason, the optical-chemical-monolithic approach to circuit construction has a number of technical advantages over the hybrid approach of mechanically attaching transistors to a previously etched chip, however small.

---

[20] Philip Siekman, "In Electronics, the Big Stakes Ride on Tiny Chips," *Fortune*, June, 1966, p. 120.

Unfortunately such technical advantages must also be reconciled with the requirements of volume production.[21] In the late 1960s the production technology required to produce the monolithic circuits in volume was not available, and management decisions were again required to resolve the dilemma presented by the engineers. Different manufacturers have gone their own ways as a consequence.

In the later 1960s IBM announced its System/360 line to replace the transistorized Model 1401s with newer and faster machines based on the hybrid, or mechanically assembled, transistor chip. This major decision by IBM had numerous internal repercussions,[22] although the reasoning behind the final production decision was clear: volume production required a process that could be automated, and the automation of monolithic circuit production was not then (and is only now slowly being) achieved. Thus, IBM moved to the mechanically constructed chip via an almost totally automated process of production, assembly, and testing. Most other firms took the integrated circuit, or monolithic, route, particularly for special purpose and military computers. The bottleneck in this form of production is the necessity for the mechanical connection of split-hair gold wires to the monolithic chip under a microscope, a process requiring manual dexterity. Although a wide number of exotic production devices have been created to speed this operation, it still exerts a basic limitation on volume as compared to a totally automated process. Since modern electronic computers can contain literally millions of components, mass production is a requirement for market penetration, and so the die was cast, at least for IBM.

In the next five to ten years we may well expect to see the development of automated methods for the manufacture of monolithic circuits and very large-scale integrated circuits which will further increase the reliability and speed of tomorrow's computers as well as cut their cost (similar remarks will be made about computer memory devices in Chapter 3).

A shift in economics

Thus, our history points to a new moral. The success of today's electronic computers is largely a feat brought about by a shift from mechanical to electronic technology, which has succeeded in rapidly increasing the speed of the computer to that of light, while reducing its components to the size of the molecule. This materials technology, which is paramount today, coupled with the greatly improved logical design of today's computing hardware, has greatly altered our way of looking at the computational and data processing scene. Formerly, because of the computing

[21] "IBM Buys Its Own Sales Pitch," *Business Week*, October 30, 1965, pp. 140–146.
[22] A. T. Wise, "IBM's $5,000,000,000 Gamble," *Fortune*, October, 1966, pp. 118–123, 138–143.

machine's high cost and relatively slow speeds we were interested in making optimum use of the machine time available to us, since human time was relatively cheaper than machine time. Today, however, the cost of computation has decreased (see Table 1.1), so that at most computing installations the cost of personnel—the user's time—is at least equal to if not greater than the cost of equipment.

The reason for this trend should be obvious: as machines become faster and more reliable, they can do more work in a given amount of elapsed time. However, someone must decide upon the work to be done and prepare the detailed instructions required for the machine to carry out the work. So with greater machine capability, we need more skilled humans to feed directions to the machines.

Unfortunately the production of skilled people is not as easily automated as hardware production, so we have a pressing personnel scarcity. This situation will grow worse in the next decade. With more than 70,000 computer installations estimated for 1972—nearly double the number in 1968 and a 35-fold increase over the mid-1950s—the problem should be clear.[23]

To compound this shift in economics and technical constraints, as computing systems become larger and more powerful they also become more complex in their organization and operation. Thus even a higher degree of skill will be needed of the many required users unless some drastic measures are undertaken to balance the human-machine equation.

Balancing the human-machine equation

The disparity between the human's ability to exploit a computer and the computer's speeds may be appreciated when we realize that while the computing system can perform many millions of instructions per second most humans could not execute more than ten or twenty. This means that the total man-machine system must be organized to exploit the strengths of both the machine and its users. A discussion of some of the methods currently in use follows.

---

[23] A current census of computer installations by manufacturer and model may be found monthly in *Computers and Automation* magazine. To get an idea of the number of persons who will be engaged in the utilization of electronic computers, we may simply assume about 10 persons will be needed per installation. Thus, by 1972, at the figures estimated, 70,000 × 10 or 700,000 persons will be directly involved in computer operation and use, not to mention those indirectly related to such information services. Some observers have placed estimates for 1975–1980 installations at over 110,000, with even more increasingly skilled personnel required. Finally, long-range observers of the information services field have estimated that in the U.S. labor force about one worker in five will within a decade be associated directly or indirectly with the use of electronic computers. No industry in world history has grown at so fast a rate.

1 / *Time sharing*

Instead of having a number of users employing machine time sequentially, they use it in parallel. In a typical arrangement as shown in Figure 1.4, many remote input/output terminals (teletype machines and similar devices) are connected to the computer by telephone lines or direct wires. Calls are answered, jobs sequenced, and stored user information is handled by the buffer and communications control unit, which swaps jobs in and out of the central processing unit. The communications control unit also sends solutions back to the appropriate user and handles storage of information upon demand of the user. When not in actual computational use, user information is usually stored in a relatively slow memory device, connected to the communications control unit. One or more jobs may be handled by the central processing unit (CPU) at once.

This approach has several consequences. First, the speed of the computer should enable it to service a large number of slow users and to give them essentially instant, or real time, service from the human viewpoint. This is the basis for using time sharing, which is a rapidly growing application of computers today.

Letting users share a computer facility at once, or as needed, has many other advantages. The cost per user is drastically reduced, since there are economies of scale in computer hardware as well as in other production facilities (the larger the installation, the less the cost per computation). Further, with shared use of and shared communication with the

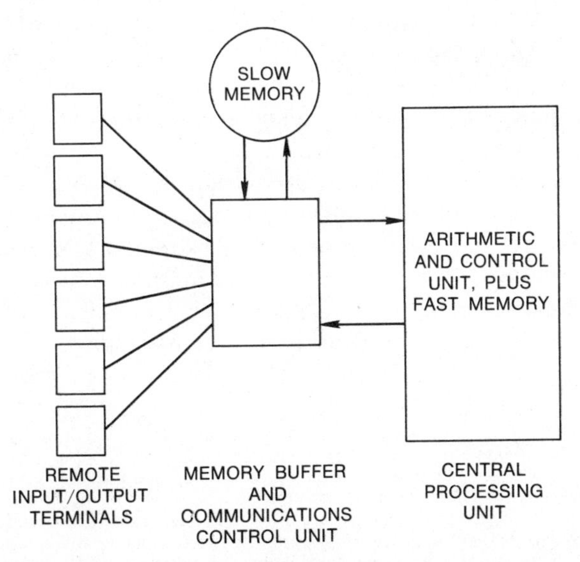

1.4. A simplified diagram of a time-sharing computer configuration. Intermediate communications devices and auxiliary peripheral computer units are not shown.

computer, many users may share the same data, the same files, and the same stored programs. Thus in business and industrial organizations there can be common access to inventory information and participants in scientific enterprises can share common statistics, mathematical routines, and computational developments. Such sharing of facilities implies a greater preponderance of communications facilities in tomorrow's computing systems and not surprisingly the trend is already in that direction.[24]

2 / *Improving the interface between human and machine*

Since the human contact with a computer is via some data input/output device, it pays to develop a better match of human and machine capabilities. Humans have some capabilities that machines generally do not. Humans, for example, can scan a large amount of data or a graphical display in parallel rather than step by step, and they can detect important or changing patterns that it would be difficult or impossible for the computer to detect. Conversely, the computer is best at quick evaluation of alternatives and intricate logic. Thus, an improvement in input/output devices, such as TV graphical devices, which exploit human capabilities is desirable. Again it is not surprising that a major new hardware market has developed in this realm.

3 / *Making conversation with the computer easier*

As we shall see in Chapter 6, computers have a language of their own, known as machine language. It is difficult to learn, and very demanding in its requirements for precision, consistency, and completeness. One early approach to matching the human and the machine was the development of user-oriented languages, which rely upon the computer to make the translation between the words of the human and those of the machine. Since computer time is relatively cheap, such automated translation is reasonable and desirable as well as extremely effective. (BASIC, a language developed at Dartmouth, is one example of a user-oriented language.) A user-oriented language permits the production of different jobs in less time and therefore aids the human-machine matchup.

---

[24] At the close of 1968 approximately 12% of the computing installations around the world were operating in what might be called a communications environment. But 21% of predicted 1969 installations will be communications-oriented and by 1975 60% will be (*Communications of the ACM*, December, 1968, p. 869). A "communications environment" is one in which a large proportion of the electronic facilities are devoted to passing information back and forth between users and the central processor. Appropriate programming and control measures are required in such installations. In advanced installations several hundred users may share the facilities at once, and because not all users will have simultaneous demand, several thousand users may have part-time access to the system.

4 / *Improving supervisory software*

Another feature of today's modern computing systems and their often complex communication with many users is the need for some supervision of the work the computer is to do at any given time. It is by no means obvious how one should create a scheme to set priorities, allocate facilities and time, or make available features that will satisfy a given group of potential users. And, indeed, such demands may change with time. For this reason, major improvements in the operation of a computing system are associated with an improvement in the supervisory procedures used. In the modern computing installation, the supervision required is reduced to a computer program, usually supplied by the manufacturer with his machine, which resides permanently in the computer's memory, thereby letting the computer do the scheduling, allocation, and bookkeeping required to handle a variety of user jobs, either in sequence or in parallel. Minor improvements in such supervisory routines may have a major effect upon the human-machine equation. Such modifications and improvements are constantly being made at most computing centers. (Because the improvements mentioned are made by the manufacturer or by experts at the computing center, and not by the novice, they will not concern us further, except in concept.)

As computing systems and communication systems connecting users with their computer (or computers) become more complex in their interconnection and more versatile in their capabilities, the importance of the supervisory routines used by the system increases. There is thus great emphasis today on the improvement of such system software and our understanding of how it may be improved.[25]

5 / *Eliminating human intervention where possible*

This form of human-machine matching is not as drastic as it sounds. For example, many input and output operations need not and should not concern the user. Once input data has been prepared for the machine, it should not be necessary to prepare it again in another form. Thus, devices such as optical readers (see Chapter 3) which can read a typewritten page for direct entry into the computer eliminate a secondary keypunch or typing operation. We may expect to see a wide range of such devices employed in the next few years.

---

[25] *Computer World*, a newsweekly for the computer trade, publishes a running financial comparison of computer stocks. It reports hardware and software suppliers separately. Because of the importance of programming, particularly supervisory programming, in today's applications, the software stocks for the past several years have greatly outstripped the hardware stocks in their percentage gains. Peripheral equipment stocks (manufacturers of input/output devices and computer memories) also show a relatively greater percentage gain than general hardware manufacturers, as do firms engaged in personnel training.

The human effort can also be reduced by having the supervisory control system of the computer anticipate human needs and supply them either directly or as available options that may be easily selected. Thus, if we ask the computer to retrieve a customer's address from its memory, we may either arrange the program inquiry to obtain other pertinent information (such as a credit limit), or cause the supervisor to call forth another program which will, say, produce the current shop status of the customer's orders in process.

Finally, in many instances it is possible to eliminate human inputs entirely, once a suitable program of instructions has been prepared. For example, when computers are set up to control a chemical process, automatic sensors can be used to report temperature and pressure to the machine (such analogue measurements are converted to digital information before they are used by the machine); and control instructions to valves and heaters can be sent directly from the computer without human intervention. By means of a suitable program of instructions, the computer can be made to control the process on its own, so that few if any workers are needed to attend the operation. These few are usually maintenance men and supervisors who are prepared to handle emergency situations. The daily routine is handled by the computer.

Such applications of the computer to industrial control problems are now standard in many fields of production, and gradually many of the same concepts of automatic control are being introduced into the more difficult paperwork and job-shop production fields where the variety of exceptional cases to be handled is greater.

In short, money spent on the areas just mentioned will generally produce a greater system improvement today than additional investment in the improvement of the computer's arithmetic, or purely computational abilities. We may expect more user sharing of facilities, better conversation with the machine—including better user-oriented languages and better problem solution methods—and also improvements in supervisory control methods as well as the peripheral computer components that help match human users to the machine (or eliminate them altogether).

Scientific and business machines: the "family" concept

As machines have become more powerful, there has also been another shift in design concept that we should note.

In the early years there were two basic types of computing machines: (1) those designed especially for scientific applications and (2) those designed primarily for business applications.

The former type required high computing speeds, little volume of input or output (the answer to a problem could be a single number), little if any alphabetic character handling, and basically mathematical data formats.

The latter type required large input/output capability, relatively small amounts of computation, large alphabetic character handling ability in variable length formats, and relatively slow computing speeds.

To see the difference, we may consider the difference between computing artillery tables and computing a payroll. The ballistic tables are computed from well-known, well-defined formulas with small data input, perhaps a few constants. The output is in columnar form, consisting mostly of numbers. The output results may consist of only a few pages. But the internal computations required to achieve these results may be very lengthy in terms of the number of instruction steps processed. The payroll computation is usually limited to a few additions, multiplications, and subtractions, but a volume of input data (e.g., time cards) and a volume of output (e.g., paychecks, financial records, tax records) are required. Moreover, the input and output data will be in various lengths, will contain much alphabetic and special character material, and will require substantial editing.

As a consequence of these disparate demands, two machine types evolved: the scientific machine and the business machine.

The new designs (e.g., IBM's System/360) attempt to create one machine which will satisfy either of the two demands, using program control to, in effect, rewire itself for either application.

In addition, it has become apparent that some concession in design must be made to facilitate the growth and expansion of the computing installation, so that drastic changes in hardware and programs will not be required to increase computing capacity. To overcome this problem, machines are now constructed on a modular concept, so that compatible families of machines may be constructed as needed from a limited number of design modules. Coupled with this trend is the standardization of the interconnections and programming specifications for a given family of modules, so that one box can be plugged into another without great difficulty and the same program can be run on several machine configurations.

The net effect of these conceptual changes in design practice is to provide a more flexible installation, which may be expanded or contracted at will and which may handle a wider range of problem types than before. Because of the increased speeds of computation and switching, little loss is suffered by either extreme demand (scientific or business), and a more generally useful machine results from the combination of alternate designs. Indeed, some current machines can process both scientific and business problems concurrently.[26]

---

[26] The ability to process a number of different jobs at one time is known as multiprogramming. Such ability is highly desirable in time-sharing installations and for utilizing fully the memory and arithmetic capacity of modern electronic computers.

If a system is to handle only one type of processing, say scientific, there is still some advantage (in cost and performance) in selecting a machine specialized for the application. However, as mass production of the generalized machine reaches greater volumes, the cost advantage of specialized construction will probably diminish.

The development of programming languages

Program language development has been a second cousin to computer hardware development until recently. Now it is apparent that concentration on hardware to the exclusion of software is not wise. When the computing system is viewed as a whole, the contributions made by software excellence often overshadow what can be achieved for the same cost or resources by hardware improvements.[27]

When, in addition, we include (as we should) the human user in our picture of the total computing system, we find that ease of efficient programming for applications is essential if wide use is to be achieved.

Historically, a number of efforts have been made to direct applications languages to a user orientation. As early as 1951, when the first UNIVACs were delivered, several proposals for user languages were made and implemented by Dr. Grace Hopper and her staff at Remington Rand. Because few UNIVACs were installed, these efforts did not gain wide acceptance in the 1950s.

IBM's introduction of its Model 650 was accompanied by similar efforts, and a partially user-oriented language, known as SOAP (Symbolic Optimizer and Assembly Program) was introduced. In 1954, IBM began work on a user-oriented language for scientists, which was released in 1957 as FORTRAN (Formula Translator). FORTRAN has now become an American Standard,[28] and after four revisions and improvements, is available on most computers.

In 1960 the initial standard specifications for COBOL (Common Business Oriented Language) were published under the auspices of the Department of Defense. This English-type language is intended for business problems involving file manipulation and the generation of special purpose reports. It includes much of the early UNIVAC work as well as con-

---

[27] It is interesting that some of the Communist countries such as Poland have used mathematical and logical excellence in program design to compensate for the lack of advanced electronic hardware, often with amazing results. Indeed, a somewhat inferior machine used with high skill can often equal or outstrip advanced hardware used carelessly. The ideal, of course, is to use advanced hardware with high skill.

[28] The USA Standards Institute in cooperation with manufacturer and user groups sets and publishes specifications for generally accepted measuring, procedural, and other operations which affect large numbers of people. Although the USASI standards are widely used in the computer industry, some local deviations from the common standards exist.

tributions from a wide range of manufacturers, including IBM. One purpose of this language was to make the many different computer types owned or rented by the Federal Government compatible—an aim approximated, but not completely achieved. Only minor modifications are necessary to move programs from one piece of equipment or one installation to another. COBOL has also passed through several stages of improvement and by 1968 also had been adopted as an American Standard.

BASIC (Beginner's All Purpose Symbolic Instruction Code), developed at Dartmouth, and designed primarily for ease of understanding by the nonprofessional user, was successfully in use by 1965. The initial specifications for BASIC have been widely accepted by computer manufacturers, although extensions to the fundamental specifications vary to some extent from supplier to supplier (see Chapter 14).

A large number of other user-oriented languages such as ALGOL, SIMSCRIPT, JOSS, DYNAMO, SNOBOL, GPSS, and LISP have also come into limited use. Each serves its own specialized applications.

By the late 1960s a move was under way—particularly at IBM—to combine the best features of the scientific language FORTRAN and the commercial language COBOL into a general language, called PL/1. At this writing results have been mixed, and the specifications for PL/1 have not been standardized. (The objective of PL/1 is in line with the trend toward general purpose hardware, described in the previous section.)

In any case, each of the language developments cited has made the computer's abilities available to a larger number of users. Because of the intensive developmental effort applied to the major languages by all manufacturers, the user-oriented languages are now highly efficient and usually can compete on a cost-effectiveness basis with programs written in the more machine-oriented languages for most applications.[29] Concurrently, a very large number of technical improvements have been made in the supervisory control programs used for today's complex machines, although because of their technical nature we will not discuss them here.

---

[29] As indicated in more detail in Chapter 6, user-oriented languages go through one or more stages of translation to convert them into a form of notation, known as machine language, which the machine can process directly. One intermediate step is the so-called assembly language, of which IBM's Symbolic Programming System (SPS), Autocoder, and Basic Assembly Language (BAL) are examples. These intermediate forms of expression are technically more complex than the user-oriented languages, and programs written according to their rules are four to twenty-five times more lengthy than the corresponding programs written in the user-oriented, or higher-level, languages. The higher-level languages put together blocks or modules of machine-language instructions at the time of translation, or "compilation," thus saving much effort. An instructional step which generates such a block of detail is called a macroinstruction. Nevertheless, where extreme efficiency is required, and where the ultimate capabilities of a given machine configuration must be exploited, programs are still prepared by professionals in machine language or assembly language. Examples are industrial process control, missile tracking, and highly repetitive commercial applications such as time-shared inventory status installations.

Finally, we should note that the developments in time sharing, supervisory control languages, and user-oriented languages free us from much further consideration of the technicalities of the equipment we will be using. We may think of the computing hardware and control programs as beginning and ending at our remote terminal or input/output device, and concentrate on our problems and a simplified user language. Our learning task will be to consider only a few rules of grammar and syntax, or sentence construction, and then go to work.

Babbage's dream: the information machine

We now come to the conclusion of our history. But in looking back to our starting point we may note that the eighteenth and nineteenth centuries were indeed remarkable times for inventors.

Ironically, most of the inventors we remember from the past—like James Watt who perfected the steam engine—devoted their attention to harnessing *physical energy.* Their development of tools to alleviate human effort and achieve nonhuman levels of physical prowess produced the Industrial Revolution. For many physically taxing jobs today, it is economic suicide—at any level of hourly wage—to use human energy where the machine can be employed. Earth moving is one example. It is impossible to feed one thousand people on a starvation diet for less than the cost of buying and operating a single steam shovel which will do an equivalent amount of work!

So, our whole society has changed profoundly as a consequence of our energy-saving or energy-multiplying inventions. Work weeks are no longer 60 or 80 hours long, as they were in the 1700s and 1800s, but half that amount for most workers. We have adjusted to, and usually benefited from, the accompanying social changes in economics, business, and industry. No one has been left untouched by the energy machines of the Industrial Revolution.

Yet while the Industrial Revolution and its energy machines were in the making, there was also a concurrent development which was less noted, but which today may turn out to be equally important, if not more profound for the further course of social development: the introduction and development of information machines—those that deal with a nonphysical quantity that is the product of organized symbols and patterns produced by the human mind.

"It is not a bad description of *man*," Charles Babbage wrote in his memoirs, "to describe him as a *tool-making animal.* His earliest contrivances to support uncivilized life, were tools of the simplest and rudest construction. His later achievements in the substitution of machinery, not only for the skill of the human hand, but for relief of the human intellect, are founded on the use of tools of a still higher order."[30]

Gutenberg's fifteenth-century invention of the printing press (which revolutionized both the printing arts and human thought by using movable type) was a forerunner of things to come. It was an information machine.

As we look back at Jacquard, Babbage, Metcalfe, Hollerith, and the later computer designers and users of our own century, we see that all were (and are) in the information business, too. True, the modern electronic computers are machines which work with physical quantities in a wholly predictable way. But their primary function is not energy conversion or doing work in the sense of multiplying human strength. The new machines expand human mental capacity. And they do this by furthering our symbol-manipulating abilities—purely human skills.

The twentieth century has, as a consequence, often been called the time of the Information Revolution, because within our own lifetimes the successful application of earlier principles has resulted in the most remarkable devices of "a higher order," those "for the relief of the human intellect."

How well and to what purpose the information machines will be used in the future rests largely with today's students. For information machines, like energy machines, are tools which man has developed in his conquest of nature. Only their users can determine how such inventions, however remarkable, will affect our lives.

For this reason more than any other, a study of present-day computer technology is important to us as well as to our society. The economics of information processing, its technology, and its applications will surely affect our later years—just as much as the Industrial Revolution affected the life of our parents. Only by understanding the potentials and limitations of the information machines can we learn to use them wisely and appreciate their power.

Lady Lovelace, in her love for an irascible inventor, best portrayed his hopes and fears. One may only hope that today's readers will treat with her care their appreciation of the information machine.

> It is desirable [she wrote] to guard against the possibility of exaggerated ideas that might arise as to the powers of the Analytical Engine. In considering any new subject, there is frequently the tendency, first, to *overrate* what we find to be already interesting or remarkable; and, secondly, by a sort of natural reaction, to *undervalue* the true state of the case, when we do discover that our notions have surpassed those that were really tenable.[31]

---

[30] Morrison and Morrison, *op. cit.*, p. 322.
[31] *Ibid.*, p. 284.

PROBLEMS

1-1 Consult one of the following sources (or others you may find on your own) and locate one or more computer applications that are of interest to you. Report on the application you found to your class. It may stimulate your interest in computers if you continue to keep a file of interesting applications, with clippings or notes for future reference.

Computers and Automation (monthly)

Computer World (weekly)

Computing Reviews (an abstracting service published semimonthly by the Association for Computing Machinery)

Communications of the ACM (semimonthly articles for the more advanced reader published by the Association for Computing Machinery)

Datamation (monthly)

Data Processing Magazine (monthly)

EDP Weekly (weekly)

In addition to these popular and widely available trade periodicals, the reader will also find frequent stories of interest in *Business Week, The New York Times*, and *The Wall Street Journal.* On occasion, *Fortune* and other periodicals in the financial field will carry survey articles of interest. *The Scientific American*, September, 1966, was devoted to a total survey of the state of the art, with extensive illustrations. This issue has been reprinted in paperback form by W. H. Freeman, San Francisco.

1-2 Why is it important to note the change which has occurred in the relative costs of computational time versus human programming and data preparation time?

1-3 Why in its contribution to human society is the electronic computer a fundamentally different type of machine than Watt's steam engine?

1-4 It has often been observed that human mental prowess (compared to that of animals) is largely due to man's symbol-manipulating ability, that is, his skills in dealing with abstractions such as numbers, words, and other representations of particular items and events. How, then, can the computer as a machine provide "relief of the human intellect"?

1-5 Recently a wide range of communications devices have been hooked up to central computing installations. Why should this new development greatly spread the use of electronic computers in everyday life?

1-6 Make some predictions of your own on the likely effects of combining the trends of the Industrial Revolution with those of the Information Revolution. How will one revolution augment the other? What are some of the possible social effects which may result?

TWO

Bistable devices and binary codes

Today's electronic computers are constructed of components which operate like switches: they can assume only two conditions, or states, *on* or *off*, and are thus called bistable devices. Depending upon the nomenclature used, the two possible states may also be *yes* or *no, true* or *false*, or *1* and *0*. The essential point is that the condition of a bistable device at any time is unambiguous. An electric light switch is either on or off at a given moment, not halfway on or halfway off. It is the function of the transistors and integrated circuits in today's computers to combine logically a number of switching operations that will control the flow of work in the machine as well as its arithmetic operations. This chapter will shed some light on how these operations are carried out and also prepare us for a later discussion of computer memory devices.

Decimal system

Accept for the moment that computers work with two-valued components. How, then, does a computer do its arithmetic? Clearly, with a number system that can take on only two values—a binary system that works with only the numbers 1 and 0. Let us first consider the familiar decimal system. When we write the number 123, or one hundred twenty-three, we mean

$$1 \times 100 + 2 \times 10 + 3 \times 1$$

or, noting that each positional move to the left in a decimal number involves an increased power of 10, we could also write decimal 123 as

$$1 \times 10^2 + 2 \times 10^1 + 3 \times 10^0$$

remembering, of course, that any number raised to the 0th power is equal to 1. As we move to the left in the decimal system, then, we understand that we are to associate with each successive column an increasing power of 10, and positional notation allows us to omit the powers of 10 when we write 123.

Ten is thus said to be the *base*, or *radix*, of the decimal system, and the multipliers for each column position in the decimal system may range from 0 through 9, that is from zero to the base minus one.

Further, to create decimal fractions, we simply extend the same scheme as above to the right of the decimal point using increasingly negative powers of 10. For example, the decimal number 123.123 may be interpreted by means of the following table, which shows the value of each column position.

Power	. . . 10^3	10^2	10^1	10^0	.	10^{-1}	10^{-2}	10^{-3}	10^{-4} . . .
Value	1000	100	10	1	.	$\frac{1}{10}$	$\frac{1}{100}$	$\frac{1}{1000}$	$\frac{1}{10000}$
Decimal Number		1	2	3	.	1	2	3	0

In short, a decimal number as normally written simply tells us *how many* of the various powers of 10 we need in each position to make the desired quantity.

We may also note that given a limited set of positions to the right of the decimal point, it is not always possible to express a fraction precisely in the decimal system. Given six places to the right of the decimal point, the fraction $\frac{1}{3}$ could be expressed as 0.333333, which approximates, but does not exactly equal the original fraction. Thus, some error may be expected when expressing certain fractions in the decimal system, in particular those fractions which cannot be reduced to a power of 10 (unlike $\frac{1}{4}$, which is equal to 0.25). The problem of rounding off does not occur with integers, or whole numbers, which may be expressed exactly, provided enough positions are available for the size of the number involved. To reduce the effect of roundoff error in the decimal system, we simply utilize more decimal positions until the precision of conversion is sufficient for our needs.

Binary systems

There is no necessity to count in the base 10; any other base, for example, base 12, 16, 8, or 2, will work as well. The available multipliers at each column position will be from zero to the base minus one, and each column position will imply multiplication by a successive power of the base.

To illustrate, suppose we agree to count using the base 2, or the binary system. The available values at each column position are 0 and 1, and each successive column will imply an increasing power of 2. To indicate any given number, we find the combination of the appropriate powers of 2 that will add up to that number.

Thus, consider the decimal number 5. To convert decimal 5 into the equivalent binary notation, consult the following table.

Power	2^3	2^2	2^1	2^0
Value	8	4	2	1
Decimal 5 in Binary	0	1	0	1

Since decimal 5 is equal to 4 plus 1, as indicated in the last line of the table, 0101 is equivalent to decimal 5.

Table 2.1 shows the corresponding decimal and binary representations that can be achieved with four binary positions.[1] Such binary "digits" are called bits to distinguish them from decimal digits, or positions. Note in the table that every combination of 0's and 1's in the four-bit sequence (representing the 8-4-2-1 values) has been utilized (from 0000 through 1111). A given decimal equivalent is made of a unique selection of the 8-4-2-1 positional values, as illustrated for decimal 5 in the preceding example and for the decimal values 0–15 in the table. Because of the unique correspondence between the two number systems, conversion from one to the other is readily accomplished, so either may be used as needed. In the computer, the needed conversions are done electronically by a method which need not concern us now. It is important, however, to realize that such a conversion is made, so that you will appreciate some of the computer manipulations described later.

To check your understanding of the notational scheme above, consider the binary equivalent of decimal 6, which is 0110. Can you explain why this conversion is correct?

---

[1] Note that the variety of distinct combinations of 0's and 1's that can be formed using *N* binary columns is 2^N, or, in the four-column case, 16, which is the same as 0–15 in decimal.

To simplify the above illustration, we have limited Table 2.1 to four binary positions and, consequently, to the decimal numbers 0–15. To represent larger decimal numbers in binary, we need more binary positions, although the conversion process remains the same. Thus, the decimal number 23 can be represented as shown below:

TABLE 2.1

Conversion from Decimal to Binary Number System for Decimal Numbers 0–15

Decimal		Binary			
tens	*ones*	*eights*	*fours*	*twos*	*ones*
0	0	0	0	0	0
0	1	0	0	0	1
0	2	0	0	1	0
0	3	0	0	1	1
0	4	0	1	0	0
0	5	0	1	0	1
0	6	0	1	1	0
0	7	0	1	1	1
0	8	1	0	0	0
0	9	1	0	0	1
1	0	1	0	1	0
1	1	1	0	1	1
1	2	1	1	0	0
1	3	1	1	0	1
1	4	1	1	1	0
1	5	1	1	1	1

Power	2^4	2^3	2^2	2^1	2^0
Value	16	8	4	2	1
Decimal 23 in Binary	1	0	1	1	1

In large computers up to 60 binary columns, or bits, may be used to represent large decimal integers uniquely.

To express decimal fractions in binary, we would need more columns to the right. A "point" is often used to separate whole numbers and fractional parts in binary as in the decimal system when such numbers are written out. Thus, if we limit the precision to four binary columns we might have

Power	.	2^{-1}	2^{-2}	2^{-3}	2^{-4}
Value	.	$\frac{1}{2}$	$\frac{1}{4}$	$\frac{1}{8}$	$\frac{1}{16}$
Decimal 0.75 in Binary	.	1	1	0	0

Again, it should be clear that although certain decimal fractions will be precisely converted into binary expressions, others cannot be handled without rounding off. For example, the decimal fraction $\frac{1}{10}$, or 0.1, cannot be made exactly with any combination of the powers of two shown in the above table, and the same difficulty remains even when a much larger number of binary positions are used. *Some* roundoff error is inherent in the conversion process for this number. Although digital computers are said to be absolutely precise in their handling of numbers (they are for integers), the process of handling fractions can be imprecise to a certain extent for the reasons cited.

Binary representation within the computer

The binary number representation just discussed has a physical meaning for the computer. First, the computer must store such numbers from time to time during a computation. The computer must also be able to transmit such numbers over its circuits from one part to another as the flow of work progresses. Each of these requirements is handled slightly differently by the machine, and the distinction is worth noting for later understanding of memory media and program execution.

First, to store a number, the computer usually provides the positional notation required for the binary number system by reference to a spatial arrangement of its "switches," or bistable devices. Thus, by referring to the position of such devices and their current states, we may symbolically store and retrieve the 0's and 1's in their proper relation, or order. Thus, one way to store the binary equivalent of decimal 5 is to set four switches to the respective states 0101. Then when the number must be referenced, those switches can be tested for 0 or 1, reading from right to left. Another way to store such information would be to magnetize given physical locations on a magnetic material, such as magnetic tape. Still the interpretation of the stored information would be by physical reference to that set of magnetic locations in a prescribed order, with tests for the presence of a magnetized spot.

When numbers must be moved from one location to another, the computer usually provides a positional reference by sending sequentially a number of 1's and 0's (electrical pulses or not) over a wire and interpreting each signal's positional meaning by reference to the *time* required to receive the number. Thus, most computers contain very precise clocks which synchronize the transmission and reception of signals, so that they may be handled in an orderly fashion and the positional meaning of the 0–1 signals may remain consistent. In this scheme, a position is indicated by an elapsed time interval, which may or may not contain an electrical pulse. By sequencing time intervals in the same order as the stored positional information, a number may be moved from one storage location to another.

TABLE 2.2

Relation Between Codes of Table 2.1 and Electrical Pulse Sequence for Transmitting Information

Decimal		Binary				Electrical pulses			
tens	*ones*	*eights*	*fours*	*twos*	*ones*	*eights*	*fours*	*twos*	*ones*
0	0	0	0	0	0				
0	1	0	0	0	1				
0	2	0	0	1	0				
0	3	0	0	1	1				
0	4	0	1	0	0				
0	5	0	1	0	1				
0	6	0	1	1	0				
0	7	0	1	1	1				
0	8	1	0	0	0				
0	9	1	0	0	1				
1	0	1	0	1	0				
1	1	1	0	1	1				
1	2	1	1	0	0				
1	3	1	1	0	1				
1	4	1	1	1	0				
1	5	1	1	1	1				

For example, a positionally stored number is typically transmitted reading from right to left at the originating storage location. The received number is then reconstituted at the new location by setting switches or magnetizing appropriate media sequentially from right to left under clock control. The original and the duplicated numbers will then be identical.

Bistable devices and computer reliability

The most important reason for using binary numbers in today's computers is to obtain computational reliability.

Since data must be passed from component to component many times during any computation and must be stored reliably during intermediate computations and for later reference, it is essential that random disturbances in the computer's operation do not alter the accuracy of such storage, transmission, or processing of data.

Unfortunately, computers, like all electronic communications devices, are subject to the effects of noise. Static and other sources of interference occur in the computer as well as on the radio. And, although static is merely annoying when one is listening to a radio program, it can create disaster in an electronic computation by altering the values of data or even changing the sequence of computations desired. For this reason, a system of number representation and communication that can be "cleaned up," or freed from noise, is an essential design feature of modern computing machines. For reasons beyond the scope of this book, the binary system possesses this ability to a greater extent than any other number system.

Another advantage of the binary system is applicable to the magnetization of computer storage media used in the spatial storage of data. When the computer uses the simplest form of number representation, slight variations in magnetic materials or in the magnetization process itself will not affect the stored data as greatly as they would if numbers to a larger base were being used. (Several other devices and coding schemes which are used to improve computer reliability will be mentioned later as they arise.)

Arithmetic manipulations in binary

We have now seen that numbers can be represented most reliably for the purposes of electronic storage and communication in the binary number system. The binary system also lends itself to economical storage, computing, and communication because of the simple on-off type of components that are needed.

You may have noted that the reliability and economy are purchased by using more column positions to represent a number than would be required if a decimal scheme were employed. This is true indeed. However, the factors of reliability, cost, and speed also must be considered. Since binary numbers may be manipulated more rapidly, cheaply, and reliably than decimal numbers, the apparent difficulty of binary with its long strings of 0's and 1's diminishes. Using binary is like making 10 inexpensive mass-produced items instead of one expensive custom-made item, when either item will perform the same function.

Still other advantages in using binary numbers or their variations will be discussed later, when the computer designer is creating computing circuits and communications switching devices. These advantages lie in the fact that binary arithmetic computations are the simplest of all that may be considered, so the circuitry required is correspondingly simplified.

For example, consider binary addition. To perform this operation manually, we need only memorize the following table:

		B	
		0	1
A	0	0	1
	1	1	10

The contents of the box indicate the result of adding the two binary numbers 0 and 1. Thus, if we are to compute C = A + B, the table tells us how to do this. If A is 0 and B is 0, the consequence, C, is also 0. If A and B have opposite values, then C is 1. And, if both A and B are 1 (producing an answer equivalent to decimal 2), the binary result is 10. In the last instance, note that the decimal number 2 cannot be represented with only one binary position. Thus, two binary positions are necessary, creating a carry from the right column to the next left column. (This process is directly analogous to the necessity for a carry when a total goes from 9 to 10 in decimal notation.)

Only four fundamental addition operations need be remembered, because with more than one binary column, the operation is simply repeated column by column, working from right to left, as we shall see below. (Compare this simplicity with the corresponding 10 × 10 table that would be required to produce the rules for decimal addition using the digits 0–9.)

To extend what we have just learned, consider the addition of decimal 5 and decimal 6 to produce decimal 11—but perform that operation using the binary number system.

	Decimal value	*Binary equivalent*
	5	0101
	6	0110
Result of addition	11	1011

The result of applying the binary addition rule is to provide a notation which tells us to add together an 8, a 2, and a 1, which is equivalent to decimal 11.

Extended binary addition

It is now useful to give two examples to show the effect of the carry in binary addition. Note the decimal equivalent shown, and that the binary carry and the decimal carry are identical in principle.

Example	*Decimal*	*Binary*
		ccc
	13	1101
	+11	+1011
	24	11000

In the example, the carry required in the binary scheme is shown by the small *c* at the head of each column. Thus, a carry is required from column one, at right, to column two, next left, because $1 + 1 = 10$ in binary. The carry 1's are simply moved to the next column as required.

Example: Although the computer will usually work with only two numbers at once and handle any multinumber problem as a series of two-number problems, it may be illuminating to see the extension of binary addition to three numbers. Here there may be multiple carry terms, which would not be desirable for the computer.

Decimal	*Binary*
	c c
	cccccc
23	10111
+19	+10011
+26	+11010
68	1000100

A similar process holds for larger numbers or for numbers with fractional parts. Moreover, once the process of binary addition has been mastered and converted to a hardware operation, it is not difficult to extend the addition idea to produce subtraction, multiplication, and division. We may recall that subtraction is just reverse addition, multiplication repeated addition, and division repeated subtraction.

Indeed, some computers have been constructed that add only, with the remaining desired operations provided by user programming. In most cases, however, modern computers will perform a large number of specific operations (such as multiplication) electronically. The choice between hardware or software implementation of any instructional step is a matter of its frequency of use and the economics of hardware construction. For simplicity, we shall not discuss binary operations other than addition.

Binary coded decimal and its variations

Thus far we have discussed how the computer can manipulate numbers using the binary number scheme. However, modern data processing requires that we handle not only numbers but also alphabetic (*A, B, C, . . .*) and special characters ($, &, %, etc.). Although there are a variety of ways to code these nonnumeric characters (each could be given a special number, for example), it is customary in most business-oriented machines or in machines which must handle both scientific and business problems to provide for a special coding scheme to handle mixtures of numeric and alphanumeric data. The method most frequently used is known as the Binary Coded Decimal scheme, or BCD for short. In fact, most modern computers can shift between pure binary and BCD forms of character representation at the user's discretion.

The Binary Coded Decimal scheme is relatively simple. By reference to Table 2.1, we note that four binary bits can generate 16 unique binary patterns, only 10 of which would be needed to generate the decimal digits 0–9. Thus, if we were to encode only the decimal numbers 0–9 with the four binary columns (and we could not use less), six possible unique combinations would be wasted. It might make sense, then, to employ these unused code combinations for something useful.

Thus, in the BCD codes used in most computers, each individual character, numeric or nonnumeric, required for the computer's "character set," or range of symbols that can be handled, is often allotted a fixed number of binary column positions, and processing is handled on a character-by-character basis.

Suppose, for example, that a computer designer wanted to provide users with 64 characters in total (the alphabet, the decimal numbers 0–9, and a number of special characters such as $). From our previous examination of binary codes, we may note that 2^6 is 64, so that six binary positions would provide the desired 64 unique codes required.

Such a scheme is illustrated in Table 2.3 in which a character set of 64 items is identified. Following the repeated binary patterns noted in Table 2.1, note that it is possible to repeat the 16 patterns available from four binary columns (four binary bits) and to tag each repetition with a variation in the 0's and 1's in additional columns to the left. In Table 2.3 there are four repetitions, each of which is identified by separating dashed lines. The distinction among the repetitions of the four columns to the extreme right is given by the block differences in the first two columns, which take on, respectively, the binary codes 00, 01, 10, and 11.

In particular, the code shown in Table 2.3 is that usually employed by the Model 33 Teletype machine when communicating with the computer. The keyboard characters are identified and sequentially numbered from 0–63 to the left. The equivalent six-bit binary coded decimal code is shown to the extreme right. (You may note that the BCD code is simply the decimal equivalent of the number in the first column of the listing.) For later reference, we also show the equivalent number that would be obtained if the decimal or the binary numbers shown in Table 2.3 were expressed to the base 8, or octal system. The latter system is sometimes used as shorthand for writing the longer binary string of numbers. By observation we may note that one octal position is identical to exactly three binary positions. Thus the octal number 17 may rapidly be translated into binary as 001 111, since the two three-bit binary numbers translate to octal 1 and 7, respectively. The conversion from octal to binary again based on three-bit blocks is equally easy. Octal to decimal conversion or vice versa is more tedious, and we need not go into it here, other than to observe that the octal numbers shown are multipliers for powers of 8, and that the multiplier may take on one of the numbers 0–7, the base minus one being the largest multiplier allowed. Thus, the octal number 17 is the equivalent of $1 \times 8 + 7 \times 1 = 15$ in decimal, as shown in Table 2.3.

Finally, it is important to note that the assignment of special characters to particular BCD codes is completely arbitrary. The 010001 shown for the letter *A* does not necessarily mean *A* to the computer, but is assigned that meaning by people using particular equipment. The code 010001—as well as the other 63 codes shown—could just as easily stand for any other character in any 64-character set; the desired character is placed on the input keyboard and the output printer in a position that provides consistent translation. It is helpful, however, to organize the special characters in a useful order and for computational purposes to assign the decimal digits 0–9 to their direct binary equivalents. In Table 2.3 this has been done. In addition, the alphabetic sequence *A* through *Z* corresponds to ever-increasing number values (in binary, decimal, and octal), thereby permitting alphabetic sorts and comparisons to be made without complex intermediate translations. In Table 2.3 the letter *A* has a smaller number than the letter *Z*, so we could say that *Z* is larger than *A* for the illustrated code. The particular ordering given to a character set by its specified code assignment is called the computer's collation sequence, since the specified ordering will determine how characters can be compared and arranged on a particular machine. (A further discussion of this point appears in Chapter 14.)

We omit consideration of manipulations with binary coded characters because of the explanatory complexity required and because our point about the binary form of encodement has already been made with regard to reliability. You should, however, understand that coding variations have been and are being used in today's electronic computers. Although all of them are based on the underlying binary representation of 0's and 1's, it is beneficial if the computer's users understand the character set available to them and the relative advantages of using a pure binary form of computation versus a Binary Coded Decimal manipulation. This choice is usually made under program control, as discussed in later chapters.

TABLE 2-3
RELATIONSHIP OF KEYBOARD CHARACTERS TO COMPUTER BCD CODES

CHARACTER NUMBER (DECIMAL)	YOUR KEYBOARD CHARACTER	THE EQUIVALENT OCTAL	THE EQUIVALENT BCD
0	0	00	000000
1	1	01	000001
2	2	02	000010
3	3	03	000011
4	4	04	000100
5	5	05	000101
6	6	06	000110
7	7	07	000111
8	8	10	001000
9	9	11	001001
10	APOSTROPHE	12	001010
11	:	13	001011
12	(	14	001100
13	;	15	001101
14	=	16	001110
15	LEFT SLASH	17	001111
16	+	20	010000
17	A	21	010001
18	B	22	010010
19	C	23	010011
20	D	24	010100
21	E	25	010101
22	F	26	010110
23	G	27	010111
24	H	30	011000
25	I	31	011001
26	BELL	32	011010
27	.	33	011011
28	QUOTE	34	011100
29	?	35	011101
30	<	36	011110
31	RETURN	37	011111

CHARACTER NUMBER (DECIMAL)	YOUR KEYBOARD CHARACTER	THE EQUIVALENT OCTAL	THE EQUIVALENT BCD
32	-	40	100000
33	J	41	100001
34	K	42	100010
35	L	43	100011
36	M	44	100100
37	N	45	100101
38	O	46	100110
39	P	47	100111
40	Q	50	101000
41	R	51	101001
42	TAB	52	101010
43	$	53	101011
44	*	54	101100
45	END MSG.	55	101101
46	>	56	101110
47	↑	57	101111
48	SPACE	60	110000
49	/	61	110001
50	S	62	110010
51	T	63	110011
52	U	64	110100
53	V	65	110101
54	W	66	110110
55	X	67	110111
56	Y	70	111000
57	Z	71	111001
58	LINE FEED	72	111010
59	,	73	111011
60	)	74	111100
61	[	75	111101
62	]	76	111110
63	FILL	77	111111

[NOTE: SOME OF THE ABOVE CHARACTERS (COLUMN 2) MAY NOT APPEAR ON YOUR TELETYPE KEYBOARD, OR MAY BE REPLACED WITH ALTERNATE SYMBOLS. CHECK FOR LOCAL VARIATIONS. ALSO SOME KEYS, SUCH AS LINE FEED, RETURN, ETC., DO NOT PRINT. OTHER CHARACTERS, SUCH AS THE APOSTROPHE AND THE QUOTE MARK DO NOT USUALLY PRINT IN BASIC.]

Extended binary coded decimal

If 64 characters can be uniquely described in a six-bit code as shown in Table 2.3, we might ask what would be required to provide a larger character set; for example, one which would provide not only uppercase alphabetics but lowercase too. Clearly, as the previous arguments indicate, more binary positions would be required.

To get a character set of 256 symbols, we would need eight binary positions (2^8 is 256). This wide range of characters has proved useful, and a number of today's computers such as IBM's System/360 line provide extended character sets of this type for commercial work. The price for this refinement is, of course, greater use of storage and communication capacity as compared to the more restricted variety of symbol use. Such tradeoffs are a general rule, but as we saw in Chapter 1, the cost of hardware and computer time may be relatively trivial compared to the need for human-machine matching and programming versatility and ease. In such applications, expanded character sets are desirable.

Parity bits and further checking for reliability

It is important for our later understanding of memory devices to know that computer designers often provide a protecting check on the transmission and storage of information over and beyond the use of the binary number representation and its variants.

To illustrate the form of protection most frequently used, consider the BCD code for the letter *A* as opposed to the letter *C*, as shown in Table 2.3. The respective codes are 010001 and 010011, the only difference occurring in the second column from the right. It is conceivable that in spite of the precautions used in handling binary information, some extraneous disturbance might alter one of the binary positions. This could be serious in computation—for example, we might pay commissions to Salesman C, rather than Salesman A!

Since the probability of having more than one binary position altered in a given number or letter is very small, a "parity check bit" is often added to the previously described BCD code.[2] Note in the codes for *A* and *C* that the count of 1's is even in the case of *A* and odd in the case of *C* (there are two 1's in the *A* code and three 1's in the *C* code). Using the two choices available in the binary scheme, it is possible to cause all of the

[2] The word "parity" means equal, or equivalent. The purpose of the parity check bit is to assure the equality of the present state of a BCD code with what was intended. The extra bit used for this check may produce either an even or an odd count of the 1's in a code scheme. If the check is even, the machine is said to be an even-parity machine; if the check is for an odd count, it is an odd-parity machine.

codes in a character set to have either an even or an odd count by adding on an extra check column, say to the left. For example, supposing that an *even* count is always desired as a check, we could write the two codes for *A* and *C* above as

A 0010001
C 1010011

By checking each character for even parity, we would detect those characters for which a bit had been erroneously added or dropped by the electronic mechanism.

Such parity bits are usually added to the code at the time of a character's initiation into the computing system and then checked at various stages of the computation to assure continued accuracy. For this reason, the six-bit BCD code illustrated in Table 2.3, would require seven binary positions for storage if the parity bit were used (see Chapter 3).

A great variety of such parity checks can be built into the computer's operation, although we need not pursue the subject further. It is useful to note, however, that most remote terminals are designed to generate a parity check for input data, so that verification is possible at later stages in the communication and computation process.

Other binary applications

In these days of remote communication to the computer, we should also note that binary forms of communication have come into their own, not only for computer and data communications services but also for voice communication as well.[3] The notion of a binary form of data handling is certainly not new and is familiar in Morse code, the beat of jungle tom-toms, and the rapping of prisoners on jailhouse pipes. But the implementation of the idea at humanly incomprehensible speeds using electronics is recent. And we should realize that the reliability of our modern computing systems rests largely upon this implementation of an ancient idea which in both primitive and historical times has used the concept of simplicity to assure reliability.

---

[3] William D. Smith, "There is No 'Maybe' in the World of Digital Communications," *The New York Times*, June 30, 1968, p. 1. When transmitting voice communication in binary codes, the amplitude of a voice signal is measured at frequent intervals (several thousand measurements per second) and the result is converted to a series of binary numbers which are transmitted. At the receiving end, the reverse translation is performed, generating a given speech pattern from the number string. The process is currently used in the U.S. telephone network, although most users are unaware of the fact. The voice quality is maintained by the large number of measurements per second.

Biblical scholars, electronic designers, and computer users may well appreciate the New Testament admonition: "But let your communication be Yea, yea; Nay, nay: for whatsoever is more than these cometh of evil."[4]

PROBLEMS

2-1 Which of the following is not a binary number?

1100 0000 1002 1101 1111

2-2 Cite three reasons for the use of binary numbers in computer design.

2-3 What are some of the disadvantages of using binary numbers in a computational system?

2-4 Give the binary equivalents of the following decimal numbers.

32 12 123 76 123.125 .0625

2-5 Compare the conversion of decimal 0.1 to the nearest binary equivalent taken to six binary positions. What is the "error" due to roundoff in this conversion? Why could this be serious?

2-6 For what sort of numbers is the electronic digital computer completely precise in its operation? Where may it fail to be precise?

2-7 By referring to Table 2.3, give the BCD codes for the following characters:

Q 3 9 $ & *S* *W*

2-8 A computer has the ability to store numbers consisting of 36 bits.

a. What is the largest decimal number that the machine can store if the storage is to be in pure binary? (Assume all positions are used.)

b. Suppose that the 36-bit block of binary positions may be segmented at will. Also assume that the six-bit BCD code of Table 2.3 can be used and that no parity check bit is employed. How many distinct symbols may be stored in the 36-bit block, or word, using the six-bit BCD code?

c. In **a** assume that one of the 36 bits available for storage is devoted to the sign of a number. What is the largest number that may then be stored in the available number of positions if the code is in pure binary?

2-9 Convert the following binary numbers into their decimal equivalents:

11 11001 11111 1001.110 0.111

2-10 In problem 7, using the same characters given there, provide an even parity bit and determine whether it should be 0 or 1 in each case.

---

[4] Matthew 5:37, from the Sermon on the Mount.

2-11 If you had your choice, when would you select a pure binary form of computation, and when would you select a BCD form of computation? Why might it be desirable to have the ability to shift from one form to another? Under what conditions would a BCD manipulation be as efficient as a pure binary manipulation?

2-12 If a blackboard is divided into 400 squares, each of which may be filled with a 0 or a 1, how many distinctly different patterns could you generate? Try to convert this number into a decimal equivalent. The estimated number of atoms in the known universe is at least 10^{76}. How can you reconcile the number you obtained with this more than astronomical figure? Does your number give you some appreciation for the power of binary number representation?

2-13 How many binary bits, or positions, would be required to store the integer value decimal 1,000,000?

THREE

Input/Output

How does the computer get, manipulate, and display data? Into his proposed machines Charles Babbage designed input/output devices as well as memories. Today, these devices work with amazing flexibility and speed. And both input/output and memory equipment are the computer system components that directly affect the user.

Various input/output devices provide the mechanical and electrical mechanisms for receiving data and instructions and showing results. These computing system components take familiar user input, convert it to the binary codes of Chapter 2, transmit it to the computer, and then, for output display, reconvert the coded computer output into symbols the user can understand.

The computer's memory devices, which manufacturers produce in different styles for different applications, provide an electronic blackboard on which the computer's arithmetic and control section can store, manipulate, and read both data and instructions.

In this chapter we consider input/output devices; in Chapter 4 we discuss memory devices, and then in Chapter 5 we show a simple input-manipulation-output sequence to illustrate the use of input/output and memory devices in combination.

Standard input/output devices

The traditional key punch (of which an estimated half-million are now in service[1]) produces the familiar 80-column tabulating card from keyboard input. A human operator may be able to prepare a few hundred cards per hour, depending upon the complexity and the amount of data per card. However, prepared cards are read into the computer at speeds of 1,000 or more cards per minute. Because it is an off-line device, that is, a device not directly connected to the computer, the key punch permits many workers to prepare data in parallel. In most installations, a large number of key punch machines are used to match human preparation capability to the computer's needs.

Variations of the traditional key punch permit operators to enter data directly onto magnetic tape, which is then read into the machine at high speeds (over 100,000 characters per second) thereby eliminating the intermediate card production. Since a large key punch installation, say 50 key punch operators, can generate over 20 million cards annually, this more direct approach greatly reduces material cost as well as space and physical handling requirements. It also results in greater efficiency by improving the match between the human operators and the machine requirements.

It is also possible to use small satellite computers (see pages 68–71) to receive data from a group of 50 or more keyboards. The small computer consolidates the data, organizes it for a large job, and then either passes it directly to a main computer or stores the total result on magnetic tape for later processing. Using this approach, another increase in efficiency is obtained.

Electric typewriter

The electric typewriter is used as a directly or indirectly connected unit. In many instances the student will encounter Teletype Corporation's Model 33 Teletype machine. Another widely used commercial input/output terminal is IBM's Model 1050 electric typewriter. Statistics on the number of teletype units currently in service, as well as projections, are difficult to obtain, since the teletype is used not only as a computer terminal, console control unit, and data preparation device but also as a standard communication unit for sending messages, telegrams, and wire service reports. By the end of 1969 an estimated 110,000 of the Model 1050's were in use, with estimates for 1972 at over 200,000,[2] this type-

---

[1] "Data Taping Gets a Bit Cheaper," *Business Week*, February 15, 1969, pp. 134–138.

[2] Arnold Wiek, "350% Growth for Terminals by 1972," *Computer World*, February 19, 1969, p. 8. An estimated 3 million terminals will be in use by 1980 (*Data Processing Magazine*, February, 1969, p. 18). Although present major use for terminals is inquiry into credit, personnel, inventory, banking, and reservation files, the trend is to greater use of terminals for interactive problem-solving applications.

writer's appeal being the low cost per unit. Similarly, by November 1969 over 100,000 additional teletype units had been ordered to supplement several hundred thousand units currently in service. The Teletype at this writing is the least expensive terminal available to the average user.

Electric typewriters for computer use operate at speeds of from 100–150 words per minute, which though fast compared to the average typewriter is relatively slow compared to the computer's input ability. Thus, pooling of such inputs and outputs again suggests itself to build up the data flow volume. Such an approach provides the basis for the time sharing of computer facilities by a number of users on a real-time basis, that is, with users connected to the computer for immediate processing.

Mechanical printers

Traditional output devices for producing reports in volume are largely high-speed mechanical printers, produce more than 1,000 printed lines (120 or 132 characters per line) per minute. Since the usual page contains 66 lines or less, 16 or more pages are printed per minute, depending upon the number of lines actually printed per page. Usually this output is produced on multiset carbon forms, so that copies are available to a number of users. The same machines are also used to print payroll checks, statements and bills, automated letters, and such business material as address labels.

Again, the output of the computer is often in excess of printing capability, and a number of printers may be used, either in parallel connection to the computer or off-line, printing from magnetic tape.

Alternate forms of computer output may also be obtained from the generation of punched cards or magnetic tape under computer control. Although the traditional input/output devices are still predominant in the computer field, they are rapidly being supplemented by a cornucopia of advanced devices and approaches, which seek to further match human and machine abilities.

It is worth knowing about some of these devices and approaches to gain an appreciation of both the expanding market in computer terminals (expected to triple or quadruple in 1969–1972) and shifts in computer system design which will affect tomorrow's users. Figure 3.1 illustrates a variety of the newer input/output devices.

Advanced input/output devices

TV tube display

A variation on the electric typewriter or its cousin the Teletypewriter is the combined TV tube display and typewriter keyboard. This device permits

3.1. A gallery of input/output terminals. From military applications, such as enemy aircraft detection (a), stock quotation devices in broker's offices (b), police interrogation systems (c), and airline reservation applications (d), remote terminal use has spread to bank transaction handling (e), direct data collection from the factory floor (f), hospital paperwork processing (g), and hospital internal medical controls. Other applications include special inquiry during data collection and processing, as on election night, often in conjunction with large briefing-room boards (i), and centralized telephone inquiry and transaction stations (j). Special terminals permit businessmen to make computations at their desks (k), or to make inquiries about customer credit or stock status with audio response from simplified, brief-case size keyboards (l). The same device types are now widely used in advanced school classes (m), as well as in introductory classes at the elementary school level (n).

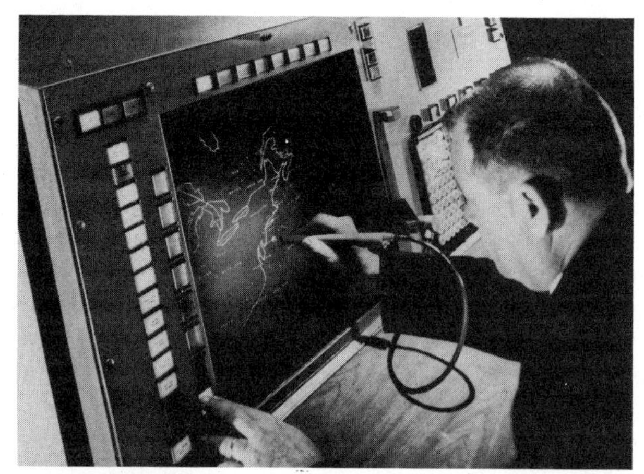

Military application

Burroughs Corporation

Brokerage application

The Bunker-Ramo Corporation

Police application

RCA

Airline application

Burroughs Corporation

Bank application

Burroughs Corporation

Factory application

Control Data Corporation

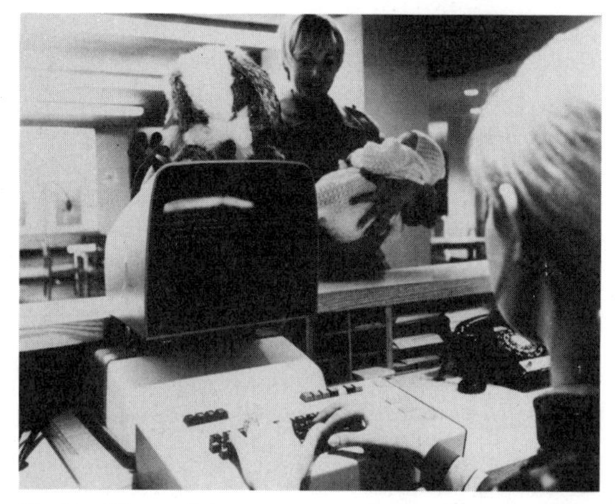

Hospital application

Courtesy of Honeywell, Inc.

Medical application

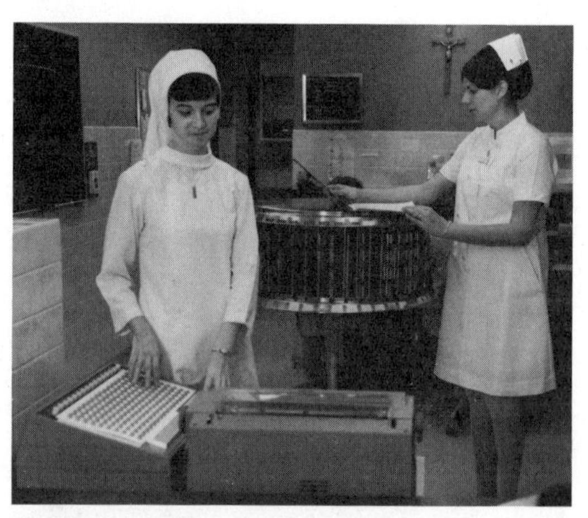

The Sisters of the Third Order of St. Francis

Election return application

RCA

Telephone application

IBM

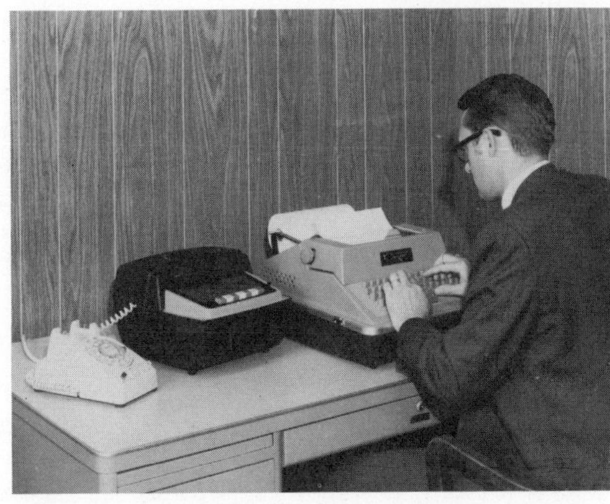

Office application

Courtesy of Data Science Group, Vernitron Corporation

Courtesy of Honeywell, Inc.

Credit application

Advanced school application

RCA

Elementary school application

RCA

the composition of material on a TV screen, instead of paper, so that flexible editing and correction ability is available. The operator of such a device is guided by a small flashing pointer which tells her the current character position on the screen where she is typing. As typing progresses, the pointer moves ahead. In the preparation of normal copy, the operation of the TV unit is no different from that of a regular typewriter. However, the operator may move her pointer, under keyboard control, to a desired correction point and enter the desired insertion, deletion, or correction. The copy is then electronically corrected on the screen. When the result is perfect, the whole page is transmitted to the computer, again under keyboard control.

When the same unit is used as an output device, tabular or graphical results may be displayed on the screen upon user request. Often, it is possible with such a device to eliminate undesired output by requesting modifications or revisions. When correct output is obtained, a paper copy may be requested from the keyboard, either from another output device or from a Xerox-type attachment to the TV console.

An extension of the same device adds graphical input capability by means of a "light pen" (see Figure 3.2) consisting of a small photoelectric cell and lens assembly connected to the electronics of the TV terminal. In the usual TV set, the picture is generated by the sweep of a projected electron beam which produces lines across the face of the tube. The timing of this sweep is precise. When the picture beam passes under the light pen as it is held to the face of the TV tube by the operator, the light pulse is detected by the photoelectric cell in the pen and passed to the com-

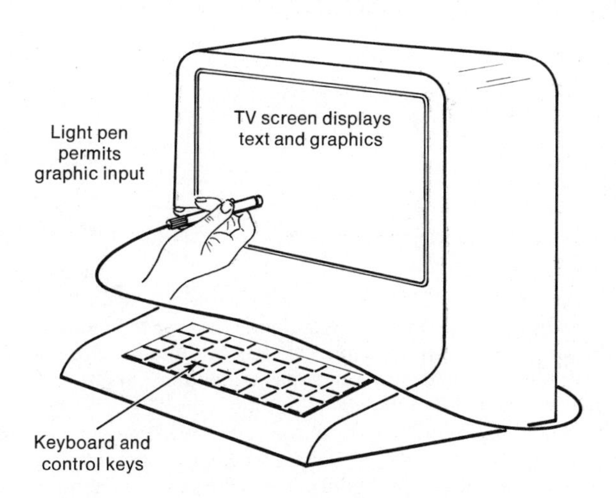

3.2. TV console input/output device with light pen.

puter. By evaluating the elapsed time from the start of the sweep to the detected pulse, the computer can determine the *X-Y* coordinate position of the pen on the tube, and with suitable keyboard instructions that point may be intensified on the tube as well as stored mathematically in the computer's memory. Continuing this process, which occurs in a fraction of a second, the operator may draw a picture on the face of the TV tube —and simultaneously have that picture's coordinates remembered by the machine (see Figure 3.3).

The applications of such a process are not obvious, but a few examples should give you an idea of the power of the graphical input idea. First, suppose the operator is a mathematician who wishes to fit a formula to a curve resulting from his experimental work. One way to accomplish this would be to take data points from the curve, enter them into the computer via the typewriter or a set of punched cards, and then proceed with the analysis. Using the TV-drawing approach, however, the mathematician could simply draw his curve on the TV screen and use the extracted *X-Y* coordinates as the data for analysis—a much faster alternative.

Or, suppose the user is a physician who needs to consult a patient record and enter medication instructions. By keying in the patient code number on the TV console, the physician may obtain the patient record on the TV screen. After consulting the record, he may ask for a medication check sheet in the same way. This form may have checkoff boxes, which

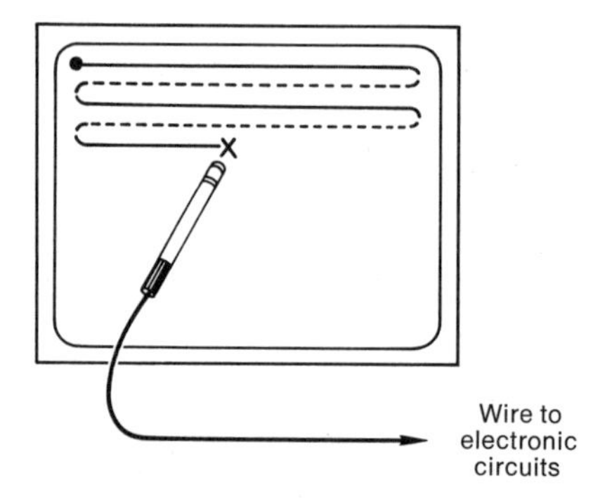

3.3. How the light pen works. The TV tube is shown with a magnified illustration of the picture sweep, a precisely timed generation of lines which form the TV picture when the horizontal lines (which should be familiar to all television viewers) are appropriately intensified. As the sweep passes under the light pen, its photoelectric cell picks up a light signal and transmits it to the console electronics. By measuring the elapsed time between the start of the sweep and the pen's signal, the unit can compute the X-Y coordinates of the pen's location. Thereafter, desired action may be taken under keyboard instruction. The light pen is an outgrowth of friend-or-foe radar developments.

may be filled in using the light pen. In this application, typing is virtually eliminated, the physician's time is saved, and the central records are automatically updated at once. Such a scheme is currently in use at several hospitals.

Other applications abound, such as engineering design, educational instruction with light pen and keyboard response by the student, graphical editing, and mathematical experimentation. The cost of the TV-type units is rapidly decreasing, largely because of extensive military procurement of these devices, and you may expect to see them in extensive commercial use within the next decade.[3]

High-speed printers

Refinements of the TV tube input/output device have also led to very high-speed output printers and to graphical applications such as the digitalized reconstruction of photographs. Using a high-precision TV tube and a combination of microfilm or Xerox devices, it is possible to obtain a printed output of 7,000 or more lines (132 characters wide) per minute, compared to about 1,000 lines per minute from a mechanical printer. It is difficult to appreciate these speeds until such devices are viewed in action. Even the mechanical printers generally used in today's computer installations produce reports faster than the human eye can follow. TV tube printers also have the ability to generate graphical output, so that charts, drawings, and other art may be included in reports as alternate displays to the familiar tabular listing of results (see Figure 3.4). Since such pictures may be generated mathematically from statistics, accounting data, or other computations, the intermediate drafting time usually required for report preparation is eliminated. One exotic example is the graphical display of an astronaut's orbital path after the spaceship leaves earth. A more commercial example is the summary of geographical statistics superimposed on county maps. Applications of this type are in current use.

Optical readers

Optical readers are another advanced form of input devices which seek to eliminate the tedious and error-prone key punching of cards traditional in the past. Modern optical readers handle a normal typewritten or printed page and produce the codes required by the computer. Current speeds for such optical recognition range to 2,400 characters *per second*, which

---

[3] Most widely accepted of the TV-typewriter terminals without light pen is IBM's Model 2260, of which an estimated 14,000 were in service in late 1969. TV terminal sales exceed all other terminals in growth today.

means that these readers can replace teams of key punch operators. It is possible, for example, to optically read gasoline charges, cash register tapes, airline tickets, subscription renewals, and similar records of everyday transactions (see Figure 3.5). Experimental extensions of the optical readers now in use enable the computer to read handwritten material.

Measurement input devices

Almost anything that can be measured can be automated for direct input into the computer. Most process control applications, such as the control of chemical plants, use a wide range of input devices which measure quantities such as temperature and pressure, convert the readings to numbers, and pass them on to the computer automatically. After computer testing and computation, appropriate correcting action can also be passed back to the process control from the computer, using output devices that will convert an output number into a valve movement, a motor control action, or a heat adjustment.

One human example of such measurement input devices (which involve analog-to-digital conversion in most cases) is the computer testing of electrocardiograms, which are usually taken in the hospital by a physician or trained technician. Some persons need to have frequent measurements of this type after a heart attack. Specialized input devices permit the patient's wife or the general practitioner to make such measurements in the home, transmit them to the hospital computer over the telephone lines, and have the computer analyze the peaks and curves generated by the measurement. The present reading may be compared to past readings by the computer, which can alert the specialist should any significant change be detected.

So the proliferation of input/output devices to feed information to the computer—and to receive humanly acceptable output from it—has been rapid. A recent count by one New York bank, for example, indicated that over 3,500 input/output devices which were currently on the market might be of use to it in its operations! We shall see more.

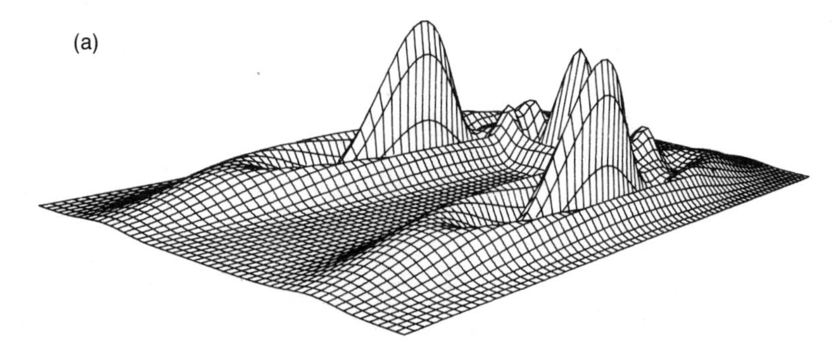

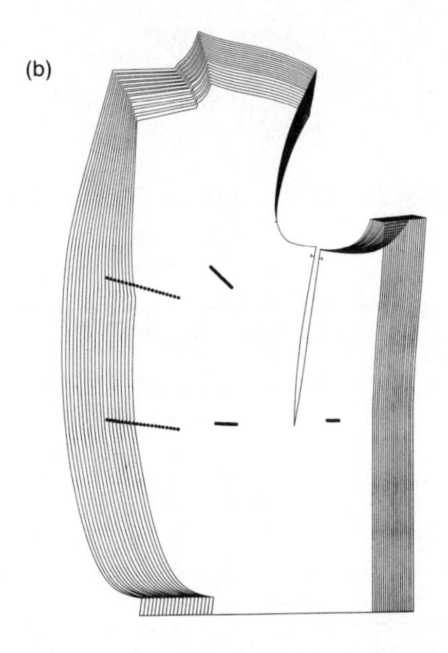

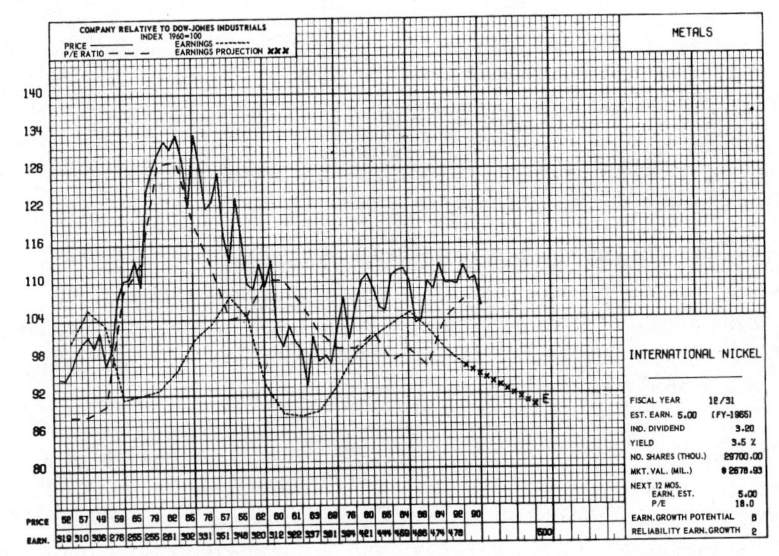

California Computer Products, Inc.

3.4. Computer graphical output. Perspective drawings from mathematic equations, automatic apparel pattern grading under computer control, and financial trend charts represent typical high-precision graphical computer output. The CalComp Plotter, which draws with pen and ink under computer direction, produces art of reproduction quality. Drawings of somewhat poorer quality can be photographed from TV tubes for reproduction.

(a) Bar code rules

0403040 04 03040

(b) Example of bar code

3.5. Simple optically-read codes, as used in gas stations. Foolproof bar codes, a special binary form of decimal conversion, can be printed by mechanical devices at filling stations. A credit card, inserted in a simple machine at the same time produces the customer account number in combination with the charge amount (in bar code and printed numbers). The lower illustration shows the numeric bar code, not a dollar amount. The combination of credit card number and the bar code dollar charge, both read optically, creates a transaction record for automated processing.

Output devices that perform work

One area of special interest to those concerned with design and production is the output device that will do useful work as a consequence of an information input from a computer. These devices wed the information and control capabilities of the computer to the energy-multiplying machines of the Industrial Revolution.

One such device is the numerically controlled machine tool, which, under instructions from a computer, will control the movement of a cutting tool to produce metal parts (see Figure 3.6). The idea is to control the movement of the cutting head or the table holding a work piece in the coordinate directions required to generate the desired item. Often such machines can be controlled in the *X*, *Y*, and *Z* directions—as well as in the rotational movements on each of these axes which may be needed to produce complex shapes. Thus, from a mathematical formula, an input drawing, or a keyboard input of certain point-to-point movements (say, for the location of holes in a plate), the computer may be used to generate incremental instructions for a numerically controlled tool, so that the tool can automatically produce the needed item without human intervention (except in mounting the material to be processed in the machine).

The implications of such technology are considerable in the field of production. Under numerical control, machine tools have little or no setup cost; little or no inventory of finished goods is required; the precision obtainable is greater than that with manual control; and few if any written specifications or mechanical drawings are required. It is thus possible to make economical production runs of specialized items—in fact, variations in design are easy, since all that must be done is to change the computer input or piece together electronically segments of previous production designs.

In other current production applications, the computer controls and supervises weaving and knitting machines, graphical drafting and plotting machines, and even generalized robots, which can be programmed to handle dangerous or heavy materials such as hot steel billets.

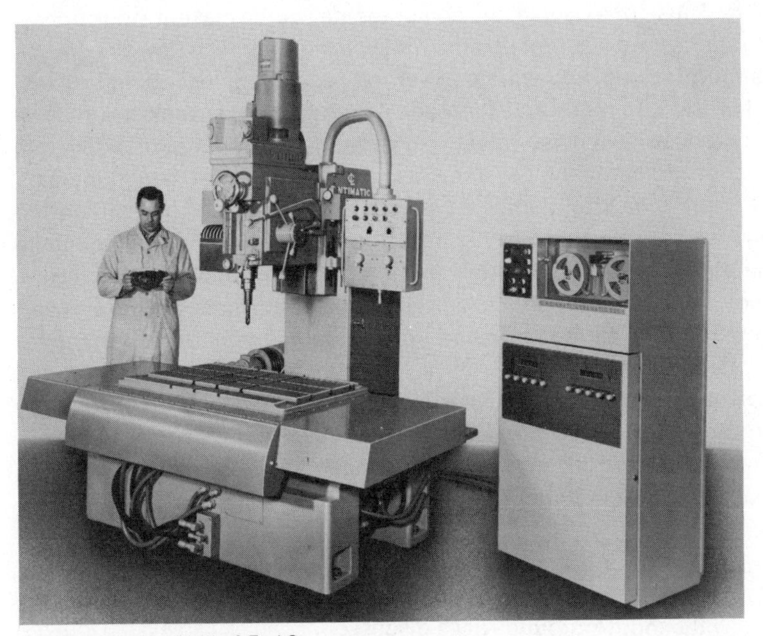

Courtesy of Cincinnati Lathe & Tool Co.

3.6. Numerically controlled machine tool. N/C Tool shown on the left is associated with the computer by the driving tape to the right. This $32,000 Cintimatic Vertical machine mills, drills, taps, and bores under computer control; this setup cuts scrap and other costs for precision operations in short runs and also permits greater flexibility in product design. Computer terminals can input instructions for production in a totally integrated system.

In the information production field, machines have been designed that set type under computer control, thereby beginning to eliminate the intermediate linotype operator, who may well be unfamiliar in the printing field of tomorrow. A study of the implications of such developments upon the labor force is beyond the scope of our present introduction to computers. However, you should realize that such machines are not only currently at work but are also increasing in number.

Output for the human ear

Another computer output scheme, which is both practical and amusing, enables the computer to talk in a human voice. Typically, such applications use a recorded voice with a limited vocabulary of, say, 150 words or a similarly limited list of recorded syllables. Under mathematical direction, the computer can cause these sounds to be combined in a variety of ways. The result, a sequence of sounds, can be used to provide the human user with information generated by or stored in the computing machine. Thus, for example, the computer may quote current stock prices, credit ratings, and inventory status with voice output. The New York Stock Exchange provides voice quotes over the phone to subscribing brokers, who dial the computer and the code for the desired stock to obtain a voice response giving the latest trade volume and price plus additional information. Experimental systems using the touch-tone telephone as a digital input device and voice as output are now in use, permitting the average telephone user to have direct access to the computer for simple computations or status inquiries. In the latter application, the small keyboard of the touch-tone phone is used to enter both limited programs and the data required for computation—or to supply the codes necessary to reach stored information.

Voice output from the computer may be combined with other forms of input/output devices to provide more effective human communication. For example, Figure 3.7 shows the combination of voice output and a TV-keyboard unit for computer-assisted instruction in schools.

Input/output devices summarized

To review the input/output devices discussed, consult Table 3.1. Note the wide range of types now in use as well as their range of application.

The newest innovations in input/output devices include not only the combination of many sensory inputs and outputs in a single device but also the expansion of sensory detail. For example, color TV-tube units increase the flexibility of the usual black-and-white unit by permitting color-coded data input and output to flow to and from the computer, so

RCA

3.7. TV console with audio response. This RCA Terminal is in experimental use in the New York City public schools. The child gets instructions visually on the tube and audially through the earphones, both under computer control. The children in the background work in the traditional manner. Many combinations of input/output, or I/O, devices and methods are currently in use.

colored forms and graphs can be handled by the operator. Laboratory developments also indicate that the familiar TV tube will eventually be replaced by solid state display devices, with large-scale "light panels," which permit the user to see more detail at once.

Designers are also rapidly expanding the capability of optical readers to handle different sizes and fonts of type. Expanded voice output and even some forms of human voice computer input are on the horizon. Various forms of touch input/output devices have been developed, both for production applications and to aid the handicapped. And inventors, using special input devices in the laboratory, have had some success with the computer analysis of scents.

Systems of input/output devices

It is not the development of this wide range of input/output devices alone that is of interest, but how they may be used in combination, that is, in a *system.* It is important to understand that in computer applications, as in most other fields, the sum of the parts can be greater than what one might expect from the individual parts.

TABLE 3.1

Input/Output Device Types and Their Uses

Device	Use
1. Standard Teletypewriters and Electric Typewriters.	Produce low-speed paper copy.
2. Typewriter-TV Combinations.	Eliminate paper. Text and corrections on screen.
3. Light Pen Devices (combined with above).	Permit graphical plus alphanumeric input/output.
4. Point-of-Use Recorders (shop transponders, data capturing cash registers).	Direct entry of both variable and semivariable production, accounting data.
5. Optical Readers (to convert familiar copy to computer codes).	Read cash register tapes, credit card slips, typed or printed copy. Some progress reading handwriting.
6. Magnetic Readers (read stylized characters, or codes on paper).	Bank check clearing, data and program entry to simple machines.
7. Various Analog-Digital and Digital-Analog Conversion Units.	
A. Digitalized Pictures (auto or manual).	Digitalize points measured at *X-Y* position for x-rays, fingerprints, maps, etc., to permit manipulation by computer, identification by matching with standards. Also for transmission electronically.
B. Digitalized Voice.	For computer voice recognition, translation, communication, and response. Stock exchange quotes, credit checks, security, instruction, etc.
C. Digitalized Measurements.	Transducers convert pressure, temperature, position, count, etc., to numeric output. Used in process control.
D. Numerically Operated Tools and Equipment.	Point-to-point and "continuous" machine tools, controls, drafting machines, type-setting devices, looms in textile field. Can control general purpose robots from computer program.
8. Specialized Devices in Several Fields.	
A. Medical Applications.	Medical "diagnostic" chair collects standard patient data. Electrocardiograms by phone. Process patient paper via TV terminal.
B. Police and Military Command.	Special radio, telephone, and input/output terminal links designed to capture and control operating data, plan deployment of the force, monitor results.
C. Airline Reservations.	Specialized terminals enter and retrieve passenger reservation data, collect statistical data.
D. Banking.	Specialized "window" machines handle input/output data needed for passbook updating, control of cash flow.

E. Other Fields.	In general, specialized input/output devices may be found in applications where (1) labor is scarce or expensive, (2) elapsed time has high value, (3) specialized operations are geographically dispersed, (4) skills are critical, (5) resources are scarce, costly, or perishable, or (6) danger exists. Thus, a missile checkout operation will have many specialized input/output devices.
9. Simplified Input Media.	Traditional punched, mark-sense, or porta-punch cards. Touch-tone telephone (key in message, get voice response). Photoelectric keyboards.
10. High-Speed Output Devices.	Traditional mechanical printers. Marriage of electronics and optics (TV tube to microfilm or Xerox). Large-scale graphical outputs (electronic briefing room displays in color).

Consider, for example, the combination of the TV-keyboard editing device as an input unit and the computer-controlled typesetting machine as an output device. Although the computer is the intermediary control and computation unit in handling the information that flows from input to output, it should be clear that an editor could perfect a document on her TV screen, introduce styling, such as type sizing and selection, and have the computer generate the detailed instructions required for an automatic typesetting machine (usually of the photo typesetting variety) to produce a series of pages from which printing plates can be made. There is little human intervention between the initial editing and the final product, thus eliminating many error-producing steps that often occur in the usual book production sequence. Furthermore, revisions in the manuscript become much easier under the new technology, since the entire record can be stored in a computer memory device and modified at will. Although wide acceptance of this approach has not yet been achieved, often for nontechnical reasons, a number of applications suggest that the trend to integrated editing-production systems will continue and expand greatly. Several interesting applications within these systems point the way. The computer can check spelling, arrange line justification and hyphenation, and produce a number of literary statistics that are of immediate use to the publisher. Such systems also greatly speed the production process, as well as preserve its accuracy. One application, now used, is the dissemination of computer-prepared stock prices for newspapers by the major wire services. Such data may be set automatically in duplicate at different locations without further proofreading.

In the same vein, consider the designing engineer who hopes to produce a new product. He may now sit down at his TV console, draw his product (in more advanced applications in three dimensions), and cause the computer to generate the instructions required by a numerically controlled machine tool to produce the finished part. In effect, the designer who sits at the TV console can think as if he were sculpturing in metal, because there will be little or no human intervention between him and the finished work. Such systems are now being used by the major automobile companies in the production of die sets for new cars.

As a last example, consider the production of a final statistical report from a series of field surveys, the results of which are recorded on forms that may be read by an optical reader (as currently used by the Census Bureau and many commerical market research agencies). These input forms are read into the computer by the optical device and analyzed according to the programs provided by the analyst. The output of this summary may be produced—with graphical displays such as bar charts—on a high-precision TV tube device that will generate either Xerox copies or master film slides for offset reproduction. If sufficient checks are built into the computer program, little if any human intervention need be used in the production of the statistical analysis from the time the field reports are received until the time the reports are mailed to the consumers of this information. The production cycle time is drastically reduced, and the probability of transcription error is dramatically diminished.

The concept of a total system can also be applied to the usually commercial transactions of order processing, inventory control, production planning, and shipping as well as to the correlated activities of cost accounting, customer analysis, and financial analysis. The idea is the same: to dispense with duplicated activities that may lead to error, to use as much as possible previously stored information, and to exploit to the extreme the capabilities of today's input/output devices in conjunction with the computer itself.

Since most of you will be working with remote terminals that act as both input and output units, it will be beneficial to realize that there are many extensions of the devices you may at first encounter in your input/output experience with the computing machine.

Pooling input/output devices

Since most input/output devices are relatively slow not only for the computer but also for most communications facilities, it is common in present installations and in those planned for the future to pool numbers of remote terminals and build the rate of information flow in both input and output directions (see Figure 3.8).

For example, through the use of a small computer dedicated to the job of communication switching and control, a large number of users may send and receive messages over one phone line, thereby greatly reducing

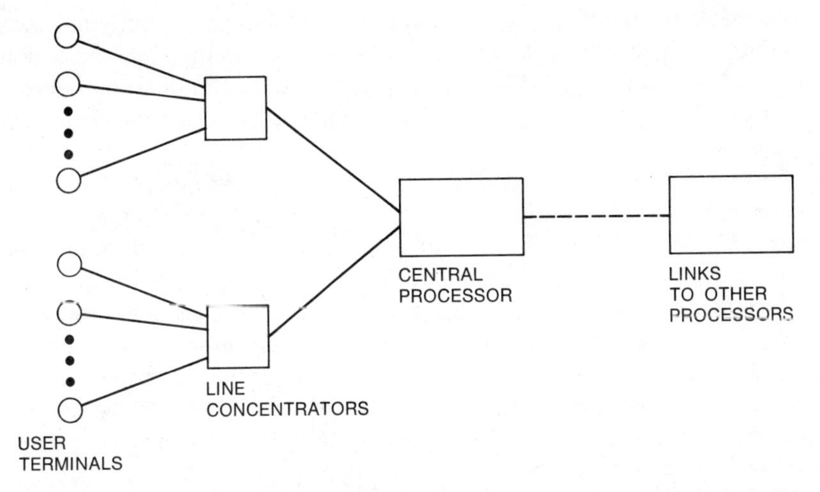

3.8. Communication system hierarchy. Use of small intermediate computers builds data volume by grouping input/output from many users, matching their data rates with communication line and computer capabilities. Variations of this "tree" presently handle both real-time and remote batch operations.

communication costs. Such "line concentrators" can group 20 to 200 or more teletype or other terminal users, pack their input together in identified form, and then transmit the total volume in an almost continuous stream to the computer. This is done by saving some of each user's input in small buffer memory areas at the line concentrator and then intermixing the individual buffer contents to provide sequential transmission to the main machine. This intermixing process is called multiplexing. The process is reversed when information comes back from the main machine. The computer output is again buffered at the line concentrator, then separated for each identified user's terminal at its slower output rate.

For obvious reasons, such concentrating schemes are growing in popularity and are in use both for real-time communication as well as for operations in which large amounts of input and output are passed back and forth from satellite locations to the main computer on a periodic basis. The latter scheme is called remote batching.

The end result of such developments is the growth of computer and communication networks which permit communication *between* main computers as well as terminal users who are geographically dispersed. For example, in early 1969 Control Data Corporation set up a national data processing network which links computers in over 25 cities. Three general classes of computers are involved: (1) the largest central processors, located in major metropolitan areas such as New York, Chicago, and Los Angeles, are backed up by (2) smaller machines which handle intermediate processing, communication switching, and buffering (see Figure 3.9), while (3) leased telephone lines provide the communication links. This system is typical of a number of private computer complexes now offering services to subscribers or handing corporate data processing on an integrated basis.

In concept and in practice, the same pooling effect may be obtained locally by having a large number of input devices feed information to a small buffer computer. This machine then accumulates the input data, usually on magnetic disc memory devices (see Chapter 4). The grouped information is then passed to the computer at high-information-transfer rates or reorganized on magnetic tape for batch processing. This approach eliminates intermediate punched card manipulations and increases the productivity of keyboard operators, often by 50 percent or more. In these mass systems, computer output and input are usually separated, and output is provided by high-speed printers.

Whether the pooling of data flow is accomplished locally or from geographically dispersed points, however, the idea is the same: to build volume and make its manipulation more flexible.

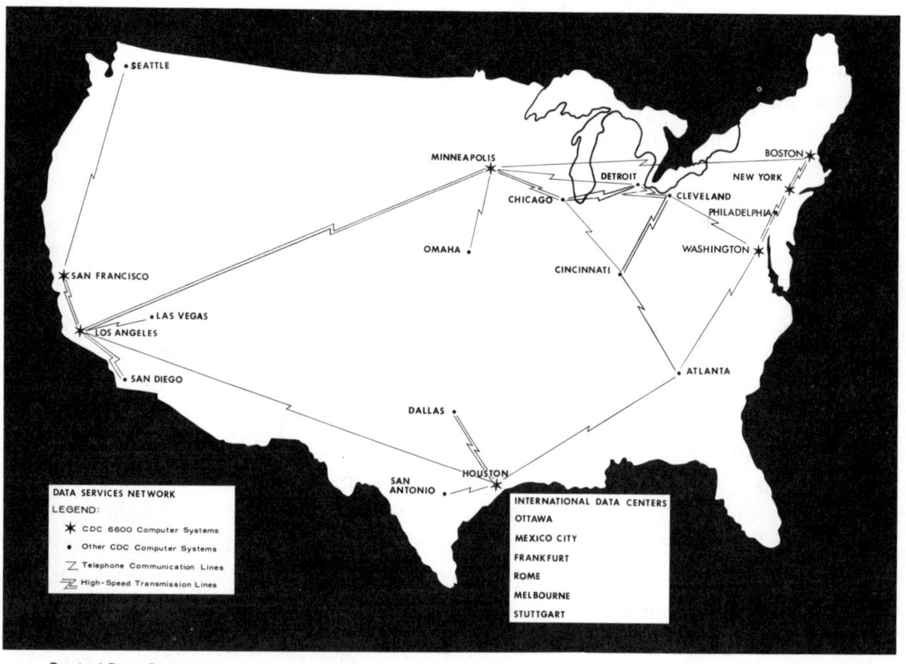

Control Data Corporation

3.9. A national communication-computer network. Control Data Corporation's system of interconnected computers, as it existed in early 1969. (*Source: Computer World*, February 19, 1969, p. 4.)

All such communication-computer complexes are invariably organized in a hierarchy of pooling arrangements, so that the "twigs" and "limbs" of the information flow "tree" may be brought together in a matched and balanced buildup of data flow.

In most cases, the success of such matching efforts lies in the exploitation of a number of computer memory device types of differing capabilities and speeds. The same may be said for the internal organization of a given main computer: its parts and functions are usually brought together by the flow of information through several memory devices which buffer and balance its internal information flow requirements.

Thus, it is helpful to know something about the characteristics of the memory devices now in use, in particular their main functions and how they are organized.

PROBLEMS

3-1 Why is it desirable to have a wide range of input/output device types available for use with a computing system?

3-2 Scan some of the periodicals listed in Problem 1 for Chapter 1 and note some of the current input/output devices advertised or illustrated there. From looking at several issues of these periodicals, what would you conclude about the technical shifts that are occurring in the input/output device market?

3-3 What measures would you suggest to assure that the input information being fed to the computer from an input device is as intended?

3-4 Why is the combination of input/output devices into a system with a central computer a powerful concept over and beyond the abilities of the input/output devices themselves? In particular, what effect do you predict when the computing and data manipulation powers of the computer are combined with machines that can do physical work under computer control—such as the numerically controlled machine tools described in this chapter?

FOUR

Memory devices

Computer memory devices may be classified by several of their characteristics, most importantly:

1. Form of access, that is, how information is placed in them and reached later;
2. Speed of access, that is, how swiftly information may be stored and retrieved;
3. Permanence, that is, how long information may be stored without deterioration;
4. Cost;
5. Storage volume.

In general, the faster the memory device and the more nearly it approaches random access capability—that is, the ability to go directly to a desired piece of information on demand—the more expensive it is, a figure often measured in terms of the cost per character or block of characters that may be stored.

Technically, each of the blocks, or words, of the memory blackboard will hold a number of characters determined by the number of binary digits, or bits, used by the manufacturer in the memory construction. Usually, the word size in bits is some multiple of 2, for reasons that will be clear in a moment. Typical sizes for the largest computers are 24, 32, 36, or 48 bits per word. The more bits per word, the larger the number that can be stored there in pure binary, and the larger the number of characters that may be represented there in the Binary Coded Decimal code of

Chapter 2. Thus, a 32-bit word may store a number up to $2^{31} - 1$ as an integer, one bit being reserved for a sign. When using an extended 8-bit BCD code, four alphanumeric characters may be stored. Or, using a 4-bit BCD code for numeric characters only, that is, just the detail portion of the code as described in Chapter 2, the 32-bit word may hold 8 numeric characters. In most machines, all of these alternatives are available; the selection is made, depending upon the application, either by the user or by the computer. Because of this variety of possibilities it is difficult to give a number for memory storage capacity without giving the corresponding method of storage that will be used. A general term that seeks to avoid this confusion rates memory size in blocks of bits, or "bytes," implying that alternate forms of storage are possible. A typical byte is defined as 8 bits. Thus, a machine having a memory of 50,000 32-bit words is rated as a 200,000-byte memory, a memory of 50,000 48-bit words as a 300,000-byte memory, etc. The user may figure out the number of characters his memory will hold, depending upon his form of storage. In the technical press, each of the above forms of description is used interchangeably.

Most modern computer memories are made of magnetic materials, which provide flexibility of design, high speed, and relatively permanent storage at low cost. Moreover, like the home magnetic tape recorder, magnetic memories permit the computer to read information nondestructively, although writing, which erases old information and replaces it with new, is also easily accomplished.

Other forms of memory devices are also used. For very fast storage and retrieval the computer's electronic switches are used to hold small amounts of information. At the other extreme, many computer systems use information that will never change; and for this purpose, high-density read-only memories—either optical spots on film or permanently wired matrices of interconnections—have been used. A list of typical current memory types appears in Table 4.1.

Access forms

The memory characteristic most important in influencing applications is the form of data access available. Sequential access, semirandom access, and pure random access form the main categories of interest.

Serial media: magnetic tape

Serial, or sequential, access memory media (of which magnetic tape, Figure 4.1, is the prime example) places memory in order as it might appear on a scroll. To reach information in the middle of a file, the computer must wheel through a number of intermediate records, passing over each one in turn until the desired point is reached.

TABLE 4.1

Memory Device Types

	Device	Use
1	Electronic Registers.	Very high-speed, used in control and arithmetic circuits.
2	Special Short-term Delay Circuits.	
3	Magnetic Tape.	Serial access only.
4	Magnetic Disc.	Semirandom access. Random access to a data block, serial search of block.
5	Magnetic Drum.	
7	Magnetic Card and Strip.	
8	Magnetic Cores.	Pure random access. Access often available to a binary character bit. The main working memory of most machines.
9	Thin Film Devices.	
10	Wire Rod Devices.	
11	Optical.	High density for permanent record of programs or data.
12	Thermoplastic.	
13	Wire and Printed.	Permits circuit alteration in machine.
14	Paper Tapes and Cards.	For communication, low-volume storage.

This process is similar to searching for a song on a prerecorded home music tape as opposed to selecting a song from a long-playing record by going directly to its track. Another analogy is the comparision between searching for information on a reel of paper tape as opposed to searching for it in an organized card file. Both the phonograph record and card file are forms of random access memory in everyday life. The term "random access" means that if we know its location, we can go to desired information directly and omit the time-consuming sequential search required by serial media. Similar random access devices, used in computers, are discussed later.

Magnetic tape applications in computer work are usually limited to the manipulation of massive files. However, since tapes can store volumes of data at low cost (say 10 million characters on a $40 reel) tape has been the traditional memory for commercial applications that occur periodically such as payroll computations.

For such jobs a file of transactions is first collected, or batched. For example, in the payroll application time cards for the week may be grouped together and copied onto a magnetic tape. The purpose of the application is not only to write payroll checks but also to update one or more master files containing historical payment, deduction, tax, and cost distribution data. Thus, the individual transactions in the transaction file must be matched against appropriate master file records. Typically, an employee number or code identifies common records in all the files in a payroll run.

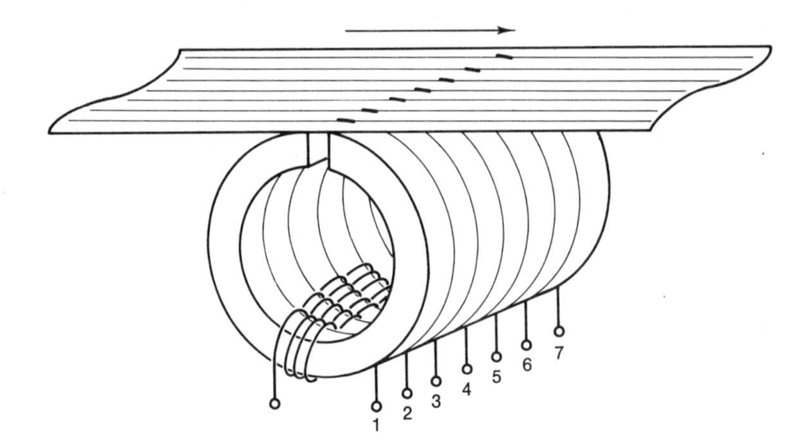

4.1. Concept of a magnetic tape unit. Magnetic tape, a plastic material coated with a ferrous oxide, passes over a bank of magnetic READ/WRITE heads. A stack of seven individual heads is shown. As the tape passes to the right, electrical impulses in appropriate combinations are applied to the head windings, causing locally magnetized orientation of the molecules in the tape. The effect is to produce magnetic spots across the tape. These spot combinations stand for alphabetic or numeric characters oriented across the tape. A message then consists of a sequence of characters read along the length of the tape. The compound seven-segment head shown records or reads a 7-bit Binary Coded Decimal code. Other head and code configurations are possible. Since typical magnetic tape is only $\frac{1}{2}''$ wide, magnetic READ/WRITE heads for computers must be manufactured to extremely high precision.

The tape files are presorted in a given order before processing, so that the records to be consulted, again in the sorted order, can be found quickly, often as the next record in sequence. Under such circumstances, retrieval time is reduced to a minimum, and tape processing of information becomes highly efficient.

In the payroll illustration, note the importance of grouping together a large number of transactions prior to actual processing. A large number of grouped and presorted transactions permit the computer to handle the transactions one after the other in an organized manner. In fact, the individual transactions may be collected from a number of different sources or may be prepared by a number of key punch operators working in parallel, which builds input volume to the computer's capacity. Thus, batch processing, as this is called, is one way to gain human-machine matching when tape memory media are used.

Finally, information from tape must be read into a random access memory form for processing so that the data from a given record can be manipulated. Thus, tape serves as a backup, or mass storage medium, in the memory hierarchy. As an example, the Internal Revenue Service and the Social Security Administration employ over 100,000 magnetic tapes each in their record keeping and processing. To store such volumes of data on other memory media would be prohibitively expensive.

A major drawback of tape, however, is the very large amount of sorting that must in fact be accomplished to achieve the desired state of efficiency. If it is a heavy tape user, up to 60 percent of a computer center's time can be devoted to sorting, as opposed to useful processing. Random access files do not suffer from this disadvantage, since information may be entered or retrieved in any sequence. Clearly, the latter ability is beneficial when a large file must be maintained that has small, but random, activity—that is, when only a few of many records need be retrieved, possibly in unsorted sequence.

Semirandom access memories: magnetic drums, discs, and cards

Attempts to create memory devices that will hold and process volume data on a direct basis have led to the creation of magnetic drums, discs, and card units as described below. Data storage volumes for such units range from a few million to more than a billion characters per unit, with the data organized in readily referenced physical locations.

These semirandom access devices correspond by analogy to the search for information in a well-organized library in which we have a book call number and a page reference, but want some detail on the cited page. We can go directly to the book and page, but must scan the page, usually sequentially, to find the desired item.

The reference process may be made faster by having smaller books or smaller pages or by giving a more detailed reference to a paragraph or line. But in general, a compromise must be struck between direct access and reference complexity for large files to avoid undue operating difficulties for users and electrical and mechanical complexity in hardware design.

Current semirandom access devices usually have some mechanical components (drums revolve, discs rotate, and cards must be shuffled). Moving parts in these devices can therefore cause some reliability problems if maintenance is not careful. For example, rotating shaft bearings can wear, temperature variations can affect alignment of parts, and vibration, dust, or grime can affect storage and retrieval accuracy.

Nevertheless, magnetic drums, discs, and card units are major components in today's communication-oriented computing systems because they offer nearly pure random access capability for data volumes whose storage in pure random access devices under present technology would be uneconomical.

The cost of storage in semirandom access devices, of course, increases with the advantages obtained by their use. For example, a magnetic disc pack that would hold 7.5 million characters of information costs from $350 to $400 as opposed to the magnetic tape's $40 cost for an equivalent volume of storage. This difference in cost per stored character becomes important for massive data files, which must be relegated to tape processing to hold down the total cost of storage.

Here are some illustrations of typical electromechanical devices currently in use as semirandom access memories.

1. The magnetic drum. Figure 4.2 shows a schematic diagram of a magnetic drum. You may think of it as a rotating blackboard.

A nonferrous drum (often aluminum) is coated with ferrous oxide recording material and rotated under fixed magnetic read/write heads, creating tracks of recorded information. These tracks are segmented into words by a synchronizing locator track with its own read head, as shown to the left in Figure 4.2. Direct access is thus possible to any given row and column combination by reference to a given track and the word within it. The speed of access is determined by the dimensions of the drum and its speed of rotation. Depending on the location of a desired word at the time of request, access time is between a half and a few milliseconds for commercial drums. Typical drum capacity is 60,000 or more Binary Coded Decimal characters, which are divided into 30 or more tracks. Transfer rate from drums can reach 1.2 million characters per second.

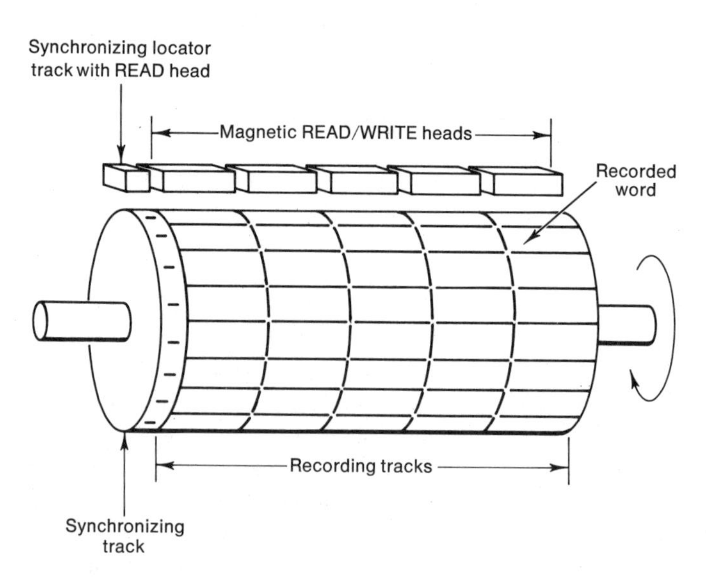

4.2. A typical magnetic drum unit.

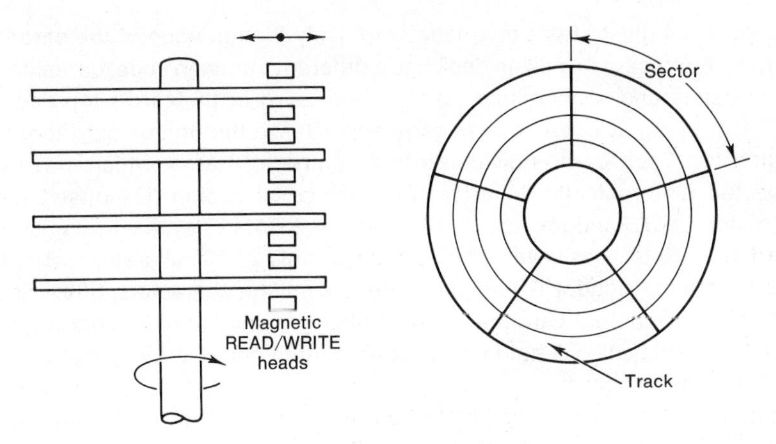

4.3. A magnetic disc file.

2. The magnetic disc. The magnetic disc is a variation on the drum design. It provides somewhat slower access to desired information, but by the same token, reduces the cost of stored information. Typical construction is illustrated in Figure 4.3.

Nonferrous discs are coated on both sides with magnetic recording material. The discs are then rotated, as shown, with read/write heads deployed on the surface of each disc. By moving the heads in and out perpendicular to the axis of rotation, tracks may be selected on the disc surface. To speed things up, each head may be allowed to traverse independently of the others. A typical large disc file may have 50 discs, with five sectors on the top and bottom of each disc. A disc surface may have 200 tracks, for a total of 100,000 tracks per disc file. At modern recording densities, such a large file may store about 250 million alphanumeric characters or a half-billion decimal digits, with information transfer rates of up to 156,000 alphanumeric characters per second. Smaller units, called disc-packs, permit manual interchange of the disc files for different jobs and generally store up to 7.25 million alphanumeric characters or 14.5 million decimal digits.

3. The magnetic card. Another design variation uses decks of magnetic cards. First, a given deck of cards is selected electrically, then one of the cards in the selected deck is retrieved mechanically, and then specific information on the selected card can be read or written at a specified row column location. You may think of this device as a large blackboard which has been cut into segments. You then refer to a specific segment as needed and work within that segment until the next source of information is needed.

Figure 4.4 illustrates a magnetic card. Only the top edge of the card is shown. Each card in a given deck has a different punched code, contained in the slots and semicircular patterns indicated in the card's top edge.

Flat rotating selector rods engage and release the unique card that is called for. Each card is divided into a number of tracks, which may be selected electronically. In a typical commercial design (National Cash Register Card Random Access Memory, or CRAM File), each magnetic card is $3\frac{1}{4}'' \times 14''$, has seven tracks, and can hold 21,700 characters. Thus, a 256-card cartridge will hold just under 5.6 million characters. Since one typical key-punched cardboard card holds a maximum of 80 characters, one 256-card deck will hold the same amount of character information as 69,000 punched cards.

Figure 4.5 is a schematic illustration of the device (National Cash Register's CRAM File) used to manipulate the magnetic cards of Figure 4.4.

When selected by rotating rods, one card drops from the box into the chute at *A*. At *B* a vacuum pulls the card into the drum, which in turn rotates the card over the read/write heads at *C*. When the desired processing terminates, a small door at *D* (not shown) opens, and the card is simultaneously released from the drum and passed onto a vertical chute. The card is then returned to the original deck at *E* and fitted back into the selector rods for the next cycle. A similar principle is used in IBM's Data Cell, which stores up to 400 million alphanumeric characters on a semi-random access basis.

Pure random access memory: magnetic core

If cost were no object, it would be ideal to maintain all the computer's stored information in pure random access form. Then any desired data

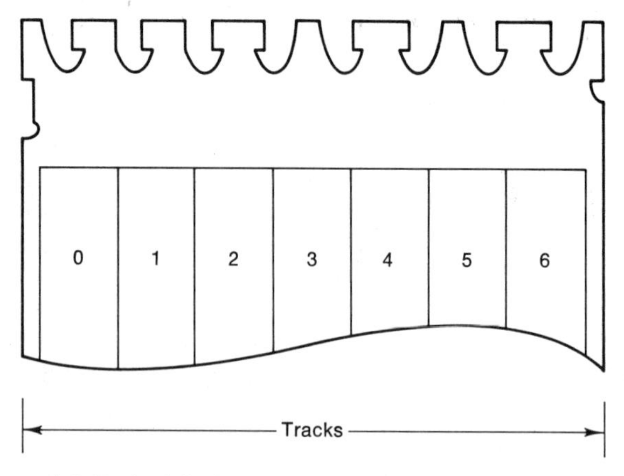

4.4. Typical design and layout of a magnetic card.

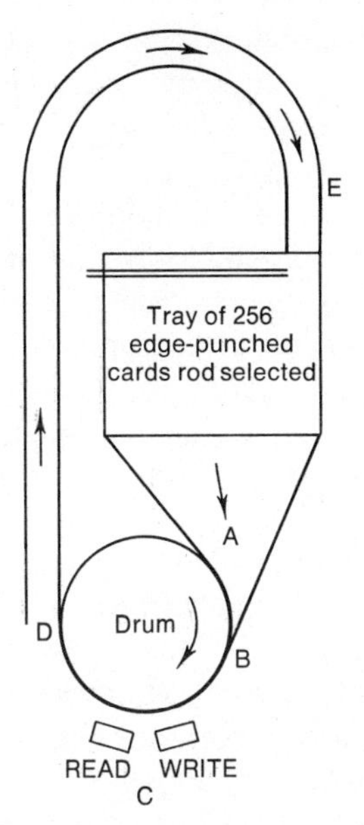

4.5. Stylized diagram of a magnetic card memory.

could be reached directly, and records could be segmented, manipulated, and analyzed on a direct basis, too. In the extreme case, it would be computationally desirable if the bit structure of a given character or group of characters could be accessed and analyzed directly in the binary codes the computer uses. Only a pure random access memory such as the magnetic core device, which is most typically used in today's machines, offers this capability.

Because the magnetic core device is the fastest memory in wide-scale commercial use and because of its pure random access capability, almost every modern computer uses some core memory, usually as the main internal computing memory of the machine. Whereas tapes, drums, discs, and card units may provide peripheral capability to build random access storage volume, the random access core memory is the workhorse which receives, processes, and returns data to these external storage devices.

The electrical principle used by magnetic core memory

As the name implies, the core memory is made up of arrays of small rings. In the following sequence, we illustrate how rings, or cores, are wired to provide memory capability. Figure 4.6 illustrates the electrical principle used in magnetic core memory.

When electrical current passes through a wire, that current generates a magnetic field about the wire. In particular, following the "right-hand rule'' familiar to most students of high school physics, there is a fixed relationship between the direction of current flow and the corresponding direction of the induced magnetic field. If you grab the wire with your right hand, pointing your thumb in the direction of current flow, the lines of magnetic force will flow in the direction of your fingertips, as shown in the top illustration of Figure 4.6. A reversal of the current will similarly reverse the direction of the magnetic field, as shown in the lower illustration. Donuts, called cores, of an appropriate magnetic material can be magnetized ''permanently'' according to the following principle: the direction of a core's magnetization may be reoriented into a clockwise or counterclockwise direction (that can represent binary 1 or 0) by a redirection of current flow or even by a directed pulse of current of sufficient magnitude. Since the magnetic core can hold its orientation until it is altered by another pulse of current, it can ''remember'' the last applied state, thus creating a memory of past events. Moreover, the whole process is symmetrical in that an abrupt reversal of the magnetic field, or core orientation, about a wire will cause a current pulse to flow in the wire. So, if a magnetic core can be made to change its state, a signal in its associated wire can be detected. This effect permits data to be read from the computer memory after it has been stored there.

A magnetic core segment

To create a memory unit from the individual magnetic cores, a specialized wiring arrangement is required. Although many variations in wiring are possible, one of the more usual arrangements is shown in Figure 4.7.

Small donuts of magnetic material are strung in a wire grid with the storage of 0's and 1's effected by the direction of the magnetization of the cores, as shown by the circular arrow for core (Y_1, X_2) in Figure 4.7. The individual cores have a sharp threshold, or critical amount of current required, to reverse their magnetic state. Moreover, a core's state can be reversed by reversing the direction of current flow passing through the grid wires. For example, if half the threshold current required to change

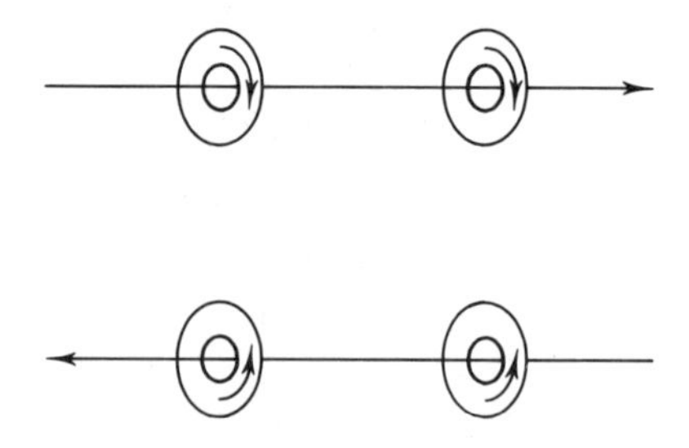

4.6. The electrical principle used in magnetic core memory.

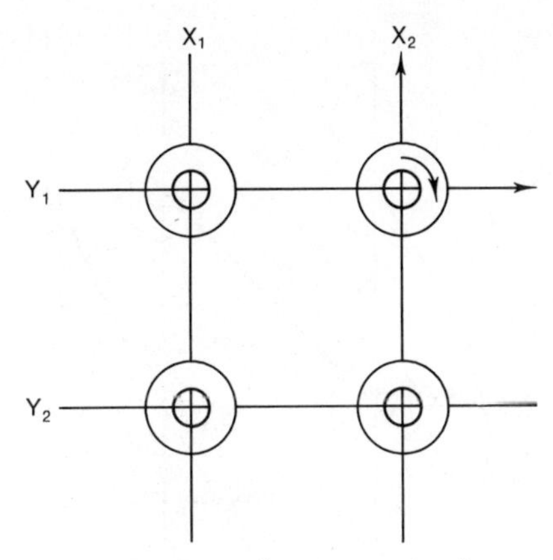

4.7. A magnetic core segment.

a core's magnetic state is passed through wires Y_1 and X_2 in the direction shown by the arrows, the current effects add only at the intersection of wires Y_1 and X_2, producing the magnetic state shown by the circular arrow. Reversal of the current direction in the same two wires will reverse only core Y_1-X_2. The other cores are not affected because the required threshold current for state reversal is not achieved. Thus it is easy to write information into the grid by appropriate switching and pulsing of the core's grid wires. In commercial design, a number of core planes are stacked, so that parallel access to a set of cores (representing a character or a group of characters in a word) may be achieved. Typically 24 to 48 cores, or binary bits, are used per word in core memory.

The core read cycle

We have seen how the state of a given magnetic core can be altered and how binary information can be written into a core memory. The process for reading information stored in the core is somewhat more complex, but is an extension of what we have already learned. Figure 4.8 shows the next step in memory construction, the insertion of a "sense wire" for reading.

To read information from a core, the computer uses a write-test-restore cycle. For example, a 1 may be written into a given core, or bit, location. If a 0 was there, the magnetic state of the core is reversed, generating a signal in a third sense wire. An existing 1 has no effect. Thus, it is possible to deduce what information was stored in a given location. However, since the read process destroys the original set of 0's which may have been stored in a computer word, the 0's must be rewritten in their original locations. This restoration process completes the memory cycle, which takes

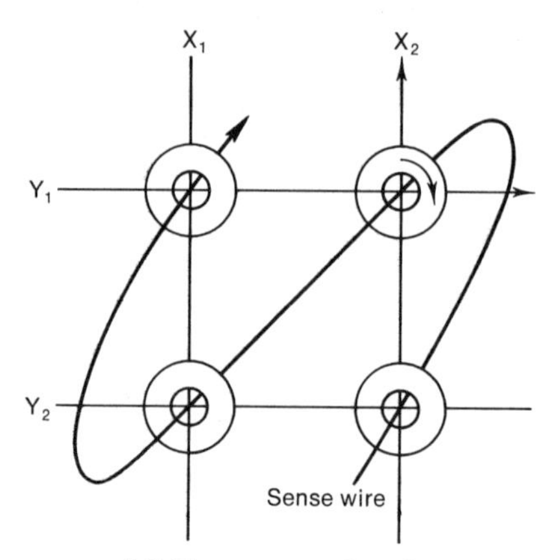

4.8. The core read cycle.

a few millionths of a second in modern machines. To speed the restoration process, a fourth wire, or "inhibit wire" (not shown in Figure 4.8) is often strung in the *X* or *Y* direction, parallel to the existing *X* or *Y* wires. This more complex memory design simplifies the electronic switching circuits which would otherwise be required for memory restoration.

The use of alternate memory devices

To take advantage of the variations in memory characteristics in the hierarchy of speed and cost (which is usually inversely related to volume storage applications) information may be passed from, say, tape to disc to drum to core and then back again during a given processing run. Such swaps are under computer control in most cases, and the beginning user is not always aware of them until he plans more complex computations and data manipulations. Yet an understanding of the functions of different memory types is beneficial to the comprehension of advanced applications.

In your early experience, you probably will not encounter tape applications, but disc, drum, and core storage in their remote terminal operations, which demand random access rather than batch serial processing. Commands from the remote terminal are often used to arrange memory swaps in time-sharing systems, so programs and data may be stored on and retrieved from disc or drum for processing in the faster core, usually limited in storage capability because of cost. After processing, results are often returned to the slower memory devices for subsequent reference. In many communication-oriented computer systems, drum and disc memories are also used as communication buffers—since they are fast enough to collect and organize incoming information for fast core processing—as well as to distribute the results of the processing to many users, either directly or through line concentrators.

A number of technical developments point the way to more and cheaper corelike memories in tomorrow's computers. Trends toward printed memories, laser memories, and similar devices offer the hope of an alternative to the expensive production methods now required for core memory production, which, as we have noted, requires three or four minute wires to be passed through a multitude of small magnetic donuts having holes only a few thousandths of an inch in diameter.

When such production breakthroughs occur commercially—as they most surely will—there will be a shift to larger and larger pure random access storage in tomorrow's computers. This trend will improve the efficiency of the total computing system, because every computation and data processing step performed requires reference to information stored in some form of memory device. Given a fast arithmetic and control unit, the faster will be the access and retrieval time for the computer's memory and the faster the total system.

The size of core memories is often a major determinant of total system cost, so that the amount purchased for a given installation is carefully evaluated. A typical business computer may have a core memory capacity of 300,000 characters, usually divided into 50,000 blocks, or words. At current manufacturing levels, core storage costs run one to two cents per bit or roughly ten cents per character for average quality memories, as compared with costs of ten cents per bit or roughly a dollar per character in core memories manufactured in the early 1960s. Very high-speed cores, which are physically small and as a result more difficult to produce are proportionately more expensive, depending largely upon access speed and flexibility. Current core speeds for cycle time range from a few millionths of a second to a few billionths of a second. Projected manufacturing costs for core-type memories in the 1970s estimate that a cost of a tenth of a cent per bit can be achieved. Even at that cost core memory or its equivalent is no place to store a billion-character file. Memory swaps with slower memory devices undoubtedly will continue to be necessary.

Magnetic memory permanence and system reliability

Although in the absence of any major physical disturbance the magnetic memory devices described will retain the information stored in them indefinitely, several forms of extraneous activity can cause damage to a magnetic memory's contents and should be of concern to any computer user who does not want to experience difficulty in processing.

Major changes in temperature or humidity (a fire or air conditioner failure), physical shocks (dropping a magnetic tape or vibrating a magnetic disc or drum), intermittent electrical conditions (defective fluorescent lights, fluctuating supply-line voltage, or sparking motors in the vicinity), or stray magnetic fields (roving janitors with powerful electric vacuum cleaners) may cause random alteration in computer memory content. Physical hazards can also affect the quality of home-recorded music tapes, but the listener is seldom aware of the minor changes that occur in his hi-fi system over time, since minute losses in fidelity are not critical to system performance. However, with the dense storage and critical coding used in computer memories, even the alteration of one binary bit in a coded number or instruction can cause computational disaster. For this reason extreme care in design and operations is exercised in computer centers. But occasionally inadvertent memory change will cause temporary suspension of computer operations.

To restore normal operations, backup memory copies (normally kept in all computing centers) are brought into play, and in most cases normal operation is resumed with little loss of current production. In well-designed systems error detection and recovery are automatic, and minor problems only "gracefully degrade" system efficiency.

Nevertheless, the user is well advised to keep copies and documentation of his work, so that he will have insurance against loss or damage.

Because difficulties similar to those described for computer memory devices can also plague input/output devices and communication circuits, protective measures (such as redundant checking of transmission, known as full-duplex communication, which returns every transmitted signal for verification at the source) are employed in circuits that connect users to the central machine as well as within the central machine's components.

As computing and communication circuits become more complex, the problem of total system reliability increases, and both equipment manufacturers and professional users devote correspondingly more care to double-checks at all stages of operation to assure the continuing success of their installations. In fact, the efforts in this direction are so great that the beginning computer user can assume that the computing system he is using is in working order; if he does have trouble its source will in all probability be his instructions to the system or the data he provides it. Even though dramatic exceptions to this general rule have occurred and will occur occasionally in the future, today's computing machines are put together with a quality seldom found elsewhere in the modern market. If our automobiles and home television sets worked one millionth as reliably as computers do, there would be no local electronic or garage mechanic who could pay his rent: they all would be out of business.

PROBLEMS

4-1 Suggest some data processing applications that could appropriately and economically be handled by serial access media, and contrast these applications with those that would require a random access form of storage and retrieval.

4-2 Why is it desirable to have a wide variety of input/output units that can feed data to and receive data from a computing system? Relate your answer to human needs and capabilities as well as to economics and technical possibility.

4-3 Scan the technical press (some suggested sources are cited in Problem 1-1) and find at least ten different forms of input/output devices that might be useful in practical applications. State some applications for each of the input/output devices you find.

4-4 Discuss the probability of disaster at your computing center and the preventive measures you could take to protect yourself from such eventualities. Expand your consideration to the problems of data and program privacy as well as security. If a large number of users have common access to a computer's memory storage facilities, what precautions must one user take to prevent access to his private information by another?

4-5 Suppose that a remote terminal input/output device can generate an information rate measured in equivalent bits per second, or "bauds" in telephone company language. If one such device has an output of ten bauds, and a telephone line can handle 2,000 bauds under ideal conditions, what is the maximum number of remote terminals that can be concentrated on the line, given an appropriate buffer, or line concentrator? What are the advantages of such pooling over the use of the telephone line by a single user? How can the same form of pooling be used to build data volume for a computer locally?

4-6 An old saw often quoted in foreman training programs is, A short pencil is better than a long memory. That statement is certainly true in regard to human memory capabilities: forgetfulness is a human trait. Make some comparisons between human memory and computer memory traits—include at least a few that are favorable to the human. Although the human memory tends to forget detail and human recall generally degrades rapidly with time, it is virtually impossible to wipe from the human memory certain of its contents, such as traumatic emotional experiences, youthful impressions, and facts which seem important to the individual. Drugs, alcohol, and physical shock may temporarily erase such memories, but nothing short of killing the individual is a guaranteed treatment for eliminating his memories of the past. The computer, on the other hand, is quite different. Its recall is essentially perfect. In the absence of physical or electrical shocks, the computer memory will generally hold reams of detail for an indefinite time without degradation. Yet the total computer memory can be erased easily, either by a disaster (corresponding to the death of the human subject) or intentionally by the machine's user. When the computer memory is erased, there is no residual, or lingering, record of the past. The user can start with a clean slate. Think of other differences and discuss them.

FIVE

Data and programs in memory

At this point you should have some idea of how computer memories and input/output devices work. Now let's shift gears from hardware to computer programming. Forget that the memory of your computing system is electronic (although some electronic detail will be mentioned hereafter). Picture your computing system not as a batch of electronic parts, but simply as a mechanism that is totally responsive to your demands and totally deterministic in its operations. In particular, it will be helpful if you can begin to conceive of your computer as a very simple device, one which symbolically shuffles information from box to box in a set of pigeonholes, much as the postal clerk sorts and retrieves letters from his address rack.

Memory layout and how it is used

Without loss of generality or understanding we may now turn from the details of memory construction and economics and look upon the computer's main memory device as a *giant electronic blackboard.* Usually, this working blackboard is a magnetic core or may be thought of as such. (Data and programs from tape, drum, and disc will be passed to the core for processing.)

Your electronic blackboard is laid out in a definite physical format, and your data and processing instructions will be stored on this blackboard in readily located blocks or squares.

Although some designs are organized about the ability to reference individual characters for processing records of varying length (a variable word-length machine), the more usual design deals with information in *blocks* of characters (a fixed word-length machine). We shall assume the latter design hereafter.

Thus, we may conceive of the electronic blackboard as being divided into a large number of squares, each of which may contain a block of characters. It is possible to address each of these blocks, or "words," by reference to the row and column of the blackboard layout (see Figure 5.1). The combination of a row number and a column number can be used to number each of the boxes, or squares, uniquely, so that later reference to that number will lead us directly to the desired location and its contents. (This standard numbering scheme for tables, or "arrays," will be useful in Chapter 11 and thereafter.)

Using an input device, you can place data in the memory boxes in several ways (to be discussed in Chapter 8). By analogy this process corresponds to placing letters in given pigeonholes in the post office address rack. The clerk does not need to know the contents of a letter to put it in its addressed location. He need only to know where it is to go (see Figure 5.2).

It is also possible to place instructions in memory boxes (again by a process we need not now discuss). For example, see the instructions stored in boxes 11, 21, and 31 of Figure 5.3. The instruction shown in box 11 can be taken to mean: "Take the contents found in box 13, add it to the contents of box 23, and place the result in box 33." To perform such a task a postal clerk, for example, would look at the letter stored in box 13, which contains a 3 and at the contents of the letter stored in box 23, which contains a 4; add the two numbers found (a task performed by the

Rows \ Columns	1	2	3
1	11	12	13
2	21	22	23
3	31	32	33

5.1. A simplified memory layout. Assume that each numbered box above can contain a coded message or data, and that we may either store or retrieve the message contained in a particular box by reference to its address or number, as shown for each box in the diagram.

Columns

Rows	1	2	3
1	11	12	13 3
2	21	22	23 4
3	31	32	33

5.2. Placing data in the memory boxes. Suppose we place data in arbitrarily selected memory boxes, as shown for boxes 13 and 23, which contain the numbers (shown in decimal for simplicity) 3 and 4, respectively.

computer's arithmetic and control circuits); and finally place the result on a slip of paper that he would insert in box 33.

Suppose we had also told the clerk as a matter of standard policy to follow the instructions he found in a given column of his rack in sequential order, starting at the top of the column and working in order to the bottom. After starting at box 11, he would progress to box 21 then to box 31.

In Figure 5.3, therefore, if he had started at box 11, the clerk would go to box 21. There he would be instructed to publish, or display, the sum he had obtained in box 11, namely, the previously computed answer, 7. (In the computing system, this answer would appear on the output device.) Having done this, our clerk would then progress to box 31, where he would be instructed by the instruction END to stop his work.

The instructions shown in Figure 5.3, of course, are not stored in the boxes of the computer's memory verbally, as we have shown them, but as a numeric code in the binary system of Chapter 2. To illustrate, sup-

Columns

Rows	1	2	3
1	11 LET 33 = 13 + 23	12	13 3
2	21 PRINT 33	22	23 4
3	31 END	32	33

5.3. Storage of computer instructions in memory. Suppose we now store in the above boxes some additional information: instructions for the manipulation of data stored elsewhere in the blackboard, or memory.

pose the codes are expressed in decimal for clarity and that we have an instruction format of the following form for the command appearing in box 11:

Operation Code: First Address: Second Address: Answer Address.

Further suppose that the decimal number 10 placed in the first position of the above format causes the computer to add. Then the instruction could be written as 10:13:23:33 or simply 10132333. The computer, by segmenting the two-digit parts of such an instruction, could unravel the meaning and then perform the operation indicated, "Add the contents of 13 to the contents of 23, and place the sum in 33." (Similar codes could also be developed for the PRINT and END instructions in Figure 5.3, with the use of an appropriate numbering and format scheme.)

Notice that if both instructions and data are numbers, the computer (or the clerk) could not tell the difference between them unless it (or he) followed the sequential operating policy described above. But given an instruction starting-point, a sequential policy of box progression, and a final instruction that stops the sequence of instructional steps, there is no confusion.

This is how computer programs work, and the steps shown in boxes 11, 21, and 31 of Figure 5.3 constitute a legitimate computer program, assuming we already have the data available for manipulation, as shown in the figure. The result of the program of Figure 5.3 is shown in Figure 5.4. The answer, decimal 7, stored in box 33, results from the execution of the instruction shown in box 11. The result of the instruction in box 21 is the display of the contents of box 33, namely, the number 7 on the computer's output device. The operation stops because of the instruction END, in box 31. Notice the sequential execution of the instructions shown in boxes 11, 21, and 31. Also note that the instructions shown refer to the locations of the memory boxes in which the required data is to be found or stored, *not to the numeric contents* of the boxes. The instructions tell the machine where to go and what to do with what it finds there, but nothing more.

Rows \ Columns	1	2	3
1	11 LET 33 = 13 + 23	12	13 3
2	21 PRINT 33	22	23 4
3	31 END	32	33 7

5.4. Execution of instructions.

Technically, the numerically coded instruction discussed above (10-132333) is called a machine language instruction, since the computing machine works with such codes internally. Obviously, the user of computing equipment does not care to deal with such unfamiliar codes and numbers; nor should he care where the computer stores his data or instructions.

Conceptually, there is no reason why a set of more familiar symbols (letters, words, or special characters such as =) could not be substituted for the numbered addresses and operations just discussed. Such a unique conversion is shown in Figure 5.5, in which each numbered address is arbitrarily assigned a letter and the instructions are accordingly modified. (As before, we show English words for commands and adopt a familiar form of statement for clarity.)

The coding for both the locations and the instructions is totally arbitrary, but unique. Compare Figures 5.4 and 5.5. Although the manipulation called for is the same as in Figure 5.4, the reference in Figure 5.5 is to more familiar, or user-orientated, symbols, rather than to absolute memory addresses such as the numbers of Figures 5.1 to 5.4.

All of these unique translations, including the assignment of storage locations (described more fully in Chapter 6), can be carried out readily by the computer. The exact process is not important to our present train of thought, but the approach is to create a small dictionary of memory assignments and their corresponding absolute addresses as well as a dictionary of operation codes. Such dictionaries can be generated by the computer and stored elsewhere in its memory.

Thus, accepting the translation possibilities shown by a comparison of Figures 5.4 and 5.5, we see that computer instructions and a sequence of instructions, or program, can be made reasonably sensible, or user-oriented (i.e., problem-oriented), rather than machine-oriented as would be the case if we dealt only with numeric codes and absolute addresses (rather than symbolic addresses and, therefore, symbolic instructions or programming). Even though this is true, it is helpful to remember that the manipulation of symbols, which we will refer to hereafter exclusively, is really a manipulation of the coded contents of physical memory locations.

Information stored in the computer does not float around at random; it is handled in a totally deterministic manner, and if we go to the trouble to make the analysis, each step, each data movement, and each intermediate result can be traced from the beginning to the end of any program.

To make this point clear in conclusion, consult Figure 5.6, which shows the same memory layout as Figures 5.1 through 5.5, but with the original contents of addresses 13, or A, and 23, or B, changed. Note that the instructions shown in the first column remain unchanged, but the answer that will be printed from the contents of address 33, or C, is now different.

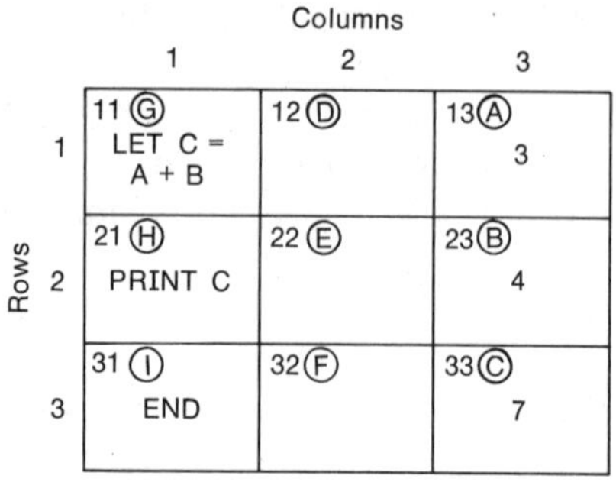

Columns

Rows	1	2	3
1	11 Ⓖ LET C = A + B	12 Ⓓ	13 Ⓐ 3
2	21 Ⓗ PRINT C	22 Ⓔ	23 Ⓑ 4
3	31 Ⓘ END	32 Ⓕ	33 Ⓒ 7

5.5. Symbolic translation of memory locations and instructions.

The same set of instructions has operated on different data; this can be done because the program is *separate* from the data values. The program refers to memory locations, *not to their contents.* So the program may be general—as Babbage observed for his machine and the corresponding Jacquard loom. Once reduced to a procedure, the weaving pattern is the same regardless of the color of the threads. Only the result is different.

The post office analogy may help to further set this important distinction in your mind. The postal clerk delivers his mail to its assigned addresses. Whether 123 Main Street, or house A, receives *Playboy* or *The Atlantic Monthly* is not his concern: the mailman follows his assigned route. The computer processes data with equal impartiality. Both the postman and the computer take things as they come and process them according to set procedures. The difference is that the computer user can design and control his own computational procedure, or program, in ways that will soon be described.

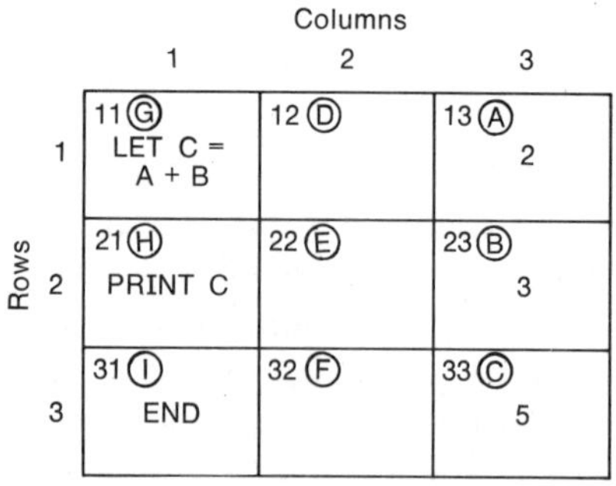

Columns

Rows	1	2	3
1	11 Ⓖ LET C = A + B	12 Ⓓ	13 Ⓐ 2
2	21 Ⓗ PRINT C	22 Ⓔ	23 Ⓑ 3
3	31 Ⓘ END	32 Ⓕ	33 Ⓒ 5

5.6. Data shown independent of instructions.

PROBLEMS

5-1 Suppose a variable called X takes on the successive values 1, 2, 3, at different points in time, as shown in time sequence in the boxes below. Also suppose that a variable called T is initially set to zero, as shown in the first box in the T column below. You are to perform the operation, LET T = T + X, step by step in time, working down the page from top to bottom, with the understanding that the statement LET T = T + X means precisely the following: Add the old value of the box called T to the present contents of the box called X and place the result of that addition in the box called T, shown at the present time. The boxes required are shown below. What is the final value contained in box T, that is, the value of variable T, after your accumulation? Fill in all the boxes and trace the progression of your result in time. Note that the contents of box T is initialized to zero at time zero, and that the progression in time is in discrete intervals. (If you have filled in the boxes correctly, you should obtain 6 as the last value of T.)

	[0]			**TIME 0**
T	[ ]	X	[1]	**TIME 1**
	[ ]		[2]	**TIME 2**
	[ ]		[3]	**TIME 3**

5-2 Repeat the previous problem assuming that there is only one box called T, and that you will update it by erasing the old value shown and replacing it with the new value determined at a given time. The contents of box T is initially set to zero before the operation starts. What is your final answer for T? Fill in and erase the contents of box T as required to get your answer. Relate the operations of this problem to those of the previous problem.

			[1]	**TIME 1**
T	[ ]	X	[2]	**TIME 2**
			[3]	**TIME 3**

5-3 Suppose instead of changing the contents of box X with time, we have three values of X as before, which are respectively stored in boxes called X(1), X(2), and X(3), as shown below. Assume also that the procedure is now to sequentially consider the contents of the three boxes in the order X(1), then X(2), then X(3). The task is to accumulate their contents in exactly that order, following the rule T = T + X(I), where I symbolically represents the numeric values 1, 2, 3 in that order. Again, as in the previous problem, trace the sequence of numbers that would appear in box T, using your eraser as needed. (Assume the initial contents of box T is zero.) What is the final answer? Compare this accumulation of numbers located in a list of successive boxes to the previous results of Problems 5.1 and 5.2, in which the values of X change with time.

		X(1)	[1]
T	[ ]	**X(2)**	[2]
		X(3)	[3]

SIX

Programming essentials

Computer programmers seldom use the machine language instructions discussed in Chapter 5. Instead, they use English-type or symbolic-type instructions, which are then translated to provide the needed machine detail. A brief discussion of the intermediate translating steps will help you bridge the gap between the preceding and the following chapters.

Figure 6.1 illustrates what happens when you provide the two things the machine needs to go to work: (1) your data and (2) your program, or the sequence of instructions expressing your data processing intent.

A supervisor at the top

The organization of internal computer operations is analogous to what you would find in many industrial production firms. To handle many different production jobs, you require a supervisor to schedule work, allocate appropriate facilities, and control the flow of work. In the computer, this is done by a *supervisory control program*, supplied by the machine's manufacturer, which resides permanently in the main core memory of the machine. As the beginning user, you will never see this complex set of instructions, nor need to. But you will become aware of the supervisor's work as you run your jobs on the machine. For example, if a number of users are simultaneously demanding machine time, as is the case in modern time-sharing applications, one function of the supervisor is to manage

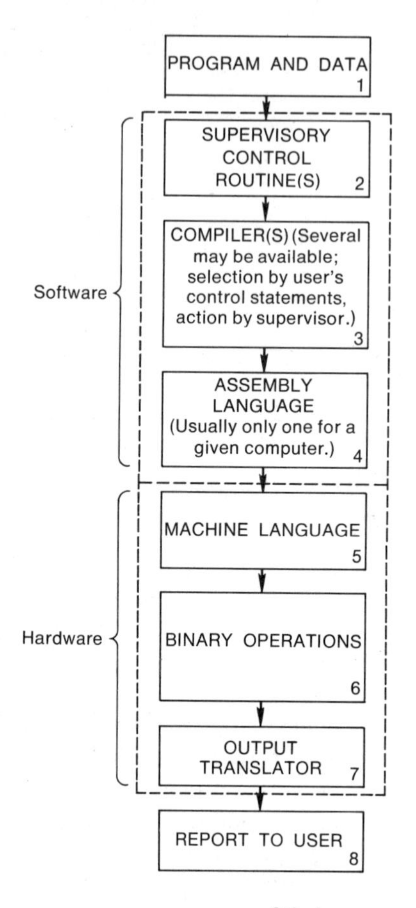

Prepared by User.

Prepared by Computer Manufacturer: selects correct compiler, schedules work flow, controls input/output.

Prepared by Computer Manufacturer: acts as an encyclopedia to generate a detailed list of assembly instructions from user's program. Detailed, but easy to read output. A one-many translation.

Prepared by Computer Manufacturer: acts as a dictionary to translate output of compiler into machine language. Usually a one-for-one translation. Allocates addresses.

Built into machine electronically as hardware. Converts input machine symbols into binary for execution.

At time of execution, operations and addresses are shown in binary. These binary codes initiate switching and sequence of steps to complete problem. Answer is then in binary representation.

Converts binary (or its possible variations) into alphanumeric that user can read.

The final result.

6.1. A programming hierarchy.

the flow of input/output information to identified users, to allocate time slots for execution of their respective jobs, and to provide the appropriate facilities required in each case. The supervisory tasks just mentioned are performed automatically. The term "system command" is used for those forms of user communication with the machine that can alter supervisory control actions. Further discussion of system commands appears in Chapter 7.

Compilers and what they do

At most installations, the supervisor has available a number of master translation programs known as *compilers.* One compiler is available for each alternative language the machine can accept for processing. Thus, if your machine can handle the BASIC language it will have a BASIC compiler or its equivalent.[1] The supervisor selects an appropriate compiler for use following the user's choice of language to be used.

The compiler has two main functions: (1) to translate the user's language into one appropriate for the given machine, and (2) to provide, for frequently needed operations, instructions that would be burdensome for the user to detail himself. For example, you may want the computer to take the square root of X and call the result Y. To accomplish this, the computer must know how to extract a square root, and a number of detailed steps may be required to complete the desired task. The compiler contains such information.

By analogy, then, the compiler may be compared to an encyclopedia to which a given reference brings out a block of detail. Thus, if we look in an encyclopedia under *dog* or *cat* we will find information about each. In the same way, a sequence of simple computer commands, by reference to the compiler, can produce a longer sequence of detailed steps for the machine to follow. (The compiler's output is often 4 to 20 detailed instructions for each user command.) The original command may be in the user's language. The detail will be in a language appropriate to the computer. Because the user's language contains less detail than the machine's, the former is often called a higher-level language.

Note that a compiler can make the user's higher-level language *machine independent* because different manufacturers provide different compilers to match a generally accepted language such as BASIC to their different machines. This ability makes possible wide use of a few user languages with varying forms of machine hardware construction.

The output from a compiler translation, which most users never see, is usually in a highly symbolic form, known as *assembly language*, that depends upon the machine type. Experienced personnel at a given location can examine this detail if necessary, since it is still in a form a trained person can understand. This possibility provides an intermediate check on the whole translation process, i.e., it permits the compiler operation to be checked.

The assembly process

At most installations yet another translation must be performed: from the assembly language output of the compiler into the machine language

---

[1] In some cases a user's instructions may be translated *and* executed one line at a time, rather than passing through a complete translation before execution, as described above. The line-at-a-time method employs a master translation and control program known as an *interpreter*, rather than a compiler. This method permits each program line to be checked grammatically as it enters the machine, but is generally less efficient than the compiler approach.

codes, often entirely numeric, that activate a particular machine. At this stage, for example, all symbols used for problem variables will be converted into specific memory location numbers, or "absolute addresses." Similarly, all symbols that specify machine operations, such as + in the user's language, become appropriate machine codes. This final translation process is usually on a symbol-for-symbol basis and is analogous to looking up equivalent terms word for word in a dictionary. The record keeping required to assign variables to memory boxes is analogous to the creation of a small dictionary appropriate to the given job.

A few assembly language steps, particularly those involving input/output operations, occur so frequently that blocks of machine language may be pieced together as the result of one assembly language statement, as in the compile step. Assembly language instructions that do so are known by the term "macroinstructions." (Almost all compiler-level statements are macroinstructions; however, the term is usually associated only with the assembly process.) If necessary, the output machine language codes from the assembly process may also be inspected by experienced personnel to permit a complete check of the entire compiler-assembly operation.

The execution

The compiler-assembly sequence described above can occur either just before a job is run (which is the usual case in compile-and-run remote terminal operations) or separately, with the execution of the job at a later date using data supplied then. In the latter case, the full machine language translation may be fed to the machine for direct execution. The term "subject program" describes the user's original set of instructions; the term "object program" describes the compiled and assembled instructions ready for the computer.

When a job is run, the computer's electronic circuits take over and convert the machine language instructions to the internal codes (binary or its variations) needed for processing. Similarly, an electronic translation reconverts the coded output into a user-oriented output before it is displayed (see blocks 5, 6, and 7 of Figure 6.1).

The costs of compilation

The compile-assembly processing the computer does before it executes the job consumes some time and therefore has a cost. And each time the user alters his original program, the entire compile-assembly sequence must be repeated. Further, a compiler that makes a machine conform to a general user language may not be able to take advantage of specific hardware details that would make that computer operate more efficiently.

The compilation step or both compilation and assembly could be avoided if users were willing to prepare their instructions directly in detailed assembly, or machine, language. When programs are run repeatedly, the effort required to work with lower-level languages becomes worthwhile. For example, to gain efficiency the supervisor and compiler programs just described are invariably written in assembly or machine codes by experts; so also are frequently run commercial or industrial control programs.

However, most users have one-time or occasionally repeated programs. Then user-programming cost dominates machine cost and the higher-level language prevails. We will concentrate on two such languages, BASIC and FORTRAN.

Features common to most computer languages

Most high-level computer languages have six fundamental abilities, as listed in Table 6.1.

TABLE 6.1

Essential Capabilities of Most Compilers

Stopping the Program
Reading or Writing Information
Performing Arithmetic Substitution
Providing Stored Functions
Branching Conditionally or Unconditionally
Using Subroutines

By first concentrating on these general commands, to be illustrated later in detail, you can get an appreciation for computer programming at the user level. The compilation-assembly process described in the previous section provides this ability to generalize.

1 / *Stopping the program*

Since all computer programs must at some point come to the end of their calculation or processing, some form of an END instruction must be included in the compiler language.[2] The END statement performs a

[2] Some applications provide an exception to the general rule. For example, process control computers may work continuously, using the same program. Nevertheless, these programs may be organized in fixed cycles or directed loops. Our point is that no written program supplied by the user goes on forever.

dual function: (a) It tells the compiler when it has come to the end of its translation task and (b) It causes the executed program to stop.

2 / *Reading or writing information*

Similarly, all computers must read and write (that is, have input and output functions) so that information can be passed to and from the machine. Instructions for this purpose are part of all computer languages (see Chapter 8).

3 / *Performing arithmetic operations*

The compiler will also provide alternative arithmetic manipulating ability in several forms. The substitution, or assignment, statement (the most important of these) causes an arithmetic expression to be evaluated, then places the answer in a specified memory location or symbolically designated variable box. A typical substitution operation, LET C = A + B, was illustrated in Chapter 5. (Chapters 8 and 9 expand on such operations.)[3]

4 / *Providing stored functions*

A function is a formula, like $y = x^2$, which provides for each value of the variable on the right (the *independent* variable, or *argument*) a unique numeric value for the variable on the left (the *dependent* variable). For example, $y = \sin x$, $y = \log x$, and $y = \sqrt{x}$ are all functions of x.

Many simple functions, such as those just cited, are used frequently in computation. Therefore, most computer languages permit you to use them by simple reference to the function type desired. The functions available directly to a user in a given language are called *stored functions*, since the compiler provides the detail needed for their use (see Chapters 8 and 9). If the user does not find the stored function he needs at his installation, most languages permit him to create his own. The functions shown above as illustrations contain only one independent variable or argument, i.e., x. Some advanced languages permit the user to define functions with several arguments, although stored functions are usually limited to one.

---

[3] Most computer languages also provide the ability to handle alphanumeric data (letters and special symbols such as $), and either display such items in titles or reports, move them from place to place during processing as required, or make tests upon such symbols against standards. Obviously, no numeric computations can be performed on such nonnumeric data. For simplicity, we hold our discussion of alphanumerics until Chapter 14.

5 / *Branching conditionally or unconditionally*

Branching instructions permit the user to break the usual sequential progression of program execution, either unconditionally or conditionally.

The purpose of a branch instruction is to cause a jump in a program's procedural sequence, either to an earlier or to a later step. By jumping backward in sequence, program statements may be repeated, thereby increasing the usefulness of those steps within the repeated loop of action. Jumps forward permit portions of a program sequence to be skipped. The distinction between unconditional and conditional branching instructions is as the names imply: an unconditional branch will force procedural change always; a conditional branch will do so only under the user's stated specifications (see the GO TO and IF/THEN commands of Chapter 10).

Most computer programs employ a large number of branching instructions. For this reason, additional special branching commands can be found in most languages to handle repetitive jobs, such as processing data from lists and tables (see Chapter 11).

6 / *Using subroutines*

A subroutine is a block of program steps you may want to use repeatedly in a given program at different places in the procedural sequence. For example, program steps that count and number output report pages will be needed whenever a new page begins. The numbering operation is the same, regardless of the content of the output pages. Thus, most computer languages permit you to prepare a subroutine, such as a page-numbering segment, then refer to or call for it as required using special commands. You can have many such subroutines in one program and you do not have to repeat the program statement groups each time you need them. The commands which activate the subroutine, in effect, electronically paste a called-for subroutine segment into the body of your program each time you ask for it. You may note that the subroutine idea is similar to that of the compiler itself, as previously discussed. A single program command can bring forth many others, thereby avoiding physical repetition and easing the programmer's task. One distinction between the compiler operation and that of the subroutine, of course, is that the latter is completely under the user's control: You may make up any subroutines you like, following the rules of your selected language.

Another advantage of the subroutine idea is that you may use the special subroutine call commands just mentioned to insert previously prepared instructions, say, from your own or another's library into a new program. In this way perfected pieces of old programs may be linked together for quick modular program construction. Although the same result can be obtained by other methods such as copying old segments in the desired order or using a series of unconditional branches to join the blocks together in order, the subroutine approach is more flexible for reasons that will be clear when we discuss and illustrate the BASIC subroutine commands in Chapter 12.

Each of the six capabilities outlined above may be combined in varying sequences to service a multitude of computer applications.

In addition to these essential capabilities, compiler designers provide us with a number of miscellaneous commands for special uses. These will be introduced as necessary. Chapter 14 groups together some useful special commands in BASIC.

Flow charts

A flow chart is a schematic picture that illustrates the action sequence a program takes from beginning to end. Such diagrams are particularly useful in the analysis of programs containing conditional branches, since the resulting action loops stand out clearly. Thus, using a flow diagram, we can trace program action sequentially from the first to the last step executed and also see how the processing sequence shifts under different input or different computational conditions.

To draw a flow diagram of a program or procedural sequence, we first isolate the steps to be performed and identify them with special graphical symbols. We will use rectangles for computer operations such as reading, writing, or substitution, and diamonds for conditional branching instructions. Circles or ovals will indicate the beginning and end of the program. Then, the sequence of operations will be shown by connecting the identified operations with arrows. To illustrate we now show several examples. In the following, look for the diamonds, since conditional branches create the logic of computer programming.

Two program types illustrated

Programs can be conditional or unconditional, as a comparison of Figures 6.2, 6.3, and 6.4 illustrates.

In the first figure, a simple numeric evaluation, we have no conditional steps, and the computation moves ahead in a direct sequence of boxes. The small number by each box indicates an arbitrary sequence number, which increases as the process progresses. In Figure 6.2 and the flow charts that follow data are not shown. Flow charts illustrate the program, not the data to be processed.

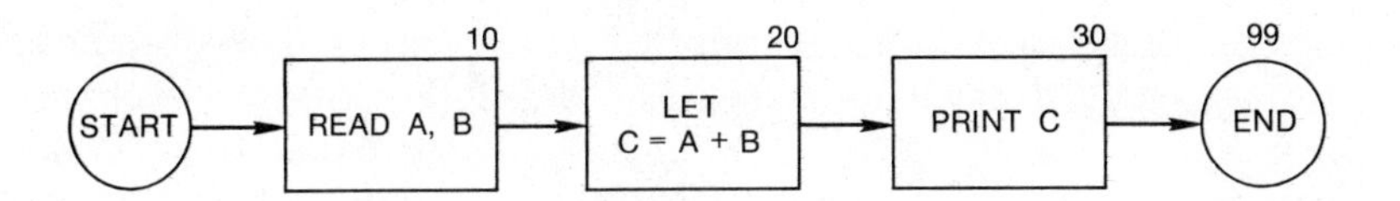

6.2. A purely sequential computation. Boxes show operations, arrows sequence. Small numbers above boxes are for reference and will later be used as program line or statement numbers in a computer program.

In Figure 6.3, we introduce an unconditional branch at box 50 to create a loop. This loop permits the same program to add and display the sum of successive pairs of numbers. In addition, we make a test (the diamond numbered 20) to see if any data appeared when we attempted to read. If NO, the job ends; if YES, it continues. Note that the unconditional branch, GO TO 10, refers to a previous box, or sequence number—a reference necessary for operational clarity. Also, a branch (either conditional or unconditional) may move the processing sequence either forward (to a higher statement number) or backward (to a smaller statement number).

The "out of data" or "end of file" test shown in Figure 6.3 is automatic in most computer installations, but the user can also control such actions, as shown in Figure 6.4.

For example, suppose we want to add only ten pairs of numbers, even though more data may be available for processing. To control this stop

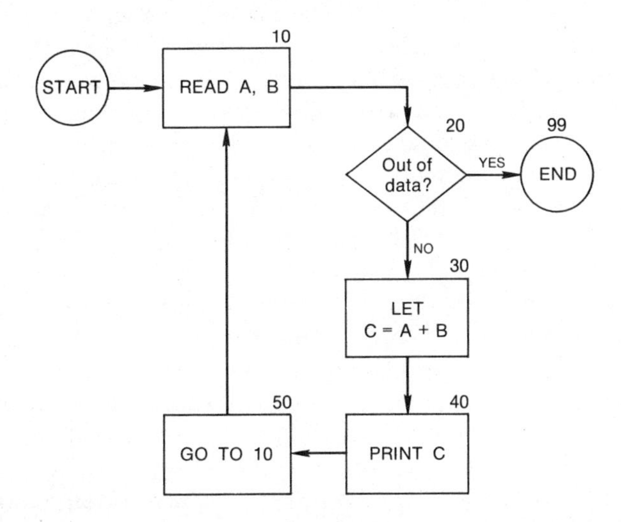

6.3. A looping with conditional test. Program illustrated continues to add pairs of numbers, A and B, until all pairs are added. The test for this out-of-data condition is shown in the above diamond. At the box labeled 50 the program goes back to step 10 and reads more data.

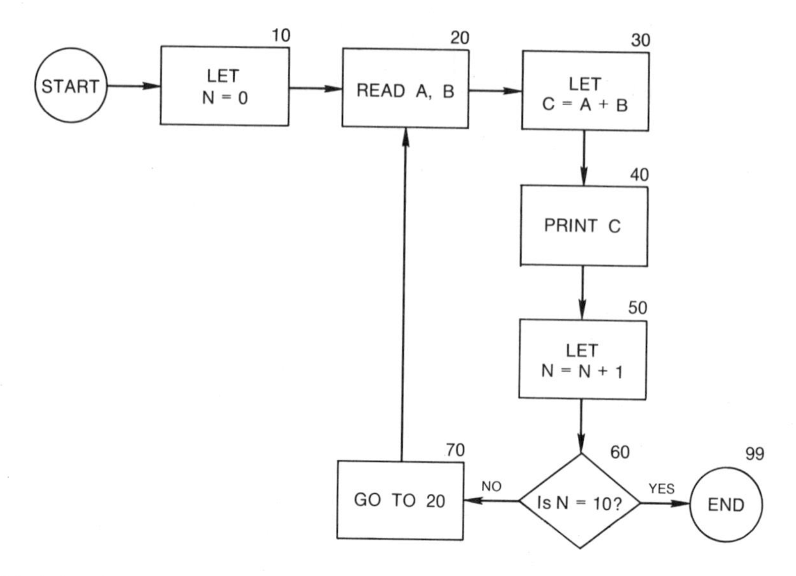

6.4. A looping procedure that counts cases. Steps required to add ten pairs of numbers, A and B, and halt after the tenth addition.

we can use the computer's testing and unconditional-branching ability by creating a "counter" and testing it after each addition. In Figure 6.4, the variable N is the counter. The substitution operation at flow chart step 50 increments the counter by 1 at each read by executing the operation, "Add 1 to the old value contained in the box called N and place the new answer in that location after deleting the old result." The counter described symbolically as variable N, of course, represents a physical memory location (assigned by the compiler and assembly translation). At step 60, the program tests the numeric contents of that box against the specified value, 10. If the counter has reached 10, we stop; otherwise, we continue.

You can get a greater appreciation of programming logic by considering the following design problem and its associated flow chart.

Suppose a vending machine delivers a product after collecting 15 cents. The machine will accept nickels, dimes, and quarters and make change. Assume that the machine will reject pennies and false coins and that it will always have a bank to make change. By what logic can we check the coins as they come in, deliver the product when we have at least 15 cents, and also provide correct change?

A method (actually used in vending machine design), as shown in Figure 6.5, is to count "equivalent nickels" using a counter we again call N for convenience. When N is equal to or greater than 3, we deliver the product, plus change equal to 5 cents times $N - 3$.

In Figure 6.5, the small circles *A* are connectors. Connectors of this type indicate that the points commonly marked should be coincident, or connected by arrows, even though direct graphical lines would confuse the art. Since the vending machine resets itself to receive new deposits after product delivery, the block GO TO START has been provided in the figure after the terminating circle, END. (Such continuous operation is not typical of most computer programs, which terminate after a fixed time.) Sequence numbers have also been omitted for simplicity of illustration, and the coin return feature of most vending machines is not shown.

Our problem is to make sure logically that each acceptable combination of nickels, dimes, and quarters will be evaluated and handled correctly. Assume that a customer can make "illogical" coin deposits, such as a nickel or a dime followed by a quarter.

To check the solution shown in Figure 6.5 develop a list of all coin combinations that could lead to product delivery, and state the change delivered in each instance (see Table 6.2). We assume in these specifications as a limiting condition that the deposit of two quarters will be handled as two separate transactions, with the delivery of a product and change for each.

TABLE 6.2

Acceptable Coin Deposits for the Vending Machine of Figure 6.5

nickel, nickel, nickel
nickel, dime
dime, nickel
nickel, nickel, dime
dime, dime
quarter
nickel, quarter
nickel, nickel, quarter
dime, quarter

To check your understanding of the vending-machine problem, trace the action taken in the logical diagram for the feasible inputs listed in Table 6.2. You should be able to give the contents of the counter, N, for the deposit of each coin in sequence, and to describe for each successful total deposit how much change will be delivered.

Decision tables

An alternate form of logical display is a decision table, such as the one for the vending-machine problem shown in Table 6.3. Decision tables summarize the logical tests and subsequent actions taken by a program. The

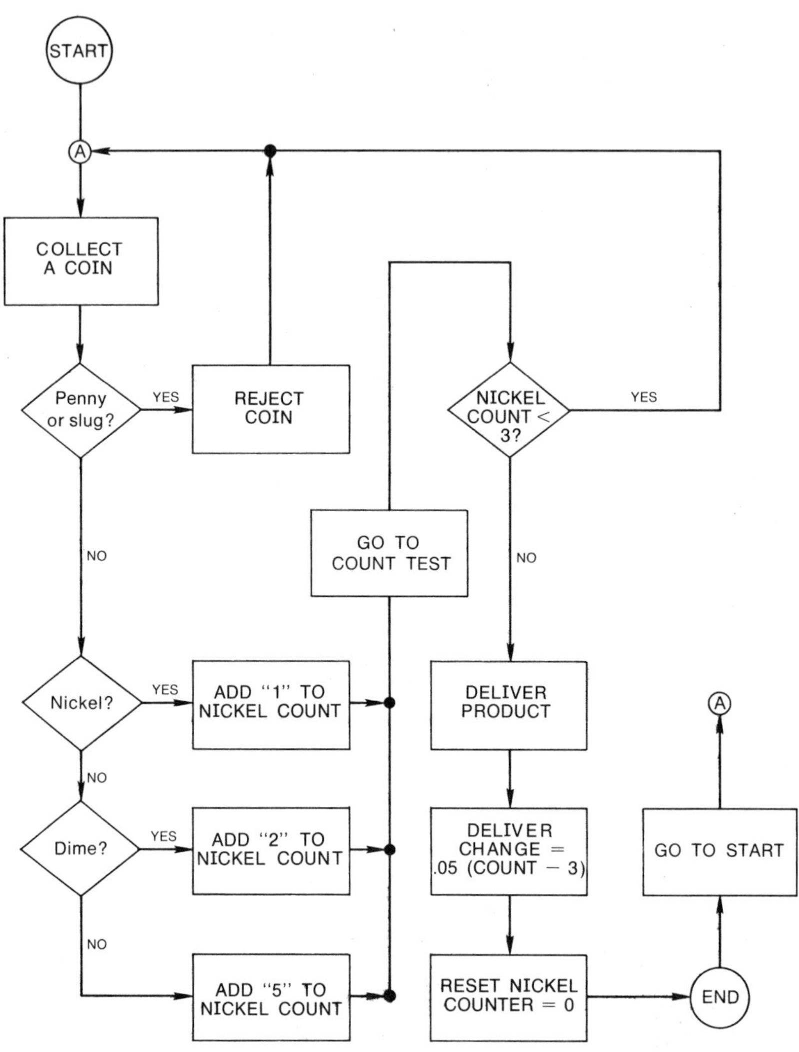

6.5. Flow diagram of vending machine logic. Machine delivers a 15-cent product plus change for any input of nickels, dimes, or a quarter. Nickel counter, N, records input of "equivalent nickels" until the count is 3 or more, then takes action. Soft-drink machine uses designs of this type. *Source:* Adapted from V. C. Hare, Jr., *Systems Analysis: A Diagnostic Approach*, Harcourt, Brace & World, Inc. (New York, 1967), p. 42.

upper half of the table lists the tests made, one row corresponding to each diamond-shaped box in the flow chart. The lower half of the table shows the actions taken, indicated by the rectangular boxes in the flow chart. Entries in the table columns relate the tests and actions. Test outcomes indicated above produce the actions indicated by X's below. Note that the possible test combinations have been numbered as column headings from left to right, following the action sequence.

TABLE 6.3

Decision Table for the Vending Problem

		Test conditions 1	2	3	4	5	6	7	8	9	10	11
Tests made	1. Penny or Slug	Y	N	N	N	–	–	–	–	–	–	–
	2. Nickel	–	Y	N	N	–	–	–	–	–	–	–
	3. Dime	–	–	Y	N	–	–	–	–	–	–	–
	4. Nickel Count	–	–	–	–	1	2	3	4	5	6	7
Actions taken	1. Reject Coin	X										
	2. Add 1 to Count		X									
	3. Add 2 to Count			X								
	4. Add 5 to Count				X							
	5. Go to Test Condition 5		X	X	X							
	6. Deliver Product							X	X	X	X	X
	7. Deliver (Count – 3) Equivalent Nickels							X	X	X	X	X
	8. Set Count = 0							X	X	X	X	X
	9. Go to Start	X				X	X	X	X	X	X	X
	10. Accept Coin	X				X	X	X	X	X	X	X

NOTE: Upper listing shows tests made; lower shows corresponding actions taken. Y stands for "yes" in tests; N for "no"; X indicates action is to be taken in the combinations indicated; – indicates the square is not considered in the test. Test sequence is from column listing 1 through 11; resulting actions follow as shown.

Often easier to draw than a flow chart, a decision table still shows the essential conditional features of a computation sequence. Some users prefer decision tables because of their compactness and summary qualities. Extremely large flow charts are hard to understand, even though they are useful in describing modular blocks of program steps. For an overall picture of a complex job, the decision table is essential documentation.

Although variations are possible, the decision table (Table 6.3) does present the total picture of Figure 6.5 in tabular form. To check this out, compare the list of acceptable coin deposits, Table 6.2, against Table 6.3.

To read the decision table, first assume the process has started with the deposit of a coin (which may be the first or subsequent deposit before product delivery). Then follow the test combination columns from left to right. If the coin is unacceptable, it is rejected, and we wait for a new coin (column 1). If the coin is a nickel, we add 1 to the nickel count; if a dime we add 2 to the count; if accepted and neither a nickel or a dime, the coin is a quarter, so we add 5 to the count. This test sequence follows the order shown in columns 1 through 4. The first test condition (2, 3, or 4) passed, the action jumps to test combination 5, i.e., we next examine the counter, which must now be at some number 1 through 7, depending upon the coins previously deposited.

Columns 5 through 11 of the decision table detail what is done under each of the possible input sequences shown in Table 6.2. Thus, the final nickel deposited in the *nickel, nickel, nickel* sequence brings us to test condition 7, as do *nickel, dime* and *dime, nickel.* The sequence *nickel, nickel, dime* and *dime, dime* bring us to test condition 8. A single *quarter* deposit brings us to test condition 9; *nickel, quarter* to test condition 10, and *nickel, nickel, quarter* or *dime, quarter* to test condition 11. The first of the conditions (7 through 11) passed causes product delivery, change delivery equal to (count − 3) equivalent nickels, i.e., .05 (count − 3) cents in nickels or dimes. After both actions, the count is reset to zero, and the whole process continues.

Computers and problem solving

To apply computers to everyday problems, the user needs to know three things:

1. What he wants to do and the specific logical steps necessary to perform that job
2. The grammar and syntax (subsequently described) of a particular computer language, so he can communicate his desires to the machine
3. Something about computer hardware, so he will understand how the computer language works and what can be accomplished with a given hardware configuration.

Ask yourself three questions about any job you propose to commit to computer execution:

1. Can you describe what you want to do in absolute detail? (Try the problems at the end of this chapter.) In particular, are you sure of all the logical conditions that must be met by your proposed job, or program? (Most people forget a few. You must be both complete and consistent.)
2. Do you understand the constraints imposed by your computer language and its implementing hardware? Look for these limitations so that you can operate successfully within them.
3. Are you sure that your input data is correct and that your proposed computer program is processing them correctly? If you supply the incorrect input to a computer program you will get an incorrect result, unless you have taken care to provide error checks on data input. Most professionals automatically take these precautions. They also test their programs with simple data to check the working order of their logic.

PROBLEMS

6-1 We have instructed a clerk to prepare the payroll for this week. As one step, the clerk must compute NET PAY = GROSS PAY LESS DEDUCTIONS. The three variables named may, of course, be referenced in English by their names. But going further in organizing the clerk's work, we provide him with a ruled sheet of paper, with column numbers 1, 2, 3, . . . , etc. We head the first column GROSS PAY, the second DEDUCTIONS, and the third NET PAY. The appropriate data are then entered in columns 1 and 2. (Each new case is entered in a new row.)

- **a.** If we now tell the clerk to "Place in column 3 what he finds as the contents of column 1 less what he finds in column 2," or, more simply, "Col. 3 = Col. 1 − Col. 2," the clerk should not get confused. Why?
- **b.** The program step described above is a substitution statement, since we have substituted the previous contents of column 3, namely blanks, with the result of the required computation. In performing this step, the contents of columns 1 and 2 are simply read by the clerk; the content is not altered. However, suppose by chance some extraneous number appeared in column 3, perhaps from a previous computation. What would the clerk logically do to obtain the correct final result? (Assume the clerk has an eraser on the end of his pencil.)
- **c.** The clerk has now made the first computation, that for row 1 of his accounting sheet. He now moves to row 2. Is there any need to change his instructions—if he is still to compute NET PAY and put that result in column 3?
- **d.** Suppose another clerk has been given the same problem, but that we letter the columns of his paper A, B, and C for columns 1, 2, and 3, respectively. If we now tell the second clerk to compute (for each row) C = A − B, would the second clerk come up with the same answers as the first?
- **e.** If we substitute X, Y, Z, respectively, for A, B, C, in part D, should the answers obtained in computing Z = X − Y differ from those obtained in part D? Why? What can you deduce from clerical and computer operations as a consequence of your answer?
- **f.** Do the numeric values of what has been placed in columns 1 and 2—or the corresponding A and B or X and Y of the later questions—in any way alter the program step? As the numeric values are changed in moving down the sheet from case to case is there any reason to change the procedure of computation?

6-2 We have been asked to find the total of both principal and interest on $1,000 invested at an interest rate of .06, compounded annually, for a period of 10 years. We seek to instruct a clerk to perform this computation.

- **a.** What is a necessary requirement before we can give the clerk detailed instructions?
- **b.** Suppose we consult a book on business mathematics and discover that the appropriate formula for computing accumulated interest and principal (as required) is $T = P(1 + R)^N$, where T is the total sought, P is the principal of $1,000, R is the annual interest rate, say, .06, and N is the number of years considered, here 10. With the data given and with the required formula, we now confront our clerk—only to find that he has no knowledge of algebra! What can be done to help him solve the problem for us?

c. Having instructed our clerk in the detailed method of arithmetic to be followed, we now wish to have him compute appropriate values of T, given other values of P, R, and N. What additional written commands in English should we give the clerk? In addition to the added command(s), what else must the clerk have before he can continue?

6-3 Returning to Problem 6-1, suppose we know that NET PAY should never exceed $1,000 per week. But let us assume that the clerk, adhering to our rules of computation, does indeed come up with a value greater than that for one or more cases.

a. By what means could such a result have come about?

b. Why would it be desirable to have the clerk report to us such exceptional cases by exact reference to the offending case numbers, or rows on his pad?

c. What form of computer command, as described in this chapter, would be required to have the computer, acting as our clerk, report the offending cases?

d. How could we have the clerk also report the cases in which NET PAY was less than $50 for the week?

6-4 We now ask our clerk to compute NET PAY, but we also ask him to keep a running tally of the number of employees for which the computation has been made. To do this specifically, we mark out a small box at the top of his accounting sheet and call it N. We then tell the clerk to place zero in box N before he starts his job, and thereafter to LET N = N + 1 after each computation, using the same box. (Again we assume the clerk has an eraser at the end of his pencil.)

a. How could the clerk perform this computation for us?

b. At any stage of the computing process, what should box N contain?

c. Notice in the above that the constant 1 must be remembered by the clerk – it is not written on his work sheet. If the clerk should forget the constant to be added to N at each computation, where could he refresh his memory? Would you conclude that a constant may be entered into the computations via a program instruction?

d. What type of command is LET N = N + 1?

6-5 Continuing with the preceding, we still have the clerk working on the NET PAY computation and still keeping the tally N. Suppose we now wish to have the clerk stop at the end of 100 cases (assuming, of course, that he has on his work sheet more than 100 cases to do).

a. In English, what type of instruction would you give to the clerk to cause him to stop work at that point?

b. Suppose at the 100th case you want the clerk to strike a total, T, of the accumulated NET PAY calculated, report that figure to you, and then go on with the next 100 cases, reporting the total, T, for the next block of 100 and so on until the data runs out, at which point T for the last set of cases, which may be less than 100, is to be reported. (For clarity, assume that "Report T" may be accomplished by a command such as PRINT T on the work sheet.) Devise in English a set of instructions for the clerk. Explain why you may need a conditional branch in this writeup.

6-6 For your English narrative in Problem 6-5 prepare a flow chart, similar to those shown in this chapter, showing (1) the start and end of the job; (2) all actions to be taken (other than tests) in rectangular boxes; and (3) all tests—for conditional branches—in diamond-shaped enclosures. You will want to indicate the sequence of execution by connecting these boxes and diamonds in proper order with arrows.

a. Why is it desirable for problem understanding to point up the conditional branches in your flow chart?

b. If the statement of Problem 6-5 is not completely clear to you, raise any questions that must be answered before you can complete your flow chart. Why is it possible that the clerk may not understand what is wanted in complete detail?

c. Why is it necessary that the clerk and the computer have such detailed and unambiguous instructional steps, which as a set will produce the result the user desires?

d. What will happen in the clerical process or in the execution of a computer program if the steps required are incomplete or inconsistent or if, even though they are complete and consistent, they do not accomplish what is intended?

6-7 Suppose your clerk did not have any arithmetic ability beyond addition. Could you provide him with a routine that would enable him to multiply—even though he would not know he was performing that operation?

6-8 Suppose each time our add-only clerk saw an asterisk (*) he summoned up the program segment produced by your answer to Problem 6-7 or a version of that solution. Then "multiply" (indicated by an "*" for the clerk) would, in effect, call for the needed detail. This is what the compiler does for operations that are not reduced to hardware. How could you devise a routine for division? Could you extend your results to the computation of other operations?

SEVEN

Getting the computer to work

The first step in using the computer is to familiarize yourself with the remote input device you will use to communicate with it. In what follows, we assume you have a Model 33 Teletype machine available. Although other terminals may differ slightly in design and application, the general functions will still follow those described.

The keyboard

Sit before your remote terminal and study its keyboard layout. Use the Model 33 Teletype keyboard in Figure 7.1 for reference.

The Teletype terminal types only in capital (uppercase) letters, so the shift key does not perform the same function as that on the office typewriter. When the Teletype shift key is depressed, the machine will type the special characters shown at the top of each key (above the letters and numbers) or will take action as called for by the depressed key. A list of the special keys and their functions is shown in Table 7.1.

In particular, note that the number 1 and the letter I have *different* keys, as do the number 0 and the letter O.

Try the Teletype off-line

Remote terminals, including the Teletype, can be connected to the computer in one of three ways:

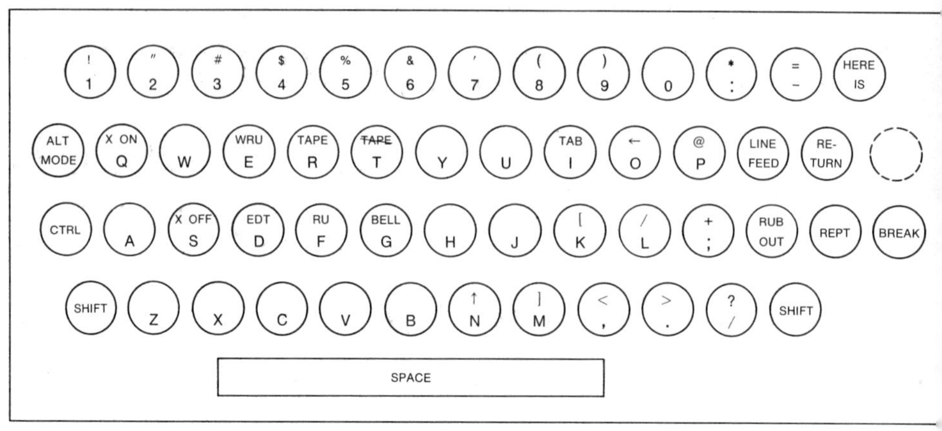

Keyboard

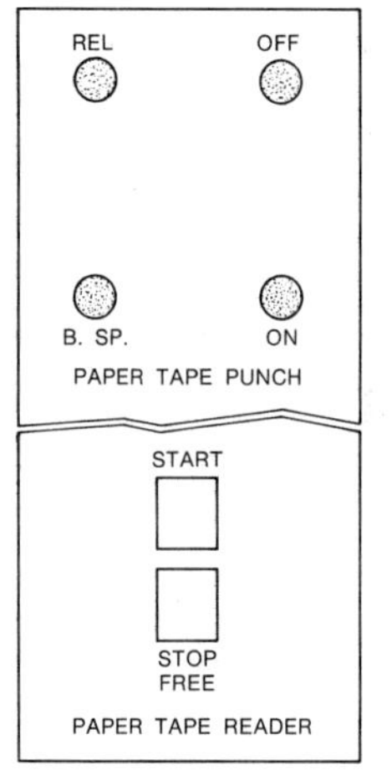

Paper Tape Punch and Reader Controls

Operator's Control Unit

7.1. Model 33 Teletype keyboard and controls. The control boxes, shown below the keyboard in the drawing, actually appear to the left and right of the keyboard on the machine itself.

1. By telephone line through the medium of a telephone company data set;
2. By direct wire;
3. By telephone line through the medium of an acoustic coupler. This is a device which produces coded tones that may be fed to any ordinary telephone without wired connections by placing the telephone receiver on the acoustic coupler in holes produced for that purpose. We shall consider Case 1 here; see Appendix C for Cases 2 and 3.

The line connection and control buttons for the Teletype are shown in Figure 7.1 below the telephone dial. To turn on the machine for "local" use, press the button marked LCL. To turn off the machine, press the "clear" button, marked CLR. When the machine is in the LCL mode you are not connected to the computer and may thus practice on the Teletype as if it were an ordinary electric typewriter and get a feel for its action.

When practicing on the keyboard, note that the RETURN button returns the type wheel to the left-hand margin and the LINE FEED button advances the paper one line each time it is depressed. When you are connected to the computer, the RETURN button will automatically initiate a line feed, as is the case with the office electric typewriter. When in the local, or LCL, mode, the line feed must be provided manually.

An interesting exercise

If your teletype is connected to a telephone line by means of a telephone company data set you may try the following experiment for further practice:

1. Find the telephone number of another Teletype machine.
2. Depress the "origin" button, marked ORIG, found below the telephone dial.
3. After receiving a dial tone, which will be audible through the small speaker on the data set Teletype, dial the number of the other machine. You will hear the usual ringing signal, then a short beep. Each teletype will type the caller's telephone number, or answerback code, as set by the telephone company.
4. You and the operator of the other machine may now type messages back and forth, and both teletypes will print the entire "conversation" in unison. (This is a common method of sending written messages by wire in commercial practice.)
5. To terminate the connection between the two teletypes, you or the other operator may depress the CLR button on either machine.

Call the computer

For simplicity, you may think of the computer as a "friend" who will now communicate with you. To connect with a given machine you will need to know the specific sequence of steps to follow at your location. However, if you use the data set Teletype, the general scheme will be as follows:

1. Find the telephone number of the computer to be used.
2. Press the ORIG button, and after you hear the dial tone dial the number correctly.

TABLE 7.1

Special Keyboard and Control Keys and Their Functions

OPERATOR'S CONTROL UNIT[a]

KEY	FUNCTION	KEY	FUNCTION
LCL	For local operation. Turns on typewriter motor. Permits local practice, or preparation of paper tape (see below).	FDX	Appears on some machines only. Press after computer tone to initiate full duplex service.
CLR	Turns off machine and clears telephone connection if present.	BRK-RLS	Break-release key. Depress to release locked keyboard after a break signal.
BUZ-RLS	Buzzer sounds when paper supply is low. Press button to silence. Replace paper roll before paper runs out.	Loudspeaker	(Not shown in Figure 7.1) Located on panel below ORIG and CLR keys. Produces dial tone, ring signal, and connection tone. Adjust speaker volume control (by speaker) to user convenience.
Telephone dial	Normal telephone dial used for dialing another teletype or the computer. Use after pressing ORIG button.		
ORIG	Connects set to phone line. Dial tone will be heard. After dial tone, use telephone dial normally.	NORMAL-RESTORE	Keep in NORMAL position.

PAPER TAPE PUNCH AND READER[b]

KEY	FUNCTION	KEY	FUNCTION
ON and OFF	Turns punch on or off as indicated. When ON copy typed on paper is reproduced on punched paper tape also.	START and STOP	Causes paper tape placed into reader to start or stop reading. (Some machines have automatic tape start under computer control. This feature is not illustrated in Figure 7.1.)
REL	Releases paper tape feed clutch, so that tape may be pulled through punch head freely. Use when reloading paper tape.	FREE	Lower position of START/STOP control lever. Provides clutch release for tape reader, so that tape may be advanced manually.
B.SP.	Backspaces punched paper tape for correction. Each depression backspaces paper tape one typed character.		

[a] Keys omitted are not used in remote computer terminal service.
[b] Not present on all Teletypes.

3. When you hear the short beep you are connected to the computer. (If your computer uses what is known as a full duplex service, you should now depress the FDX button above the dial; if not, omit this step. At some installations the computer may automatically check your teletype phone number or your answerback code. If so your own check number will appear on your teletype page.)

TELETYPE KEYBOARD

Key	Function
RETURN	Causes print wheel to return to left margin.
LINE FEED	Each depression advances paper one line.
REPT	Causes repetition of character when held down simultaneously with character key.
SHIFT	Causes special character or control operation when depressed simultaneously with other character key.
RUBOUT	Nonprinting. Causes deletion of backspaced characters in paper tape. One character deleted per depression.
HERE IS	Causes Teletype to be identified automatically by its telephone number or its answerback code, as set by phone company. Not usually employed in automatic sign-on sequences as described in text.
ALT MODE	(Sometimes marked ESCAPE) Causes incorrectly typed line to be deleted when teletype is under computer control.
CTRL	A control key used in combination with other characters for specialized actions.
BREAK	Disconnects machine from phone line and computer. Should not be pushed.
Special Characters	Special characters in the keyboard set shown on upper half of keys, e.g., $, *, +, obtained by holding down shift key and pressing desired key. Keys with words on upper half have not been mentioned as they are not generally used in computer communication.
SPACE	Produces space as on normal typewriter.

4. The computer will now ask you a series of questions, which may vary slightly from one installation to another. The following sequence is typical.

(a) You will be asked for your user code number. When the computer asks this question, you respond with your assigned user number on the same line, then depress the RETURN button. Your supplier or instructor will give you the required code number, which is used for accounting and security purposes.[1]

(b) You will be asked for the SYSTEM you desire. This refers to the language you want to speak when preparing your program. Type BASIC, then depress the RETURN button.

(c) You will then be asked whether you want to write a new program, or use one previously stored in the computer (by a procedure to be discussed later). Type NEW, and depress RETURN.

(d) You will be asked next for a program name. Since we are going to write a new program now, type TEST1. (Most systems permit a program name of up to six or eight characters in length. In some cases, embedded spaces are considered important, i.e., TEST1 and TEST 1 would be considered different names. Check your supplier's specifications.)

---

[1] At some installations you must inform the computer of your readiness to communicate by typing an initial HELLO followed by depression of the RETURN key. This step, if necessary at your installation, precedes step (a). Also, some installations use a password in addition to a user number as a double security measure. Should this added information be necessary it will be provided by your vendor or instructor.

(e) You will finally be informed that all is well (if you have passed through the above steps correctly). The typical computer response is READY or OK. If you have made a mistake, most systems will ask you for additional or corrected information before terminating your connection. The exception to this rule is the input of an invalid user code number, which generally cuts you off at once. Once a correct sign-on sequence has been completed, you are ready to use the computer's facilities.

The computer will now recognize two types of input: (1) program statements and (2) system commands.

Program statements

A program statement is composed of words either taken from a particular language or made up by the user according to the rules of a particular language, in our case BASIC.

The computer distinguishes between program statements and system commands by the fact that each program statement is given a one- to five-digit line number. (System commands, as discussed below, have *no* line number and with few exceptions are always typed at the left margin of the page.)

Program statements may be typed with any legal starting line number. However, when you LIST or RUN a program, all program statements are first sequenced in ascending line number order. In case two lines have the same number the *last* one typed takes precedence; the former is deleted. Thus, we can make additions, deletions, or corrections to our program text during the course of composition, using the line numbers as reference.

Later in this chapter we will illustrate the grammatical structure of typical program statements in BASIC and show how a sequence of program statements makes a computer program.

System commands

Before continuing, however, we must pause and consider a few typical system commands that will be of continual use throughout the remainder of this text.

A system command directs the computer to perform one of a limited number of acts which are *independent* of the program language you have chosen. (System commands generally involve information needed by the computer's supervisory control system in order to handle or execute program statements, hence their name.[2])

For example, if you tried the computer sign-on sequence, you have already encountered one system command in disguise. The word NEW, your answer to the computer's question, NEW OR OLD?, is a system command advising the computer that you want to prepare a new program. Similarly, when you supplied the NAME of your program, the computer was informed that it should identify your new program thereafter by the name stated. Had you typed OLD instead of NEW, the computer would have asked you for the name of a program you had previously prepared, named, and filed using the system command SAVE (see Table 7.2).

If you had forgotten which programs you had previously saved, you might type the system command CATALOG, and the computer would list the names of your currently stored programs. If you wanted to see the list of library programs available to all users at your facility, you would type the system command CATALOG*** and would then receive the list on your teletype page. The system command UNSAVE followed by the name of a previously stored program would cause that program to be eliminated from your file.

The most frequently used system commands are LIST and RUN. LIST, when typed without a line number at the left margin of the page, causes all the program statements in the program you are currently working on to be displayed in line number order. The program thus listed may, of course, be either a new program currently under composition or an old program which has been retrieved from the system's file. The system command RUN, typed after you have completed a new program or supplied the data for execution of an old program (see Chapter 8) causes the computer to process that program in line number order.

Other typical system commands are explained in Table 7.2, and the examples which follow will show them in use.

User files

To fully appreciate the range of system commands in Table 7.2, a few words about user files are in order. When the user prepares a new program, the computer stores that program and its associated data in its

---

[2] Since the exact system commands used by different suppliers vary, we have necessarily chosen a typical set for illustration. Both the text and Table 7.2 follow the conventions of General Electric's time-sharing service. Other services provide analogous commands, but you should check your own installation for the precise system commands in current use, i.e., ask for a local system command listing such as that in Table 7.2. Fortunately, the system commands LIST and RUN are not only most frequently used but are also almost universally adopted by all suppliers in their system command specifications. It is the other commands of Table 7.2 that are likely to vary from one installation to another.

TABLE 7.2

Frequently Used System Commands and Their Functions

COMMAND	FUNCTION
RUN	Causes user's current program to be executed.
LIST	Causes current program to be listed in line number order.
LIST—xxx	Causes the current program to be listed in line number order starting at line xxx and continuing to the last line of the program.
STOP	This special system command may be typed at any time while a program is running, and will cause execution of the program to halt. STOP need not be typed at the left margin. In most systems, striking S key while a program is running is equivalent to typing STOP. (The system command STOP should not be confused with the program command STOP, to be discussed in later chapters.)
NEW	Indicates user wishes to create a new program. User will be asked to name the new program, then may proceed to type it.
OLD	Indicates the user wishes to use a previously created program which he has stored in his file (see SAVE). User will be asked to name old program desired. If name is stated incorrectly or if name is not in file, user will be informed of error.
RENAME	Permits user to change name of current program. Program itself remains unchanged. User will be asked for new name.
CATALOG	Provides list of program names currently in user's file (see SAVE).
CATALOG***	Provides list of program names currently in the computer center's library which are available to all users upon request. To retrieve a library program listed in the CATALOG***, type OLD, then type the desired program name followed by three asterisks as in CATALOG***.
SAVE	Causes user's current program to be filed under its current name for later use.
SCRATCH	Destroys the program currently being worked on, but preserves the current program name. Permits user to start from "scratch" in revising his program.
UNSAVE	Eliminates currently named OLD program from the user's file.
SYSTEM	Announces to computer that user wishes to change language currently in use to another language. User will be asked what alternate system he wishes to use. Some systems use name of desired language as a system command to change language, e.g., BASIC, FORTRAN.
HELLO	Sometimes needed to inform the computer you want its services and are ready to sign on. Check your own installation.
GOODBYE, or BYE	Terminates your connection with the computer automatically after giving you a report on computer time you have consumed and current time of day. (Depressing the CLR control button on the Teletype, and other forms of disconnection do not provide such information before cutoff.)

TAPE	Informs the computer you will be providing input information, program lines, or data via paper tape. Inhibits automatic line advance, which tape will provide. Corrects timing for tape input.
KEY	Informs computer you will now provide input from the keyboard. Restores automatic line advance after each RETURN depression.
Other System Commands	Most systems provide a variety of editing commands that merge sections of new and old programs according to stated line number specifications, delete specified sections of programs by line number, and renumber lines in a program according to specified rules. Some advanced systems also provide "string-editing" commands, which scan a program; locate specified variables, characters, or program commands; and permit detailed user alteration. For example, such detailed edit commands permit the user to find every line number in which the variable X appears in a program, or to change every X in a program to Y. Although a discussion of such capabilities is beyond the scope of this book, the user as he progresses may wish to look into the advanced system commands at his location. The advanced system commands mentioned here add greatly to the user's ability to combine program segments, diagnose program errors, and correct erroneous program details.

fast memory area (usually core) in preparation for processing. When the system command SAVE, or its equivalent, is used, the program currently in use is copied into a slower memory file area (usually disk) and is identified there by the user's number as well as the current program name. Then, when the user requests one of his old programs by name, a copy of the filed program is made from the slow to the fast memory areas (e.g., from disk to core). If a computer center library program is requested (see system command CATALOG***) a similar copying process is followed. Thus, one function of the system command is to control the files a user may employ.

All program modifications, as is program execution, are carried out in the high-speed memory area, which is sometimes called the working area (as opposed to the file area). When you disconnect your terminal from the computer the work then in high-speed memory is erased; only that filed remains for later use.

An editing exercise: four correcting methods

In addition to typed system commands most supervisory systems also provide a number of keyboard manipulations that provide editing and correcting ability in any language.

To illustrate some editing features of the supervisory system before you write a computer program in a particular language, try the following:

We assume that you have correctly signed on to your computer, following the routine described previously, and are ready to write a *new* program. We use ordinary English for illustration. Strictly speaking, our example is not a computer program, but it serves to illustrate system commands and manipulations, independent of programming techniques. The example also illustrates how you may use the terminal for editing letters and manuscripts, should you care to do so. For example, Table 2.3 was prepared using the editing methods in the following exercise:

Type the following sequence of lines in English on your computer terminal. Include the leading line numbers as shown below and depress the RETURN button at the end of each line. (The intended word sequence is NOW IS THE TIME FOR ALL GOOD MEN TO COME TO THE AID OF THEIR COUNTRY, and some errors have been introduced on purpose.) Note that the lines are numbered in increments of 10. By skipping lines, we leave room for later insertions, if necessary.

```
10 NOW IS
20 THEY
30 FOR
40 FOR
50 ALL GOOD MEN TO COME
60 TO THE AID OF THEIR COUNTRY.
```

At the end of your typing job, the computer has received your six-line message, including the errors shown: (1) the intended THE was misspelled, (2) the word TIME was omitted, and (3) the word FOR was repeated twice.

In most conversational computer systems you can make the needed corrections easily according to the following rules:

1. To delete a given line, type the line number and push the RETURN key without spacing. The line in question will be erased.

2. To introduce a new line or to replace an old one, type the desired line number and text. The new line will be inserted after the existing line of the same number if any has been deleted.

Thus, to correct the above example, type the following lines and push the RETURN key at the end of each:

```
20 THE
25 TIME
40
```

Now, if you type the system command (left-margin justified, with *no* line number) LIST and then push the RETURN button you will get the corrected text reproduced on your teletype page. Indeed, since the system commands (with no line numbers) are independent of the particular language used, the add, correct, or delete features we have described will always work, even though the text makes no sense.

```
LIST

10 NOW IS
20 THE
25 TIME
30 FOR
50 ALL GOOD MEN TO COME
60 TO THE AID OF THEIR COUNTRY.
```

Sometimes you will discover an error before you have completed a line. Most installations provide the following means of correcting them.

3. To delete one or more mistyped characters on a line *before* you have pushed the RETURN button, depress the shift key and then the letter O key. On most machines, the symbol displayed is a left-pointing arrow (←). Repeat the process for each character to be erased. Retype the correct ones, then terminate the line by pushing RETURN. All the errors will appear on your work sheet, but if you again type the system command LIST, the computer will display the corrected text. For example, suppose you want to type the word Mississippi and have gotten thus far

100 MISSISSS

Realizing that you now have one too many S's you perform the operation above, and your paper now reads

```
100 MISSISSS←IPPI
```

After typing LIST and pushing the RETURN button, you would get

```
LIST

100 MISSISSIPPI
```

4. To delete a whole line, again *before* depressing the RETURN button, depress the key marked ALT MODE. This wipes out the erroneous line, and, since the type wheel automatically returns to the left-hand margin of your paper, you may start again from scratch. Since the ALT MODE key is nonprinting, no illustrations of its action are provided here. Try it on your own. (On some Teletype machines the ALT MODE key is marked ESCAPE. In most systems an alternate way to delete an entire line before

RETURN has been pushed is to simultaneously depress the key marked CTRL (control) and the letter X key.)

The system command SCRATCH (see Table 7.2) can be used to eliminate *all* numbered lines in the listing currently in your working area. After the command SCRATCH is executed, you have a clean slate to work with, although the name identifying your work will remain unchanged. To get both a clean work area and a new name, type the system command NEW, then supply the new name when requested. (In most systems, requests for either a NEW or an OLD program will eliminate the program previously in the working area.) Finally, note that the system command RUN would not be appropriate for the lines used in this editing exercise. We have used for illustration a series of arbitrary English words and statements: an executable program requires us to conform to the rules of a particular computer-programming language, to be illustrated after a brief discussion of the Teletype's paper tape device.

Paper tape use

For Teletype terminals that have a paper tape unit, you may prepare a program and its associated data in the LCL mode, then transmit it using paper tape.

To prepare a paper tape, turn the paper tape punch ON. Then as you type in the LCL mode, your text will be reproduced in the punched coded holes of the paper tape. Remember that in the LCL mode you must type both a RETURN and a LINE FEED at the end of each typed line. In addition, most systems require that you also hit the RUBOUT key at the end of each line. The purpose of this action is to provide one "do-nothing" character in the paper tape which will give the print wheel time to return to the left margin as the tape is read into the computer at high speed.

To assure that you have a leader at the beginning and end of your tape, it is also good practice to hold down the RUBOUT and RPT keys simultaneously to generate ten or twelve RUBOUTS before you start and after you end your tape. This will facilitate loading the tape reader. (You will see the RUBOUT character as eight holes across the tape. The small ninth hole is a sprocket feed for the tape reader.)

Should you make an error when punching tape you may use the editing features described previously. These editing operations will be effected when your tape is read into the computer. Or, you may use the tape backspace key followed by a RUBOUT (see Table 7.1). The former method is easier.

After punching tape, turn the punch OFF. Grasp the tape as it comes from the punch and pull upward smartly. The punch housing will tear the tape cleanly and produce a torn V at the end, so you will know the direction in which the tape was cut. The total effect will be that of an arrowhead at the start and a tail at the end. You may now store your tape for later use or read it on the Teletype.

To store the tape, roll it up, then compress the roll gently and secure the resulting band with a paper clip or rubber band. The contents of the tape may be identified on a small piece of attached paper or on the tape with a felt-tipped marker. The tape should not be folded sharply, since creases and other such irregularities may jam the tape reader.

To read the tape, first make sure the reader is OFF. Then insert the leading end of the tape into the reader after releasing the plastic reader guard (not shown in Figure 7.1). In loading the tape, note that the tape sprocket holes are *not* symmetrically located; three holes appear on one side, five on the other. This difference forces you to align the tape correctly in the reader head. With the tape aligned and the sprocket in the sprocket holes, close the plastic guard cover. About an inch of leader should protrude from the guard and you should make sure that you have not moved part of your message beyond the reader head, for then it would not be reproduced. Also make sure the tape is not twisted or at an angle in the reader. After such checks, you are ready to start the reader.

When you turn the reader ON, the effect is the same as if you were typing on the keyboard, except that the machine will type at a constant rate of 100 words per minute. You may read your tape in the LCL mode to check it, use it for message transmission at high speed to another Teletype, or use it to feed input to the computer.

In the latter case, one additional operation is required before turning on the tape reader. Assume that you have dialed the computer and have gone through your sign-on sequence, as earlier described. You now wish to read into the computer a program you have prepared on tape. First, type the system command TAPE (see Table 7.2). This informs the computer you will input tape and inhibits the automatic line feed, since you will have line feeds in your tape.

After the TAPE system command, turn the reader ON. The tape will be read, and you will see on your Teletype paper a copy of the tape as it is transmitted. The tape will stop reading when it reaches the end. (The tape reader will also stop automatically if it encounters any tear, sharp fold, or other restriction in tape movement. Make sure the tape is feeding freely.) Once the tape input is complete, type the system command KEY at the left margin of your page. This informs the computer you will revert to keyboard input and restores the automatic line advance. You may now proceed on the keyboard.

If you have a paper tape feature on your input terminal, you should learn how to use it. It will be useful not only for the preparation of programs before you hook up to the computer, i.e., off-line, but also for saving copies of your work which you may not wish to file in the computer's magnetic memory.

You may also make tape copies of programs you have perfected while hooked up to the computer, or of stored or library programs. To do this you type the system command LIST and turn on the paper tape punch just before you push RETURN. The program currently in your working area will then be listed on your Teletype paper and also punched on tape.

In many installations, both terminal connect time (that is, the number of minutes you have the telephone connection going) and file storage are charged for. The paper tape feature can save you money if you use it wisely. In addition, a tape copy of valuable programs provides security in case of a major malfunction at the computer center, which might obliterate your magnetic files.

Now try a program

Before going into the details of the BASIC language, try typing and running a simple computer program in BASIC so you will understand its form. Here is a problem. You want to prepare a solution. Given the number of hours you worked this week, H, your hourly rate of pay, R, and your income tax deduction percentage, T, find and print your net pay for the week, N. In particular, suppose you worked 40 hours ($H = 40$), your rate is \$4.85 per hour ($R = 4.85$), and your tax deduction rate is 18% ($T = .18$). Then, of course, $N = (H \times R) \times (1 - T)$ or, numerically, $N = (40 \times 4.85) \times (1 - .18) = 159.08$. (The problem is easy, so that you can check your hand-computed result against the computer result and gain some confidence in the machine.)

Here is a computer program that will give you a numerical result identical to that computed above. (We assume you have signed on to your computing system and that you have named your NEW program.)

```
10 READ H,R,T
20 LET N = (H * R) * (1 - T)
30 PRINT "YOUR NET PAY IS  $";N
40 DATA 40,4.85,.18
50 END

RUN
```

After typing in the program above, you may type the system command
RUN
(remember: no line number). After you have depressed the RETURN key following RUN, the computer will begin its execution of your program, and produce the following result:

```
YOUR NET PAY IS  $ 159.08

   50,  NORMAL EXIT FROM PROG.

TIME:     0.046 SEC.
```

The above program illustrates only a few of the forthcoming BASIC features, but at least you can see what happens before you go on.

1. Each line of the program starts with a line number.
2. The words READ, LET, PRINT, DATA, and END are BASIC language words that either tell the computer to do something or give it information.
   a. READ H, R, T causes the numbers in the line headed DATA to be identified with the variables H, R, T in that order.
   b. LET causes the numeric value of the expression (H * R) * (1 – T) to be computed. This is possible because H, R, and T have numeric values after the READ statement is executed. The final numeric result is then substituted for, or called, N. In the program, to avoid confusion with X, which might be used as a variable name, the symbol * is used to indicate multiplication.
   c. PRINT causes the title in quotation marks to be displayed literally as shown, followed by the computed value of N, your net pay. The semicolon following the second quotation mark controls the spacing between the dollar sign and the dollar amount.
   d. DATA identifies the numbers that follow it, separated by commas, as the data required for the problem.
   e. END tells the computer it has reached the end of the current problem.
3. The final word RUN is a system command which causes the program to be executed and the answer to be produced, as shown. In addition to the answer the computer tells you how long the program ran and that it ran normally.

Each of the above statement types as well as others will be discussed in the following chapters, but the form of a BASIC computer program should now be evident. To test the operation of your remote terminal when executing a program, duplicate the preceding program on your machine and see how it works.

The structure of BASIC language statements

The BASIC computer language, like English and all other languages, has a specified structure. Each BASIC statement has a required form with possibly one or more variations. To illustrate the standard form for each statement, we shall employ a general form of description. For each statement we shall

1. Underline all *required* words, symbols, or numbers except where underlining might cause confusion;
2. Capitalize all BASIC words;
3. Enclose all optional choices in brackets or parentheses.

For example, looking back to the net-pay program of the last illustration, we have for the first line:

```
10 READ H,R,T
```

This specific line has the following general form:

line number READ (list of variable names)

The user supplies an appropriate line number and the list of variables chosen for the problem at hand separated by commas.

A variable (as opposed to a constant) is a quantity that may assume a succession of numeric values. A variable name is that symbol or symbols which denote one particular variable as opposed to others. (Remember from the computer's viewpoint that a variable name identifies a specific memory box, or location.) In BASIC simple variable names may be composed of one of the 26 alphabetic characters, A through Z, or one of the alphabetic characters followed by a decimal digit, e.g., A5. The variable names shown in line 10 of the program meet these requirements, as do all others in the program. Finally, in most BASIC installations a variable when first mentioned is assumed equal to zero until that variable is given another value by reading data, a substitution, or other means. This fact is usually assumed in all program examples to follow.

For the evaluation statement, we had

```
20 LET N = (H * R) * (1 - T)
```

which has the general form

$$\text{line number LET (variable)} = \begin{Bmatrix} \text{numeric literal} \\ \text{variable} \\ \text{expression} \end{Bmatrix}$$

In the above statement, the line number is required, and LET is a BASIC word indicating that a substitution is to be made. A single variable will follow the word LET. Although the symbol = is required next, to avoid confusion it is not underlined. Finally, the three lines in the brackets to the right indicate a choice of alternatives. We may LET the value of a variable equal

1. A single number, sometimes called a numeric literal, or constant, because the number itself, e.g., 5, appears directly in the statement. (A nonnumeric literal, e.g., A, may not be used in a substitution except in special cases which will be discussed later.)
2. A single variable, e.g., LET X = Y, in which X and Y would have the same numeric value.
3. The numeric value of an expression, i.e., the numeric result of the arithmetic operations indicated to the right of the = symbol. An expression may contain both variables and constants, or numeric literals.

Some statement forms offer no choice. Thus, the last line of the previous program was

```
50 END
```

which has the general form

line number END

In BASIC, no program statement may be longer than one typed line; there is no provision for continuation from one line to the next. But BASIC does permit you to space a line as you like, since spaces are disregarded. Thus, line 20 of the illustrative program could have been written

```
20LETN=(H*R)*(1-T)
```

which, although somewhat confusing, is compact. By the same rule, note that LET, L ET, LE T, and L E T would all be considered the same. You may thus arrange the one-line BASIC statements across the page with great flexibility. (In most systems, blanks within line numbers or system commands are not tolerated; the flexibility mentioned above applies to BASIC language statements only.)

With this scheme of presentation in mind, we will now take up individual BASIC language statements in turn. The sequence of presentation follows approximately the frequency of use of the statements described.

EIGHT

END, PRINT, READ, and DATA

We assume you have become familiar with the line numbering and line correcting conventions of the previous chapter and know the difference between a system command and a program statement. All computer languages have conventions that must also be observed when preparing program statements. Let us now consider those essential to BASIC.

Language conventions

Numbers

In BASIC numbers may be expressed in one of three forms, or *modes*:

1. *Integers*, or numbers with no fractional part, e.g., 123;

2. *Real*, or *fixed-point*, numbers that have a decimal point and a fractional part, e.g., 123.45;

3. *Floating-point*, or *exponential form*, numbers in which decimal point location is modified by specified powers of ten, e.g., 123.45E +4 is taken to mean 1234500. The factor following the E means "times the specified power of ten." By this rule 123.45E −3 is equal to .12345, since multiplying a number by a negative power of ten is the same as moving the decimal point to the left a number of positions equal to the specified power. This form is useful for expressing very large or very small numbers. An omitted sign following the E is assumed to be plus; an intended negative sign must be shown.

Most BASIC installations limit numbers in the above forms to nine or fewer digits, not counting the decimal point or the exponent. When numbers are too large or too small to be represented within the specified limitation, the floating-point form is used. Numbers must be rounded to the maximum allowable number of significant digits, unless they can be expressed precisely in fewer places.

Variables

BASIC numeric variables, as opposed to numeric constants (numeric literals), may be identified by one of the 26 letters A to Z, or a letter followed by one of the 10 digits 0 to 9. Thus, A, X, Y, A1, Y3, Z9, etc., are legal variable names. The names A26, 9Z, ABC, and A2$ violate the rules and are not legal. Thus, you may have up to 286 variable names using the above rules. (Subscripted variables are discussed in Chapter 11.) At many installations, variables are initialized to zero until otherwise defined by a given number. Hereafter that convention is followed in the text.

Arithmetic operations

Numbers and variables may be combined into arithmetic expressions by using one or more of the arithmetic operators

+	Add	*	Multiply	↑	Raise to a power (exponentiate)
−	Subtract	/	Divide		

(The symbol * is used for multiply to avoid confusion with the letter X, which may be a variable name.)

In writing an expression, each arithmetic operation must be shown; none may be assumed. No two operations may be adjacent, nor may two numbers or variables be adjacent in an expression. For example, 2 + 2, A + B, X * Y, and 2 − X are legal expressions. The expression AB + 2 has two adjacent variables and is illegal; one possible correct form is A*B + 2. The expression X/−2 is also illegal because it contains two adjacent operations; the negative sign is taken to mean subtraction. Parentheses may be used to avoid the latter error; e.g., X/(−2) is legal. Parentheses may also be used to control the order in which an arithmetic expression is evaluated by the machine. Normal evaluation proceeds as follows:

1. Exponentiation, then
2. Division and multiplication, then
3. Subtraction and addition.

If parentheses are used, the expression segment within a parentheses pair will be evaluated first (in the above order). The computer then works outward until the entire expression is reduced to one number. Thus, by these rules,

4 + 6/2 has the value 4 + 3, or 7
(4 + 6)/2 has the value 10/2, or 5
4 + 6/2 ↑ 2 has the value 4 + 6/4, or 5.5
(4 + 6/2) ↑ 2 has the value 7 ↑ 2, or 49
((4 + 6)/2) ↑ 2 has the value (10/2) ↑ 2, or 25

Parentheses used in arithmetic expressions must always occur in pairs, otherwise you will get an error message from the computer. Without parentheses and in case of a tie in priority, evaluation is from *left to right*, e.g., 1/10/10 is .01, *not* 1.

Spaces

Most installations disregard spaces in BASIC statements and expressions. Thus, spaces are not necessary in expressions; for example, (4 + 6)/2 and (4 + 6) / 2 are equivalent.

We next treat four BASIC words—END, PRINT, READ, and DATA—that will enable us to write simple computer programs.

END

Each program you write must have a conclusion. The BASIC statement which indicates program termination has the general form

line number END

Because every BASIC program must be terminated by an END statement, END will be associated with the *largest* line number in your program. (You may wish to use the same line number for your END statement in all your programs, e.g., 9999 END, so references to that line number may be readily interpreted as references to the END statement. The utility of this practice will be evident in later examples.)

As we progress, it will be helpful to distinguish between two types of program statements:

1. Those that are *executed*, or cause some direct action, e.g., PRINT;
2. Those that are *declarative* and serve only to provide information to the computer.

The END statement is a declaration indicating that the program is finished. That fact, of course, causes compilation to stop and the machine to turn from its translating tasks to that of running the job, but no *program* action is called for. This point will be of later importance.

PRINT

BASIC uses the command PRINT to display results. PRINT is a flexible executable command and offers the user a number of options. The general form of the command is

line number PRINT { numeric literal / expression / nonnumeric literal / variable value }

The options in the brackets consist of

1. Printing a stated number or constant (line number PRINT 3.14 displays the number 3.14). A special case is to PRINT nothing (line number PRINT) and produce a line of blanks, or, in effect, a line feed, useful in vertically spacing output reports.
2. Presenting the numeric value of an expression which the PRINT command will evaluate before displaying (line number PRINT 2 + 2 displays the answer, 4).
3. Printing a nonnumeric literal, usually for a title or similar report purpose (line number PRINT "THIS IS PROBLEM 1" displays THIS IS PROBLEM 1). The text to be printed is enclosed between quotation marks, and may consist of any string of keyboard characters, except quotes.
4. Printing the current value of a variable. (If the value of X is 2, the statement line number PRINT X prints the number 2.)
5. Combinations of the above may be specified on one line, separated by commas or semicolons, as described in the next section.

PRINT editing symbols

In BASIC the comma and semicolon are used in the PRINT statement to permit several PRINT actions to be specified on one program line. Although some variations occur among installations, the usual effects of the comma and semicolon in the PRINT statement are as follows.

1. Comma: Use of the comma in a PRINT statement list causes the teletype page to be automatically divided into five columns of 15 spaces each. (The total teletype page is usually 75 characters wide.) Then if the text fits, a printed list will be spread into these five fields. If not, the machine usually skips to the next available field until the effective output line of 75 characters has been used. For example,

line number PRINT V, W, X, Y, Z,

will print the current numeric values of the five variables in five columns *across* the page, reading from left to right.

The comma may also be used to intermix the above options. For example,

line number PRINT "X", X, "Y", Y

will print the literal values X and Y in columns 1 and 3 and the numeric values of the variables X and Y in columns 2 and 4. Column 5, in this instance, will remain blank.

Most BASIC installations assume a comma format following an ending quote if the comma is omitted. In this case

line number PRINT "THE ANSWER IS" X

is equivalent to

line number PRINT "THE ANSWER IS", X

as illustrated in the programs hereafter.

2. Semicolon: Like the comma, the semicolon may also be used to separate a list of PRINT options. However, the semicolon does not spread the results into five equally spaced columns, but seeks to pack the results as tightly as possible across the page. You must check your own installation for the exact semicolon packing rules used there. In general, the semicolon editing feature provides *variable* packing, depending upon the length of the text to be displayed. The computer scans the output to be displayed and packs it according to predetermined spacing rules, with more space for larger text material. To illustrate using the General Electric time-sharing specifications, the semicolon will provide a print field

6 spaces long	for 1-, 2-, or 3-digit numbers
9 spaces long	for 4-, 5-, or 6-digit numbers
12 spaces long	for 7-, 8-, or 9-digit numbers
0 spaces	for two labels (alphanumeric literals) separated by a semicolon

Thus, the semicolon option may not result in equally aligned columns on the printed page. The comma option, above, should usually be used when column alignment from a series of PRINT statements is desired.

3. Line Feed Inhibition: Use of either a comma or a semicolon to terminate a PRINT statement will inhibit the line feed associated with each PRINT. Thus, the pair of print statements

```
100 PRINT X, Y,
110 PRINT Q, R
```

will cause the four numeric values of X, Y, Q, R, to be displayed on a single line and is equivalent to the single statement

100 PRINT X, Y, Q, R

In other words, the terminating comma inhibits the line advance and perpetuates the standard format rules. The terminating semicolon inhibits line feed and perpetuates the semicolon packing rules, which, as above, will vary depending on the length of the upcoming text.

4. Line Overrun: If you ask the computer to PRINT more text than can be accommodated on one printed line, the machine will usually continue to the next line, following the specified comma or semicolon used until the required printing is accomplished.

For reasons that should be clear, commas or semicolons enclosed in quotation marks will not have any editing effect, but will be printed. The statement

line number PRINT "YEA, YEA; NAY, NAY"

will print the text between the quotation marks, spaced as shown, on one line.

Applications of PRINT

You can see the versatility of the PRINT command in the following examples.

1 / Evaluate and print a literal expression

An arithmetic expression to be evaluated may be handled directly in a PRINT statement.

100 PRINT 3.1416 + 2

would cause the number 5.1416 to be displayed on the teletype. All the other operations may also be used in this form. Thus,

100 PRINT (3.1416 + 2)/4 − 2.2 ↑ 2

is a possibility. Note the use of parentheses to avoid ambiguity in the order of operations.

This first application of the PRINT statement enables us to write the easiest form of program possible. By putting together the PRINT and END statements (plus the *system command* RUN–*without* a line number after END) we can execute our first (two-line) program. Thus,

```
100 PRINT 3.1416 + 2
9999 END
RUN
```

is a correct program that will be executed if you type it as shown on your remote terminal. The system command RUN *does not have a line number* so that the computer can distinguish the program to be executed (which has line numbers) from direct commands to take some control action. Finally, notice that no program can be shorter than two lines (plus a RUN) because every program must terminate with a numbered END statement.

2 / *Evaluate expressions containing variables*

The PRINT statement can also handle expressions in variables, if those variables have been previously defined, that is, if they have been given a numeric value by some previous command by methods we shall soon discuss. Thus,

```
100 PRINT X ↑ 2 + Y ↑ 2
```

can be evaluated and printed in one step if X and Y have been given previous numeric values. In the same way

```
100 PRINT X ↑ 2 + Y ↑ 2 + 3.1416
```

will also work.

3 / *Display results without manipulation*

We may need to display the results of one or more computations that result in several answers, say, A, B, C, D, and E.

```
100 PRINT A, B, C, D, E
```

would place on one line the numeric values of the stated variables and space them into five columns. (Again, the numeric values of A, B, C, D, and E must have been previously determined.) The statement

```
100 PRINT A, B, C, D, E, F, G
```

would place the first five numeric values on one line, then advance to the next line and place F and G in the two left-most columns. The statement

```
100 PRINT A, B
```

would place the numeric values of A and B in the two left-most columns, then when another PRINT is encountered in the program, a *line feed* (or single space to the next line) is automatically initiated.

4 / Display numeric and nonnumeric literals

A numeric literal is just a number; other literals might be alphabetic and/or special characters. A PRINT statement will enable them to be used as titles, column headings, or for other informational purposes. Although numeric literals will be printed as they stand, following the rules given in (1), nonnumeric literals must be enclosed in quotation marks. Literals and variables may be intermixed by the application of quotation marks, as illustrated below. Thus,

```
100 PRINT "THIS IS PROBLEM NUMBER 1"
```

will cause the nonnumeric string of characters between the quotation marks to be displayed (left-justified) on the page. The quotation marks *will not* be printed. Between the quotation marks you may have any alphabetic, numeric, or special characters (including spaces)—except, of course, quotation marks, which would confuse the computer. Obviously, in any line of a PRINT command, there must be an even number of quotation marks, i.e., pairs of opening and closing quotation marks. Here are some further variations:

```
100 PRINT "THIS IS PROBLEM NUMBER 1. THE ANSWER IS "X
```

The statement above will display the text between the quotation marks, then print the numeric value of the variable X, which must have been defined previously.

```
100 PRINT "THE ANSWER IS "X/Y
```

will display the text between the quotation marks, and also evaluate and print the numeric result of the expression X/Y, provided both X and Y have been previously defined.

100 PRINT 150 <u>or</u> 100 PRINT "150"

will simply print the numeric literal 150. Column headings will be correctly aligned (for the standard five-column format) if the headings are short (in most systems under 12 characters). Thus, the *pair* of PRINT statements

```
100 PRINT "A", "B", "C", "D", "E"
110 PRINT A, B, C, D, E
```

will not only print the literal column headings, but will correctly align the numeric values of the indicated variables under them.

If you understand the above PRINT operations, you may write a wide range of programs without any further knowledge of other PRINT options.

READ and DATA

In the BASIC language, the executable command READ and the declarative statement DATA go together. If one or more READ statements appear in a program, that program must also contain one or more DATA lines. However, they need not be equal in number.

The general form of the READ statement is

line number READ {list of variable names}

and the general form of the DATA statement is

line number DATA {list of numeric data values}

The simplest form of the READ statement is 20 READ X. When such a READ command is encountered in the sequence of processing, the computer scans the DATA lines, which (in the simplest version) would have the form 900 DATA 3.1416 (when 3.1416 is the numeric value to be assigned to the variable X). The first numeric value encountered in this search is set equal to X, which is now defined. Thus, a READ statement is one method by which a variable may be given a numeric value.

By extension, several variables may be read at once. Thus the lines

```
20 READ A, B, C, D, E
```

and

```
900 DATA 1, 2, 3, 4, 5
```

would cause the five numeric values to be substituted for the five variables in their respective order (A would be set equal to 1, B to 2, etc.). A simple program using the READ and DATA statements in conjunction with the PRINT statement follows:

```
20 READ A, B
30 PRINT "THE ANSWER IS" A ↑ 2 + B ↑ 2
40 DATA 2.7, 3
99 END
RUN
```

(We have used 99 END instead of the previous 9999 END to illustrate that line numbers are arbitrary: They only indicate sequence. So long as END has the *largest* line number, you have met the computer's needs.)

The illustration just given may at first seem a less efficient way to compute the required result than the alternate method of placing the data values directly in the PRINT statements, as illustrated in the last section. However, as we shall see later, we may want to use the same set of computations over and over again, changing the data at each repetition. In these instances, a READ command is absolutely necessary.

Applications of PRINT, READ, DATA, and END using READ and DATA

To illustrate the four BASIC words presented thus far, here are several alternate methods of creating simple programs. Try to understand each before you proceed.

1 / Simple arithmetic

Let your GROSS PAY for the week be A, your DEDUCTIONS be B, and your NET PAY be C. Suppose A is $150, B is $40. Cause the computer to print out your NET PAY, or variable C, after making the required subtraction.

The solution may be obtained in two ways: by a direct evaluation using the PRINT statement, or by a combination of the READ and PRINT statements. Both methods follow.

Method A

```
100 PRINT "YOUR NET PAY IS "150 − 40
999 END
RUN
```

If you want to show a dollar sign in the answer you can change line 100 to

```
100 PRINT "YOUR NET PAY IS $"150 − 40.
```

Method B

```
100 READ A,B
200 PRINT "YOUR NET PAY IS $"A − B
300 DATA 150, 40
999 END
RUN
```

The comma in the DATA line is the "delimiter," which separates the values of A and B. This delimiter *must* be a comma, not another character or a space. In particular, because of visual problems and their proximity on the keyboard, the comma and period are often confused. A period in a DATA statement is considered a decimal point. If you had 300 DATA 150.40 you would get an error message "OUT OF DATA AT LINE 100" indicating the computer looked for a value of B and could not find it! You might want to try this erroneous DATA statement and see what happens. (Note that variable C is never mentioned, for reasons discussed in Example 5 below.)

2 / *PRINT a small table*

Suppose the value of X is 2. Given that value, produce a five-column table in which you will show X, X/2, 2X, X^2, and the square root of X, or equivalently X raised to the .5 power. Display a title as well as the numeric results.

Again, either of the former two approaches is possible.

Method A

```
100 PRINT "X", "X/2", "2X", "X ↑ 2", "X ↑ .5"
200 PRINT 2, 2/2, 2 * 2, 2 ↑ 2, 2 ↑ .5
999 END
RUN
```

Method B

```
100 READ X
200 PRINT "X", "X/2", "2X", "X ↑ 2", "X ↑ .5"
300 PRINT X, X/2, 2 * X, X ↑ 2, X ↑ .5
400 DATA 2
999 END
RUN
```

In both examples, note the necessity for using the symbol * for multiply. PRINT 2X will not work, since it does *not* communicate the symbol for multiplication to the computer. Also, note that in BASIC a numeric literal or a variable may be raised to a fractional power as well as an integer power. To ask for X ↑ .5 is to ask for the square root, just as to ask for X ↑ .333333 is one way to obtain a cube root, and so on. (We could also ask for the evaluation of an expression such as X ↑ 2.5.)

3 / Get several evaluations in one program

Suppose we want to find the values of (2)(3.1416), (3)(3.1416), and (4)(3.1416). An efficient way to do this would be to compute all the values at the same time in the same program. Again, there are two approaches, but you may now see the greater power of the READ statement.

Method A

```
100 PRINT 2*3.1416
200 PRINT 3*3.1416
300 PRINT 4*3.1416
999 END
RUN
```

Method B

```
100 READ X,A,B,C
200 PRINT A*X,B*X,C*X
300 DATA 3.1416,2,3,4
999 END
RUN
```

Not only does Method B involve less chance of typing error in transmitting data to the machine, it also permits the same program to be used with different data, as illustrated below. Since commas are delimiters in BASIC, omission of spaces in the READ, PRINT, and DATA statements of Method B is allowed.

One further comment regarding a difference between Method A and Method B in this problem may be in order. Note that the answers in Method A will be displayed one below the other, with single values on three successive lines. On the contrary, in Method B, the three answers will appear on the same line, in three separate columns. Can you explain why? Answer: Because in Method A we have used three PRINT statements, whereas in Method B we have used only one. Each separate PRINT statement causes a line advance.

4 / RUN an existing program with different data

Now suppose we require the same computation as above, but would like to change the value of 3.1416 to 7.8973. To use Method A above, we would have to retype the entire program. However, with Method B, we could change the single DATA line to

```
300 DATA 7.8973, 2, 3, 4
```

type RUN, and obtain the new result. In BASIC retyping a new line with an existing line number will replace the old line with the new one. This editorial capability makes it possible to use one program over and over, simply by entering new data. (Similarly, to type a line number, say, 300, followed by an immediate carriage return has the effect of erasing line 300. Further, to insert a new line as an afterthought, say a title in the above problem, we may type a presently nonexistent line number and have it inserted automatically at RUN-time in the proper sequence. Thus

```
150 PRINT "X", "Y", "Z"
```

when typed before RUN in Method B would cause those column headings to be displayed above the numeric values computed.)

5 / *Evaluating more complicated expressions*

Suppose you have been asked to evaluate the following expression

$$X = \frac{-B + \sqrt{B^2 - 4AC}}{2A}$$

in which A is 2, B is 5, and C is 2. Find the numeric value of X.

The purpose of this problem is to indicate how arithmetic operations are handled in more difficult cases. Again, we have the two alternatives, one using numeric literals in a PRINT statement, the other using the READ statement with variables.

Method A

```
100 PRINT "THE ANSWER IS" ((-5) + ((+5) ↑ 2 - 4 * 2 * 2) ↑ .5)/2 * 2
999 END
RUN
```

Method B

```
100 READ A,B,C
200 PRINT "THE ANSWER IS" ((-B) + ((B) ↑ 2 - 4 * A * C) ↑ .5)/2 * A
300 DATA 2, 5, 2
999 END
RUN
```

Note the use of parentheses to make the meaning of the arithmetic expression unambiguous. It is not harmful to have *extra* parentheses (such as those shown enclosing —B and B in Method B, or the equivalent literal values in Method A), but to leave out the first and the last parentheses shown in both cases would produce the wrong answer. Why? Answer: Division would have been applied only to the most adjacent term, 4 * A * C, not to the entire expression to the left of the /. The parentheses make the evaluation proceed from the innermost parentheses to the outermost, which, as shown, produces the correct result.

Another question may be asked. Why does the variable X never appear in the program? (We *do* mention it in the problem specifications!) Answer: The variable X is not needed, although it could be mentioned as an alphabetic literal in the PRINT statement for clarity if we so desired. Since we will make no further use of X, there is no necessity for this reference—all we want is the numeric value of the right-hand side of the equation, which we obtain upon execution of the PRINT statement. In fact, it would be illegal to ask for

```
100 PRINT Y = X ↑ 2,
```

since such a statement would imply that we want to do two things at the same time: namely find the numeric value of X ↑ 2 and *remember* that Y should equal that value later on. The PRINT statement is not intended to perform that dual function. (In the next chapter, we will encounter a statement that can simultaneously evaluate and remember—the LET command. But that is another subject.)

Input

In some applications we may want a program to pause momentarily so we can enter data at the time of execution or after seeing previous results. An alternative to the READ and DATA statements permits us to do this. It has the general form

line number INPUT {list of variable names}

When the computer comes to an INPUT statement in its *execution* phase, it stops execution, presents a ? to the user, and pauses until the remote terminal user types in the required numeric values of the variables specified in the INPUT statement.

Usually a PRINT statement is used before the INPUT statement to remind the user of what is needed. Here is an example.

```
100 PRINT "WHAT ARE YOUR VALUES OF A, B AND C"
110 INPUT A, B, C
120 PRINT "THE SUM OF A + B + C IS "; A + B + C
999 END
RUN
```

The output after RUN would be the question of line 100. You would then type in the numeric values of A, B, and C in that order with a carriage return. The program would then proceed to produce the sum required for the numbers you had just typed in, and would print the answer with the title shown in line 120. The uses of the INPUT statement will appear in later problems and examples.

PROBLEMS

8-1 Why is an END statement necessary in any BASIC language program? (This same question could be asked for other computer languages, too. There are two main reasons in BASIC. See if you can name them.)

8-2 Which of the following PRINT statements is illegal, according to the rules given in this chapter?

a. 10 PRINT A, B, C, D

b. 10 PRINT 1 − A/2

c. 10 PRINT 2*(A + B)/3

d. 10 PRINT (3.14 + 7.86)*X

e. 10 PRINT A + C + D + E

f. 10 PRINT "THE ANSWER IS" X

8-3 Write a program to compute the numeric value of the expression

$$AX^2 + BX + C$$

where A is 1, B is 2, C is 3, and X is 4.

8-4 Write a program that will cause the computer to print your name on your remote terminal.

8-5 Write a program to compute the same expression as in Problem 8-3, but include the title "THE ANSWER IS Y EQUALS", where

$$Y = AX^2 + BX + C$$

and the values of A, B, C, and X are those given in Problem 8-3.

8-6 Write *one* program which will produce successive values of X^2, where X has the values 1, 2, 3, 4.

8-7 Add to (or modify) the program which is the result of Problem 8-6, so that the title "A", "B", "C", "D", will be printed above the values of X^2 for the four values of X, i.e., 1, 2, 3, 4. Place the title on one line and the four values of X^2 on the next line.

8-8 How can you cause a line space to appear between the title and the results of Problem 8-7? That is, how can you double space the results?

8-9 Is there any difference among the following program *segments*? (The entire program is not shown, and the dashes indicate lines not shown. We concentrate on the READ and DATA statements.)

a.
```
20 READ X, Y
- - - - -
- - - - -
100 DATA 10
110 DATA 20
```

b.
```
20 READ X, Y
- - - - -
- - - - -
100 DATA 10, 20
```

c.
```
20 READ X
25 READ Y
- - - - -
- - - - -
100 DATA 10
110 DATA 20
```

d.
```
20 READ X
30 READ Y
- - - - -
- - - - -
100 DATA 10, 20
```

8-10 In the program below, specify

a. The numeric values of A, B, C, D, E, and X.
b. The sequence of the numeric values that will be printed and the numeric value of these results.
c. Whether the numeric results will be printed in one row or below one another. Why?
d. What would happen if the numeric value of the line number 99 END were changed arbitrarily to 9999 END.

```
10 READ X
20 READ A, B, C
25 READ D
30 READ E
35 PRINT X
40 PRINT A + B + C
50 PRINT D/E
60 PRINT (A + B + C) ↑ (D/E)
70 PRINT "THIS IS THE END OF THE JOB"
80 DATA 10, 20, 30, 40, 50, 25
99 END
```

8-11 You are now interested in finding out how much you will have in the bank after 12 years if you invest $1,000 at the start of the first year and if interest at your bank is compounded:

a. Annually at the rate of $5\frac{1}{4}$%?
b. Annually at the rate of 5%?
c. Monthly at the rate of $4\frac{4}{5}$%?

Indicate how you would make the required evaluations using your computer terminal and the BASIC language with the least effort. What would you need to know—in addition to your present knowledge of computer programming—to obtain the required results?

8-12 Why are the READ and PRINT statements (or their equivalent) an essential feature of *any* computer programming language?

NINE

LET and stored functions

The next command to learn is LET, which causes expressions to be evaluated and the answer to be stored *within* the computer, rather than printed on the remote terminal as would happen in an evaluation using the PRINT statement.

In particular, the LET command is a "substitution" statement because it causes the evaluation of an expression to be substituted for the current value of a variable. In general, the form of the LET statement is

$$\underline{\text{line number}}\ \ \underline{\text{LET}}\ \{\underline{\text{variable}}\} = \begin{Bmatrix} \underline{\text{numeric}}\ \underline{\text{literal}} \\ \underline{\text{variable}} \\ \underline{\text{expression}} \end{Bmatrix}$$

In standard BASIC, only one evaluation of an expression may be accomplished for each LET command, unlike the multiple possibilities of a PRINT command, as described in the previous chapter. In the general form given above, the equals sign is also required, but for clarity it has not been underlined; remember that the symbol = is associated with a LET command, but in this case it does not denote "equals" in the usual algebraic sense of equality of both sides of an equation. Instead, it requires that a numeric value obtained from the arithmetic evaluation of the expression on the right should be substituted for and identified by the name of the variable on the left. The same holds true for the substitution of a numeric literal.

The operation thus proceeds from the right to the left in either case, and to ask that an expression or a numeric literal be set equal to a variable will not work.

Here are some typical LET statements. The line number shown here is completely arbitrary, but in a computer program it would have to be in the correct sequential order.

```
100 LET X = 0
100 LET X = A + 2
100 LET X = A * X + B * Y
100 LET A1 = 25 * A3 + X * 2.5
100 LET A = ((X + Y)/2 + 3.96 * W) ↑ 4
100 LET X = 1.968
```

In the above examples, of course, every variable must be given a numeric value before the expression containing it can be evaluated. An undefined variable will cause the computer to halt. (If you do not remember why the variables A1 and A3, shown in the fourth example above, are legal consult the definitions of variables in Chapter 8.) In the first and the last examples above, the variable X is given a numeric value by the LET command. Thus, the substitution of a numeric literal for a variable by means of a LET statement is yet another way data may be introduced into a program.

Unlike the PRINT statement, the LET statement does not produce visible results at the remote terminal. The effect of LET is to cause the result of the evaluation and substitution to be stored in the computer under the name of the variable shown in the LET statement. Thus, by referring later to any of the variables shown to the left of the equality sign in the above examples, we will obtain a numeric value. (For obvious physical reasons, only one variable may appear to the left of the equals sign in a LET statement; the single variable refers to a single physical storage location in the computer's memory. For this same reason, *some* variable must always appear to the left of the equals sign!)

As an extension of the previous examples, look now at some LET statements that may appear contradictory from an algebraic viewpoint.

```
100 LET N = N + 1
100 LET A = A * B
100 LET A = A ↑ 2
100 LET A = A + A
100 LET A = 2 * A
100 LET A = -A
```

All of the above substitutions are frequently used in computer programs. When the same variable appears on both sides of the equals sign, this implies that the new value of the variable should be computed from the old. For example, the statement

```
100 LET N = N + 1
```

causes the new value of N (on the left) to be set equal to the old value of N (on the right) plus 1. (As we shall see in later chapters, this form of substitution is often used in program sequences that count the number of cases handled, number pages, or record transactions processed. Therefore, an understanding of this operation is fundamental for further progress.) Similarly,

```
100 LET A = -A
```

has the effect of changing the sign of A from whatever it was to a new (alternate) plus or minus value.

You may well wonder how the substitution operation is performed physically in the computer. For example, if the variable name A actually refers to a single memory storage location, how is it that

```
100 LET A = -A
```

is performed?

The possibility of performing such a substitution lies in the sequential operation of the computer's arithmetic circuits and the intervention of intermediate storage registers associated with the arithmetic unit of the machine. Thus, the LET statement of the last example calls up several sequential machine operations, which can be described as follows:

1. Pick up the existing value of A and hold it in an arithmetic register, a nondestructive operation with respect to the memory location A;
2. Perform the required arithmetic operation, namely, reverse the algebraic sign of the numeric value of A now in the storage register;
3. Place the current contents of the storage register in the physical location called A, a destructive operation that deletes the old contents of A and puts in the new value.

Other more complicated substitution operations work fundamentally in the same manner.

With these preliminaries out of the way, let us now look at some programs involving LET.

1 / Introduction of data via the LET statement

```
100 LET A = 2
110 LET B = 2
120 PRINT A + B
999 END
```

The number printed will be 4.

```
100 LET A = 3.1416
110 LET B = 5.9138
120 LET X = A * B
130 PRINT X
999 END
```

The number printed will be the product of 3.1416 and 5.9138.

The user of the remote terminal would, of course, have to type RUN—with no line number—at the end of each of the above programs. We shall hereafter assume that you will remember to type RUN when you want the program executed.

2 / Introduction of data via the READ statement, evaluation by LET

```
100 READ A,B,C,D
110 LET X = A + B + C + D
120 PRINT X
500 DATA 1,2,3,4
999 END
```

It is not yet obvious why the LET statement is needed in this type of problem, since the PRINT statement alone or its combination with READ could provide the same numeric answer, 10. However, we shall later see the value of being able to store intermediate answers. In the above example (as well as in the two former examples) the values of all the variables are available for other uses, until we type END and the system command RUN. Thus, if you also wanted X ↑ 2 in the above problem, you could insert

```
130 PRINT X ↑ 2
```

or retype line 120 as

```
120 PRINT X, X ↑ 2
```

and the new required result would be instantly available when you typed RUN. There are other important extensions.

3 / Break up a long computation, use the same result many times

```
100 READ X,A,B,C
110 LET Y = A + B + C
120 LET W = X + Y
130 LET R = X + Y ↑ 2
140 LET S = X + Y ↑ 3
150 PRINT W,R,S
500 DATA 3.14, 9.87, 8.76, 3.49
999 END
```

Note that it is possible to use the original evaluation of Y in several later evaluations because the LET statement stores and holds the numeric value of Y until a later value is substituted for it (which is not done in the above program). The LET statements of lines 120, 130, and 140, could, of course have been combined in a single PRINT statement, such as

```
150 PRINT X + Y, X + Y ↑ 2, X + Y ↑ 3
```

since the necessary variables have been defined. If the new line 150 were introduced, it would be desirable to delete lines 120, 130, and 140 by typing in those line numbers with a carriage return.

Although the illustrations given here show the uses of the LET statement in elementary cases, the true power of the substitution operation will become evident only when we show in Chapter 10 how to depart from strict sequential execution of a program and permit loops and branches to occur. However, it will be useful to introduce another topic here, namely, the use of stored functions and user-defined functions.

Stored functions

The designer of a total computing system (i.e., one that includes hardware and the associated software, or programs) can choose either hardware or software implementation of the desired instructions. For example, it is possible to build a general purpose machine that can only add and to have the special commands required for a given application provided by the program. The opposite alternative is also available. The designer could create a piece of hardware with a wide instruction repertoire which would make the machine particular with respect to those operations and thereby simplify programming. Each manufacturer estimates the needs of his users and strikes a balance between the two extremes. Customarily, the frequently used operations, such as add and multiply, are committed to hardware, and the less frequently used commands, such as finding the logarithm of a number, are left to software, usually the compiler, which implements a given language. (Hardware implementation gives faster results than software but is expensive.)

From the average user's viewpoint, it is impossible to detect the difference between hardware or software implementation of instructions. Indeed, as we shall see, the user may add to the machine's effective instruction repertoire in several ways. Such programming approaches to instructional versatility are an aid in solving complex computational problems.

First, each programming language usually makes available to the user (in addition to the essential arithmetic operations) a number of special operations, called stored functions. A complete list of those available in BASIC is presented in Table 9.1.

TABLE 9.1

BASIC Stored Functions and Useful Conversions

Function[a]	**Use**
SIN(X)	Gives sin x, where x is measured in radians.
COS(X)	Gives cos x, where x is measured in radians.
TAN(X)	Gives tangent x, where x is measured in radians.
ATN(X)	Gives arctangent x, where x is measured in radians.
EXP(X)	Gives e^x (exponential function).
LOG(X)	Gives natural logarithm of the absolute value of x, that is, the sign of x; plus or minus is disregarded.
ABS(X)	Gives the absolute value of x; the sign is deleted.
SQR(X)	Gives square root of the absolute value of x.
INT(X)	Gives the integer part of x (greatest integer $\leq$ x).
SGN(X)	Gives sign of x: +1 for positive x, 0 for 0, −1 for negative x.

Useful conversions

1. X (in radians) = 3.1416/180 * D (in degrees)

2. D (in degrees) = (180/3.1416) * X (in radians)

3. log to base B of the number X = LOG(X)/LOG(B)
where B is the desired base and LOG(X) and LOG(B) are the natural logarithms of X and B provided by the BASIC stored function.

4. LOG(X) = LOG(10) * $\log_{10}(x)$

5. $\log_{10}(x)$ = LOG(X)/LOG(10)

[a] $\pi = 3.1416$.

A typical stored function is LOG(X), which provides the natural logarithm of the variable X, previously given a numeric value.[1] Thus, the statement

```
100 LET Y = LOG(X)
```

---

[1] A natural logarithm, as opposed to a common logarithm, is one taken to the *base* e = 2.718, . . . rather than to the base 10. The reason for this base choice is that natural logarithms are easier to compute than those to the base 10. Appropriate conversions are shown in Table 9.1.

will cause the computer to substitute for Y the numeric value of the natural logarithm of the numeric value of X. The operation of the other functions indicated in Table 9.1 is similar. Thus,

```
100 LET Y = SIN (X),
```

where X is expressed in radians (not degrees) will set Y equal to the numeric value of the appropriate sine.[2]

The numeric values generated by such stored functions are not obtained by looking up a table, as one might expect by reflection upon his own experience in flipping the pages of handbooks. Each required value is computed from a formula, so that *any* value of X, called the argument of the function, may be evaluated and so that memory space may be conserved. The required formula is part of the compiler for a given language and need not in any way concern the beginning user. A simple knowledge of how the functions are used will suffice.

In this vein, we will now present only one example of the use of stored functions, and leave further applications to later chapters.

Logarithms

A suitable example is the application of logarithms. Thus, suppose we have the equation $2^X = 1000$ and wish to solve for X. In the usual way (remembering our algebra), we could write

$$(x)\log(2) = \log(1000)$$

or $$x = \log(1000)/\log(2)$$

A suitable program in BASIC to implement this solution would be

```
100 LET X = LOG(1000)/LOG(2)
110 PRINT X
999 END
```

Or the evaluation could be effected directly in a PRINT statement.

In the above problem, the base of the logarithms used is not important, since the result desired is the quotient of two logarithms to the same base. However, in the next example, we have a different requirement.

---

[2] A circle is divided into 360 *degrees* using the everyday method of measurement, and alternatively into 2π *radians* in most scientific work. The latter method of measurement permits easy computation of the trigonometric functions. (In both the natural logarithm and trigonometric computations, power series techniques are used. See any mathematics handbook under *power series* for details.) The note to Table 9.1 provides the formulas for radian-degree conversions. In the table we have shown the value of π as 3.1416; for more precision you may use all nine significant figures for π, 3.14159265.

To take the simplest case, let us multiply two numbers together by adding their logarithms. Let A be 2 and B be 5, and the answer desired be X = A * B. Omitting the obvious direct evaluation, we could use logarithms and obtain the required result in the following manner.

```
100 LET X = LOG(2) + LOG(5)
110 LET C = EXP(X)
120 PRINT C
999 END
```

The function EXP(X) finds the *antilog* of X and thus produces the required answer, C.

With the methods just outlined, any logarithmic operation may be performed, thereby greatly expanding the versatility of the BASIC language. Since finding the logarithm, manipulating it, and then finding its inverse, or antilog, are all done to the same base, it is immaterial whether we use common or natural logarithms. We could come out with the same numeric result regardless of the base employed.

Of course, if you are not in the habit of using logarithms, you may ignore the computer's ability to handle them! No harm will be done, but your repertoire of possible instructions will be constrained. You will not have made yourself familiar with a potential problem-solving aid.

Similarly, a knowledge of the functions provided in any computer language will expand your command ability greatly. The problems at the end of this chapter will bring out more useful applications of the stored functions in BASIC.

User-defined functions

A second approach to an expansion of the computer's instruction repertoire, or the list of things it can do directly, is the use of user-defined functions. By means of the command DEF, which stands for "definition," the user may define his own functional relationships and have them available for shorthand evaluation in his programs.

How this is done is best illustrated by example. In what follows remember that a function's purpose is simply to substitute one numeric value for another, which is given.

Suppose in a sequence of computations we are required repeatedly to compute various values of the expression

```
A * X ↑ 2 + B * X + C
```

where A, B, and C are given and where X may take on various values in the computation. Moreover, suppose that other terms, such as X^3, may be added to the expression during the course of your work. (Problems of this type arise in many scientific computations.)

Since the expression is to be evaluated repeatedly, we now define a function, which in BASIC can be done as follows:

```
100 DEF FNA(X) = A * X ↑ 2 + B * X + C
```

where the DEF indicates a definition, and the declaration FNA names the specific function desired. (The third letter of FN__ may be any alphabetic character, so that 26 different functions may be defined in one BASIC program if necessary.)

The argument, X, may now take on any numeric value, by means of a READ, LET, or numeric literal input. Here is a working program.

```
100 READ A,B,C
110 DEF FNA(X) = A * X ↑ 2 + B * X + C
120 PRINT FNA(2.5), FNA(3.6), FNA(9.8), FNA(10.76)
500 DATA 4.5, 6.7, 8.9
999 END
```

We have used the PRINT statement to produce the evaluation and the printout, the DATA statement with READ to define A, B, and C, and the numeric literal in the argument of FNA(X) to define the four values of X required. All variables are defined, and the economy to user time is obvious. (Try getting the same results in another legal way.) To convince yourself of the usefulness of this approach, try the above problem on your remote terminal.

The user-defined function is even more versatile than may be obvious at first, since such a function may include in its definition stored functions and previously defined user functions, as well as numeric literals, variables, and arithmetic operations. However, there is one limitation: a user-defined function may be no longer than one line in length. Thus, the user-defined function is suitable only for relatively short computational sequences.

A third method of increasing the machine's instruction repertoire with programming is to employ subroutines, as discussed in Chapter 12. Conceptually, the subroutine is an extension of the user-defined function, but it will be treated separately because of its importance.

PROBLEMS

9-1 Why are the following forms of the LET statement *incorrect*? You may assume all variables given to the right have been defined.

a. 100 LET X + Y = 2 * A
b. 100 LET 2 * X = A + B
c. 100 LET X = 0, Y = 0, Z = 0
d. 100 LET Y > A
e. 100 LET Z = A/−B
f. 100 LET A28 = Z

9-2 Give some applications in which a LET statement of the form

100 LET N = N + 1
might be useful.

9-3 Write a LET statement that will evaluate the following expression, assuming that all variables to the right have been previously defined. (Use parentheses as necessary, and remember the asterisk is used for multiplication.)

$$Y = \left(\frac{AB + BC}{A^2 + B^2}\right) \div \left(\frac{B^2 - BC}{A^2 + AB}\right)$$

9-4 Since no evaluation by a LET statement can extend for more than one line, comment on how you might break the expression in Problem 9-3 through the use of several LET statements and then shorten the final evaluation. Write a suitable program to accomplish this alternative result.

9-5 Suppose you want to raise the number 2.78 to the power 1.56. Write two alternate programs to accomplish the same result, the first using the exponentiation symbol (↑), the second using the stored functions LOG(X) and EXP(X).

9-6 We are going to do a number of computations of interest and principal using the standard formula

T = P * (1 + R) ↑ N

where T is the total of interest and principal after N years, P is the principal, and R is the annual interest rate. Thus, we decide to create a user-defined function. First, we must decide which variable will take on different values as the argument. For example, suppose we propose holding the principal P and the annual interest rate R constant and varying N. A suitable definition would be

```
50 DEF FNA(N) = P * (1 + R) ↑ N
```

and this definition would have to occur *before* we referred to FNA(N). Further suppose we want P to be $1000 and R to be .06 while we compute the value of the defined function for N is 1, 2, 3, 4, and 5 years. A suitable program follows:

```
10 LET P = 1000
20 LET R = .06
50 DEF FNA(N) = P * (1 + R) ↑ N
100 PRINT FNA(1), FNA(2), FNA(3), FNA(4), FNA(5)
999 END
```

Now as an extension of this problem, suppose we want to compute the same values of FNA(N) but change the values of P and R to $2000 and .07 respectively. Modify the program to do this in the easiest way.

9-7 It is not necessary or useful to employ the user-defined function DEF unless the defined function is to be mentioned two or more times in a given program. Why?

9-8 The following program will print out the numeric value of the sine of 60 degrees. Why is line 20 necessary, and how can you explain the constants, or numeric literals, used there? (If you cannot, refer to the conversions of Table 9.1.)

```
20 LET P = 3.1416/180
30 LET A = 60
40 LET S = SIN(P * A)
50 PRINTS
999 END
```

9-9 Using the LOG(X) function, find how many years it would take to double your money at an annual compound interest of .06. (The required formula is given in Problem 9-6.)

9-10 Consider the following definition of a nonnumeric function.

```
50 DEF FNA(X) = "THIS LINE IS NO GOOD"
```

Why is it illegal?

9-11 Following the reasoning of Problem 9-10, is the following statement legal?

```
100 LET X = "PAGE NUMBER"
```

9-12 Why is the LET statement called a "substitution" statement or an "assignment" statement, rather than an equation?

9-13 Two user-defined functions which you may use frequently are

<u>line number</u> DEF FND(X) = X * (3.1416/180)

which converts X (in degrees) to radians, the value of the function FND(X), and

<u>line number</u> DEF FNL(X) = LOG(X)/LOG(10)

which produces the logarithm of X to the base 10 as the numeric value of FNL(X). A slight roundoff error may be experienced in these conversions, but it will not usually be serious in practice.

- **a.** Why is it useful to have a user-defined function for making conversions of the type described above?
- **b.** Using the first user-defined function above, what number of radians would be equivalent to 30 degrees? To 45 degrees?
- **c.** The natural logarithm of the decimal number 10 is 2.30259. The natural logarithm of the decimal number 8 is 2.07944. What is the logarithm to the base 10 of the decimal number 8?
- **d.** Employ the second user-defined function above and write a program that will print out a comparative list of the integer numbers 1, 2, 3, 4, 5, their natural logarithms, and their logarithms to the base 10. (You may use more than one PRINT statement to do this.)

TEN

REM, GO TO, IF/THEN, and INPUT

We now come to the commands which truly give the computer its power: those which allow us to divert the strictly sequential processing of program steps studied so far. These commands do not make the computer less deterministic in its work: its efforts are still foreordained by the user's program of instructions. However, by means of the GO TO and IF/THEN statements described in this chapter the user may skip backward or forward in the program unconditionally or conditionally as needed. The jump made by either of these commands is always to another *line number*, another reason for numbering lines in BASIC.

As you may imagine, the programs will be more complicated than the previous ones. You must be able to follow a sequence of happenings which may branch in various ways. To aid you we now discuss a miscellaneous but extremely useful command in BASIC—REM—which introduces a *comment* into a program. This is a nonexecuting statement (that is, the computer ignores it during computation), but when a program is listed (by typing the system command LIST) REM statements will be shown as they were typed in. The form of the REM statement (which stands for "remark") is

line number REM {Any string of characters}

Thus, REM may be used to introduce a program name, to define variables for the reader, and to indicate what is being done by the program. *Every* program that is to be stored (either within the computer or on paper) for later use should have some REM statements indicating, or documenting, the program's actions.

For example, the following lines might head a program:

```
10 REM *** THIS PROGRAM COMPUTES THE STANDARD DEVIATION
20 REM *** OF OBSERVATIONS PROVIDED AS DATA. N IS THE
30 REM *** NUMBER OF OBSERVATIONS, X IS THE VALUE OF AN
40 REM *** OBSERVATION, A IS THE ARITHMETIC AVERAGE, S
50 REM *** IS THE SUM OF SQUARES OF OBSERVATIONS, AND D
60 REM *** IS THE DESIRED STANDARD DEVIATION. THE LAST
70 REM *** DATA ELEMENT 9999 IS NOT USED AND INDICATES
80 REM *** END OF FILE. AUTHOR: J. JONES, DATE: 10/28/70,
90 REM *** REVISED 11/3/70. PROGRAM FILED AS STAT2. ENTER
99 REM *** DATA LINES 500-998. TEST DATA NOW AT LINE 500.
```

The above comments state what the program is to do (perform the statistical manipulation indicated) and spell out some of the operational details such as how to bring the program to a halt and how to enter data. The latter may prove very important if more than one person is to use the program. Pertinent facts such as the author's name, date of origination and revision, and file code are supplied; and the variables are identified, enabling the program to be read more easily. The asterisks at the beginning of each line have no meaning here other than to illustrate how special characters may be used in a REM statement to set off the comments from the REM command, which will be printed on each line (as shown) when a program is made. Special characters may also be used as needed in the comments; for example, see the dates and punctuation in the above REM lines.

REM is also used to indicate what the segments of a program are to accomplish, or how a program reaches a given point in its execution. Examples of these uses will follow. Remember REM is not executed; upon reaching a REM statement the computer simply progresses to the next non-REM line for processing.

Branches

Let us consider the main subject of this chapter: branches, (1) unconditional, and (2) conditional.

As we saw in Chapter 6, a program's execution may either take a direct route from the first to the last statement or deviate from that strict progression at the programmer's command. The detours which occur in the latter case are called branches, or jumps. Like a detour because of highway construction, an unconditional branch is one the program sequence must always take. A conditional branch is one that may or may not be taken, depending upon the programmer's specification, and is analogous to the motorist's turnoff from a turnpike if he has reached his destination, is hungry, or needs gas.

We may note that the unconditional (GO TO) and conditional (IF/THEN) commands in BASIC have certain prototype applications which occur so frequently in practice that we may concentrate upon them with benefit. The remainder of this chapter is organized around these standard applications, with variations appearing in the problems. (You may recall from Chapter 1 that the concepts of looping and branching were originated in the field of textile weaving and incorporated into the original computer designs of Charles Babbage. Although Babbage could not implement his ideas during his lifetime, modern technology permits us to do so now.)

GO TO

The command GO TO has the following form:

line number GO TO line number

When the computer encounters such a statement in its sequential progression from the lowest to the highest (which is always an END statement) line number, the sequential progression stops *in every instance*, and the sequence of operations is transferred to the line number last mentioned in the GO TO statement. Thus, GO TO is called an unconditional branch: There are no *ifs* or *buts* at this point: control of the program is unconditionally altered in sequence. The required jump, of course, may be either forward or backward (that is, to a higher or to a lower line number than that of the GO TO statement itself).

The GO TO statement has two main uses:

1. To cause a program to continue processing in a loop of action until it runs out of data (in which case in the BASIC language the machine will stop automatically).
2. To cause a loop of action or a skip in sequence to occur after (or until) a conditional branch halts or diverts the course of action.

1 / Repeat action until out of data

In many programs computations or procedural manipulations are repeated in the same form, but with different detail. Thus, to add 10 numbers we may consider writing a PRINT statement containing the necessary 10 numeric literals

```
100 PRINT 1 + 2 + 3 + 4 + 5 + 6 + 7 + 8 + 9 + 10
```

or the combination of a series of READ and/or LET statements together with PRINT

```
100 LET X = 1 + 2 + 3 + 4 + 5 + 6 + 7 + 8 + 9 + 10
110 PRINT X
```

to accomplish the desired result. However, since the same operation is to be done repeatedly, the idea of repeating the same program segment may well come to mind. A GO TO statement will let us do that, just as Jacquard's looped cards let him weave repeated patterns of fabric from a single stored program. Here is a simple program that will add 10 numbers and print a running accumulated total, i.e., the output will be 1, 3, 6, 10, . . . printed one below another.

```
10 REM PROGRAM ACCUMULATES NUMBERS
15 LET T=0
20 READ X
30 LET T=T+X
40 PRINT T
50 GO TO 20
60 DATA 1,2,3,4,5,6,7,8,9,10
99 END

RUN

 1
 3
 6
 10
 15
 21
 28
 36
 45
 55

   20,  PROGRAM OUT OF DATA

TIME:     0.073 SEC.
```

In the above program, the computer follows the loop from line 20 to line 50 and back to line 20 until the READ statement (moving across the DATA statement from one data element to another) runs out of data. At that point the computer will come to a halt, and the program will be ended.

(You will also get a message from the machine that it stopped because it ran out of data!)

Note, however, the economy of looping, rather than repeating. Had we not known how to loop, we would have been required to write a specialized program for the 10 data elements. To imagine the real difference, suppose we needed to add up 10,000 data elements! However, only the DATA line in our present program would have to be changed in order to handle more—or different—data. If we attempted to add 10,000 numbers with the last program, we would generate a large output with one accumulated answer per line! Generally, of course, we would want only one result—the final one. We have thus not completely solved our looping problem and will not be able to do so until we take up the IF/THEN command. There are nevertheless many problems for which the GO TO statement is of immediate use. To illustrate, the following program is completely reasonable in its approach to the stated problem.

```
10 REM Z=X↑2+Y↑2 FOR THE DATA PAIRS SHOWN IN
20 REM THE DATA LINES AS X,Y,X,Y,X,Y,...ETC. THE
30 REM PROGRAM WILL HALT WHEN OUT OF DATA.
40 READ X,Y
50 PRINT "Z =" X↑2+Y↑2
60 GO TO 40
70 DATA 8,9,1,2,3,4,9,8,7,6,5,4,3,6
99 END

RUN

Z =                145
Z =                5
Z =                25
Z =                145
Z =                85
Z =                41
Z =                45

   40,  PROGRAM OUT OF DATA

TIME:     0.070 SEC.
```

In the DATA line of this program, there are 12 numbers (or 6 pairs). The numbers are considered in pairs by the program's READ statement, which picks up X first and then Y. Thus, the first pair read is 8,9, and the first answer printed is 64 + 81, or 145. The machine then loops back and considers the second pair (1,2) and so on until the end of the data set. (The mixture of integers and real numbers—those with a decimal point—makes no difference to the machine in BASIC.) When the end of the data list arrives, the program halts, but all of the required answers have been computed and displayed.

Question: In the last two programs, why would it have been incorrect to interchange the order of the PRINT and GO TO statements, e.g., in the last program to number the PRINT statement 60 and the GO TO statement 50?

Answer: The computer would come to a halt (due to lack of data) but no answers would have been displayed, since running out of data stops everything before the PRINT statement is reached.

In the latter program, it is interesting to note what would have happened if the user had put in an *odd* set of numbers. For example, if the last number (representing the last value of Y) had been omitted, the computer would not have completed the last evaluation for lack of data—another illustration of how demanding the machine is in its requirement for consistency.

2 / *Repeat on condition of user's test*

The second, and most common, reason for using a GO TO statement is to cause the program sequence to be diverted after one or more *conditional* branches, or tests, have been made.

For example, looking back at the first program of the last section (the number accumulation), suppose we knew in advance that there were 10 numbers to be accumulated and could keep track of each case considered in turn. Then we could arrange our affairs to repeat the accumulation without printing (using a GO TO)—IF the number of cases considered was less than or equal to 10. If the number of cases had reached 10, THEN we could print the final total. It is not possible to illustrate this application in detail without first describing the conditional branch, so we move forward to that subject without further hesitation.

Computed GO TO

Many installations of the BASIC language provide a useful and optional form of GO TO that will direct the program sequence to one of *several* line numbers, depending upon the value of a previously evaluated variable. The form of the computed GO TO is

line number ON {variable name} GO TO $\{n_1, n_2, n_3, \ldots\}$

where the variable name is a previously defined integer and the n's represent alternate line numbers to which branching may be desired. The value of the variable name is 1, 2, 3, . . . to a maximum equal to the number of line numbers mentioned in the statement. To illustrate, the statement

```
50 ON N GO TO 100, 200, 300, 400
```

will cause the program to branch to line 100 if N is 1, to 200 if N is 2, to 300 if N is 3, and to 400 if N is 4. If N were 5 at the time line 50 was encountered—in fact if N were any number but 1, 2, 3, or 4—it would be considered an error, and the computer would stop. Thus, the index, denoted by N in the example above, must agree in its count with the count of line numbers shown in the computed GO TO, and the numeric value of the index must agree logically with the position of the desired line numbers in the list shown. For example, if we intend to branch to line 200 when using the computed GO TO above, then N must have the value 2, and line 200 must be the second line number mentioned in the list. The list of line numbers may be in any order, but the value of the index must be consistent with the specific listing. (For an application of the computed GO TO, see footnote 1 on page 174.)

Since the computed GO TO is not a command in standard BASIC, but is one of the extensions made to the language at most computing installations, you may wish to check the specific details of its execution at your location.

In what follows you may note that the computed GO TO may be replaced by several conditional branching statements. The value of the computed GO TO in programming is simply that it replaces several lines of programming with one.

IF/THEN

The IF statement in BASIC causes a diversion of the program sequence *only* under stated test conditions, THEN the sequence branches off to a designated line number.

The general form of the IF/THEN statement is

$$\underline{\text{line number}}\ \underline{\text{IF}} \left\{ \begin{array}{l} \underline{\text{variable}} \\ \underline{\text{expression}} \end{array} \right\} \left\{ \underline{\text{relation}} \right\} \left\{ \begin{array}{l} \underline{\text{numeric literal}} \\ \underline{\text{variable}} \\ \underline{\text{expression}} \end{array} \right\} \underline{\text{THEN}}\ \underline{\text{line number}}$$

In the IF/THEN command the relation may be *one and only one* of the following:

Relation	*Symbol*
1. Equality	=
2. Less Than	<
3. Greater Than	>
4. Not Equal To	<>
5. Less Than *or* Equal To	<=
6. Greater Than *or* Equal To	>=

Some examples of *correct* IF/THEN commands follow:

```
200 IF X = 9999 THEN 9999
200 IF Y = X THEN 8000
200 IF N > 2 THEN 100
200 IF S > = (2000 + X) THEN 600
200 IF SQR(X) > 10 THEN 600
200 IF (S ↑ 2 + 3) < (X ↑ 2 + 8) THEN 300
```

The line numbers indicated after THEN must be line numbers that exist in the final version of the program. In standard BASIC, alphanumeric literals may not appear in an IF/THEN expression. The user may be tempted to vary the format of his IF/THEN statements from the required specification, thinking the desired results will be obtained because the proposed statement sounds reasonable in English. Unfortunately, this is not so. The following IF/THEN forms are *incorrect*:

```
200 IF X = 9999 THEN GO TO END
200 IF N > 2 THEN LET Y = 0
200 IF S ↑ 2 > = 2000 THEN PRINT "S IS" S
200 IF "NET PAY" > 1000 THEN 8000
```

If the condition stated in the IF/THEN command is *false*, i.e., if the numeric comparison called for at the IF/THEN statement does not result in a YES result, the sequential processing of the program is not altered, and the IF/THEN statement is, in effect, completely ignored. Diversion of the processing routine will occur to the stated line number only when the IF/THEN statement is *true.*

Frequently, the position of the IF/THEN statement in a program can be altered, depending upon the relation used, without altering the effect of the test. Thus, when X > 10 is true, X <= 10 is false, and either alternative would be satisfactory if the following work segments were appropriately sequenced. (This point will be illustrated in later examples. However, note here that the second relation above is the complement of the first and vice versa.)

Finally, the relation = which demands strict equality of two numeric values should be used only when testing *integers* (see Problem 10-2 B and E). For example, to the computer, 1.000000 is not the same as 0.999999, and a test for equality such as

```
200 IF X = 1 THEN 9999
```

would be false if in fact X were 0.999999. Thus, use the equals test only when you are sure of an integer result. Such certainty may be had, for example, when you are counting by incrementing a result by 1 (e.g., LET N = N + 1, in which N was originally an integer). A division operation in the process of defining an equals test variable invites disaster, since division most often converts integer numbers into a real, or floating point, result. Thus, 4 and 3 are both integers, but 4/3 results in 1.333333, which is not an integer. (In some cases, round-off error can also occur when decimal fractions are converted by the machine into its internal arithmetic codes, which are usually to the base 2, rather than 10. Without going into further detail, this technical point presents another reason for confining equals rests to integer comparisons. See Problem 10-2 E.)

With these rules in hand, we may now proceed with some applications of the IF/THEN statement.

Clearly, because of the six relations that can be used in an IF/THEN statement and because a number of IF/THEN statements (and associated GO TO statements in a given application) may be used in combination, there are many possible variations of sequential processing with unconditional branches. This new ability can greatly complicate a computer program's sequential routes of execution, but that is precisely the purpose of the GO TO and IF/THEN statements! We need a greater variety of action so we can handle more different jobs.

For the purposes of exposition, however, we may divide the IF/THEN applications into three main headings: (1) Count and test; (2) READ and test, and (3) Compute and test. Each of these applications results in one of two actions. Either the computer is directed to stop its work or it is directed to take one or more alternate actions, i.e., the program may branch off to another program line if the test is passed (or to one of several possible program lines if a sequence of tests is employed). We thus have six prototype applications to consider, and we shall take them up in turn.

1 / *Count and test*

a. Stop after a predetermined count. Consider again the first program of the last section (the accumulation of 10 numbers) in which we had to print out 10 answers to get the (last) one we wanted. Suppose we could have instead kept track of the numbers added, and printed out the wanted answer only after the tenth data element had been accumulated. That could be done, using a combination of the IF/THEN and the GO TO statements, as follows:

```
10 REM PROGRAM ACCUMULATES 10 NUMBERS
20 LET N=0
25 LET T=0
30 READ X
40 LET N=N+1
50 LET T=T+X
60 IF N=10 THEN 80
70 GO TO 30
80 PRINT "THE ACCUMULATED TOTAL IS " T
90 DATA 1,2,3,4,5,6,7,8,9,10
99 END

RUN

THE ACCUMULATED TOTAL IS        55

   99,  NORMAL EXIT FROM PROG.

TIME:    0.081 SEC.
```

In the program above, only one answer would be printed, that in line 80. However, it would be necessary to know how many items there were to add, i.e., the maximum value for N would have to be known and correctly tested (see Problem 10-2 D.) Note that to add a much longer list of numbers, only minor modifications would need to be made in the program. For a maximum of N = 100, we would have only to change 10 to 100 in line 60 and supply the additional data. *A single answer would still be printed.*

b. Count and take alternate action. In some problems, it is necessary to take action periodically, instead of continuously. For example, suppose we were required to generate and print out only *odd* numbers from the sequence 1, 2, 3, 4, 5, ... (Why we should want to do such a thing is immaterial to our argument, but it is a motivating influence to know that many practical applications abound. For example, the auditor may want to examine every tenth account at your bank, the statistician may wish to take a systematic sample of the population consisting of the name of every hundredth member of the population roster in your community, your professor may want to give two exams to your class—one to the odd-numbered students on his roll, another to the even-numbered. You can probably think of more extensions.)

The following program prints out the odd numbers from the set 1 through 19. It is a somewhat harder program than those preceding, but, since it is full of REM statements, you should be able to find your way through it. The essential trick is the counter N, which takes on the alternate values 0 and 1—and permits printing only when N = 1, which is true only on alternate numbers. N = 1 to start, so 1 is the first number printed, then 3, and so on. To fully understand this program, you may want to flow chart it, following the methods of Chapter 6. (Flow charts come into their own when a program has many conditional branches in it. They are of little use in strictly sequential programs!)

```
1 REM PROGRAM PRINTS ODD NUMBERS TO X = 19
5 REM INITIALIZE SWITCH N AND COUNTER X
10 LET N = 1
20 LET X = 0
25 REM INCREMENT COUNTER AND TEST SWITCH
30 LET X = X + 1
40 IF N = 0 THEN 70
45 REM IF NO BRANCH AT ABOVE STATEMENT, X IS ODD,
50 REM SO PRINT, TEST FOR END, REVERSE SWITCH AND REPEAT
55 PRINT X
58 IF X = 19 THEN 9999
60 LET N = 0
65 GO TO 30
70 REM THE NUMBER IS EVEN IF BRANCH IS TO HERE
80 LET N = 1
90 GO TO 30
9999 END
```

2 / Read-and-test

a. Stop at end of file. Again, consider the problem of adding the numbers from 1 to 10, but suppose that we do not know the exact number of data elements in the DATA statements and would like to have the computer determine *under our control* when the end of the data file has been reached. To do this, we may employ as the last data element in the file a dummy number, which will not be used, but which will be an end-of-file indicator. Typically, a suitable indicator is a very large (or a very small) number that will not be encountered anywhere in the program's data. For example, suppose we use 99999. Then, if we test for 99999 at each READ statement, we can detect the end of the file and cause the program to take any desired action with the data read in—before the machine cuts off automatically. In the following program, our objectives are to (1) count and print the total number of data elements handled and (2) print the accumulated total of those numbers.

```
100 LET N = 0
110 LET T = 0
120 READ X
130 IF X = 99999 THEN 400
140 LET N = N + 1
150 LET T = T + X
160 GO TO 120
400 PRINT "THE NUMBER OF OBSERVATIONS IS "N
410 PRINT "THE ACCUMULATED TOTAL IS "T
500 DATA 1, 2, 3, 4, 5, 6, 7, 8, 9, 10, 99999
999 END
```

In the above program, the first two lines initialize the memory spaces representing N and T to 0, we then read X and test for the end of file. If not at the end, we add 1 to the number of observations and add X to the accumulated total, T. If we have come to the end of the file, the value of X last read (99999) is ignored, and we branch to line 400, where the current values of N and T are printed, thus ending the job.

Notice that this program is perfectly general: It would total any list of numbers (provided, of course, that list did not contain within it the tag 99999 which signals the end of the file). The only modification necessary to add more numbers is to provide more data, the last element of which is 99999. For example, if we put in new lines 500 and 510

```
500 DATA 2.3, 4.5, 7.6, 1.23, 4.678, 1,5.4, 12.34
510 DATA 3.45, 6.12, 2.98, 6.07, 99999
```

then the 12 numbers supplied as data would be accumulated and the total printed. Further, our observation counter, N, would tell us how many elements were in the file list.

When writing a program, it is useful to take such a general approach so that the program may have a large number of applications.

Several technical points should be noted in the preceding program. First, it is desirable to test for an integer using an equals test, because our end-of-file tag is an integer, and we do indeed want to test for a unique value. A READ statement will in no way alter what is read in as an integer. Second, if you are worried that your end-of-file tag (here 99999) will possibly be encountered in your data, you may use an extremely large or small number in its place. A typical value, expressed in the *exponential* form, would be, say, 4E37, which would be acceptable to the READ statement and would represent 4 with 37 zeroes after it. Since this extreme is near the limit the average computer can handle, and since it is not likely to be encountered in any practical student data, library programs often make use of such a tag in READ tests. Finally, it is important to note that the READ test is made immediately after the READ statement. To illustrate an *incorrect* alternative, note what happens if line 130 is moved between lines 150 and 160 by giving it line number 155. The end-of-file tag would be counted as an observation and added to the total, yielding, of course, not only the wrong observation count but also an incorrect total. Such a mistake is called a logical error. The program would "work," but produce the incorrect numerical results, and the machine would provide no diagnostic error messages to warn the user. In this instance, the error would be obvious because of the large value of the end-of-file tag in relation to the other data, but in general this may not be so. To avoid such logical errors, every computer program should be tested using simple data for which a hand solution can be computed. If the hand solution and the machine solution do not agree, then a logical error should be suspected and searched for! Removal of logical errors is "debugging" a program, and techniques for speeding this process of diagnosis and cure are given on page 180.

b. Read and take alternate action. Depending upon the input data it receives, a program may cause its sequence of events to alter. This ability is very useful in making a general purpose program act as a specialized program.

As one example, consider the computation of a payroll in which different benefit deductions are to be made for weekly and monthly employees. If the computer can identify these two categories, based upon data received about an employee, it may branch off to an appropriate set of operations to perform the required computations. Credit tests offer another illustration (see Example 8 of Chapter 13, page 165). And, in general, the same approach may be applied to decoding an input signal which should lead to further elaboration or action.

The following program includes several features. The allowable inputs are 1, 2, 3 or 4, and the computer will PRINT in English various statements indicating the decision to be taken as a consequence of interpreting those inputs. Further, if an input other than 1, 2, 3 or 4 arrives, an error will be detected and the erroneous data element identified by the machine. (In most commercial programs, such error checking of input data becomes an ever-present and important program segment, since erroneous data input can also lead to wrong answers or a computer halt. When data are in error, the machine cannot by itself aid the user: The machine can detect only grammatical errors in the language used. To screen data, the user must build appropriate tests into his program.)

```
5 REM PROGRAM INDICATES ALTERNATIVE ACTION DEPENDING
6 REM UPON OBSERVATION, WHICH MAY BE ONLY 1, 2, 3 OR 4.
7 REM DATA ERRORS ARE DETECTED. N IS OBSERVATION COUNT,
8 REM X OBSERVATION VALUE. PROGRAM TERMINATES AT
9 REM X = 99999 E-O-F TAG.
10 LET N = 0
15 LET N = N + 1
20 READ X
25 REM END OF FILE TESTED AND ERRORS SCREENED FROM DATA
30 IF X = 99999 THEN 99999
35 IF X < 1 THEN 500
40 IF X > 4 THEN 500
45 IF X <> INT(X) THEN 500
50 REM TEST ALTERNATIVES AND PRINT (X NOW 1, 2, 3 OR 4)
55 IF X = 1 THEN 100
60 IF X = 2 THEN 200
65 IF X = 3 THEN 300
70 IF X = 4 THEN 400
100 PRINT "USE PLAN 1, SELL SHORT"
110 GO TO 15
200 PRINT "USE PLAN 2, GO LONG"
210 GO TO 15
300 PRINT "USE PLAN 3, STAND PAT"
310 GO TO 15
400 PRINT "USE PLAN 4, LIQUIDATE HOLDINGS IMMEDIATELY"
410 GO TO 15
450 REM AN ILLEGAL OBSERVATION WILL BE INDICATED BY N
500 PRINT "ILLEGAL OBSERVATION AT "N "PLEASE CHECK"
510 GO TO 15
800 REM TEST DATA FOLLOWS
900 DATA 0, 1, 2, 3, 4, 99, 1.2, 99999
99999 END
```

The program above will take one of five actions (indicated at lines 100, 200, 300, 400, and 500). The first four alternatives indicate a proper interpretation of the inputs 1, 2, 3, or 4.[1] The fifth alternative, at line 500, in-

---

[1] Using the computed GO TO previously mentioned, lines 55, 60, 65, 70 of the "Alternate Action" program above could be replaced with the single line

```
50 ON X GO TO 100, 200, 300, 400
```

so that four lines would be reduced to one The power of the computed GO TO statement increases as the number of possible alternatives increases.

dicates a data error. Line 500 will be reached if the input is less than 1 (see line 35), greater than 4 (see line 40), or lies between 1 and 4, but is not an integer (see line 45). After this screening, the only possible result is that the input is one of the four integers 1, 2, 3 or 4, so equals tests can be used without error. For simplicity in exposition, the possible conditional branches are then considered in order of the possible inputs remaining (see lines 55, 60, 65, 70). Obviously, one of the branch routes must now apply, and we will get one of the outputs indicated at line 100, 200, 300, or 400. After each of the possible five actions, there is an unconditional branch back to the next READ statement via the counter N − N + 1 at line 15. The program terminates when X = 99999. Since the test for X = 99999 is made immediately after the READ X statement, the value 99999 will never be evaluated.

In the test data for the program, each of the three illegal conditions will occur. Thus, observations 1 and 6 will be in error since both are outside the range 1 to 4. Similarly, observation 7 is in error because it is not an integer, and it will also cause an error message. Since there are generally many ways to write branching programs to accomplish a given set of specifications, you may wish to try writing an alternate program to accomplish the same results. (The reader who is not yet familiar with the stored function INT(X) may wish to refer to Chapters 8 and 9 for clarification. Briefly, INT(X) simply truncates the decimal part of X and discards it: the value 1.2 becomes the integer 1. Thus, when the test datum 1.2 arrives, a branch will occur due to line 45 because 1.2 is not equal to 1.)

Without illustration, we may observe that the branches that occur in a program can be made dependent, or conditional, upon several values of input, not just one. Thus, we may read in several variable values *before* tests are made—and then devise a test sequence to examine them in combination (see Example 8 of Chapter 13).

3 / *Compute and test*

a. Compute and test for stop. In many applications, we would like to have the computer make computations until some desired result is achieved and then come to a halt. We may wish to approximate a desired result only within a given precision and then work no more (see Example 12, Chapter 13). Or we may wish to cease a given operation (e.g., disbursement of funds) when a given critical value (e.g., the maximum budget) is reached.

For example, given a list of numbers as shown in the following program at line 120, find how many of them, N, starting from the beginning, are required to equal 100 or less, but not more.

Program STOP below provides both the count and also the confirming totals, that desired and the next which exceeded the specified upper limit, 100. After reading a data element, X, a total, T, is computed at line 50. The computed total is compared to 100 at line 70. The test is <=, since T could be exactly 100 depending upon the input data.

The program must "look ahead" one data element to meet its specifications. When T first becomes greater than 100, the count, N, is reduced by one, line 80, and the total, T, is reduced by the last value of X, line 90, producing the desired result. As a check, the value of T which halts the operation is provided. The variable P is introduced in line 90 to avoid loss of the check total, T, which we wish to display.

```
10 REM PROGRAM STOP -- HALTS AT A GIVEN TOTAL
20 LET T=0
30 LET N=0
40 READ X
50 LET T=T+X
60 LET N=N+1
70 IF T <= 100 THEN 40
80 LET N=N-1
90 LET P=T-X
100 PRINT "THE FIRST ";N;"NUMBERS TOTALED";P
110 PRINT "THE NEXT NUMBER MADE THE TOTAL";T
120 DATA 15.6,7.9,26.5,19.6,24.5,9.8,7.3,13.7
999 END

RUN

THE FIRST  5 NUMBERS TOTALED 94.1
THE NEXT NUMBER MADE THE TOTAL 103.9

  999,  NORMAL EXIT FROM PROG.

TIME:    0.096 SEC.
```

b. Compute and take alternate action. Reverting to the alternate-action problem of page 174, suppose that instead of directly reading in the test data (using the READ and DATA statements) you desired to make some intermediate computations on the data before the test for the integer values (1, 2, 3 or 4) was made. There is no reason why this could not be done! Thus, we could compute and then test for alternate courses of action. For example, suppose some conversion of the input data to the alternate-action problem had to be made before testing. This conversion could be lengthy or short. If the input data had been the *square* of the desired test data, then we could have inserted

```
32 LET X = SQR(X)
```

or

```
32 LET X = X ↑ .5
```

in the original problem and continued.

More generally, the sequence of program execution might well depend upon the value of an intermediate computation (e.g., the value of one or more variables at a given stage of computation; the sign of a value, plus or minus, etc.).

To illustrate again simply, suppose we wish to pay a salesman's bonus of 2.75% of gross sales—if the salesman's gross for the year is greater than or equal to $50,000 more than his base salary. The award is not to be made otherwise. Thus, for several salesmen, we could compute the annual bonus as follows:

```
10 REM PROGRAM NAME: BONUS—COMPUTES BONUS Z > 0 IF
12 REM GROSS SALES X $50,000 OR MORE THAN BASE SALARY Y.
14 REM VARIABLE A IS SALESMAN NUMBER.
18 READ A,X,Y
20 IF A = 9999 THEN 99
22 LET D = X - Y
24 IF D >= 50000 THEN 30
26 LET Z = 0
28 GO TO 32
30 LET Z = .0275 * X
32 PRINT "SALESMAN ";A, "BONUS $";Z
34 GO TO 18
50 DATA 1, 100000, 20000
52 DATA 2, 12000, 10000
54 DATA 3, 50000, 50000
56 DATA 4, 70000, 8000
60 DATA 9999, 0, 0
99 END
```

In this program, the sequential route of program execution takes a different route depending upon the computed value of D, because of the test at line 24.

Finally, those with a scientific bent should consider the following exercise:

A train starts out from rest at time T = 0 and distance X = 0 and then accelerates down the track at A = 2 feet/second^2 until it reaches a terminal velocity of V1 = 60 miles/hour (88 feet/second). Thereafter, the train has an acceleration of zero and continues its travel at the velocity V1. Print out a tabulation of the train's progress showing T, X, and V every 4 seconds from T = 0 to T = 64 seconds. The necessary equations are given below:

1. X = (.5) * A * T ↑ 2 and V = A * T

where the symbols are defined in the above paragraph, and where the velocity, V, is less than 88 feet/second. Variable X will be given in feet from the origin.

2. X = X1 + V1 * (T − T1) and V = V1

where X1 is the distance achieved at the time V achieves the velocity V1 and T1 is the time when that occurs.

This problem is therefore in two parts: (1) a computation to be made with one formula until the train reaches terminal velocity and (2) a computation with a second formula after that specified state has been reached. Thus, we have another application of compute-and-test method to an alternate-action problem. An appropriate flow chart (Figure 10.1) and program follow. The output for the specified conditions is also shown.

```
5 REM PROGRAM NAME:TRAIN -- COMPUTES DISTANCE VERSUS
6 REM TIME FOR GIVEN ACCELERATION AND TERMINAL VELOCITY.
10 LET T=0
20 LET X=0
30 LET V=0
35 LET N=0
40 LET A=2
50 LET V1=88
60 LET T1=V1/A
70 LET X1=.5*A*T1↑2
80 PRINT "TIME-----------DISTANCE--------VELOCITY"
90 LET X=.5*A*T↑2
100 LET V=A*T
110 IF V > V1 THEN 190
120 GO TO 300
190 LET N=1
200 LET V=V1
210 LET X=X1+V*(T-T1)
300 PRINT T,X,V
310 LET T=T+4
315 IF T>64 THEN 999
320 IF N=1 THEN 210
340 GO TO 90
999 END
```

```
RUN

TIME-----------DISTANCE--------VELOCITY
 0              0               0
 4              16              8
 8              64              16
 12             144             24
 16             256             32
 20             400             40
 24             576             48
 28             784             56
 32             1024            64
 36             1296            72
 40             1600            80
 44             1936            88
 48             2288            88
 52             2640            88
 56             2992            88
 60             3344            88
 64             3696            88

  999,   NORMAL EXIT FROM PROG.

TIME:      0.238 SEC.
```

Before considering the program, several comments are in order. We are tabulating the results at 4-second intervals, but the cutover from formula (1) to formula (2) does not necessarily have to occur at a multiple of 4 seconds for all values of A and V1. To preserve the accuracy of the computation (for any value of A and V1), we preevaluate the point of desired cutover as follows:

T1 = V1/A

X1 = .5 * A * T1 ↑ 2

With these numbers in hand the tabulation may be adjusted to produce the precise results required, even though the tabulation is in uniform increments.

Another feature of the program is the use of the counter N which is 0 when formula (1) is to be used and 1 when formula (2) is to be used. This counter, or "switch," controls the program logic, so that the appropriate line of computation is followed.

To illustrate an extension of this program, we now run it for A = 2.5 (feet/second^2). The reader who wants a hand check of the program may try A = 10 or any other value, and compare his hand-computed results with those of his program.

```
40 LET A=2.5

RUN

TIME-----------DISTANCE--------VELOCITY
 0              0               0
 4              20              10
 8              80              20
 12             180             30
 16             320             40
 20             500             50
 24             720             60
 28             980             70
 32             1280            80
 36             1619.2          88
 40             1971.2          88
 44             2323.2          88
 48             2675.2          88
 52             3027.2          88
 56             3379.2          88
 60             3731.2          88
 64             4083.2          88

  999,   NORMAL EXIT FROM PROG.

TIME:     0.236 SEC.
```

The example just cited illustrates the sixth and last variation on the use of the conditional branch, or IF/THEN, statement. In large programs it is not unusual to have tens or even hundreds of conditional and unconditional branches, using mixtures of all the prototype examples presented here. Although such lengthy examples do not make suitable illustrations for a textbook, you should now be able to work your way through more complex cases which are merely mixtures and compounds of the fundamental applications in this chapter.

A note on debugging

In programs involving many branches it may be difficult to follow the line of computation for comparison with a hand-computed solution (which is always suggested to confirm the logic of your programs). In such programs it does no harm (and indeed is beneficial) to insert a number of superfluous PRINT commands in the original construction of the program so that the initial progression of the computation may be checked in detail.

For example, you may wish to see the value of intermediate variables or a counter at any given point of computation, or the exact point at which a program takes alternate action.

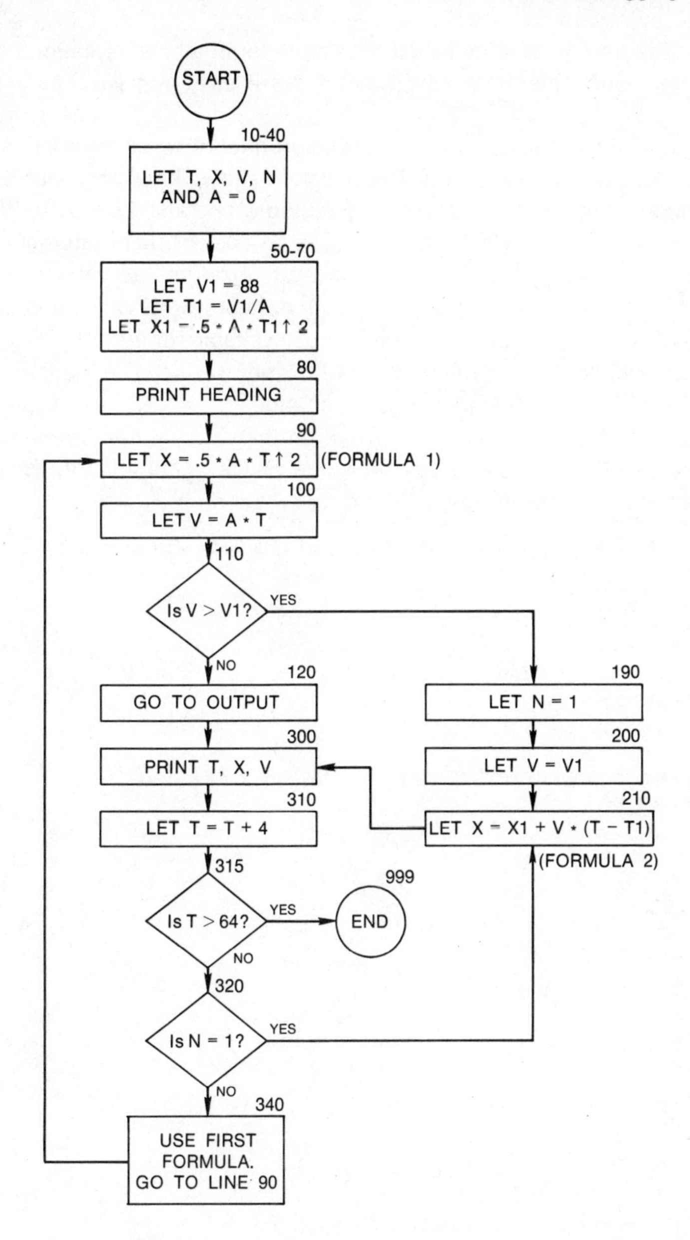

10.1. Flow chart for Program TRAIN.

Once the program has been validated by a comparison of a machine-computed solution versus a hand-computed solution, the extra PRINT statements may be deleted by typing in their line numbers with a carriage return. This is one of the virtues of remote terminal conversational programming: such additions and deletions are easy and virtually instantaneous.

The following short program finds the product of two integer numbers, J and K, by repetitive addition. The program shows how a computer with only the ability to add can be made to multiply, and also how extra PRINT statements (lines 45 and 55) can be used to check computational progress. The variable P represents the desired "product" as determined by the repetitive addition of J to itself. The variable N, initially set equal to K, is used so the original value of K will be available for output. Then each addition reduces N by 1 until N = 0, at which point P is the desired product. The program halts after printing the changes in N and P and the final answer (at line 70) showing J, K, and P. In the *variable trace* provided by the extra PRINTs, P is the current value of the accumulation, N is the number of additions yet to go before termination.

```
10 REM PROGRAM MULTIPLY -- MULTIPLIES USED REPEATED ADDITI
20 LET P=0
30 READ J,K
35 LET N=K
40 LET P=P+J
45 PRINT "P IS";P
50 LET N=N-1
55 PRINT "N IS";N
60 IF N>0 THEN 40
70 PRINT "THE PRODUCT OF";J;"AND";K;"IS";P
80 GO TO 20
90 DATA 3,4
99 END

RUN

P IS 3
N IS 3
P IS 6
N IS 2
P IS 9
N IS 1
P IS 12
N IS 0
THE PRODUCT OF 3 AND 4 IS 12

   30,  PROGRAM OUT OF DATA

TIME:     0.108 SEC.
```

After checking the program's operation you may type

```
45
55
```

to eliminate the extra PRINTs and the resulting diagnostic detail. Then the program will print only the last line of output, the final answer.

Obviously an astute selection of checkpoints will be helpful in tracing computational progress and correctness. For this reason it is helpful if you can think of your program construction in *modular* terms, that is, as blocks of computations, each of which is reasonably self-contained. When this approach is taken, each module may be checked using the superfluous PRINT commands and possible logical errors (which can only be detected by a human) more readily isolated.

How to prepare a computer program in six steps

Most of you now have some knowledge of the BASIC computer language. What will probably trouble you most is going from a poorly defined, or an informally defined, problem statement to the detailed formalization required to write a computer program (in any language). It is entirely possible to organize yourself, so that this apparently mysterious transition is no great hurdle, using the steps suggested in Table 10.1.

TABLE 10.1

How To Prepare a Computer Program in Six Steps

1. Define All the Variables You Must Use in the Problem.
2. What is the Exact Input and Output Form You Desire?
3. What Test Combinations Will Be Encountered, and What Actions Should Be Taken in Each Case?
4. Draw a Rough Flow Chart of Your Proposed Process.
5. Draw a Detailed Flow Chart and Write the Program.
6. Run the Program and Test It.

To illustrate this orderly approach to problem refinement and programming, reconsider now the vending-machine problem of Chapter 6, which we have already analyzed in some detail. You also know by now all of the BASIC language statements required to produce a computer program that will logically simulate the vending machine. That is, in general both the problem and the language available are now reasonably clear—but what do we do in particular to go from the problem to the desired particular programming result?

1 / Define all the variables you must use in the problem

In the vending-machine problem, we have only a few variables to define, some because of the problem statement itself, and one because of the computer's requirements. Let X be the deposit of a coin, which must take on the value 5, 10, or 25 (simulating a nickel, dime, or quarter). Further, if we wish to model our program after actual vending-machine operation, we will keep track of accumulated deposits in terms of "equivalent nickels." Let the variable K be the equivalent nickel count, and note that this variable may run from 0 through and including 7 before a product is delivered. (We assume that a customer may be illogical and deposit first a dime and then a quarter, producing a maximum nickel count of 7 before a product is delivered and change is made.) Finally, we note that a computer program, as written by the user, must at some point come to a stop, although the vending machine continually repeats its action in cycle after cycle. Thus, we propose to ask the user of our computer program (which for student use cannot be made to cycle continuously on a conditional basis to avoid tying up the remote terminal facility) if he wants to continue depositing coins. The variable used to answer this question, which we arbitrarily call Z, will be either 1 to continue or 0 to quit. The three specific variables X, K, and Z will then constitute all those we shall use, and further, they must observe the ranges and specific values cited above.

2 / What is the exact input and output form you desire?

In this problem, the input may be only the numbers 5, 10, and 25 for success; all other numeric values, corresponding to wrong deposits and false coins, should be rejected. We decide that we want the program to take input from the user from the remote terminal, so the input of X will be from the remote terminal, using the INPUT X command. The variable K is an internal operation, so it does not directly affect input or output operations. However, the variable Z, which is the "continuation decision" will also come from the remote console operated by the user of our program. Therefore, Z will come into our program via the statement INPUT Z. On the output side of the question, we want to print "DEPOSIT REJECTED" if we do not receive a deposit of 5, 10, or 25. If we have not received sufficient deposits to deliver the product (which costs 15 cents) we wish to give instructions to deposit another coin, which on the console can be indicated by

"TYPE 5, 10, OR 25 TO INDICATE DEPOSIT."

If the accumulated deposit, however, had reached 15 cents or more (i.e., K >= 3), we wish to inform the user as follows:

"PRODUCT DELIVERED. CHANGE IS" ;5 * (K − 3); "CENTS"

Finally, we will check the buyer's desire to continue depositing coins after each deposit. Should the buyer wish to stop, we shall print

YOU TERMINATED OPERATION

and also refund any existing deposit by printing

"YOUR PRESENT DEPOSIT OF" ;5 * K; "CENTS RETURNED."

3 / *What test combinations will be encountered and what actions should be taken in each case*

In all computer programs that involve conditional branches, if he can, the programmer should make a list of all the input conditions that will lead to specific outputs.[2]

In Figure 6.5 we displayed all of the logically possible inputs to the vending machine, assuming that when 15 cents had been received, by any sequence of deposits, a product and appropriate change would be delivered.

In addition to checking all the input variations that may occur in a given program's application, we also want to know what to do in each input case. Thus, for each input possibility, the programmer should outline in detail the actions to be taken.

In this problem, there are three essential tests, some of which are summarized in the following program.

a. Is the coin good? If the deposit X is not exactly 5, 10, or 25, we want to reject the deposit and so inform the depositor.

b. At each deposit, after incrementing the equivalent nickel counter, K, we want to know if K is equal to or greater than 3. If it is we want to inform the customer that his product has been delivered and that he has received 5 * (K − 3) cents change. If not, we want another deposit, i.e., if K is less than 3, we continue.

---

[2] In very complex computer programs, it may not be possible to list all of the *conceivable* input conditions and their associated outputs, since the number of possible input combinations may be too great to enumerate. Thus, the programmer faces the danger that someone will deliver an input to his program for which the programmer has not prepared himself. The vending-machine problem is a good one for illustration since we can in fact enumerate all of the inputs than even an idiot would create. But to illustrate in payroll and order-processing systems used in business, we would be hard pressed to think of all the idiot inputs that could possibly occur. We might try, yet the only final test would be experience.

c. After each deposit we want to know if the customer wants to continue. This question is necessary if we want to stop our program at some point. The specific test for this decision is whether the console operator inputs 0 or 1 (i.e., Z = 0 or 1) after the question has been asked.

Figure 6.5 and the decision table of Table 6.3 detail the input combinations and their associated actions as called for by the problem specifications. Similarly, in more complicated programming problems, the same form of detailed displays will be useful to your understanding and progress.

4 / Draw a rough flow chart of your proposed process

It is important to realize that most formalizations of a given problem's specifications proceed in steps. We do not expect at first to produce the ultimate refinement. So, we continue in steps from roughness to perfection.

Figure 6.5 shows a flow chart of the vending-machine logic necessary to understanding the problem—which is an essential first step. But, Figure 6.5 is not a suitable flow chart for creating a computer program. Thus, the moral of this suggested step is first to sketch in the outlines of something which seems feasible or might work—without regard to the details of programming. If the initial result is reasonable, we can refine it later.

5 / Draw a detailed flow chart and write the program

Looking back at Figure 6.5, which explains the vending-machine logic in general, we see that some of the tests made in that diagram are not compatible with our present knowledge of computer programming. For example, how could we test to see if a deposit were a slug or a false coin? We have no way to test such vague statements. Yet with our knowledge of computer programming and its logic, we may realize now that if a deposit is not *precisely* 5, 10, or 25 cents, the deposit is defective and should therefore be rejected. That decision is easily programmable, following the rules cited in this chapter. So we think of revising the original flow chart to conform to the constraints required by our language. Further, we have noted that to be practical as a remote terminal simulation the program must come to a halt under user control. And we also can introduce this constraint into our computer flow chart—as well as our program.

The revised result, shown as Figure 10.2, incorporates these constraints and provides the basis for a direct production of a computer program in BASIC conforming to them. The program, shown as Program COIN hereafter, illustrates the possible correspondence between a detailed flow chart and a program by associating block numbers in the flow chart with line numbers in the program. Note in the program that all of our previ-

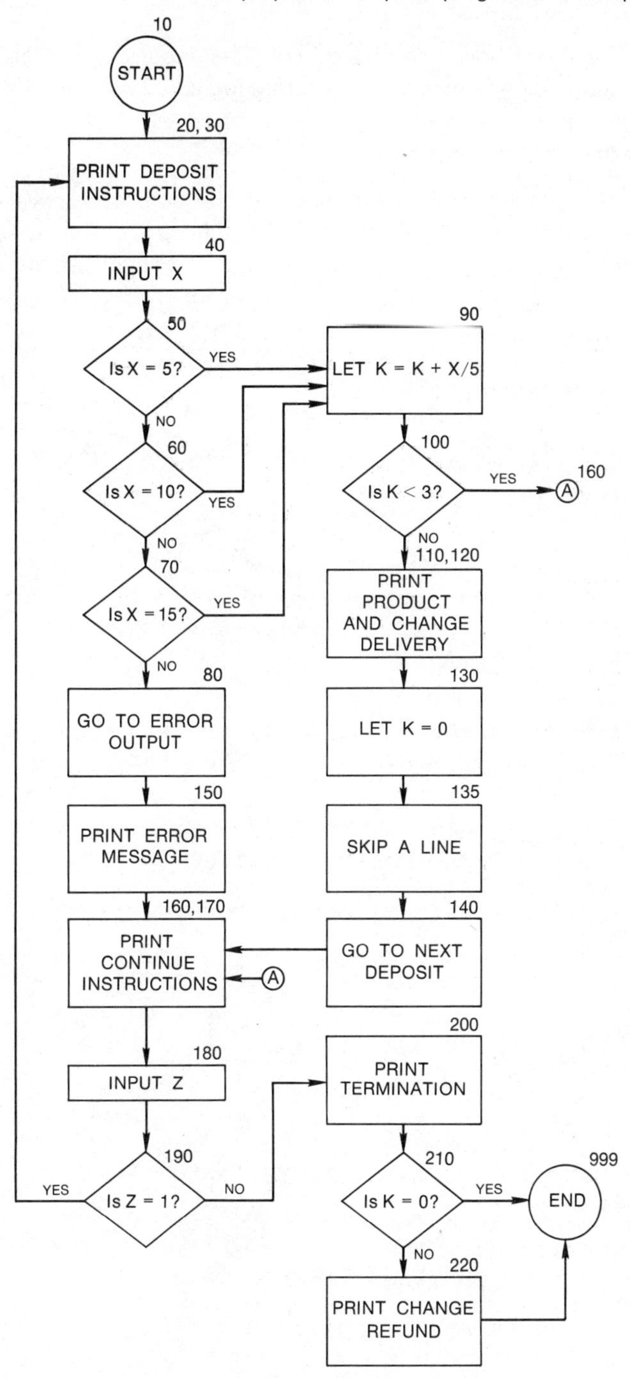

10.2. Flow chart for Program COIN.

ous specifications have been used: variables, input/output details, tests versus actions, and diagrammed program logic.

6 / Run the program and test it

Associated with Program COIN you see the output for several cases, which test some of the possible input conditions. To save space, all of the possible test conditions have not been evaluated for the vending-machine problem.

```
10 REM PROGRAM COIN -- SIMULATES VENDING MACHINE
20 PRINT "TYPE 5,10,OR 25 FOR DEPOSIT."
30 PRINT "YOUR DEPOSIT";
40 INPUT X
50 IF X=5 THEN 90
60 IF X=10 THEN 90
70 IF X=25 THEN 90
80 GO TO 150
90 LET K=K+X/5
100 IF K<3 THEN 160
110 PRINT "PRODUCT DELIVERED"
120 PRINT "YOUR CHANGE IS";5*(K-3);"CENTS"
130 LET K=0
135 PRINT
140 GO TO 160
150 PRINT "UNACCEPTABLE DEPOSIT OF";X;"CENTS REJECTED"
160 PRINT "DO YOU WANT TO CONTINUE? 1=YES, 0=NO"
170 PRINT "YOUR DECISION";
180 INPUT Z
190 IF Z=1 THEN 20
200 PRINT "YOU TERMINATED OPERATION"
210 IF K=0 THEN 999
220 PRINT "YOUR PRESENT DEPOSIT OF";5*K;"CENTS RETURNED"
999 END

RUN

TYPE 5,10,OR 25 FOR DEPOSIT.
YOUR DEPOSIT?25
PRODUCT DELIVERED
YOUR CHANGE IS 10 CENTS

DO YOU WANT TO CONTINUE? 1=YES, 0=NO
YOUR DECISION?1
TYPE 5,10,OR 25 FOR DEPOSIT.
YOUR DEPOSIT?10
DO YOU WANT TO CONTINUE? 1=YES, 0=NO
YOUR DECISION?1
TYPE 5,10,OR 25 FOR DEPOSIT.
YOUR DEPOSIT?25
PRODUCT DELIVERED
YOUR CHANGE IS 20 CENTS
```

```
DO YOU WANT TO CONTINUE? 1=YES, 0=NO
YOUR DECISION?1
TYPE 5,10,OR 25 FOR DEPOSIT.
YOUR DEPOSIT?10
DO YOU WANT TO CONTINUE? 1=YES, 0=NO
YOUR DECISION?1
TYPE 5,10,OR 25 FOR DEPOSIT.
YOUR DEPOSIT?1
UNACCEPTABLE DEPOSIT OF 1 CENTS REJECTED
DO YOU WANT TO CONTINUE? 1=YES, 0=NO
YOUR DECISION?0
YOU TERMINATED OPERATION
YOUR PRESENT DEPOSIT OF 10 CENTS RETURNED

  999,  NORMAL EXIT FROM PROG.
TIME:     0.261 SEC.
```

In complex computer programs, it would be impractical to generate all the possible distinctions that could occur for a computer's input and to test the correspondingly desired output. In really complex programs, which involve many tests, the combinatorial possibilities for input exceed what any reasonable man would want to see—or could—in his lifetime! (See Program MAZE and its notes in Chapter 15.)

Thus, in practice, we pick the variants most likely for test or those most critical to the operation of our programs in terms of cost, disaster, or program abortion.

The most serious unexpected difficulty that can occur in a complex programming effort involving conditional branches is that an unexpected input can cause an unexpected program diversion in sequence that will be never-ending. Such "infinite loops" of action within the computer not only do the user no good but also are a fatal logical fault. The program will never come to an end unless some ultimate test has been provided for its termination. (For students who use BASIC, all computer centers guard against this infinite loop tragedy by holding compute time to a given maximum. Should you exceed this maximum limitation, you will be cut off automatically. But in the world of practical application, you must guard yourself against the same revolving door by your own wits.[3])

Similarly, in highly conditional programs an unexpected input can cause a branch to an unexpected program statement, unless you have screened out all of the false input possibilities—which may be extremely difficult, since you can never be aware of every conceivable input except in the simplest combinatorial cases.

---

[3] One obvious ploy is to introduce one or more gross test constraints to eliminate undesirable inputs; or you might accept only a given set, as in Program COIN. Thus, input variety is controlled.

Thus, to prevent trouble you may view all your programs as an extrapolation of the vending-machine problem just analyzed. Most consequential programs become a variation on the testing required in this problem, and most computer program planning is a variation on the six steps just enumerated. The only difference is scale, or variety of input to and output from the machine: the more complex the problem or the greater the variety of its possible input/output relationships, the greater the care that should be taken in program planning before execution.

You will see these six steps in preparing a program again in Chapter 11. They are important to your orderly understanding of how to go from a problem to a computer program, regardless of the computer language you use. And that transition is the secret of your ultimate success when using the computer.

If you understand a computer language, such as BASIC, but cannot understand how to make the transition from a problem to its expression in the statements a computer language, such as BASIC, requires, you have not yet mastered the art of computer application.

To make sure you do in fact understand the necessary problem-to-language transition, we will not hesitate to repeat the above six steps in what follows.

Two miscellaneous commands

We complete this chapter with two miscellaneous commands that are part of the standard BASIC language. Both may be used as optional methods of performing actions we have discussed thus far.

STOP

The command STOP has the general form

line number STOP

and is equivalent to a GO TO command which references the last line of the program, which will be an END statement. Thus, if the last line of your program is 9999 END, then a program statement such as 100 STOP is entirely equivalent to 100 GO TO 9999. STOP will therefore cause termination of the program under program control and may be used as a shorter and more easily recognized version of the equivalent GO TO. The command STOP may appear one or more times in a program, where as only one END may appear. Finally, do not confuse the program command STOP, which causes a program halt under program control, with the system command STOP (or the equivalent depression of the "S" key on your keyboard), which may be typed while a program is running to halt its execution. The distinction is that the system command STOP permits manual termination of the program during its execution; the programmed STOP operates without manual intervention.

RESTORE

The command RESTORE has the general form

line number RESTORE

and causes the list of data currently being READ to revert back to the beginning. Thus, RESTORE permits the same data to be used more than once without repeating that data in the DATA lines of a program. For example, suppose you wish to have the variable X take on the six successive values 1,2,3,1,2,3, which will then be printed. Method A achieves this end by repeating the data in a DATA line; method B achieves the same end using RESTORE. Method B is longer, but provides multiple use of the data shown.

Method A

```
100 LET N = 0
110 READ X
120 LET N = N + 1
200 PRINT X
300 IF N < 6 THEN 110
800 DATA 1,2,3,1,2,3
999 END
```

Method B

```
100 LET N = 0
110 READ X
120 LET N = N + 1
130 IF N = 6 THEN 999
140 PRINT X
150 IF N = 3 THEN 170
160 GO TO 110
170 RESTORE
180 GO TO 110
800 DATA 1,2,3
999 END
```

In effect, the command RESTORE "rewinds" the data list to its beginning *whenever* the RESTORE command is encountered in a program. The command is most useful in performing a number of different manipulations on the same set of data values. See Example 13 of Chapter 13.

PROBLEMS

10-1 Why are the following branching statements not correct?

```
100 GO TO LINE 200          100 IF X = 0 THEN GO TO 200
100 GO TO END               100 IF X => 1 THEN 200
100 GO TO READ X            100 IF X = 1 OR X = 2 THEN 200
```

10-2 What is wrong with the following programs? Each contains one or more errors.

a. The purpose of this program is to test for equality of X versus the sum of Y + Z and to print out in English the result of the test.

```
10 READ X, Y, Z
20 IF X > Y + Z THEN 500
30 IF X < Y + Z THEN 500
40 PRINT "X IS EQUAL TO Y + Z"
50 PRINT "X IS NOT EQUAL TO Y + Z"
60 GO TO 10
70 DATA 1, 2, 3
75 DATA 10, 2, 3
80 DATA 5, 2, 3
99 END
```

b. The purpose of this program is to print the powers of 2 until a power of 2 equals 5000. The program fails to stop.

```
10 LET X = 2
20 LET N = 1
30 LET Y = X ↑ N
40 IF Y = 5000 THEN 99
50 PRINT N,Y
60 LET N = N + 1
70 GO TO 30
99 END
```

c. This program is supposed to accumulate, then print the numbers in the DATA line. It does not accumulate.

```
20 LET T = 0
30 READ X
40 IF X = 9999 THEN 90
50 LET T = T + X
60 GO TO 20
90 PRINT T
92 DATA 1, 2, 3, 4, 5, 9999
99 END
```

d. This program is supposed to accumulate 10 numbers in the DATA line. The correct sum is 55; the program gives 45.

```
10 LET T = 0
20 LET N = 1
30 READ X
40 LET T = T + X
50 LET N = N + 1
60 IF N < 10 THEN 30
70 PRINT "THE TOTAL IS" T
80 DATA 1, 2, 3, 4, 5, 6, 7, 8, 9, 10
99 END
```

e. This program is supposed to print out numbers from 10 to 20, but the last number printed exceeds 20. Can you explain? The program appears to work logically. (In fact, at most computer installations, this program will continue to print until halted manually! Why?)

```
10 LET N = 1
20 PRINT 10 * N
30 IF N = 2 THEN 99
40 LET N = N + .1
50 GO TO 20
99 END
```

10-3 Discuss the difference between the commands REM and PRINT. Why is it desirable to have both forms of command available in a programming language?

10-4 Consider a table having 3 rows and 4 columns (thus 3 × 4 = 12 cells, or row-column intersections). Let I = row number and J = column number, starting the numbering from row 1, column 1, in the upper left-hand corner of the table. Then any cell in the table may be referenced by a pair of numbers (I,J). For example, in the specified table cell (1,1) is the top cell furthest to the left, and cell (3,4) is the bottom cell furthest to the right (see diagram).

		Column 1	2	3	4
	1	(1,1)	(1,2)	(1,3)	(1,4)
Row	2	(2,1)	(2,2)	(2,3)	(2,4)
	3	(3,1)	(3,2)	(3,3)	(3,4)

Now a small ladybug presently resides at cell (1,1). When the spirit moves her, she jumps to the next column in her present row, i.e., to (1,2) next, and so on to the right at progressive intervals until the end of a row is reached. Continuing in this regular sequence, our ladybug hops back to the first column of row 2, cell (2,1), and traverses row 2, then hops to the start of row 3, and carries on step by step to the end of the table, where she stops.

The following program, using combinations of IF/THEN, GO TO, and LET statements will print out sequentially the progression of the ladybug from cell (1,1) to cell (3,4).

```
5 REM PROGRAM NAME: LADYBUG--ILLUSTRATES NESTED LOOPS.
10 LET I = 1
20 LET J = 1
30 READ M, N
40 PRINT I,J
50 LET J = J + 1
60 IF J > N THEN 80
70 GO TO 40
80 J = 1
85 LET I = I + 1
90 IF I > M THEN 999
100 GO TO 40
110 DATA 3,4
999 END
```

a. Flow chart this program and note that the loop involving J is inside the loop involving I in your chart (or should be!). This problem illustrates the use of nested loops and you will want to compare its solution to the procedures used in Chapter 11.

b. How many times does the program sequence go around the J loop for each time it goes around the I loop? How many total looping actions are there in this program? Notice how the nesting of the loops, in effect, multiplies the power of the program by letting one loop control another.

Note: The notation used in this problem is standard nomenclature in mathematical literature defining matrices, or two-dimensional, tables. Also, the progression followed by the ladybug follows the progression the computer would use in reading data into a table and in defining the location of the numeric values located there. The numbers indicated in parentheses above, i.e., the (I, J) values, will correspond to the indices of the subscripted variables described in the following chapter.

eleven

FOR/NEXT, subscripted variables, and DIM

In Chapter 10 we saw how the BASIC branching commands can make your programs more versatile and useful by permitting you to alter the sequence of statement execution. In this chapter we expand upon that idea.

You will recall from the last chapter that we often use conditional and unconditional branches *in combination* to provide repetitive action until some specified condition is achieved. That sequential repetition shows in our flow charts as a *loop* from a later program step to an earlier one. The termination, or exit from the loop, occurs when the specified condition is reached. For example, when we read and accumulate 10 numbers, the read-and-accumulation sequence continues until the count of 10 is reached.

Such repetitive loops with conditional exit occur so frequently in advanced computer programs that an abbreviated form of programming them is useful. The FOR/NEXT *pair* of BASIC commands, as discussed below, provides automatic looping control with fewer program statements than would be possible using only IF/THEN and GO TO. The FOR/NEXT pair also simplifies the logic of most programs and makes them easier to understand.

Automatic loops

FOR/NEXT is a compound command. That is, in a given program, a FOR statement will *always* be associated with a NEXT statement. The FOR statement has the general form:

$$\underline{\text{line number}}\ \underline{\text{FOR}}\ \underline{(\text{variable})} = \left\{\begin{array}{l}\underline{\text{numeric literal}}\\ \underline{\text{variable}}\\ \underline{\text{expression}}\end{array}\right\}\ \underline{\text{TO}}\ \left\{\begin{array}{l}\underline{\text{numeric literal}}\\ \underline{\text{variable}}\\ \underline{\text{expression}}\end{array}\right\}$$

$$\text{STEP}\ \left\{\begin{array}{l}\underline{\text{numeric literal}}\\ \underline{\text{variable}}\\ \underline{\text{expression}}\end{array}\right\}$$

The modifier STEP and the following alternatives are optional. If it is not specified, the STEP is assumed to be 1. The entire command must appear on one line, although here for clarity, the option, STEP, has been shown on a second line.

Thus, some suitable FOR commands are

```
100 FOR J = 1 TO 10
100 FOR I = 1 TO N
100 FOR X = 1 TO Y STEP .5
100 FOR W = X + Y TO Z + R
100 FOR A = −10 TO 0 STEP + 1
```

Each FOR command is associated with a later NEXT command of the form:

$$\underline{\text{line number}}\ \underline{\text{NEXT}}\ \underline{(\text{variable})}$$

The variable following NEXT is that stated in its corresponding FOR statement, as shown to the left of the equals sign. Thus, each of the above FOR commands would be associated respectively with later NEXT commands of the form:

```
500 NEXT J
500 NEXT I
500 NEXT X
500 NEXT W
500 NEXT A
```

1 / Single loops

The implication of the FOR/NEXT statements is that the line numbers between those shown for a FOR statement and the NEXT statement corresponding to it are to be repeated successively, each time increasing the value of the variable shown to the left of the equality sign in the FOR statement by the STEP specified (or 1 if STEP is not specified) until that variable is *greater* than the limit shown after TO.

Thus,

```
100 FOR J = 1 TO 10
– – – – –
– – – – –
– – – – –
500 NEXT J
```

would cause the intermediate lines between 100 and 500 (indicated by dashes) to be repeated 10 times. (The test is for J > 10 for termination.) After that repetition, control continues to the line following line 500.

Compare the two programs below. Program A adds 1 through 10 the integers by the methods of Chapter 10. Program B uses the FOR/NEXT pair to accomplish the same result and to provide identical execution.

Program A	*Program B*
10 LET T = 0	10 LET T = 0
15 LET N = 0	15 FOR N = 1 TO 10
20 LET N = N + 1	20 LET T = T + N
25 IF N > 10 THEN 50	30 NEXT N
30 LET T = T + N	40 PRINT T
40 GO TO 20	99 END
50 PRINT T	
99 END	

Program B is shorter and easier than Program A, and since the two forms of looping are equivalent, the FOR/NEXT approach is usually preferred by most programmers. The relative benefit of the FOR/NEXT command pair over the corresponding IF/THEN and GO TO sequence rapidly increases as more loops are added to a program.

Note in particular that the variable name on the left of the equality sign in the FOR statement *must* be identical to the variable name in the corresponding (or next encountered) NEXT statement. Note also that FOR/NEXT statements are always used in pairs, and to have FOR without NEXT or vice versa will abort the program. (A diagnostic message usually results when these errors are encountered by the computer.)

2 / *Nested loops*

Nested loops are also possible and frequent in the application of FOR/NEXT commands. For example, here is the solution to Problem 10-5,

Program LADYBUG,[1] using two FOR/NEXT statement pairs.

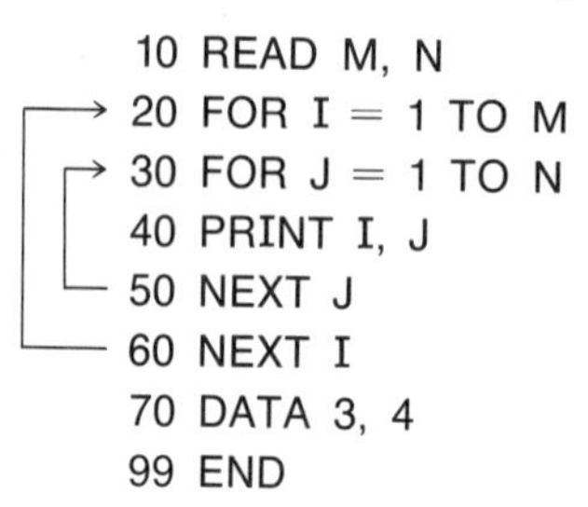

```
10 READ M, N
20 FOR I = 1 TO M
30 FOR J = 1 TO N
40 PRINT I, J
50 NEXT J
60 NEXT I
70 DATA 3, 4
99 END
```

The appropriate nesting of the loops is shown in the program by the arrows to the left of the line numbers. To interchange lines 50 and 60 would be disastrous because the counts for I and J would become confused and the computer would halt—again with a diagnostic message to the user.

The FOR and NEXT for the inner loop must be contained within the FOR and NEXT for the outer loop. This requirement may be checked by drawing connecting arrows between corresponding FOR and NEXT statements. If the arrows do not cross, the loops have been nested properly. In most BASIC installations, you have wide latitude in the number of loops nested and the manner of nesting, so long as the "no-crossing" rule is observed. Here are a few schematic examples of correct and incorrect nestings: (Note that when loops are nested the NEXT corresponding to a given FOR is not necessarily the first encountered in line sequence. Only the "innermost" loop will have such adjacency.)

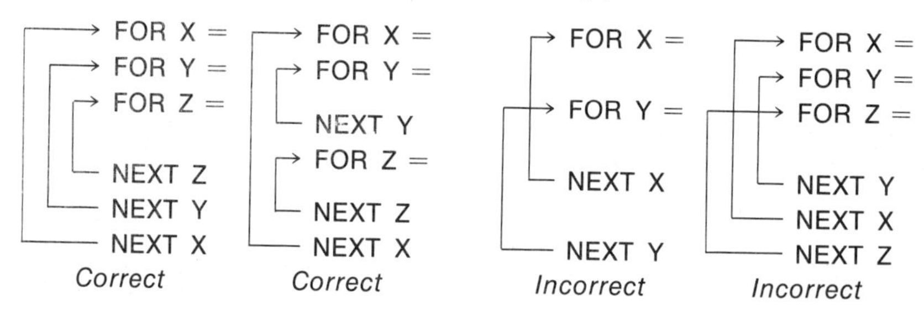

Within the FOR/NEXT loop IF/THEN statements may be used (1) to branch *out* of the loop to stop the looping prematurely or (2) to branch from one statement *within* the loop to another *within* the loop. In general it is not possible to branch *into* a FOR/NEXT loop, either conditionally or unconditionally. A few exceptions to this rule exist and they will be

[1] In this program we wanted to print out the row-column steps, indicated by the indices (I, J), which a hypothetical bug would follow if it progressed from the upper left-hand corner of a table to the lower right-hand corner moving sequentially from left to right and from top to bottom. If you do not remember this problem, refer to it before continuing.

mentioned later, but by and large the general rule applies. The essential idea is that the test routine set up by the FOR/NEXT pair of statements cannot be bypassed. To illustrate, if a branch were made into the middle of a FOR/NEXT loop, the controlling variable and test set up by the FOR statement may not be correctly defined. Thus, the following program which is supposed to add the numbers 10 through 20, will not work at many BASIC installations, or worse, may operate, but with unexpected results if your compiler does not detect the into-loop branch. (Deleting line 20 would correct the program.)

```
5 LET T = 0
10 LET X = 10
20 GO TO 40
30 FOR N = X TO 20
40 LET T = T + N
50 NEXT N
60 PRINT T
99 END
```

In addition, you should make no computations within a FOR/NEXT loop that will disturb the variable first specified in the FOR statement. Such action will alter the FOR specification. Thus, Program A below will print the numbers 1 through 10. Program B will print only the number 1, because the first encounter of line 30 of Program B changes the test value, or index I, from 1 to 11—a value greater than 10—which terminates the loop and, in this case, the program.

Program A	*Program B*
10 FOR I = 1 TO 10	10 FOR I = 1 TO 10
20 PRINT I	20 PRINT I
30 NEXT I	30 LET I = I + 10
99 END	40 NEXT I
	99 END

One added technical point is worth noting. If a branch is made *out* from a FOR/NEXT loop *before* the looping is terminated by the FOR test, then the *current* value of the indexing variable indicated to the left of the equals sign in the FOR statement is available for later reference. For example, in the program segment

```
– – – – – – – – – – –
– – – – – – – – – – –
20 FOR I = 1 TO 100
30 READ X(I)
40 IF X(I) = 9999 THEN 100
```

```
50 NEXT I
100 LET N = I - 1
- - - - - - - - - - -
- - - - - - - - - - -
500 DATA 8,5,3,99999
999 END
```

a branch outside the loop (to line 100) will occur when the fourth observation, 9999, has been detected, leaving the current value as I = 4. Line 100 may then be used to determine the number of useful observations (exclusive of the end-of-file tag) as N = 3. (This device is used in line 50 of Program RANGE, page 204.) Similarly, in most implementations of BASIC if the loop terminates normally at the upper limit defined in the FOR statement, that upper value of the indexing variable will also be available for later use until it is redefined or altered by subsequent program statements. Check this point at your location; some variations do exist.

With these few rules, FOR/NEXT statements provide a powerful way to increase the looping power of computer programming, particularly when nested FOR/NEXT loops are used. Since a major use of the FOR/NEXT statements is in the processing of data in tabular form, we now turn to that subject.

Subscripted variables

In the discussion of legal BASIC variable names in Chapter 8, you discovered that an "unsubscripted" variable could consist of one letter (A–Z) or one letter plus one decimal digit (A1 or Z9). In BASIC, subscripted variables may also consist of one letter plus one or two subscripts in parentheses.[2] To understand the meaning of these subscripts, we now consider the standard notation used to define data arranged in lists and tables. However, before continuing, we note that the following are appropriate subscripted variables.

A(1), A(J), A(1,3), A(I,J), A(I + 1, J − 1), A(2 * I, 3 * J), A(X − Y, X + Z)

where the variables named within the parentheses have been defined with a numeric value before the subscripted variable is mentioned. Note that a subscript may include simple additions, subtractions, and multiplications in the forms shown above. More complex expressions leading to

[2] Subscripted variables with two subscripts refer to tables, whereas those with a single subscript refer to lists. The discussion of table manipulations, and therefore the manipulation of variables with two subscripts, will be postponed until later in the chapter. Note now, however, that the first subscript in a double-subscripted variable refers to a row in the table, the second to a column.

subscript definition would be evaluated in a previous LET statement. Moreover, the subscript used should be an integer. (If it is not, most BASIC compilers will take the integer part of the number stated to be a subscript, and unwanted results may ensue.) A subscript itself may be a subscripted variable, i.e., A(X(I)) is legal if X(I) has been previously defined with a numeric value. This variety of possibilities will take on more meaning after you consider the following sections and examples.

Lists and list definition

A numeric list, or a "vector" or a "single-dimensional array," is what the name implies, a set of numeric values arranged in an orderly fashion. For example, we may have a set of six numbers introduced into a program by the following data line.

```
800 DATA 1.2, 3.6, 1.9, 12.7, 6.3, 7.8
```

Suppose we would like to have all these values available and distinctly identified for use *at one time* or by appropriate reference throughout a program. One way to make such values available would be to introduce a corresponding READ command of the form

```
100 READ A, B, C, D, E, F
```

which would define the variables and store them for later use. (Each named variable, remember, becomes a given memory location containing the current numeric value appropriate to it, which may be referenced by the variable name.)

This process, however, becomes tedious when the list of values to be held for later reference is lengthy, say, 100 values, since we must create 100 variable names of the form A1 or Z9 and then keep track of these definitions in later work.

A more suitable approach is to use subscripted variables and handle the list by one name. For example, suppose we call the list of data above List A and then simply number the values in the list (from left to right) as A(1), A(2), A(3), . . . , A(6), the subscript, or number within the parentheses, indicating uniquely the position of the desired number in the list. This approach is not only possible but desirable in BASIC as well as in other computer languages.

All we need to do is read in the list incrementing the subscript by 1 for each new value. To do this we can use the FOR/NEXT statement pair as follows. (The dashes, as before, indicate program lines not of immediate interest.)

```
10 FOR I = 1 TO 6
20 READ A(I)
30 NEXT I
— — — — — — — — — — —
— — — — — — — — — — —
— — — — — — — — — — —
800 DATA 1.2, 3.6, 1.9, 12.7, 6.3, 7.8
999 END
```

After the loop ending at line 30 has been completed, the six numeric values in the DATA line will be stored in the computer memory for later reference. *We may now refer to any item in the list by its subscripted name.* Thus, the statement

```
100 LET X = A(6)
```

would cause the value of X to be set to 7.8. We may output a list in a similar manner (or otherwise manipulate it at will). Thus, by insertion of

```
200 FOR I = 1 TO 6
210 PRINT A(I);
220 NEXT I
```

we would print out the values in the DATA line [assuming there were no other intermediate operations that altered the values of A(I)]. Note that because of the semicolon in the above lines, all six values would appear on one line, rather than vertically, on the Teletype or other remote terminal page.

1 / Dimensioning a list

For a list of up to 10 numbers or cells in BASIC, you do not have to advise the computer to reserve room in its memory. The use of a single-subscripted variable automatically sets up a 10-cell list, as in line 20 of the program on the previous page. However, if we plan to have longer lists, we should make it known at the outset of the program by the use of a dimensional statement, which in BASIC is DIM. The general form is

line number DIM {list of subscripted variables with integer numeric literals indicating maximum subscript required}

For example, if we intend to have a one-dimensional list of 100 cells we might say at the start of a program involving such a list

```
10 DIM X (100)
```

and if we intend to have two such lists, one called X and the other Y,

```
10 DIM X(100), Y(100)
```

It is necessary to make the dimension declaration *before* any reference is made to the list or any element in it. Thus, the DIM statements required in a program are usually the first statements in that program.

It is possible to dimension lists under 10 cells in length, and this is often done to alert the reader that one or more lists will come up in the program. Further, it does no harm to overdimension a list since the purpose of the dimension declaration is only to make sure that there is *enough* storage space. (Obviously, however, it is possible to overdo a good thing, and reckless overdimensioning can sometimes exhaust the available computer memory, so that no room will be left for the actual program or its data! If you actually need DIM X(20) and ask for DIM X(1000), you are being grossly extravagant in your reservation.) Overdimensioning is necessary when the programmer does not know how much data will be received as illustrated by Program RANGE in the next section. In such cases, a reasonable estimate must be made in advance of the maximum list size to be handled, and the program dimensioned accordingly. Usually the maximum allocation dimensioned will not be used. But if more data than the list size provided for must be handled, the program itself must be adjusted.

BASIC compilers (as well as those for other languages) require that the maximum dimension indicated in the parentheses of a DIM statement be a *numeric literal* and, in particular, an *integer.* The BASIC compiler will not permit you to use a variable name for a dimensioning subscript, even though that variable has been "previously defined." This requirement is somewhat at variance with the consistency one would expect from the flexibility available in the use of subscripted variables themselves, as illustrated above. There is a good reason for the rigid requirements for a DIM statement, however. DIM is a *nonexecuting* statement which serves *only* as a declaration to the compiler that a given amount of space will be needed for a list or table at the time of execution. At the time of compilation, none of the executable statements can supply a numeric value to the DIM statement, and thus, although it may appear from the program sequence that a variable could be defined for a DIM statement, this is not the case.

For example, although

```
10 READ M
20 DIM X(M)
- - - - - - - - - - -
- - - - - - - - - - -
```

looks reasonable, it is not. The values within the parentheses of the DIM statement must be numeric integer values themselves. It is entirely reasonable, however, to read upcoming dimension sizes *after* an original DIM statement has appeared. For example,

```
10 DIM X(100)
20 READ M
30 FOR I = 1 TO M
40 READ X(I)
50 NEXT I
— — — — — — — — — — —
— — — — — — — — — — —
90 DATA 3, 1, 2, 3
99 END
```

is a program that somewhat overdimensions the space needed at time of execution. Yet the READ correctly places the three values 1, 2, 3 in the first three cells of the list, or vector X, disregarding the remaining cells which are not used.

The only way to avoid overdimensioning in a BASIC program is to write a specific DIM statement for each application; this is another reason for placing all DIM statements at the first line or beginning of any program. The usefulness of having a total list of data available at once may not yet be obvious, and so two examples follow.

2 / *List illustrations*

Suppose we want to find the largest and the smallest numbers in a list of data and then to compute the statistical range of the data as the largest minus the smallest. It is possible to make such tests by sequentially examining the data as it is read by remembering the largest or the smallest value seen to date. However, if we wish to arrange the numbers in order from largest to smallest and then print out the result, it would be necessary to have a complete list of them with which to work. The ordering of numbers in ascending or descending order by their value is known as sorting. This important operation, illustrated extensively in Problem 11-6, is an extension of Program RANGE.

```
3 REM PROGRAM NAME: RANGE -- FINDS LARGEST AND
4 REM SMALLEST DATA VALUES.
5 REM READ IN DATA AND DETERMINE N<=100
10 REM ENTER DATA LINES STARTING AT LINE 500
15 REM TEST DATA AT LINE 500 UNLESS YOU ENTER NEW DATA
20 DIM X(101)
```

```
22 FOR I=1 TO 101
24 READ X(I)
26 IF X(I) = 99999 THEN 50
40 NEXT I
50 LET N=I-1
60 PRINT "THE NUMBER OF OBSERVATIONS IS ";N
100 REM NOW FIND THE LARGEST VALUE IN LIST
110 LET A=X(1)
115 FOR I=2 TO N
120 IF X(I) <= A THEN 140
130 LET A=X(I)
140 NEXT I
150 PRINT "LARGEST VALUE IS ";A
160 REM NOW FIND SMALLEST VALUE IN LIST
165 LET B=X(1)
170 FOR I=2 TO N
180 IF X(I) >=  B THEN 200
190 LET B=X(I)
200 NEXT I
205 PRINT "SMALLEST VALUE IS ";B
206 PRINT "RANGE IS ";A-B
500 DATA -1,-2,-3,-4,-5,1,2,3,4,5,99999
999 END

RUN


THE NUMBER OF OBSERVATIONS IS  10
LARGEST VALUE IS  5
SMALLEST VALUE IS -5
RANGE IS  10

  999,  NORMAL EXIT FROM PROG.

TIME:    0.179 SEC.
```

In Program RANGE we assume the total number of data elements will not exceed 100 and the list will be terminated by an end-of-file tag, 99999, as illustrated in Chapter 10. We thus dimension a list of maximum length 101 (at line 20) and proceed to read the data into storage. When the end of file is encountered, reading halts, and N, the number of data elements to be considered, is set to the number read less 1 (this subtraction excludes the last data element, which is the end-of-file tag). We next scan the list looking for the largest observation (lines 110–150). This is done by comparing the first observation with the second, then retaining the larger, and continuing until the list is exhausted. At that time the largest value has been found and we print it.

The process is repeated (with a reversal of the IF/THEN test between lines 120 and 180) to find the smallest data element. The difference between the smallest and the largest is then printed as the range. Of course, in the entire computation we are interested in the *algebraic* difference between observations, as illustrated by the test data at line 500. Negative numbers are considered smaller than zero, and "large" negative numbers smaller than "small" negative numbers, e.g., −5 is less than −3.

Tables and table definition

There are also problems in which it is convenient to have available an entire table for repeated reference or for the storage of results. (Tables are also called matrices, or two-dimensional arrays.)

To provide such ability, the BASIC language (as well as most others) uses double subscripts in its variable names and corresponding DIM statements.

Thus DIM X(20, 20) will reserve in the computer memory space for a table of size 20 × 20 (or 400 cells in total). Similarly, DIM X(3, 4) will reserve space for a 3-row by 4-column table. In BASIC a table smaller than 10 × 10 (as with a list smaller than 10 cells) need not be formally dimensioned with a DIM statement. However, we suggest that a DIM statement always be used when tables (or lists) are involved.

Although the BASIC language permits only two indices (or subscripts) referencing row and column respectively, more advanced languages, such as FORTRAN, permit "deeper" indexing, or subscripting. Thus, in such languages, the subscripted variable X(I, J, K) might refer to page I, row J, column K, permitting further refinement of data classification. With some thought, however, the capability available in BASIC may be extended. (See Problem 11-6.)

As with a list, any element (or cell) in a table (or matrix) may be referenced by defining the pair of subscripts desired, in row-column order. Problem 10-5 was intended to illustrate the standard nomenclature used by most computer languages (as well as most mathematics texts) in referencing cells in a table. By reference to that example, we see that the upper left-hand corner of a (standard) table is located at the intersection of row 1, column 1, and therefore may be referenced by the subscript (1, 1), which is a unique identification.[3] Similarly, the value of the variable X(2, 3) is the value found at the intersection of row 2, column 3 of the table called X.

Since a large number of practical commercial and scientific problems require the use of tables for their solution, it is now worthwhile to look at a variety of examples that deal with tables.

---

[3] Although some computer implementations of BASIC and some mathematics texts index rows and columns from 0,0 rather than from 1,1 (that is, the first row and first column [the "northwest" corner of a table] are given the index 0 instead of 1), the notation cited here is more common and will be followed hereafter.

1 / Table manipulations

Study carefully the following problems involving the manipulation of data in a two-dimensional table. An understanding of these standard manipulations will be useful in later work.

First, consider an $M \times N$ table (where M is 3 and N is 4) which is to be filled with data from a DATA line. Suppose that we will want eventually to compute row and column totals from this table, as well as a grand total, and therefore must provide space for those solutions. Thus, we will dimension our table one row and one column larger than that needed for data, the additional space and data to be used as described in the following diagram:

1	2	3	4	
5	6	7	8	
9	10	11	12	

Number of rows	$M = 3$
Number of columns	$N = 4$
Total data elements	$M \times N = 12$

Extra row and column added for answers, thus total table is $(M + 1) \times (N + 1) = 4 \times 5$.

With the above conventions, we may now introduce the following program segments. In what follows, the dashes indicate program lines that are not of immediate interest. Line numbering is such that the program segments may be grouped together at will.

Each one of the following program segments may be considered in turn. Note the manipulation of the subscripts in the programs, since the following segments provide practice in subscript manipulation using the FOR/NEXT statements.

Let us now read the 12 data elements into the properly dimensioned table.[4]

[4] Note that the data read in by the program segment shown will occupy the upper left-hand 3×4 table in the overdimensioned 20×20 table A(20,20). However, since the READ subscripts have been set at 3×4, we may now think of Table A, containing the body of the data, as a 3×4 table. The added row and column for storage of the sums to be computed are obtained by the later subscripting to $M + 1$ and $N + 1$, which is permissible with the overdimensioning provided.

```
10 DIM A(20, 20)
20 LET M = 3
30 LET N = 4
40 FOR I = 1 TO M
50 FOR J = 1 TO N
60 READ A(I, J)
70 NEXT J
80 NEXT I
– – – – – – – – – – – – – – – –
– – – – – – – – – – – – – – – –
900 DATA 1,2,3,4,5,6,7,8,9,10,11,12
999 END
```

Assuming that the data values have been read into the computer's memory by the program segments above, perform the following:

a. Sum all of the values in the table (i.e., find the grand total) and place the answer in A(M + 1, N + 1).

```
– – – – – – – – – – – – – – – –
– – – – – – – – – – – – – – – –
100 FOR I = 1 TO M
110 FOR J = 1 TO N
120 LET A(M + 1, N + 1) = A(M + 1, N + 1) + A(I, J)
130 NEXT J
140 NEXT I
– – – – – – – – – – – – – – – –
– – – – – – – – – – – – – – – –
```

b. Compute the total of column 1, store at A(M + 1, 1).

```
– – – – – – – – – – –
– – – – – – – – – – –
200 LET J = 1
210 FOR I = 1 TO M
220 LET A(M + 1, 1) = A(M + 1, 1) + A(I, J)
230 NEXT I
– – – – – – – – – – –
– – – – – – – – – – –
```

c. Compute the total of row 1, store at A(1, N + 1).

```
– – – – – – – – – – –
– – – – – – – – – – –
300 LET I = 1
310 FOR J = 1 TO N
```

```
320 LET A(1, N + 1) = A(1, N + 1) + A(I, J)
330 NEXT J
- - - - - - - - - - -
- - - - - - - - - - -
```

d. Produce the sum of each column, store in cells A(M + 1, J), i.e., at the foot of each column of the table.

```
- - - - - - - - - - -
- - - - - - - - - - -
400 FOR J = 1 TO N
410 FOR I = 1 TO M
420 LET A(M + 1, J) = A(M + 1, J) + A(I, J)
430 NEXT I
440 NEXT J
- - - - - - - - - - -
- - - - - - - - - - -
```

e. Produce the sum of each row, store in cells A(I, N + 1), i.e., to the extreme right of each row.

```
- - - - - - - - - - -
- - - - - - - - - - -
500 FOR I = 1 TO M
510 FOR J = 1 TO N
520 LET A(I, N + 1) = A(I, N + 1) + A(I, J)
530 NEXT J
540 NEXT I
- - - - - - - - - - -
- - - - - - - - - - -
```

By inserting program segments (a), (d), and (e) into the program which read in the original data, the complete set of totals will be obtained, and the complete table, including data and totals may be printed out by inserting also:

```
- - - - - - - - - - -
- - - - - - - - - - -
600 FOR I = 1 TO M + 1
610 FOR J = 1 TO N + 1
620 PRINT A(I, J),
630 NEXT J
640 PRINT
650 NEXT I
- - - - - - - - - - -
- - - - - - - - - - -
```

The final output table will be of the form:

```
1     2     3     4     10
5     6     7     8     26
9     10    11    12    42
15    18    21    24    78
```

Clearly, the sum of the row totals and the sum of the column totals must equal the same number, namely 78, as shown above in the lower right-hand corner, i.e., A(M + 1, N + 1). (This is the usual accounting format in which the row and column totals on a "spread sheet" must "cross-foot" to the same value.) The comma terminating line 620 in the printing segment above inhibits the line advance and provides the five-column spacing shown. When index J reaches N + 1, or 5, line 640 is executed, providing a line advance and the start for the second table row.

A complete understanding of the above manipulations is desirable before continuing, since manipulation of tabular data is an important aspect of computer programming. If you are not entirely at home with the subscripting method of referencing tables, some practice on the computer terminal will help fix the standard nomenclature in your mind. In the above examples, note, in particular, the order in which the indices are incremented by the FOR/NEXT pair of statements in BASIC. Reversing the order of the nesting of two FOR/NEXT statements, e.g., for I and J, will reverse the sequence of row and column operations, as illustrated in (d) and (e) above.

Also remember that once the data has been read into a table and once the row and column totals have been generated by the program segments, the table is available for later reference by any program statement before the END statement occurs. Thus, we could easily generate the sum of squares of the values in the table (or indeed any other computation using those numeric values). For example, the insertion of the program lines

```
125 LET S = S + A(I, J) ↑ 2
- - - - - - - - - - -
700 PRINT "THE SUM OF SQUARES OF THE DATA IS" S
- - - - - - - - - - -
```

would cause the sum of squares to be printed out (after the table) with the title shown in line 700. Other intermediate computations of the same sort can be carried out. Remember that when subscripted variables are used, the usual purpose is to make a number of computations from data which must be available *in toto* for the computation to be a success. (Matrix operations are a case in point. For special commands to manipulate matrices, see Chapter 14.)

A table application

To confirm what you have learned in the past few pages about table manipulations (particularly the row and column totaling of pages 207 to 210), consider the following practical problem.

A clothing store has an inventory of a given item, which comes in three sizes, small, medium, and large, and three colors, red, white, and blue. The number of units presently in stock is available. Similarly, there is a different unit-price for each of the nine classifications of goods, i.e., from small red through large blue.

The store owner wants to get a listing of the value of his inventory, not only in detail by size and color but also by a summary on size, a summary on color, and a summary of the total value.

We propose to handle this problem using tables.

1 / Decide upon the variables to use

We first propose to set up three tables, X(I, J), Y(I, J), and Z(I, J), which will represent respectively units on hand, unit price, and the results of all the price computations. In particular, the first two tables will be 3 × 3, the last 4 × 4, so that we can show the row and column totals by size and color. Again, specifically, we will understand these tables to look like those following, with the specific row-column designations shown. (Note: one of the main practical reasons for using tables is so data may be organized and manipulated in classified form. Size and color are the classifications shown.)

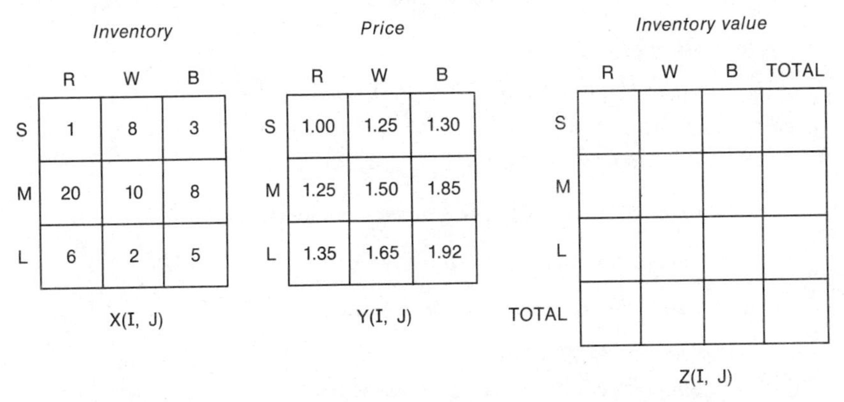

Inventory

	R	W	B
S	1	8	3
M	20	10	8
L	6	2	5

X(I, J)

Price

	R	W	B
S	1.00	1.25	1.30
M	1.25	1.50	1.85
L	1.35	1.65	1.92

Y(I, J)

Inventory value

	R	W	B	TOTAL
S				
M				
L				
TOTAL				

Z(I, J)

In the tables shown, the dimensions are, left to right, DIM X(3, 3), Y(3, 3), Z(4, 4). The input data we shall use for testing the program has also been shown for reference in Tables X(I, J) and Y(I, J) as it should appear after we have gone through the read operations. (Note: We do not have to dimension these tables since they are all under the 10 × 10 size; however, we shall do so in any case, to indicate in the program that we are dealing with tables of the size stated above.)

2 / What specific input data and output report forms are to be used?

a. Input. We shall read in the data for this problem at lines 800 and 810 of our program. Line 800 will give the values of X(I, J), line 810 the values of Y(I, J):

```
800 DATA 1, 8, 3, 20, 10, 8, 6, 2, 5
810 DATA 1.00, 1.25, 1.30, 1.25, 1.50, 1.85, 1.35, 1.65, 1.92
```

Note that *nine* data elements appear on each line. In line 810 take great care not to type in a "." for a "," or you will not get a correct result.

b. Output. From Z(I, J) we want to print out a table of summary computations that the store owner can read directly. Therefore, we must supply a title and use table headings in English, as shown below. (Asterisks are used arbitrarily in the tabular heading to set off the totals.)

INVENTORY VALUE REPORT

	RED	*WHITE*	*BLUE*	***TOTAL*
SMALL				
MEDIUM				
LARGE				
**TOTAL	___	___	___	___

We will use the automatic formatting feature of BASIC to space the columns from 5 fields of 15 characters each. The output titles and computed numbers will be left-justified in these fields, since BASIC always shows printed output to the left in each available field.

3 / What tests are to be made?

In this program there will be no conditional branches other than those automatically set up by the FOR/NEXT statements we will use to read in the data, make the computations, and print out the output.

4 / Draw a rough flow chart of your proposed computations

The major steps to be performed are as shown in Figure 11.1.

5 / Draw a detailed flow chart and write the program

Since this job does not involve any conditional branches, we may safely omit the detailed flowchart, and go ahead with the program. The program steps, except for the output detail follow the instructions given in the last section. To avoid one FOR/NEXT loop, we will make the computation for Z(I, J) in the main body of the output table as soon as we have the needed value of Y(I, J). Also, in order to get the complete set of titles needed in the specified output report, we will use a brute-force method of printing

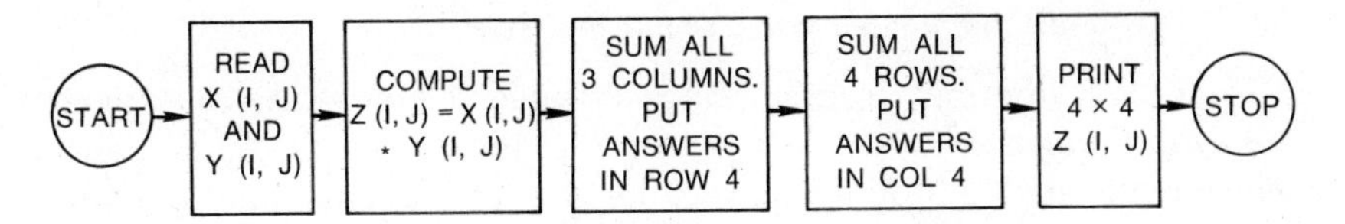

Fig. 11.1

out the final values of Z(I, J) for the entire 4 × 4 table, including row and column totals. The index to I = 4 of the row total routine (line 145) will automatically generate the grand total, to be shown as Z(4,4). This device again avoids a separate computational loop.

```
50 REM PROGRAM NAME: INVENTORY -- PRICES INVENTORY AND
55 REM COMPUTES VALUE DISTRIBUTION BY SIZE AND COLOR.
57 REM ENTER INVENTORY DATA LINES 800-809, PRICE 810-819.
120 DIM X(3,3),Y(3,3),Z(4,4)
125 FOR I=1 TO 3
130 FOR J=1 TO 3
135 READ X(I,J)
140 NEXT J
145 NEXT I
150 FOR I=1 TO 3
155 FOR J=1 TO 3
160 READ Y(I,J)
165 REM YOU CAN COMPUTE Z(I,J) HERE
170 LET Z(I,J)=X(I,J)*Y(I,J)
175 NEXT J
180 NEXT I
185 REM COMPUTE COLUMN TOTALS
190 REM PLACE RESULT IN ROW 4
200 FOR J=1 TO 3
210 FOR I=1 TO 3
220 LET Z(4,J)=Z(4,J)+Z(I,J)
225 NEXT I
230 NEXT J
235 REM SUM ROWS INCLUDING ROW 4 TO GET
240 REM GRAND TOTAL AND ROW SUMS, TOO.
245 FOR I=1 TO 4
250 FOR J=1 TO 3
255 LET Z(I,4)=Z(I,4)+Z(I,J)
260 NEXT J
265 NEXT I
270 REM PRINT ALL COMPUTATIONAL RESULTS
280 PRINT
285 PRINT
290 PRINT "INVENTORY VALUE REPORT: FIGURES SHOWN IN DOLLARS"
300 PRINT
310 PRINT "      ","RED","WHITE","BLUE","**TOTAL"
315 PRINT "      ","---","-----","----","-------"
320 PRINT "SMALL",Z(1,1),Z(1,2),Z(1,3),Z(1,4)
325 PRINT "MEDIUM",Z(2,1),Z(2,2),Z(2,3),Z(2,4)
330 PRINT "LARGE",Z(3,1),Z(3,2),Z(3,3),Z(3,4)
335 PRINT "      ","---","-----","----","-------"
340 PRINT "TOTAL",Z(4,1),Z(4,2),Z(4,3),Z(4,4)
800 DATA 1,8,3,20,10,8,6,2,5
810 DATA 1.00,1.25,1.30,1.25,1.50,1.85,1.35,1.65,1.92
999 END

RUN
```

6 / Run and test the program using simple test data

The output from our program follows below. Of course, we must type the system command RUN with no leading line number and a carriage return to initiate the program's execution. Notice that the output directly conforms to the desired specifications. Further note that this output was obtained by reference to each individual cell in the Z(I, J) table, using a numeric pair of values for each possible row-column designation. (This output illustrates that you may always make reference to the data stored in a table, by reference to a specific row-column combination, and that this may be accomplished by using specific subscript numbers, rather than subscript symbols.)

Finally, we may check the accuracy of the computation by evaluating a few of the computer-computed answers by hand. For example, there are 3 units of small blue units in inventory, and the unit value of small blue items is $1.30. Thus, the inventory value for that category is (3) * (1.30), or 3.90, as shown for the small blue category in the output report. You can check other cells in the output similarly.

Although the output figures are shown in dollars and cents, we have not shown dollar signs in the output table. This requirement was not part of our output specification. Although the dollar signs could have been put in the output report using BASIC by inserting a series of "$"; symbols (with the semicolon following as shown), this additional refinement would have complicated our output program lines, and we might have had to experimentally adjust our column headings (line 190) to center them perfectly over the output columns of numbers.

```
INVENTORY VALUE REPORT: FIGURES SHOWN IN DOLLARS

                RED              WHITE            BLUE              **TOTAL
                ---              -----            ----              -------
SMALL            1                10               3.9               14.9
MEDIUM          25                15              14.8               54.8
LARGE            8.1               3.3             9.6               21
                ---              -----            ----              -------
TOTAL           34.1              28.3            28.3               90.7

  999,  NORMAL EXIT FROM PROG.

TIME:     0.350 SEC.
```

In standard BASIC all leading and training zeros are suppressed in the output, and the printed numbers are always left-justified, as above. Without precise format control, which is eliminated in BASIC for simplicity, it is difficult to align decimal points. This shortcoming is not usually a problem in student work, but for professional business work a more complex language would be chosen to provide the needed format control (see Chapters 16 to 18). Some extensions to BASIC do provide format control, although the formatting extensions offered by various suppliers differ greatly. (See Chapter 14 for a selection of such extensions to BASIC.) In particular, IBM's Call/360 BASIC provides full output format control, as shown in Chapter 14.

The six steps of problem analysis and program creation are those suggested in Chapter 10. You will find them useful in the analysis of programs others have written, as well as in the creation of your own programs. You will find a pencil and eraser helpful, particularly at the beginning of the sequence of problem development. Ball-point pen and ink efforts are a waste of time. Also, use plenty of paper and skip lines between your proposed pencil-written program, so that you may make insertions as needed.

Some effort at your pencil and paper planning now will save time and grief at the teletype later, particularly when you plan problems involving subscripted variables and/or conditional branches.

An extension of the inventory problem

Now return to the clothing store problem, just solved. Suppose that our clothing store manager now has three stores, not just one, and that he has inventory records on the item in question (again by size and color) for the stock at all three locations. Assume the unit-value table remains the same.

We now want to repeat the same computations, this time summarizing the detail for all three stores into the same output table we used before. Two tabular alternatives immediately suggest themselves.

Method 1. We could read in three small 3×3 inventory status tables, one for each store. These tables might be called A(I, J), B(I, J), and C(I, J). Then we would add all the corresponding cells of the store inventory tables, and proceed as before with the summarized inventory figures. However, this method requires three FOR/NEXT Loops, one for each table, to read in and accumulate the data if you have one data line per store.

Method 2. It is also possible to read in all of the three-store inventory data on one 3×9 table called X(I, J), as shown below, with each three successive columns representing a different store.

		COLOR								
Col. No.		1	2	3	4	5	6	7	8	9
		R	W	B	R	W	B	R	W	B
	S									
Size	M									
	L									
			Store I			Store II			Store III	

As before, I is the row number and J is the column number. The columns are numbered for easy reference.

With this method of data organization, note that the entire table can be read in using one FOR/NEXT loop, although the corresponding DATA statements would have to show first the total record for smalls, then the total record for mediums, and finally the total record for larges.

With this data read in as shown, the following program segment would produce the required price values for Z(I, J) in one computational line.

```
- - - - - - - - -
100 FOR I = 1 TO 3
110 FOR J = 1 TO 3
120 LET Z(I, J) = (X(I, J) + X(I, J + 3) + X(I, J + 6)) * Y(I, J)
130 NEXT J
140 NEXT I
- - - - - - - - -
```

We assume that the price tables, Y(I, J), is the same as in the previous program. The line numbers shown in the above program segment are arbitrary and do not necessarily agree with those needed nor with those shown in the previous program.

Why might you prefer Method 2 to Method 1 when setting up your problem planning? Also try a less obvious method, but one that has considerable merit.

Method 3. We enter our store inventory data in a table, X(I, J), again of size 3 × 9, but use the stores as the rows and indicate at each column the size-color combination that would be found in the cell of successive squares of a 3 × 3 table corresponding to each row. The size-color combinations shown above each column correspond to the exact order we would get if we read out the original 3 × 3 table in row-column order. With this arrangement, we may now enter our DATA lines, one for each store. We would have to hold to the exact format indicated below:

SIZE-COLOR COMBINATION

	1 SR	2 SW	3 SB	4 MR	5 MW	6 MB	7 LR	8 LW	9 LB
Store 1									
Store 2									
Store 3									

With this scheme, we could still read in the whole table with an I TO 3, J TO 9 FOR/NEXT loop as in Method 2. And, with a little thought, we could make the same computation as we did above for Z(I, J) in the two-line set of computations.

```
- - - - -
100 FOR I = 1 TO 3
110 FOR J = 1 TO 3
120 LET M = M + 1
130 LET Z(I, J) = (X(1, M) + X(2, M) + X(3, M)) * Y(I, J)
140 NEXT I
150 NEXT J
- - - - -
```

The effect of the line

```
120 LET M = M + 1
```

within the inner loop is to convert the subscripts for the 3 × 3 table of Z(I, J) into the subscript M, which runs from 1 to 9, as required to read across the 3 × 9 table, X(I, J). We then use numeric literals, i.e., 1, 2, 3, in the expression of line 130 to sum the store data down each column for each of the 9 size-color combinations. (Use of the index M at line 120 presents a general method of converting a list to a table, should that be necessary in other problems.[5])

[5] Without comment, we offer the following program segment that will convert a 3 × 3 table into a 9-element list. (The program below is the reverse operation of that above and may be generalized as needed.)

```
- - - - - - - -
100 FOR I = 1 TO 3
200 FOR J = 1 TO 3
300 LET X(M + J) = Y(I, J)
400 NEXT J
500 LET M = M + 3
600 NEXT I
- - - - - - - -
```

In this segment Y(I, J) is a 3 × 3 table and X(M + J) is a 9-element list.

Another variation on the inventory problem is handling the input data for the three stores as one long 27-element list, which could then be divided and manipulated as needed, using appropriate subscripting. Other variants are possible, but we will not detail any more of them.[6] The moral of these inventory examples is that many approaches to problem definition and solution usually can be found for a given application. It is up to the programmer to select the approach he wants, then follow it consistently to the end. The orderly six-step approach to problem analysis, definition, and solution will help greatly in eliminating confusion when you move to more complex problems.

PROBLEMS

11-1 The following program is supposed to print the squares of a number that ranges from 1 to 10 in steps of 1. Thus, the output should consist of 10 lines. This is what one student wrote, together with his output.

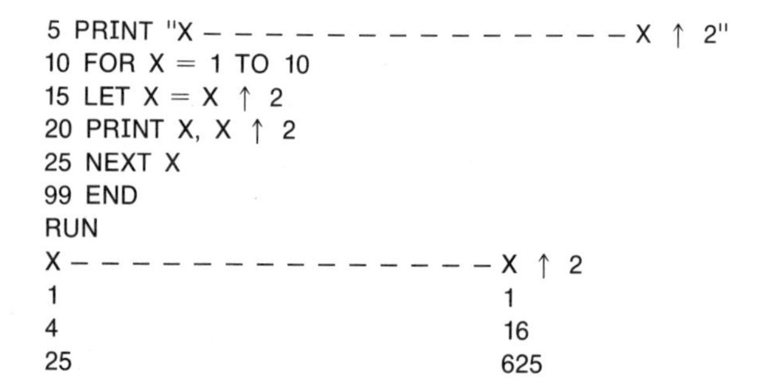

```
5 PRINT "X – – – – – – – – – – – – – – – X ↑ 2"
10 FOR X = 1 TO 10
15 LET X = X ↑ 2
20 PRINT X, X ↑ 2
25 NEXT X
99 END
RUN
X – – – – – – – – – – – – – – – X ↑ 2
1                                1
4                                16
25                               625
```

a. What corrections are needed?

b. Why did the program work at all?

c. How did X get to 25 in the last line of output?

d. What moral can you draw from this example, specifically with regard to alterations of an indexing or control variable (here X) *within* the control loop?

---

[6] One possibility which is not legal in BASIC—BASIC permits only two subscripts to be used in defining a table, e.g., X(I, J), not X(I, J, K)—is to use more subscripts in subscripted variables to define more clearly the classification categories that may be used to describe a given data element. We may use multiple subscripts in FORTRAN. However, using the devices shown in the inventory examples above, we may accomplish the same result with two subscripts, or even one, through proper manipulation of the subscript numbers.

11-2 New York City and New York State retailers are obliged to collect a sales tax on retail purchases. This tax is categorized in the following table:

	Class	Tax[a]
New York City	1	6%
New York State[b]	2	2%
Out of State	3	0%

[a] Percentage applied to gross sales.
[b] New York State except New York City. Point of merchandise receipt determines class.

Assume that data on each purchase at a store are available in the form

```
800 DATA 1, 125.63
```

where the first number to the right of the DATA statement is the customer class, the second is gross sales.

a. Using the customer class as an index, I, write a program in BASIC that will read in each customer record and print out on one line (1) customer class, (2) tax rate applied, (3) gross sales, (4) tax added, and (5) total bill. At the end of the file of customer data, provide for a grand total of columns (3), (4), and (5). (This is a simple list-lookup problem, with direct access to the list via the subscript, I, determined by the class number.)

b. If the customers are not coded by class, what other ways might the computer use to determine the appropriate tax rate?

11-3 Read in record X(I) consisting of four decimal digits (integers) in the range 0 through 9. (A typical record is 8, 0, 2, 5, and it is to be held as a list for future reference.) A file of records is also available in the form Y(I), consisting of five decimal digits (integers) in the range 0 through 9 for cells Y(1) to Y(4). Cell Y(5) may be an integer from 1 to N, where N is the total number of records in the file and acts as a record serial number.

a. Write a BASIC program to print out the serial number of all records in the Y file which exactly match the test record, X(I). By an exact match, we mean that the values X(I) and Y(I) from $I = 1$ to 4 are identical. Make up your own test data and run the problem.

b. Why is it necessary to store permanently the test record for the complete run, although the Y records may be examined one at a time?

11-4 We again return to the tabular data of page 207. (Refer to the last sections on table manipulation if you have trouble with this problem.)

1	2	3	4
5	6	7	8
9	10	11	12

a. For the 3×4 table in question, find the sum of the perimeter values, i.e., those in the outermost rows and columns. Be careful not to duplicate the summation at the corners. (There are at least three ways to solve this problem.)

b. Find the sum of the values for all cells in the table for which the sum of the subscripts (I + J) is *odd.*

c. As an extension of this problem, use the concepts illustrated in Program RANGE, page 204, to devise a program that will find the largest value in the table.

11-5 A clothing store presently keeps inventory records of garments in stock by (1) style, (2) size, and (3) color. At present, this information is kept on three pages, one page for each style. On each page is a 3 × 3 table for that style. The rows represent small, medium, and large respectively; the columns red, white, and blue respectively. In BASIC we may not directly index any specific inventory item by asking for X(I, J, K), where I is the page representing style, J is the row representing size, and K is the column representing color. Only two subscripts are permitted.

To avoid this constraint, a proposal has been made to place all this data on one page in a table consisting of 9 rows and 3 columns, so an inventory item may be obtained by asking for X(I, J), where I is the new row number and J is the old column number of the new consolidated table.

a. How could you reach a specific inventory item if the request were still in the form of style, size, color?

b. Can you devise a method that will allow you to carry the total inventory file as a list of 27 cells? How would you locate the required specific inventory item in this new list, given style, size, and color?

11-6 Many computer applications require that data be ordered in ascending or descending order. The popular term for this operation is "sort," which means to group equal items together. However, if we sort numbers in the order of their value we simultaneously sequence them correctly, so "sort" and "sequence" are often used interchangeably.

A large number of different sorting schemes have been developed, depending upon the equipment available, the character of the lists to be sorted, and the various arrangements that may be desired as output. Two basic methods are illustrated in this problem, with one extension. The approach illustrated is to sort items in computer core memory using the lists and tables that have been discussed in this chapter. Three programs follow, labeled SORT1, SORT2, and SORT3. The purpose of this problem is for you to understand each of the three sort programs and then run SORT3 under conditions different from those given here.

a. In SORT1 sorting is accomplished by first reading in a list of numbers to be sorted. As in Program RANGE, we look for the largest value in the input list, and copy it into the first cell of the second list, which will be used for output. The largest value found is then deleted. In this example this is done by setting it to a very negative number at line 170. We then continue the scan-and-copy procedure until the output list is filled, and then we print the list.

```
50 REM PROGRAM NAME: SORT1 -- SORTS LIST IN DESCENDING ORDER
55 REM BY COPY METHOD USING TWO LISTS
100 DIM X(100),Y(100)
102 REM -----READ DATA-----
```

```
105 READ N
110 FOR I=1 TO N
115 READ X(I)
120 NEXT I
122 REM-----------SORT STARTS----------
125 FOR I=1 TO N
130 LET Y(I) = X(1)
135 LET L=1
137 REM -----COMPARE REMAINDER OF LIST WITH CURRENT HIGH VALUE-----
140 FOR J=2 TO N
145 IF X(J) <= Y(I) THEN 165
150 Y(I) = X(J)
155 REM -----REMEMBER WHERE LARGEST WAS FOUND-----
160 L=J
165 NEXT J
167 REM -----DELETE LARGEST FROM LIST X(I)-----
170 LET X(L)= -9E57
175 NEXT I
177 REM -----PRINT SORTED LIST-----
180 FOR I=1 TO N
185 PRINT Y(I);
190 NEXT I
200 PRINT
210 PRINT
800 DATA 4
805 DATA 1,3,-6,2
999 END

RUN

 3  2  1 -6

  999,  NORMAL EXIT FROM PROG.

TIME:    0.181 SEC.
```

b. SORT2 uses a transposition method and only one list, thereby saving memory. SORT2 also requires less searching, since there are only N(N − 1)/2 comparisons as opposed to N(N − 1) for SORT1. The idea here is to locate the largest value in the input list, and exchange its position with the first value (if the first value is not itself the largest). With the two numeric values changed in position, the search now proceeds from the *second* list position until N − 1 scans have been made across the list. At that point, the smallest value will be in the final position, so that the Nth scan is not needed. In making the swap (which occurs at lines 160 to 175 of the program) a dummy variable, Q, is introduced, so that both values to be swapped will be available at one time. Recall that a substitution statement will wipe out or alter the previous value of a variable to the left of the equals sign, so if we did not use Q and only stated LET X(I) = X(L), then the original value of X(I) would be lost. Obviously we still need it, since the value of X(I) is to be placed in the position where we found X(L). Nothing else is tricky about this program, and, as you can see, it is a somewhat more efficient way to get the job done than SORT1, although perhaps not so obvious an approach.

```
50 REM PROGRAM NAME: SORT2 -- SORTS LIST IN DESCENDING ORDER
55 REM BY SWAP METHOD USING ONE LIST.
57 REM -----READ DATA -----
100 DIM X(100)
105 READ N
110 FOR I=1 TO N
115 READ X(I)
120 NEXT I
122 REM -----SORT STARTS-----
125 FOR I=1 TO N-1
130 LET P= I + 1
135 LET L=I
137 REM -----SCAN UNSORTED LIST FOR LARGEST-----
140 FOR J= P TO N
145 IF X(J) <= X(L) THEN 155
150 LET L=J
155 NEXT J
157 REM -----SWAP LARGEST WITH CURRENT X(I)-----
160 LET Q=X(I)
165 LET X(I)=X(L)
170 LET X(L)=Q
175 NEXT I
177 REM -----PRINT SORTED LIST-----
180 FOR I=1 TO N
185 PRINT X(I);
190 NEXT I
200 PRINT
210 PRINT
800 DATA 4
810 DATA 1,3,-6,2
999 END

RUN


 3  2  1 -6


  999,  NORMAL EXIT FROM PROG.

TIME:     0.176 SEC.
```

c. SORT3 is an extension of SORT2 that permits the user to select the sort "key" that he wants. Thus, if we have a set of records showing (1) salesman code, (2) units sold, and (3) dollars sold, we say that each record contains three data elements, or fields. In the usual case we will get a different sequence of listing, or sort, depending upon the data element we select to consider, since there will in general be no necessary relation between the salesman code and what a man sold either in units or in dollars. Thus, the key indicates what field to consider in the sort. In SORT3 the data are arranged in an N × E table, or file, in which N is the number of records and E is the number of data elements in each record. K is the key desired and is an integer between 1 and E indicating from left to right the column of the table on which the sort is to be performed. For test data we have used four records of three fields each (as defined above for the salesmen), and have chosen to sort the total file (consisting of all the records) on salesman number, K = 1. The method is simply an extension of SORT2, using tabular notation instead of list notation. When the largest sales value has been found the entire corresponding record is swapped with the first record, analogous to the swapping of single data values in SORT2. This operation occurs in lines 165 to 185.

The searching continues as in SORT2 until N − 1 records have been put in order.

Try this program using different data, perhaps with more data elements and a different key. Prove to yourself that it is a *general* program which is specialized by the specification of the parameters N, E, and K. Why is it desirable to write programs in this general form, rather than to be specific for a given application?

```
50 REM PROGRAM NAME: SORT3 -- SORTS N RECORDS OF E-ELEMENTS
55 REM ON SINGLE KEY, K, IN DESCENDING ORDER BY SWAP METHOD.
57 REM -----READ DATA-----
100 DIM X(100,5)
105 READ N,E,K
108 PRINT "SALESMAN-------UNITS SOLD-----DOLLARS SOLD"
110 FOR I = 1 TO N
115 FOR J = 1 TO E
120 READ X(I,J)
125 NEXT J
130 NEXT I
132 REM -----SORT STARTS-----
134 FOR I = 1 TO N-1
135 LET P = I + 1
140 LET L = I
142 REM -----SCAN FOR LARGEST ON SORT KEY, K-----
145 FOR J = P TO N
150 IF X(J,K) <= X(L,K) THEN 160
155 LET L = J
160 NEXT J
162 REM -----SWAP RECORDS, LARGEST KEY VALUE FOR CURRENT-----
165 FOR S = 1 TO E
170 LET Q = X(I,S)
175 LET X(I,S) = X(L,S)
180 LET X(L,S) = Q
185 NEXT S
190 NEXT I
192 REM -----PRINT RECORDS SORTED ON KEY,K-----
200 FOR I = 1 TO N
205 FOR J = 1 TO E
210 PRINT X(I,J),
215 NEXT J
220 PRINT
225 NEXT I
230 PRINT
235 PRINT
800 DATA 4,3,1
805 DATA 1, 500, 250
810 DATA 3, 500,1000
815 DATA 2,1750, 450
820 DATA 4,1000, 500
999 END

RUN

SALESMAN-------UNITS SOLD-----DOLLARS SOLD
 4                1000          500
 3                500           1000
 2                1750          450
 1                500           250


  999,  NORMAL EXIT FROM PROG.
TIME:    0.277 SEC.
```

Note that we have specialized the program to some extent by entering a specific output title at line 108 to identify the data elements. However, this special line occurs just after the parameter read at line 105 and can easily be changed for another program. Thereafter, the program is perfectly general. Note also, following our discussion of DIM statements in this chapter, that DIM(100, 5) at line 100 limits the range of N to 100, and the range of E to 5—unless, of course, the program is redimensioned for greater scope.

A variation of SORT3 may be obtained using the concept of SORT2. Thus, instead of swapping records, we could make a secondary list of indices, one for each record in the file and swap the indices rather than the record. When the *indices* have been sorted using the element values specified by the "key" field selection, the file may be printed out in sorted index order. This process saves much internal data shuffling, and is suggested for an exercise, as well as application.

d. Extensions: In general a file may be sorted on one or *more* keys. Thus, suppose we sorted the salesmen data shown at lines 805 to 820 of SORT3 by units sold. Since two men have sold the same number of units, we may wish to specify the order in which equalities on the "major key" can be sequenced—by the specification of a "minor key," such as dollars sold. It may not be entirely obvious, but if the sort is performed first on the minor key, say K2, and then upon the major key, say, K1, then we will have arranged the salesmen by dollars sold *within* the units sold categories. Thus, the rule is to sort from the least important key to the most important. When this has been done the output will be arranged from the most important to the least important—just the reverse of the sorting keys selected. To convince yourself of this make records on a few 3″ × 5″ cards and sort them manually. Then modify SORT3 to handle a major key and at least one minor key.

You may note that the number of records that may be sorted by the methods suggested here will be limited by the size of core memory (or other random access memory for slower sorts) available to the user in a given application. When very large-scale files are used, alternate sorting media (usually tape) and alternate programming methods are required. The variety of methods available is beyond the scope of this text, but the interested reader may benefit from a comparison of alternate sort methods as well as different methods of file organization. (See R. S. Ledley, *Programming and Utilizing Digital Computers*, New York: McGraw-Hill, 1962, Chapter 11, "Searching, Sorting, Ordering, and Codifying." Most computer handbooks and advanced texts contain comparative chapters of the same type as Ledley's. Look in the index for *merge-sort* or *tape-sort* citations.)

Finally, you may want to consider how SORT3 and its extensions may be made even more general by permitting the output of the sort to be in either *ascending* or *descending* order under the control of an input parameter (say, 1 or 2) read in from the first DATA line (say, via a new variable, D). Note that in the computer the final sorted list appears in descending order as a result of this program. However, there is no reason that the list may not be printed out or otherwise considered from the last element to the first, thereby reversing the order of the sort at output time. This treatment applies to all of the sort programs given here, although it has not been shown in any of them.

To illustrate the program for other sort keys, DATA line 800 is altered to select the second and then the third column of the record as keys:

```
800 DATA 4,3,2

RUN


SALESMAN-------UNITS SOLD-----DOLLARS SOLD
 2              1750           450
 4              1000           500
 1              500            250
 3              500            1000


  999,  NORMAL EXIT FROM PROG.

TIME:    0.277 SEC.
```

```
800 DATA 4,3,3

RUN


SALESMAN-------UNITS SOLD-----DOLLARS SOLD
 3              500            1000
 4              1000           500
 2              1750           450
 1              500            250


  999,  NORMAL EXIT FROM PROG.

TIME:    0.277 SEC.
```

TWELVE

Subroutines and their use

In many programs a block of lines may be needed on more than one occasion. Since the physical repetition of such lines in a program is burdensome, commands have been made available that will electronically "paste in" the required steps when they are called for.

A review of stored and user-defined functions

We have already seen two simple illustrations of this concept, the stored functions and the user-defined functions of Chapter 9. Recall that the compiler provides for the evaluation of stored functions by steps contained within itself. Such steps are "called" from the compiler as needed to evaluate the specified function and to generate the necessary machine language at the time of compilation.

In addition, the user can make up his own functions by means of the DEF statement [e.g., DEF FNA(X) = 1/(1 + X)]. When the function is called for in a program sequence it is evaluated as defined.

It is important to understand that the variables specified as arguments in both stored and user-defined functions are dummy variables, since the function is evaluated using the numeric value of the variable in the calling statement. Thus,

```
LET Y = FNA(W)
```

causes the function FNA to be evaluated using the argument W, and the numeric value of W to be substituted for the dummy variable in the definition. Finally, after a function has been evaluated, the single numeric value passed back to the program, i.e., the numeric value of Y in our example, is the value resulting from the evaluation using W.

In short, once defined by a DEF statement, both stored and user-defined functions are used in an identical manner; and the sequence of control required to evaluate both functions is provided by the compiler and need not concern the user.

A GO TO patch

Suppose a program sequence which has to be executed only once has been forgotten in the initial writing of the program, and there is not a large enough gap in the line numbering to insert the required steps. One way to put them in is with a programming "patch," which may be created with a pair of GO TOs. Thus, if *one* line number is available, we may unconditionally branch off to a set of available line numbers, complete the desired programming sequence, and then unconditionally branch back to the line following the original GO TO.

Schematically, this "patching" could be diagrammed as follows:

Main Program	*Patch*
— — — — — — — — —	500 LET X = A + B
100 PRINT A,B,C,D,E	505 LET Z = B + C
101 GO TO 500	510 LET Q = D/3
102 FOR I = 1 TO E	515 LET R = SQR(D)
— — — — — — — — —	520 GO TO 102

The pair of GO TOs cause the insertion of lines 500 through 515 between lines 100 and 102. This, of course, is a very handy method of fixing defective programs without renumbering the lines, and it is a desirable approach when the patched-in segment is to be referenced only once.

Subroutines

On the other hand, if the program segment is to be inserted in a number of places (without being rewritten several times) a pair of GO TOs will not work, because the final GO TO in the patch must refer to a *specific* line number, which in this instance would not be constant, but would vary with the origin of the initiating GO TO. In such cases, we resort to a subroutine pair of statements: GOSUB and RETURN. A subroutine consists of a sequence of BASIC statements which may be used to accept a number of variables for evaluation and to return one or more (or no) values to the main program. Except for the few exclusions noted hereafter, any legal BASIC statement may be used in a subroutine block.

The GOSUB statement has the general form

line number GOSUB line number

and, like the GO TO command, it causes the transfer of the program sequence to the second line number mentioned. The statements following the stated line number are then executed in order until the sequential operation encounters a RETURN statement, which has the general form

line number RETURN

at which point the sequence automatically shifts back to the *line number immediately following the initiating GOSUB statement.* That is, when a GOSUB statement is encountered, the computer remembers the line number from which the GOSUB was initiated. The next RETURN is therefore able to transfer control back to that line number plus one (or to the next available line in numerical sequence).

The following program segment is equivalent to the previous GO TO in its execution:

Main Program	*Subroutine*
- - - - - - - - - - - -	500 LET X = A + B
100 PRINT A,B,C,D,E	505 LET Z = B + C
101 GOSUB 500	510 LET Q = D/3
102 FOR I = 1 TO E	515 LET R = SQR(D)
- - - - - - - - - - - -	520 RETURN
- - - - - - - - - - - -	

Before continuing, we should note the similarities between the cases just shown.

In both the patch and the subroutine, the variables in the main program are passed to the inserted lines of programming. That is, the numeric values of the variables at the time of the GO TO patch or the GOSUB jump are moved to the subsequent computations and, of course, must be defined before those computations can be made.

The distinction between the subroutine and the patch is that the subroutine may be called as often as necessary, because the compiler-generated machine codes will initiate the last equivalent GO TO as required by the RETURN statement. Thus, the subroutine GOSUB/RETURN pair of statements comes into its own *only* when the program segment referenced by the GOSUB statement is used more than once in a given program to call the same block, or group, of program steps for an electronic paste-up.

Also note the distinction between a GOSUB/RETURN and either the stored or user-defined functions, just reviewed. Although all three may be "called" many times in a given program, the subroutine in BASIC does not use the argument idea, so the variable names that appear in a BASIC subroutine must be carefully chosen so they do not undesirably duplicate those in the main program (or vice versa). Except for this point, the subroutine provides the most general method of inserting program steps "on call."

A GOSUB application

Here is a simple example of the GOSUB/RETURN pair in action. In the following program segments, three READ statements occur. In each READ, we are interested in detecting if variable C has a numeric value of less than 100 and, if so, in printing out a statement to that effect, together with the line number of the READ statement which found that result. Since the test will be applied in different parts of the program, we use the subroutine approach. For brevity, only a program segment is shown; and for clarity, although the same program segment could be accomplished with fewer commands using a FOR/NEXT operation (see next problem), the complete detail appears here.

Main Program	*Subroutine*
- - - - -	
200 LET N = 1	500 IF C >= 100 THEN 515
210 READ A,B,C	510 PRINT "C <= LINE", 200 + 10 * N
215 GOSUB 500	515 LET N = N + 1
220 READ A,B,C	520 RETURN
225 GOSUB 500	
230 READ A,B,C	
235 GOSUB 500	
- - - - -	

The solid arrows indicate GOSUB transfers, the dashed arrows RETURNS. (Note that the transfers and returns from the main program to the subroutine at the right initiate and complete three patches with one GOSUB/RETURN subroutine, instead of three pairs of GO TOs.)

Each GOSUB command must be associated with at least one RETURN command. The first RETURN command encountered by a GOSUB takes control, so that you may have more than one RETURN which can terminate a subroutine, if conditional branches select the desired RETURN statement. However, in such a case your RETURN would still be to the appropriate line, since the compiler keeps track of GOSUB branching.

The combination of GOSUBs and FOR/NEXT commands

Another variation on the screening example just given follows. Program SCREEN tests incoming data values, then indicates by count those less than 5 or more than 10.

```
LIST


2 REM PROGRAM SCREEN -- REJECTS DATA NOT IN
4 REM RANGE 5 TO 10 INCLUSIVE.
6 DIM X(10)
10 READ N
15 FOR I=1 TO N
20 READ X(I)
25 IF X(I) >=5 THEN 35
30 GOSUB 500
35 IF X(I) <=10 THEN 45
40 GOSUB 510
45 NEXT I
47 STOP
50 REM ==================SUBROUTINE=============
500 LET J=1
505 GO TO 515
510 LET J=2
515 ON J GO TO 520,530
520 PRINT "DATA ELEMENT ";I;"<5."
525 RETURN
530 PRINT "DATA ELEMENT ";I;">10."
535 RETURN
800 DATA 5
805 DATA 1,9,6,26,7
999 END

RUN

DATA ELEMENT  1 <5.
DATA ELEMENT  4 >10.

   47,  NORMAL EXIT FROM PROG.

TIME:    0.149 SEC.
```

Note in Program SCREEN that line 515 shows the computed GO TO, mentioned in Chapter 10. Depending on the current value of J, which may be 1 or 2, the branch proceeds from line 515 to line 520 or 530, respectively, the first and second numbers given after GO TO.

The GOSUB selected by the program depends upon the incoming data. Either GOSUB 500 or GOSUB 510 or neither may be used for a given set of input values.

Also note four other points:

1. The RETURN at line 525 refers to GOSUB 500, or line 30, and the RETURN at line 535 refers to GOSUB 510, or line 40. (Trace the processing progression for several numbers to check this.)

2. When either subroutine is executed, the current value of I is passed to the subroutine. Neither GOSUB returns a numeric value to the main program: Variable I is printed, but not altered.

3. The GOSUB is used within a FOR/NEXT loop and then branches out and returns. This operation is normally illegal. But since the GOSUB is not encountered before the FOR/NEXT loop is defined in line 15, the branch out and back can be accommodated.[1] Obviously, you should not unwittingly make any computations in the GOSUB/RETURN sequence that would disturb formal progression of the FOR/NEXT's index, I. Thus, to insert a line such as

```
522 LET I = I + 1
```

would alter the index, I, after each test of X that resulted in a value of less than 5. With this error, the reading would stop prematurely (before 100 cases) and the X(I) values read would be indexed inconsistently. (A similar error has been illustrated in the FOR/NEXT use of Problem 11-1.)

4. The command STOP at line 47 is necessary so that the subroutine section will be skipped after the Nth, or last, data element has been processed. If STOP were omitted, the program would indicate the last number as less than 5, regardless of the previous printout or the last number's numeric value.

Nested GOSUBs

One GOSUB may logically call another, in which case we have nesting similar to that used with FOR/NEXT loops. Figure 12.1 shows one possibility in block form.

[1] Most BASIC systems also permit you to insert a patch within a FOR/NEXT loop. The error is to branch into such a loop before its index and limit have been defined.

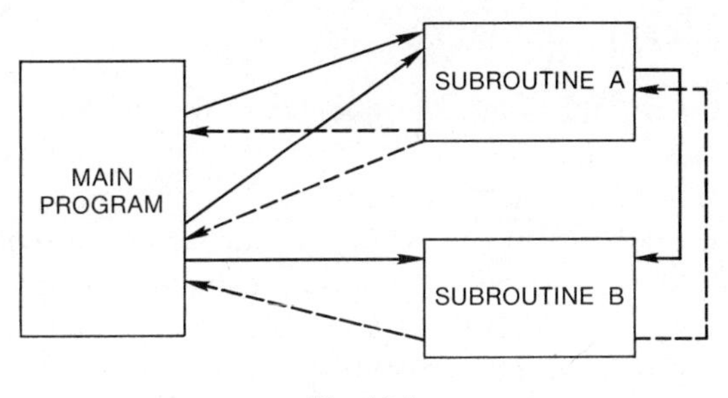

Fig. 12.1

The main program calls subroutine A twice and subroutine B once. However, subroutine A may call subroutine B one or more times. The effect is multiplicative (like nesting FOR/NEXT loops). As shown in Figure 12.1, subroutine B will be used three times, subroutine A only twice.

You must keep track of the current status of all variables as your computation progresses, because the variables passed from one subroutine to another (and back to the main program operations) will be logically interrelated by the structure of the GOSUB nesting used. In particular, the same variable may appear in one or more subroutines as well as in the main program. All of these computations work in concert in BASIC, and either a subroutine computation or a main program computation may affect your results.

The progression of a computation using nested subroutines may be difficult to trace. If you use a subroutine developed by another be careful to avoid possible duplication and inconsistent use of variable names when inserting the borrowed routine in your BASIC program.[2]

Finally, no subroutine in BASIC may be nested so that it calls itself. That is, "recursion" of subroutines is not allowed (see Figure 12.2). The reason for this constraint is clear: We do not want to create "infinite loops of action," the bugaboo of the programmer. All programs must come to an end, and the sooner the better!

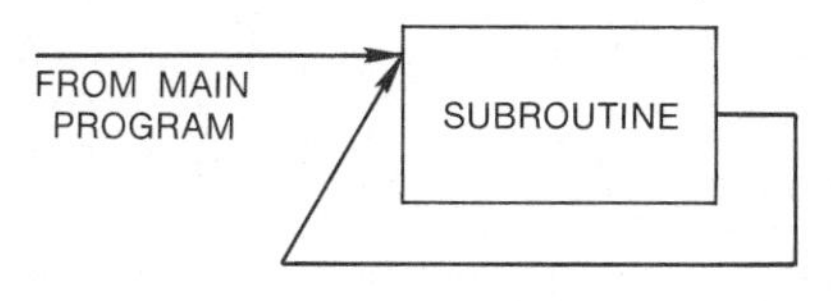

Fig. 12.2

[2] BASIC does not use the argument concept in its GOSUB/RETURN subroutine operations, as it does in its stored and user-defined functions. Other languages use such concepts, so that their subroutines can be more general. In FORTRAN, for example, variable names are specified at the time of a subroutine call, as they are in a BASIC stored or user-defined function call. This FORTRAN approach, compared to BASIC, produces more flexibility.

Two main uses of subroutines

You will use subroutines most frequently to introduce repetitive mathematical computations into a program when those computations cannot be reduced to a single line, as required by the simple user-defined function, or when more than one input number would be required for the numeric evaluation. (Remember that only a single argument can be used in BASIC stored or user-defined functions.) Subroutines are also used to introduce repetitive data processing procedures, such as page numbering, line counting, and spacing into a given procedure.

1 / Mathematical subroutines

Consider the problem of finding the greatest common denominator (GCD) of three numbers, represented by A, B, and C. For example, if A is 18, B is 21, and C is 27, the largest number that will divide into those three figures (without producing a fractional part) is 3, since six 3's are 18, seven 3's are 21, and nine 3's are 27. Program GCD uses a subroutine to evaluate first the numbers indicated by A and B and then the third number, indicated by C. The method used to find the greatest common denominator is an algorithm formulated by the mathematician Euclid.[3] The BASIC stored function INT(X) used in Program GCD and its explanation, recall, discards the fractional value of a number or expression to provide an integer result, e.g., INT(3/2) = INT(1.5) = 1.

```
10 PRINT "A","B","C","GCD"
20 READ A,B,C
30 LET X=A
40 LET Y=B
50 GOSUB 200
60 LET X=G
70 LET Y=C
80 GOSUB 200
90 PRINT A,B,C,G
100 GO TO 20
200 LET Q=INT(X/Y)
```

[3] A step-by-step procedure which guarantees a solution is called an "algorithm" after the ninth-century Arabian arithmetician al-Khuwarizmi, who wrote on how to solve numerical problems in a cook-book manner. An algorithm, which corresponds in business applications to a data-processing procedure, is the opposite of a "heuristic" (which means roughly *"learn by doing,"* from the Greek), that is, a method which is likely, but not guaranteed, to produce the desired results. Although both approaches have their place in computer programming and may be programmed, the programmer must first know *how* to solve the problem at hand before he can direct the machine to help him.

```
210 LET R=X-Q*Y
220 IF R=0 THEN 300
230 LET X=Y
240 LET Y=R
250 GO TO 200
300 LET G=Y
310 RETURN
320 DATA 60,90,120
330 DATA 38456,64872,98765
340 DATA 32,384,72
350 DATA 18,27,21
999 END

RUN

A              B              C              GCD
 60             90             120            30
 38456          64872          98765          1
 32             384            72             8
 18             27             21             3

    20,  PROGRAM OUT OF DATA

TIME:     0.187 SEC.
```

To understand Program GCD, we need to review (1) how and why Euclid's algorithm, or step-by-step method of problem solution, works and (2) the detailed numerical progression of Program GCD, which implements the solution. We proceed in that order (see Figure 12.3).

Euclid's method. Follow the mathematical argument below, which although presented formally is simple. The argument, which is Euclid's, proceeds by a series of simple propositions to the desired result: the method will work in all cases.

A. Given two integer numbers, X and Y, of which Y is the smaller, a common denominator of both X and Y must also be an integer, and cannot be greater than Y itself. (By definition, a greatest common denominator, or GCD, will be the largest common factor of both X and Y.)

B. If Y is in fact a common denominator of both itself and X then

$$Q = INT(X/Y) > 0 \quad (1)$$

and

$$R = X - Q * Y = X - (INT(X/Y) * Y) = 0 \quad (2)$$

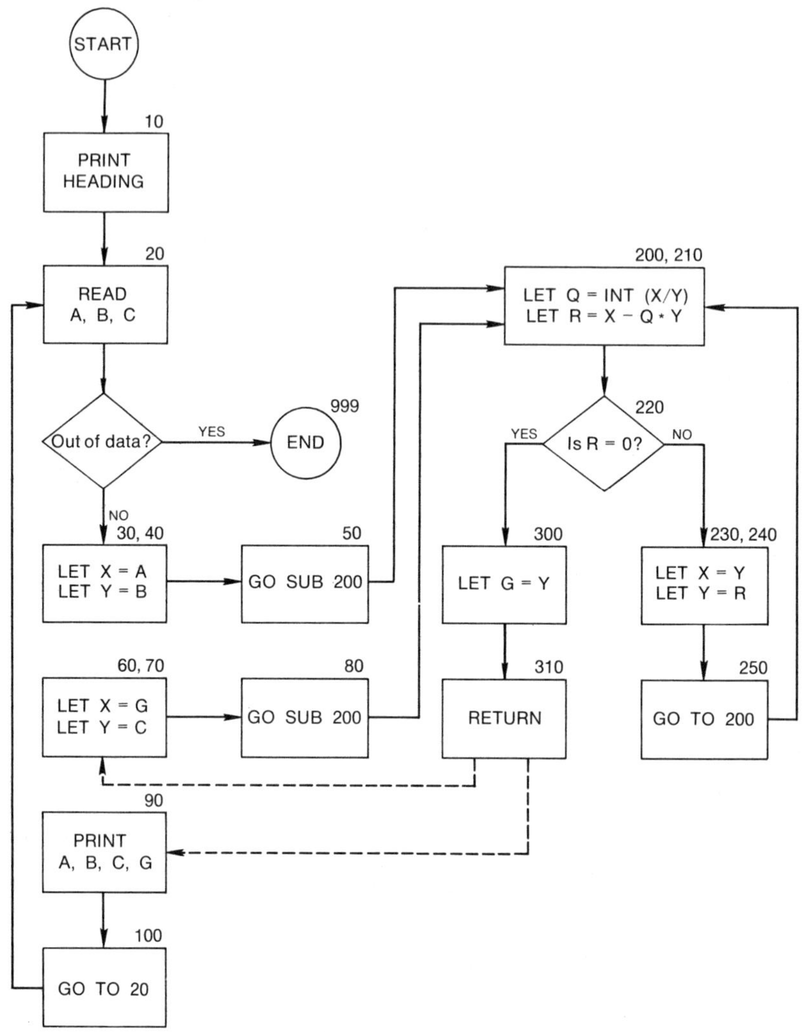

Fig. 12.3

C. If $Q = 0$ in the first test above, then Y is greater than X, so the two numerical values for X and Y should be reversed before continuation of the process.

D. If $Q > 0$ and $R = 0$, then Y is the greatest common denominator of X and Y, and the search may stop.

E. If $Q > 0$ and $R \neq 0$, then Y is not the greatest common denominator of X. However, by a simple rearrangement of the terms in (2) we see that

$$X = R + (Q * Y) = R + (\text{INT}(X/Y) * Y) \qquad (3)$$

F. If we can now prove that R is a common factor of Y, then (3) could be rewritten as

$$X = (R + Q) * Y = R * (1 + Q * Y') \tag{4}$$

where Y′ is another common factor of Y (e.g., $Y = R * Y'$).

G. Further, if R is a common factor of Y, it is also a common factor of X, by virtue of (4), since we have clearly factored X in factoring Y. [Equation (4) simply states that X = X.]

H. Moreover, R is the *largest feasible integer* that could be a common factor of both X and Y. Because of the 1 within the parentheses on the right-hand side of (4), any greater increase in R would cause the numeric value within the parentheses to become a noninteger, in violation of the initial definition in (A). That is, all factors of the numbers X and Y must be integers to be feasible, and R is the largest feasible integer that will preserve the required relationship. Thus, R is the largest feasible candidate for a greatest common denominator.

I. If we can prove R to be a common factor of Y, we have solved the problem of obtaining the GCD of X and Y. The way to prove that R is this GCD is to repeat computations (1) and (2), replace the largest number (the former X) by the present value of Y and the smaller number (the former value of Y) by the present value of R, and continue.

J. If R passes test (2), it is the GCD. If R does not meet the test, we should then continue to repeat the argument of steps (E) through (I) until a newly defined value of R does pass test (2). That is, we will continue to search for successively smaller common factors of Y until we find a value of R that will satisfy condition (2). At that point, the last value of R tried will be the GCD of both the original values of X and Y, by an extension of the argument proposed above.

K. Having found the GCD of two numbers, we can now proceed to find the GCD of more than two numbers by a reapplication of the process, using the "new" number as the initial "larger" test value (the new value of X) and the current GCD, R, as the smaller test value (the new value of Y) in tests (1) and (2). This procedure, by just extending the initial argument, eventually will produce the GCD for all the integers considered.

L. Finally, note that the GCD for a set of N numbers must be an integer less than or equal to the smallest number in the set, and also a number greater than or equal to the integer 1, which will divide commonly into any other integer.

Steps A to L complete the formal argument, but two numerical examples may aid in the transition to the program application. All that Program GCD does is to implement the mathematical procedure outlined above.

Example 1	*Example 2*
X = 21	X = 21
Y = 18	Y = 19
- - - - - - - - - - -	- - - - - - - - - - -
Q = INT(21/18) = 1	Q = INT(21/19) = 1
R = 21 − (1 * 18) = 3	R = 21 − (1 * 19) = 2
- - - - - - - - - - -	- - - - - - - - - - -
Q = INT(18/3) = 6	Q = INT(19/2) = 8
R = 18 − (6 * 3) = 0	R = 19 − (8 * 2) = 1
- - - - - - - - - - -	- - - - - - - - - - -
Thus, the GCD is 3	Q = INT(2/1) = 2
	R = 2 − (2 * 1) = 0
	- - - - - - - - - - -
	Thus, the GCD is 1

Before detailing Program GCD, however, let us consider why the method Euclid proposed for finding a greatest common denominator for two or more numbers is beneficial, as opposed to a more obvious approach which consists of making tests (1) and (2) and hoping that X will have the common denominator Y. In this obvious, or "brute-force," method, if Y is not a common denominator of X, then the greatest common denominator must be some number between Y and 1. And we would have to successively decrement Y by 1 (or subtract the integer 1 from Y at each new trial), repeat tests (1) and (2), and stop when we came to the first success. This first successful number would be the GCD of both X and Y.

However, this brute-force method is short-sighted, lengthy, and inefficient, as compared to the approach proposed by Euclid, which *jumps to the next feasible alternative at each step*, rather than running through all the possibilities. The relative disparity between the two approaches increases when X and Y are very large. (Consider the second numerical illustration computed by program GCD!)

The moral to the exercise you have just completed is that a good method of computation is highly desirable. Such an algorithm can greatly multiply the effectiveness of a computer's computational capacity by eliminating unnecessary computations.

Indeed, many scientific computations and many business applications computationally will be unfeasible unless there is available an algorithm that screens out all impossible or unfeasible combinatorial cases.[4]

---

[4] For further illustration of this point, see Program MAZE in Chapter 15. Note in that program's description the possible combinatorial alternatives generated by a chess game. In business the same sort of impossible situations can occur. An algorithm can convert a brute-force approach to problem solution (which may fail either economically or technically) into a feasible and efficient problem solution, and algorithmic development is an advanced specialty in the computer field.

Now turn to the second point we wish to make in the example of Program GCD. You should be able to trace the numeric progression of the variables in a given program in order to understand the program fully. Further, your understanding of the numeric progression of a program's variables will be essential in your later diagnosis of a program's logical difficulties, should your ideas or your implementation of them fail to work. (Remember that you can have the computer trace the numeric progression of your program's variables automatically by inserting a number of superfluous PRINT commands at significant places in your program. Having satisfied yourself that your program works in detail, you can then remove the extra PRINT commands from your final program by typing in the line numbers of each of the to-be-deleted PRINT statements with a carriage return for each. This action will immediately erase the extra detail, as outlined in Chapter 7.)

Now turn to Table 12.1, which shows the numeric progression of the variables in Program GCD for the three numbers A = 60, B = 90, C = 120. The final answer is obviously 30, but we want to trace how we get that result using the Euclid algorithm, as implemented in Program GCD.

In Table 12.1, we show the variable names and their values in sequential succession on the left. The line number which produces the numerical result to the left is shown on the right. Further, at each branch from normal sequence, and at each test, we also show the detail necessary to follow or trace what happens. To confirm your understanding of this important point and to build your skill in its application, create tables similar to Table 12.1 for the other numeric examples computed in Program GCD.

TABLE 12.1

Variable Trace for First Numeric Case of Program GCD

	Line number
A = 60, B = 90, C = 120	
X = 60	30
Y = 90	40
GOSUB 200 FROM LINE 50	
Q = INT(60/90) = 0	200
R = 60 − 0 * 90 = 60	210
TEST AT 220 FALSE	
X = 90	230
Y = 60	240
GO TO 200	
Q = INT(90/60) = 1	200
R = 90 − 1 * 60 = 30	210
TEST AT 220 FALSE	
X = 60	230
Y = 30	240
GO TO 200	
Q = INT(60/30) = 2	200
R = 60 − 2 * 30 = 0	210

```
     TEST AT 220 TRUE, SO 300
G = 30 (FIRST GCD FOUND)                                      300
     RETURN TO INITIATING GOSUB AT 50
X = 30                                                         60
Y = 120                                                        70
     GOSUB 200 FROM LINE 80
Q = INT(30/120) = 0                                           200
R = 30 - 0 * 120 = 30                                         210
     TEST AT 220 FALSE
X = 120                                                       230
Y = 30                                                        240
     GO TO 200
Q = INT(120/30) = 4                                           200
R = 120 - 4 * 30 = 0                                          210
     TEST AT 220 TRUE, SO 300
G = 30 (FINAL GCD FOUND)                                      300
     RETURN TO INITIATING GOSUB AT 80
PRINT 60, 90, 120, 30                                          90
     END OF FIRST CASE
```

2 / *Data processing subroutines*

Subroutines are also used in data processing. In business applications, which are essentially simple computations, the difficulty lies, among other things, in the production of suitable output reports that anybody can read. The editing of output reports from the results of a given computation is not BASIC's strong point, but it can be done. We now show how a very simple computer language like BASIC can be used to produce a commercial output report that may run to any number of pages depending upon the length of the output of a given computation (shown in sample form at lines 230 through 260 of the following program to generate 80 lines of output).

Program FORMS provides titles, running heads, and column headings, as well as page numbers, spacing, and computational output in an artistic and commercially acceptable form. You will find ample documentation in the program, using REM statements, as described in Chapter 10.

The general procedure is as follows. The typewriter page—as well as a computer high-speed printer page—is normally spaced at 6 lines per inch, or 66 printed lines per 11-inch page. If you are going to generate a Teletype output report you should plan to print your data and any headings that may be needed to explain your work on a standard sheet, usually 66 lines long. (The continuous roll used by the student Teletype can be handled this way by Program FORMS.)

Note that Program FORMS has many subroutines. The subroutine at line 6100 inserts appropriate column heads on each page. The subroutine at line 6200 counts lines used in the printing of column heads, main titles, spaces, and program results. At the end of the page subroutine 6200 passes control to the NEXT PAGE ROUTINE subroutine at line 6300. The whole process continues until the end of the computation, at which point we make a direct branch (a GO TO) to line 6400, the END OF PAGE ROUTINE (which is used only once, at the last page, and need not be a GOSUB) to complete the report.

Segments of the first and second page titles with a few of the test computations and the final lines of the last page (in this example the second page) show how the program works using the test sample at lines 230 through 260.

```
10 REM PROGRAM FORMS-- TESTS FORMS CONTROLS SUBROUTINES
20 REM (INCLUDED HERE). INITIALIZE PAGE AS FIRST PROGRAM STEP.
30 REM WHEN USING SUBROUTINES, P IS PAGE, K IS LINE COUNT
40 REM SAMPLE DATA GENERATED BY LINES 230-260.
60 LET P=1
70 REM SUBROUTINE STARTS FIRST PAGE
80 GOSUB 6300
90 REM THE MAIN PROGRAM FOLLOWS
95 REM PRINT ANY DESIRED MAIN HEAD PAGE 1. GOSUB 6200
96 REM AFTER EACH PRINT.
100 PRINT"                         THE FOLLOWING TEST SHOWS"
101 GOSUB 6200
102 PRINT"                     ALIGNMENT OF COLUMNS ON EACH PAGE"
103 GOSUB 6200
130 REM NOW DOUBLE SPACE TO HEADING OF TEXT FIRST PAGE
140 PRINT
150 GOSUB 6200
160 PRINT
170 GOSUB 6200
172 REM NOW USE GOSUB 6100 TO INTRODUCE COLUMN HEADS
175 GOSUB 6100
220 REM SAMPLE COMPUTATIONS NOW START. NOTE GOSUB 6200 AT EACH PRINT.
230 FOR I=1 TO 80
240 PRINT 1234,1234,1234,1234,1234
250 GOSUB 6200
260 NEXT I
270 REM NOW PERFORM LAST PAGE ROUTINE
280 GO TO 6400
290REM------------------SUBROUTINES------------------------------------
6100 REM RUNNING COLUMN HEAD ROUTINE, REPLACE LINE 6102 AS NEEDED.
6102 PRINT 1,2,3,4,5
6104 PRINT
6106 LET K=K+2
6108 RETURN
6200 REM LINE COUNT AND TEST ROUTINE
6210 LET K=K+1
6220 IF K<62 THEN 6270
6230 REM-------------END OF PAGE ENCOUNTERED------------------------
6240 GOSUB 6300
6270 RETURN
6300 REM NEXT PAGE ROUTINE
6310 REM MAKES PAGE DIVISION, ADVANCES, PRINTS PAGE NUMBER
6320 PRINT
6330 PRINT
6340 PRINT
6350 PRINT"-------------------------------------------------------"
6362 PRINT
6364 PRINT
6366 REM CHANGE RUNNING HEAD IN NEXT LINE AS DESIRED.
6368 PRINT"FORMS CONTROL TEST USING SUBROUTINES              PAGE ";P
6370 PRINT
6372 PRINT
6374 LET K=6
```

```
6376 REM INSERT COLUMN HEADS IF P>1
6378 IFP=1 THEN 6382
6380 GOSUB 6100
6382 LET P=P+1
6399 RETURN
6400 REM END OF PAGE ROUTINE (USED LAST PAGE ONLY).
6410 FOR Q=K TO 64
6420 PRINT
6430 NEXT Q
6450 PRINT"                                                  END OF JOB"
6460 PRINT"--------------------------------------------------------------"
9999 END
```

RUN

```
------------------------------------------------------------


FORMS CONTROL TEST USING SUBROUTINES                      PAGE  1


                    THE FOLLOWING TEST SHOWS
                 ALIGNMENT OF COLUMNS ON EACH PAGE


 1               2               3               4               5

 1234            1234            1234            1234            1234
 1234            1234            1234            1234            1234
 1234            1234            1234            1234            1234
 1234            1234            1234            1234            1234
 1234            1234            1234            1234            1234
 1234            1234            1234            1234            1234
 1234            1234            1234            1234            1234
 1234            1234            1234            1234            1234
 1234            1234            1234            1234            1234
 1234            1234            1234            1234            1234
 1234            1234            1234            1234            1234
 1234            1234            1234            1234            1234
 1234            1234            1234            1234            1234
 1234            1234            1234            1234            1234
 1234            1234            1234            1234            1234
 1234            1234            1234            1234            1234
 1234            1234            1234            1234            1234
 1234            1234            1234            1234            1234
 1234            1234            1234            1234            1234
 1234            1234            1234            1234            1234
 1234            1234            1234            1234            1234
 1234            1234            1234            1234            1234
 1234            1234            1234            1234            1234
 1234            1234            1234            1234            1234
 1234            1234            1234            1234            1234
 1234            1234            1234            1234            1234
 1234            1234            1234            1234            1234
 1234            1234            1234            1234            1234
 1234            1234            1234            1234            1234
 1234            1234            1234            1234            1234
 1234            1234            1234            1234            1234
 1234            1234            1234            1234            1234
 1234            1234            1234            1234            1234
 1234            1234            1234            1234            1234
 1234            1234            1234            1234            1234
 1234            1234            1234            1234            1234
 1234            1234            1234            1234            1234
 1234            1234            1234            1234            1234
 1234            1234            1234            1234            1234
```

```
1234          1234          1234          1234          1234
1234          1234          1234          1234          1234
1234          1234          1234          1234          1234
1234          1234          1234          1234          1234
1234          1234          1234          1234          1234
1234          1234          1234          1234          1234
1234          1234          1234          1234          1234
1234          1234          1234          1234          1234
1234          1234          1234          1234          1234
1234          1234          1234          1234          1234
1234          1234          1234          1234          1234
```

The last dashed line above indicates the end of the first page of FORMS test output. We now show below only a sample of page two of this output. Note that lines 230 and 240 of the program call for 80 lines of test output, the 1234's shown. The first page terminates after 50 test output lines so a lower margin may be provided. The running heads, page number, and column headings in addition to the next 30 lines of test output (although all are not shown here) appear on the second page. Thereafter program lines 6400–6460 generate enough white space to complete the page, print "END OF JOB", and the terminating line. Only one dashed line will divide pages 1 and 2, although two are shown here for clarity. Further, the actual termination of page 2 is not shown.

```
FORMS CONTROL TEST USING SUBROUTINES                    PAGE  2

1             2             3             4             5

1234          1234          1234          1234          1234
1234          1234          1234          1234          1234
1234          1234          1234          1234          1234
1234          1234          1234          1234          1234
1234          1234          1234          1234          1234
1234          1234          1234          1234          1234
1234          1234          1234          1234          1234
1234          1234          1234          1234          1234
1234          1234          1234          1234          1234
1234          1234          1234          1234          1234
1234          1234          1234          1234          1234
1234          1234          1234          1234          1234
1234          1234          1234          1234          1234
1234          1234          1234          1234          1234
```

The purpose of this FORMS example is not only to show the possibility of controlling output report format in a reasonable manner with BASIC but also to indicate that the same structural principles of subroutine and unconditional branching may be used to produce a commercially useful report in a very simple computer language. (Obviously the test computations shown are only for generating a check of the FORMS control line count, the critical subroutine at line 6200. To use this same program in other applications you would have to change only the main report headings, the running heads, and the column headings, as indicated by the REM statements in each subroutine, and provide a GOSUB 6200 after each PRINT to make the line count for your alternate program, to be inserted at lines 230 through 6099.)

If you tried to write Program FORMS without subroutines you would need many more programming lines than in the program duplicated above.

Program SCREEN and Program FORMS illustrate both input and output editing, respectively. In commercial data processing programs you will find that 80 percent of a program's lines may be devoted to these two functions: (1) input editing to make sure the data used by your program is acceptable and (2) output editing to produce reports that are easy to read.

The sixth essential program command

In Chapter 6 we outlined the *six* essential features of any computer programming language that you should learn and began our discussion of appropriate commands. We have now come, in this chapter, to the last command, and you should realize that the subroutine can be the most powerful as well as the most complicated programming command.

Can you follow a subroutine's digressions? Can you give the numeric value, or the output display that will be produced at each stage of the programs you now see? If you cannot, please go back and review the material. Then work the following problems on your computer terminal before you go on to the next chapter.

PROBLEMS

12-1 Create a program that may be used as a subroutine which will generate the factorial of a given number N and supply that result F(N) to the main program upon request. Recall that the factorial of a number N is defined as

$$1 * 2 * 3 * 4 * \cdots * (N - 1) * N$$

and that the factorial of $N = 0$ is, by definition, equal to 1, as is 1!, due to the formula above. (The symbol ! is used in most texts to indicate factorial computation.) Limit the range of your computation to $N = 40$ to avoid excessively large numbers.

12-2 Compare the advantages that may occur from using the one-shot computation described above to those which might result from the computation of all the factorials from 0! through 40!, which could be stored in a list for later reference in a program. (In this case you would need to dimension your proposed list. Suppose you dimensioned it DIM F(41). How would this dimensioning affect the possibility of running a large program, as compared to the one-shot computation?)

12-3 The present value, P, of an amount A(N), due in N years at an interest (or discount) rate, R, is

At interest compounded annually
P = A(N)/((1 + R) ↑ N)
And at interest compound Q times a year
P = A(N)/((1 + R/Q) ↑ (N * Q))
For example, if $1000 is due in 10 years at 6% yearly, but compounded monthly, A(10) is $1000, R is .06, Q is 12, and, of course, N is 10 in the second formula above.

a. Write a general program to compute present value for both cases by proper specification of the parameters.

b. Extend the program and compute the present value of the future payments due as follows, using 6% annual interest.

Year	*$ Amount Due*
1	1000
2	1250
3	1500
4	1500
5	2000
6	1750
7	1600
8	1000

c. Repeat the above computation, but now use monthly compounding at 6% annual interest. Compare the results of (B) and (C). (In both examples above, display the appropriate titles with your output answers.) You can, of course, perform computations (B) and (C) in one program. The present value of the total payment stream in each case is *the accumulated sum* of each future yearly payment brought back to present time using the present value formula. Use a subroutine in (B) and (C) to compute the present value of future yearly payments, and use the main program to accumulate the sum, as well as to read in the necessary data and to print out the results.

d. Could you use a BASIC stored function or user-defined function to get the results in (B) and (C)?

e. If the future payments A(N) were all equal to $1000 for each of the 8 years, could you employ a user-defined function in BASIC to get your result?

12-4 Refer to Program GCD in this chapter. The text shows the progression of the variables in the program as the subroutines are called for one case.

a. Trace the numeric progression of the variables for A = 32, B = 384, C = 72.

b. Repeat the above, but this time for A = 18, B = 27, C = 21, the progression which produced the greatest common denominator 3, as shown in the last line of Program GCD's illustrative output.

c. Why is it important that you know how to trace the numeric progression of your proposed computations in detail?

12-5 Devise an alternate program to give the same result as Program GCD, which finds the greatest common denominator of four numbers. Why would you call Program GCD, as based on Euclid's method, a good algorithm? If you have several methods to solve and then program a given problem (many are usually available) how would you pick the one to use? Would your choice necessarily be the shortest solution, considering your own time and the cost of present computational services?

12-6 Recall the clothing inventory problem in Chapter 11, first illustrated in Program INVENTORY. Also recall the report-generating program in this chapter, Program FORMS. Now consider the following. Our clothing store manager has not one item stocked at one store, as in the illustrative program, but stocks 1000 different items in each of three stores; each item is graded in sizes small, medium, and large, and, for simplicity, in the colors red, white, and blue. We have available the stock status at each of the three stores for each of the 1000 items, and also the prices for each of these items, classified by size and color.[6] You may assume any input data form you wish.

a. How could you piece together appropriate READ statements, what you know about Program INVENTORY and its variants, and modifications of Program FORMS to produce a detailed inventory report for each of the 1000 items with the output for each item in the exact specifications shown in Program INVENTORY for one item at one store? (Do not write this program but outline the steps you would use.)

b. If you were a data processing consultant to the store manager, would you recommend that he buy such a report, which would contain 1000 detailed tables, or would you suggest another alternative? Why? What sort of a reporting alternative would you suggest?

c. Suppose the store manager's problem is not to get a summary report with all the detail, but to be able to make spot inquiries on inventory status by item, size, and color, at any of his stores. What sort of computing equipment and data organization would he need to get this information (1) if he only needed the answer in one week, (2) if he needed the answer in five seconds? Which response time would be the most expensive in terms of equipment, programming, and data input?

---

[6] In the specifications for this problem there are 27,000 "stock-keeping units" to consider (1000 items × 9 size-color classes × 3 stores). The classification combinations, or problem dimensions, multiply, rather than add. So, a slight increase in the complexity of classification greatly complicates the problem or greatly increases the processing volume. (In most practical problems, the maximum combinatorial number of distinctions may not exist, because some of them either do not actually exist physically or are ignored as being unimportant.) In any case, a major decision in all large-scale information-processing problems is "How much detail shall we keep—and how much shall we summarize?"

d. Suppose the store manager decides he does not want to make spot inquiries about his inventory, but wants the computer system to advise him automatically of any impending shortages of stock or actual out-of-stock conditions for any of the 1000 items at any of his three stores. What sort of screening procedures—and consequent computer program statements—would be necessary to provide a processing routine to advise the store manager of "exceptional conditions" in his inventory status?

12-7 A major distinction to note when using subroutines in program construction is that you are dealing with modular program construction rather than line-by-line construction. (This is analogous to building a house with 4′ × 8′ plywood panels, rather than bricks or small sticks of wood.) Although modular construction is faster than the more detailed method, it limits the variety of action available to a program (just as a house of plywood cannot be more ornate than a house of bricks). The modular form of thinking has often been compared to "adult-learning" as opposed to "infant-learning," because as we grow older we become accustomed to thinking, or learning, in combinations of our previous experience blocks. The child, on the other hand, who does not have such large blocks of experience to work with, deals in bits and pieces. And, as a result, the child may come up with novel ideas we never think of as adults. Discuss the advantages and disadvantages that modular program construction offers in terms of speed, economics, and practice as opposed to the variety of possibilities and the possibly novel results a programmer might obtain if he concentrated on the absolute detail of each and every program line. Under what conditions is each approach preferable?

THIRTEEN

A Baker's Dozen

In this chapter we recapitulate much of what has been learned in the previous chapters in order to check your understanding of the grammatical rules of BASIC and also to provide an increasingly difficult progression from the most rudimentary applications of a computer remote terminal to those that are less obvious.

All of the standard BASIC statements are illustrated in one or more of the examples in this chapter. Stress is given to list and table manipulation, since such applications seem to cause the most difficulty.

In Chapters 17 and 18 these thirteen examples will be presented again, but written in another computer language, FORTRAN.

An additional purpose of this and Chapter 15 is to move the reader from a computer language orientation to a problem orientation, that is, from a direct concern with the grammar and syntax of the BASIC language to a wider appreciation of that language in practice.

Detailed comments are provided for each example, with a detailed, line-referenced explanation of what was done. Attempt to follow each example thoroughly, and if you cannot do so return to the earlier chapters and review any unclear points. In effect, this chapter is a test. If you cannot understand all the examples here, you should not go on until you do.

Example 1 (Using the computer terminal instead of a hand calculator.)
Evaluate the numeric expression

$(3.1416)^2$

Solution

```
100 PRINT (3.1416)↑2
200 END

RUN


 9.86965056

  200,   NORMAL EXIT FROM PROG.

TIME:     0.025 SEC.
```

Comment For very simple calculations, such as the one above, the desk calculator may be more efficient than the computer terminal. The computing time shown above does not include the time required to type in the problem. For very simple problems, the total time required for compilation plus running can be greater for the terminal than for the calculator. (The time shown above includes both compile and run time, but not typing time.)

Example 2 (Using the computer terminal as a calculator in more difficult cases.)

Evaluate the single numeric expression

$(12.963 \times 42.312)^2/(3.753 - 1.212)^3$

Solution

```
100 PRINT (12.963 * 42.312)↑2/(3.753 - 1.212)↑3
200 END

RUN


 18336.8256

  200,   NORMAL EXIT FROM PROG.

TIME:     0.030 SEC.
```

Comment With this more difficult case, the computer begins to gain advantage over the hand calculator. First, several intermediate storage registers, or hand notations, would be required for desk calculation. Second, the actual speed of computation is faster on the computer than on the calculator.

Example 3 (Using the computer terminal in multiple evaluations.)
Evaluate the numeric expressions

$(2.42)(3.17)^2 + (4.73)\sqrt{1.96}$
$(1.73)(1.93)/(7.42) - \sqrt[3]{1.96}$
$(1.73)(1.93)/((7.42) - \sqrt[3]{1.96})$

Solution

```
100 PRINT (2.42)*(3.17)↑2 + (4.73)*(1.96)↑.5
200 PRINT (1.73)*(1.93)/(7.42) - (1.96)↑.33333
300 PRINT (1.73)*(1.93)/((7.42) - (1.96)↑.33333)
400 END

RUN


 30.940338
-.801475619
 .541278999

  400,  NORMAL EXIT FROM PROG.

TIME:    0.063 SEC.
```

Comment Because the computer has been asked to do more work—evaluate three expressions instead of one—with approximately the same setup, greater efficiency can be obtained. The computer is now considerably faster than the hand calculator.

Example 4 (The power of stored programs and repetitive loops.)
For the ten values of X from .5 through 5, in steps of .5, compute and print the values of X^2, the natural logarithm of X, the value e^X, and $\sqrt{X}$. Show a title for each column of this table.

Solution

```
100 PRINT "X","X↑2","LOG(X)","EXP(X)","X↑.5"
200 FOR X = .5 TO 5 STEP .5
300 PRINT X,X↑2,LOG(X),EXP(X),X↑.5
400 NEXT X
500 END

RUN

X             X↑2           LOG(X)         EXP(X)         X↑.5
 .5            .25          -.69314718      1.64872127     .707106781
 1             1             0              2.71828182     1
 1.5           2.25          .405465108     4.48168907     1.22474487
 2             4             .69314718      7.38905609     1.41421356
 2.5           6.25          .916290731     12.1824939     1.58113883
 3             9             1.09861228     20.0855369     1.7320508
 3.5           12.25         1.25276296     33.1154519     1.87082869
 4             16            1.38629436     54.59815       2
 4.5           20.25         1.50407739     90.0171313     2.12132034
 5             25            1.60943791     148.413159     2.23606797

 500,   NORMAL EXIT FROM PROG.

TIME:     0.137 SEC.
```

Comment This problem deserves special attention. Note the program contains the FOR/NEXT pair of statements in lines 200 and 400. This programming feature causes the computer to repeat a given set of instructions in a "loop of action" until an upper specification ($X = 5$ in this case) has been reached. In this way a few computer instructions can produce a volume of results, as illustrated in the table. The ability of a stored program to loop from one step to another is one of the major conceptual (as well as utilitarian) workhorses of computer instruction: you need not describe every repetitive detail, only request that the detail be repeated with minor modifications.

In addition, in this program we have asked the computer to make use of another of its major features: the ability to store a reserve of other programs, which will be executed on call. To find the natural logarithm of X, or compute the value e^X, or even $\sqrt{X}$ would usually require the preparation of individual computer programs. However, if these often-used programs are already stored in the computer, they may be asked for directly—as functions of X—thereby saving much time and effort for the user. In general, the greater the number of available stored functions, the easier it is for the user to solve a problem.

Finally, it should be obvious that in a race with the computer no human could produce the table shown in the solution for this problem. Even though handbooks and desk calculators are available, the number and variety of results required preclude human success in the few seconds required for the computer to compute and type out the results. As the problems become more complex, this gap widens markedly as will be seen in the examples that follow.

Example 5 (Using the FOR/NEXT loop to handle input data as a single-dimensional table.)

For the 10 values of X shown in line 700 of the following program, evaluate the expression

$$Y = 1 + 3X^2 + 4X^3$$

Print out the answers with column headings for "CASE NO.", "X", and "Y." Note the index I which selects the input value from left to right in line 700.

Solution

```
100 PRINT "CASE NO.","X","Y"
200 FOR I=1 TO 10
300 READ X(I)
400 LET Y(I) = 1 + 3*X(I)↑2 + 4*X(I)↑3
500 PRINT I,X(I),Y(I)
600 NEXT I
700 DATA 2.75,3.43,4.56,1.23,8.74,7.92,9.98,8.70,4.73,8.21
800 END

RUN

CASE NO.        X               Y
 1               2.75            106.875
 2               3.43            197.709128
 3               4.56            442.656064
 4               1.23            12.982168
 5               8.74            2900.67329
 6               7.92            2176.35155
 7               9.98            4275.84916
 8               8.7             2862.08199
 9               4.73            491.413968
 10              8.21            2416.76294

  800,   NORMAL EXIT FROM PROG.

TIME:    0.131 SEC.
```

Comment The number of cases to be computed could be increased by providing more data and increasing the range of computation in line 200, e.g., by showing a larger value of I than 10. There is no real need for using a subscripted variable in this problem (although no harm is done). We have used a subscripted variable in anticipation of the two following examples.

Example 6 (Handling the input data for two variables as two one-dimensional tables.)

Let 10 values of X be those given in line 930 of the following program, and let 10 corresponding values of Y be those in line 940. For these cases, evaluate the expression

$$Z = 1 + 3X^2 + 4Y^3$$

Print title and answers.

Solution

```
100 FOR I=1 TO 10
200 READ X(I)
300 NEXT I
400 FOR I=1 TO 10
500 READ Y(I)
600 NEXT I
700 PRINT "CASE NO.","X","Y","Z"
800 FOR I=1 TO 10
900 LET Z(I) = 1 + 3*X(I)↑2 + 4*Y(I)↑3
910 PRINT I,X(I),Y(I),Z(I)
920 NEXT I
930 DATA 12, 24, 46,  3,  72,  12.43,  9.72,  9,  2,  46
940 DATA 24,  2,  5,  7,  63,   7.36,  2.16,  3,  7,  46
999 END

RUN

CASE NO.        X               Y               Z
 1               12              24              55729
 2               24              2               1761
 3               46              5               6849
 4               3               7               1400
 5               72              63              1015741
 6               12.43           7.36            2059.26772
 7               9.72            2.16            324.745984
 8               9               3               352
 9               2               7               1385
 10              46              46              395693

  999,  NORMAL EXIT FROM PROG.

TIME:    0.180 SEC.
```

Comment In this problem, the data are read in in their entirety before computation is started. Although the programming language shown (BASIC) provides for 10 table positions without notice, larger tables would require reservation of storage space in the computer. Such notice of things to come is usually provided with a dimension statement at the start of the program. Thus, if 20 cases were to be read in and computed, the program could start

```
90 DIM X(20), Y(20), Z(20)
```

thereby reserving 20 spaces for each of the variables. Note in addition the convenience of having all values of X together on one (or more adjacent) lines, and all values of Y together. With this arrangement, values of X (or Y) can be changed for another run without affecting the other variables. Note also the different input and output values for integer and decimal variables. Cases 6 and 7 are decimal input and output values, and the decimal point is shown in both. All other cases are integer values, and the integer value is shown for both input and output. You may want to write a program for "paired data," in which successive values of X and Y are provided for computation. In this case, the data shown in lines 930 and 940 would be as follows:

```
930 DATA 12, 24, 24, 2, 46, 5, 3, 7, 72, 63, 12.43, 7.36, 9.72, 2.16
940 DATA 9, 3, 2, 7, 46, 46
```

In this arrangement, neither indexing nor dimensioning would be required; but to change values of X for a new run, we would also have to retype Y. The next example illustrates a further advantage in grouping data in orderly tables and in using multiple indexing.

Example 7 (Handling the input data for a two-variable problem as one two-dimensional table.)

Repeat the computations required in Example 6, using the same data input as shown in the solution to that problem, but consider the input to be handled as one 2-row × 10-column table. Following the usual convention, use the index I to represent a row and the index J to represent a column.

Solution

```
100 FOR I = 1 TO 2
200 FOR J = 1 TO 10
300 READ A(I,J)
400 NEXT J
500 NEXT I
```

```
600 PRINT "CASE NO.","X","Y","Z"
700 FOR J = 1 TO 10
800 LET Z(J) = 1 + 3*A(1,J)↑2 + 4*A(2,J)↑3
900 PRINT J, A(1,J), A(2,J), Z(J)
920 NEXT J
930 DATA 12, 24, 46,  3,  72,  12.43,  9.72,  9,  2,  46
940 DATA 24,  2,  5,  7,  63,   7.36,  2.16,  3,  7,  46
999 END

RUN


CASE NO.        X              Y              Z
 1               12             24             55729
 2               24             2              1761
 3               46             5              6849
 4               3              7              1400
 5               72             63             1015741
 6               12.43          7.36           2059.26772
 7               9.72           2.16           324.745984
 8               9              3              352
 9               2              7              1385
 10              46             46             395693

   999,  NORMAL EXIT FROM PROG.

TIME:     0.180 SEC.
```

Comment This computation introduces two independent variables, X and Y. Suppose we now want to introduce another independent variable, say, W. In the present format, much of what has been done can be saved. To add the third variable, we add another *row* to the table of data, with the columns again representing the different cases. In the program we need only change the upper index for I from 2 to 3, and tack on the computation for A(3,J)—which would be the various values of the third variable—in line 800. For this reason, the tabular arrangement of data is often advantageous when we may want to add (or delete) variables to a computation.

We have also used a special device to read in the tabular data in this problem, namely the "nested loops" shown in program lines 100 through 500. Notice what these steps do. For row 1, we first read in all of the column entries for that line, then for row 2, we read in the column entries. Thus, we complete a range for J from 1 to 10 each time we increase the value of I. For this reason, the statements FOR J . . . and NEXT J must be written *within*, or be bracketed by, the statements FOR I . . . and NEXT I. In other words, the inner loops, which occur more frequently, *must* be nested within the FOR/NEXT statements that indicate the less frequently executed loops. In particular, if the indices in lines 400 and 500 are interchanged, the computer will not know what to do, and you will get an error message. If your problem requires it you may further nest loops (e.g., for I, J, K, L, etc.), but some care is required to assure correct nesting, as illustrated on the left.

Example 8 (Using the Computer's Testing Ability—IF/THEN statements.)
Suppose we have asked loan applicants for their (1) annual salary, (2) years employed on same job, (3) years residence in same location, (4) monthly rental or mortgage payments, added (5) an arbitrary serial number to each case, and let each of these numeric values be denoted by A, B, C, D, and E, respectively. In other words, we have a *record* for each case (A, B, C, D, E) in which the letters denote the *data elements* in the record. Further, suppose our bank will accept a loan application automatically if salary is $7,500 or more a year *and* if residence *or* employment tenure is 3 years or more, *and* if rent (or mortgage) payments are not greater than one week's pay—but will reject it otherwise. Write a program to evaluate the cases shown in lines 1000 through 1040. Print "CASE NO. ( )" and "CREDIT APPROVED," or "CREDIT REJECTED" as appropriate.

Solution

```
100 READ A,B,C,D,E
110 IF A < 7500 THEN 800
120 IF D > A/52 THEN 800
130 IF B >= 3 THEN 900
140 IF C >= 3 THEN 900
800 PRINT "CASE NO." E "CREDIT REJECTED"
805 GO TO 100
900 PRINT "CASE NO." E "CREDIT APPROVED"
905 GO TO 100
1000 DATA 8600,2,10,200,1
1010 DATA 7400,3,7,200,2
1020 DATA 6200,6,5,150,3
1030 DATA 4800,10,20,125,4
1040 DATA 15000,3,3,285,5
9999 END

RUN


CASE NO.          1                 CREDIT REJECTED
CASE NO.          2                 CREDIT REJECTED
```

```
CASE NO.          3                CREDIT REJECTED
CASE NO.          4                CREDIT REJECTED
CASE NO.          5                CREDIT APPROVED

  100,  PROGRAM OUT OF DATA

TIME:     0.129 SEC.
```

Comment By using the IF/THEN statement (or conditional branch) we can cause the program to treat each input case differently. For more complicated problems, the logical AND, OR, and NOT combinations possible with a number of IF/THEN statements in combination can be displayed in a *flowchart*, as shown in Figure 13.1, or a *decision table.* The number of distinct actions the computer can take can be increased by using more IF/THEN statements, as shown in the following example.

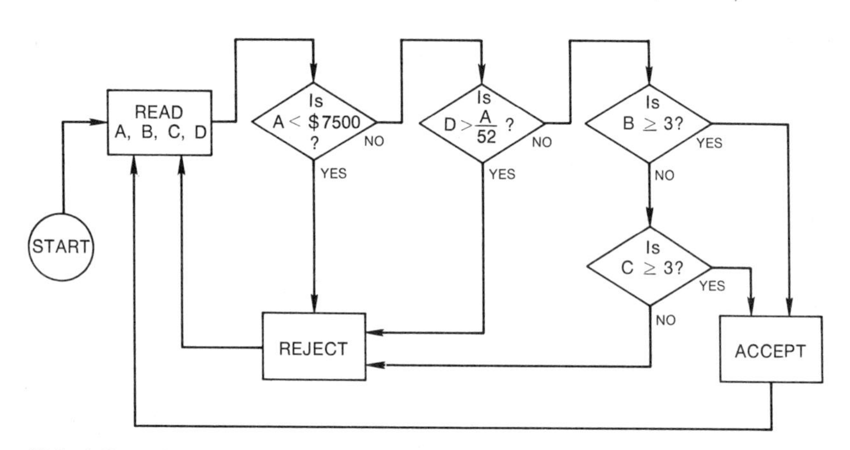

13.1. A flow chart for Example 8. In this program cases will be evaluated in turn until the data available is used up. Both of the first two conditions must be met, *and* one of the latter two to accept the loan application.

Example 9 (Using FOR/NEXT and IF/THEN statements in combination.)

Consider the evaluation of a poker hand. For simplicity, let the cards in a 52-card deck be numbered 1, 2, 3, . . . , 13 by face value without regard to suit, Ace low, King high. From such a deck, deal a 5-card hand (X, X, X, X, X) at random. Write a program to examine the hand and specify NO PAIR, ONE PAIR, TWO PAIR, THREE OF A KIND, FULL HOUSE (three of a kind and a pair), or FOUR OF A KIND. Again for simplicity in this example, let a straight be denoted by NO PAIR. Sample hands are provided in lines 900 through 913.

```
020 DIM X(13)
025 FOR I=1 TO 13
030 LET X(I) = 0
035 NEXT I
036 LET S2=0
037 LET S3=0
038 LET S4=0
050 FOR N=1 TO 5
100 READ I
110 LET X(I) = X(I) + 1
120 NEXT N
150 FOR I = 1 TO 13
160 IF X(I) = 2 THEN 500
170 IF X(I) = 3 THEN 520
180 IF X(I) = 4 THEN 540
200 GO TO 575
500 LET S2 = S2 + 1
510 GO TO 575
520 LET S3 = S3 + 1
530 GO TO 575
540 LET S4 = S4 + 1
550 GO TO 575
575 NEXT I
600 IF S4 = 1 THEN 700
610 IF S3 = 1 THEN 750
620 IF S2 = 2 THEN 800
630 IF S2 = 1 THEN 850
640 PRINT "NO PAIR"
650 GO TO 999
700 PRINT "FOUR OF A KIND"
710 GO TO 999
750 IF S2 = 1 THEN 780
760 PRINT "THREE OF A KIND"
770 GO TO 999
780 PRINT "FULL HOUSE"
790 GO TO 999
800 PRINT "TWO PAIR"
810 GO TO 999
850 PRINT "ONE PAIR"
860 GO TO 999
900 DATA 1,2,3,4,5
901 DATA 7,7,7,7,8
902 DATA 2,3,4,3,2
```

```
903 DATA 13,13,13,11,11
904 DATA 11,13,12,1,2
905 DATA 2,4,2,4,4
906 DATA 3,6,6,6,6
907 DATA 5,12,5,5,12
908 DATA 1,2,8,12,12
909 DATA 4,4,9,9,9
910 DATA 4,5,6,12,4
911 DATA 2,7,12,2,2
912 DATA 2,7,4,6,2
913 DATA 5,8,8,12,8
999 GO TO 25
1000 END

RUN


NO PAIR
FOUR OF A KIND
TWO PAIR
FULL HOUSE
NO PAIR
FULL HOUSE
FOUR OF A KIND
FULL HOUSE
ONE PAIR
FULL HOUSE
ONE PAIR
THREE OF A KIND
ONE PAIR
THREE OF A KIND

  100,  PROGRAM OUT OF DATA

TIME:     0.463 SEC.
```

Comment This example is more difficult than Example 8, and combines FOR/NEXT with IF/THEN statements to read in data and simplify an otherwise lengthy logical process.

First, a small one-dimensional table is set up with 13 row-positions, or vector cells, at zero. These cells will be used to develop a count of cards by their face value. Three counters (variables S2, S3, and S4) are first set at zero to record, respectively, the pair count or the presence of three

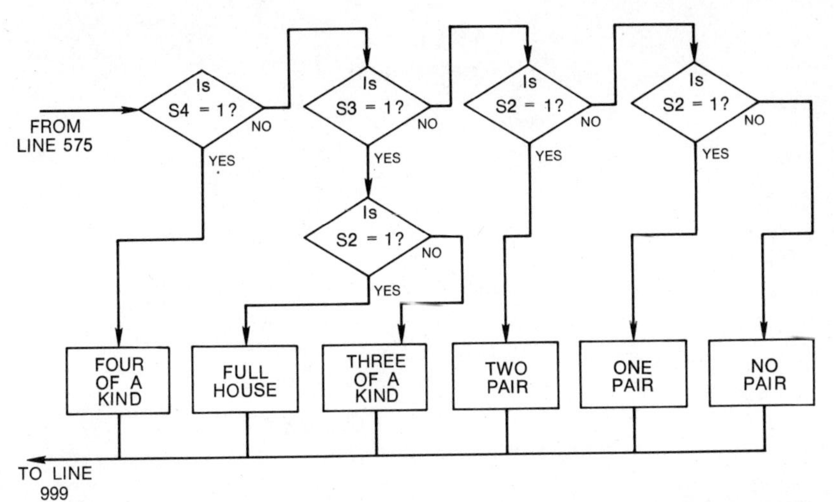

13.2. Flow chart for a portion of the program of Example 9 (starting at line 575). This chart shows the tests required of the counters, S4, S3, and S2, to evaluate the poker hands.

of a kind then four of a kind. For the first hand we then read the hand values and add 1 to the vector cell position indicated by each card's value.

Having read in the data for a given hand, we next examine each cell of the record vector for matches and increment the appropriate counter if one or more matches are found.

Finally, the three counters are tested, so that the appropriate evaluation can be printed to complete the job. Successive hands are evaluated by repeating the steps above until we run out of data. (The printed evaluations may be compared to the data to verify the program's correctness.)

The flowchart in Figure 13.2 shows the logic used in evaluating the poker hands. As an alternate summary of these tests, the decision table (Table 13.1) shows the contents of the counters and the associated actions to take. The decision table, which is more compact than the flowchart, is often used to summarize the logical conditions and associated actions required in large-scale computer programs.

In the foregoing examples you applied the FOR/NEXT pair of statements to produce a loop of action and thereby greatly multiplied the work that can be done with a few program lines. You have used the IF/THEN statement to test for special conditions that should be handled differently by the program. You have also seen the use of a few simple functions, or stored subprograms, e.g., log(X), which are automatically executed in the BASIC language. We now turn to four final examples to illustrate selected methods and techniques. In these examples you will need some knowledge of the problem area in addition to your current knowledge of the BASIC language.

TABLE 13.1
Test Number

Counter	1	2	3	4	5	6
S4	1	0	0	0	0	0
S3	0	1	1	0	0	0
S2	0	1	0	2	1	0
Four of a Kind	X					
Full House		X				
Three of a Kind			X			
Two Pair				X		
One Pair					X	
No Pair						X

Decision Table for Example 9.

Example 10 (The Subroutine and Its Use: The GOSUB/RETURN Pair.) This example introduces the GOSUB XXXX statement, where the X's indicate the starting line of a set of program steps you want to use, or "electronically paste" into a program repetitively. When the computer reaches a GOSUB statement, it executes the lines from XXXX to the first RETURN statement encountered in sequence, and then at RETURN automatically goes back to the program line following the initiating GOSUB statement. Subroutines may be repeated anywhere in the program, as is the case with GOSUB 1080; the computer keeps track of the appropriate line that should follow RETURN. For obvious reasons GOSUB and RETURN statements always occur in pairs.

In the following example two other statements, INPUT and REM, also appear. The INPUT statement allows the user to enter variable information from the computer terminal at the time of program execution, so that the same program can be run for different conditions, immediately after the previous result has been seen. (The input required in this problem is marked for identification in the solution output.) The REM statement permits nonexecuted comments to be made in the program for user reference.

Now, suppose a fabric designer wants to "weave" different patterns on the computer so he can see the results of different repetitions of the patterns shown in lines 1010, 1050, and 1090. (The sequence of these patterns is given by the sequence of subroutines which may be written between lines 115 and 169, as noted in the REM comment of line 180. Only four of the available lines are used in this illustration. The number of repetitions will be determined by the INPUT of data, A, B, and C.) One possible solution to the designer's problem follows.

Solution

```
1 REM JACQUARD LOOM PROBLEM -- PRINTS SELECTED PATTERNS
70 LET R = 0
80 LET R = R + 1
90 PRINT "FABRIC DESIGN CASE NO.";R
100 PRINT "WHAT ARE YOUR VALUES OF A,B,AND C?"
110 INPUT A,B,C
111 PRINT
112 PRINT "THIS IS CASE NO.";R
114 FOR I = 1 TO 2
120 GOSUB 1000
122 GOSUB 1080
125 GOSUB 1040
130 GOSUB 1080
170 NEXT I
175 PRINT
176 PRINT
180 REM TO CHANGE DESIGN SEQUENCE REWRITE LINES 115-169
182 PRINT
200 REM PROGRAM  NOW GOES TO START OR ENDS
205 PRINT "DO YOU WANT ANOTHER DESIGN. 0 = NO, 1 = YES"
208 INPUT K
210 IF K=1 THEN 80
220 GO TO 9998
900 REM THESE ARE THE SUBROUTINES
1000 FOR J = 1 TO A
1010 PRINT "XXXXX     XXXXX     XXXXX"
1020 NEXT J
1030 RETURN
1040 FOR L = 1 TO B
1050 PRINT "     XXXXX     XXXXX     "
1060 NEXT L
1070 RETURN
1080 FOR M = 1 TO C
1090 PRINT "XXXXXXXXXXXXXXXXXXXXXXXXX"
2000 NEXT M
2010 RETURN
9998 PRINT "PROGRAM TERMINATED AT YOUR REQUEST"
9999 END

RUN
 FABRIC DESIGN CASE NO. 1
 WHAT ARE YOUR VALUES OF A,B,AND C?
 ?2,2,0

 THIS IS CASE NO. 1
 XXXXX     XXXXX     XXXXX
 XXXXX     XXXXX     XXXXX
      XXXXX     XXXXX
      XXXXX     XXXXX
 XXXXX     XXXXX     XXXXX
 XXXXX     XXXXX     XXXXX
      XXXXX     XXXXX
      XXXXX     XXXXX
```

```
DO YOU WANT ANOTHER DESIGN. 0 = NO, 1 = YES
?1
FABRIC DESIGN CASE NO. 2
WHAT ARE YOUR VALUES OF A,B,AND C?
?2,0,2

THIS IS CASE NO. 2
XXXXX     XXXXX     XXXXX
XXXXX     XXXXX     XXXXX
XXXXXXXXXXXXXXXXXXXXXXXXX
XXXXXXXXXXXXXXXXXXXXXXXXX
XXXXXXXXXXXXXXXXXXXXXXXXX
XXXXXXXXXXXXXXXXXXXXXXXXX
XXXXX     XXXXX     XXXXX
XXXXX     XXXXX     XXXXX
XXXXXXXXXXXXXXXXXXXXXXXXX
XXXXXXXXXXXXXXXXXXXXXXXXX
XXXXXXXXXXXXXXXXXXXXXXXXX
XXXXXXXXXXXXXXXXXXXXXXXXX


DO YOU WANT ANOTHER DESIGN. 0 = NO, 1 = YES
?1


FABRIC DESIGN CASE NO. 3
WHAT ARE YOUR VALUES OF A,B,AND C?
?1,1,1

THIS IS CASE NO. 3
XXXXX     XXXXX     XXXXX
XXXXXXXXXXXXXXXXXXXXXXXXX
     XXXXX     XXXXX
XXXXXXXXXXXXXXXXXXXXXXXXX
XXXXX     XXXXX     XXXXX
XXXXXXXXXXXXXXXXXXXXXXXXX
     XXXXX     XXXXX
XXXXXXXXXXXXXXXXXXXXXXXXX


DO YOU WANT ANOTHER DESIGN. 0 = NO, 1 = YES
?0
PROGRAM TERMINATED AT YOUR REQUEST

 9999,  NORMAL EXIT FROM PROG.

TIME:    0.327 SEC.
```

Comment It is of historical interest that the Jacquard loom (invented in 1801) operated under the control of punched cards formed into repetitive loops to generate repetitive patterns. This program provides a deterministic simulation of the Jacquard loom's operation.

It is of current interest that computer output, such as that shown, can be converted to punched cards or similar media that will directly control the operation of a Jacquard loom, thus providing automatic execution in cloth of the computer designer's artistic selection. This current application of computers in the garment industry greatly increases the designer's ability to devise alternate patterns and to speed them into practical implementation.

Note that this example has given only an introductory application of the subroutine concept. The programmer may greatly extend the subroutine idea. By first constructing modules of frequently used program steps and then patching these blocks together with a few lines of programming to create useful programs, the speed and accuracy of programming can be vastly increased. Further, the modules once written and perfected need not be written again, but can be stored on tape, cards, or in the computer memory. Such planning leads to an *accumulation* of stored "skills" that may be shared instantly with others and executed with little or no setup cost to the user. Thus, the subroutine concept has major implications for the design of instructional, operational, and control procedures which are at the heart of the information revolution.

Finally, we should note that the GOSUB/RETURN pair can be used with the FOR/NEXT and IF/THEN statements to generate more program variety. The combinations possible are essentially without limit.

Example 11 (Simulation Using Random Numbers.)

The computer is often used to solve problems through its ability to generate a volume of experimental results quickly, inexpensively, and safely. One such application is to problems of risk and uncertainty, i.e., probabilistic simulation problems—as opposed to the deterministic simulation of Example 10.

Consider a game of Russian roulette. In this game of chance, the player places one shell in the chamber of a six-shooter pistol, or revolver. He spins the chamber, points the pistol at his head, then pulls the trigger. [His probability of survival, according to theory, is $\frac{5}{6}$ on one trial, and for a game of N independent trials is $(\frac{5}{6})^N$, since the player must survive on each of the N trials to survive the game. For example, a player who engages in a 10-trial game has a survival probability of $(\frac{5}{6})^{10} = .161506$.]

Although we may compute the survival probability analytically for any game of N trials (if we remember the multiplication law of probability illustrated in the last paragraph), we may also estimate the survival probability for such a game by experimental means. One way to conduct such an experiment would be to have a large number of men engage in the stated game, and then record the percentage who survive as our best estimate of the required survival probability. But this approach is wasteful of personnel.

An alternate and much safer approach is to generate a sequence of numbers between zero and one at random, with the definition that, at a given trial death will occur if the random number generated is $\leq \frac{1}{6}$. (With this approach, in a series of N trials, survival cannot occur unless *each* of N random numbers generated for that game is $> \frac{1}{6}$.)

With this background, we may now turn to a specific example. Suppose we ask for the survival probability at Russian roulette after *ten* trials. (We know the answer, .161506, but want to compute it experimentally.)

Show the survival probability (which equals the number of games survived/total number of games played) for sets of 250 games of 10 trials each, up to a total of 2,500 games. Compare the theoretical and experimental results as the experiment continues.

In the following solution program and in the output results the abbreviation ITERS stands for "iterations," or repetitions of the experimental games. In the output, the simulated probability is shown in column 2, and the actual (theoretical) probability is shown in column 3. The difference, shown as ERROR in column 4, is the difference between the experimental and theoretical probabilities.

Solution

```
5 LET D = 0
8 LET G = 0
10 PRINT "NO OF ITERS","SIM P(SUR)","ACT P(SUR)","ERROR"
35 FOR I = 1 TO 10
40 FOR J = 1 TO 250
45 FOR K = 1 TO 10
50 LET W = RND(X)
55 IF W <= 1/6 THEN 70
60 NEXT K
65 GO TO 75
70 LET D = D + 1
75 NEXT J
80 LET G = G + 250
85 PRINT
86 PRINT G,(G-D)/G,(5/6)↑10,(G-D)/G-(5/6)↑10
90 NEXT I
100 END

RUN
```

```
NO OF ITERS    SIM P(SUR)     ACT P(SUR)     ERROR

 250           .176           .161505582      1.44944171E-2
 500           .17            .161505582      8.49441711E-3
 750           .166666666     .161505582      5.16108378E-3
 1000          .161           .161505582     -5.0558288E-4
 1250          .169599999     .161505582      8.09441711E-3
 1500          .167333333     .161505582      5.82775045E-3
 1750          .162285714     .161505582      7.80131405E-4
 2000          .1635          .161505582      1.99441711E-3
 2250          .160444444     .161505582     -1.06113843E-3
 2500          .158           .161505582     -3.50558288E-3

  100,  NORMAL EXIT FROM PROG.

TIME:     1.516 SEC.
```

Comment In this solution we have *three* nested FOR/NEXT loops—for I, J, K, the number of experimental sets (10), the number of games per set (250), and the number of trials per game (10), respectively. In line 50, the function RND(X), provided by the BASIC language, is used to generate automatically a random number between zero and one. In line 86, G is the total number of games played, D is the number of those resulting in death, and (G − D) is the number resulting in survival. Thus (G − D)/G is the estimated survival probability for any given number of games played, or iterations.

In probabilistic simulations of this type, the simulated probability estimate (and therefore the error term which can be computed in this case) oscillates about the "true" value (or zero for the error) because of sampling fluctuations in the random number generation. Such variation in the estimates is typical of all sampling procedures, and can be expected to diminish in amplitude as the number of experimental, or sample, games increases, provided that the random number generator is indeed random and that the roundoff error in a string of lengthy computations does not become excessive.

One moral of this example is that precision in probabilistic simulation requires a larger sample size, or number of iterations, than one may at first expect. For example, in this Russian roulette problem, the estimate is (apparently) good to three significant figures (for the set of random numbers used) only after 2,500 simulated games. As the following technical note indicates, we can only be assured of two significant figures. And to increase the precision requires geometrically increasing sample sizes.

Technical Note In this case it is possible to compute limits on the variation in possible estimates. In particular, since a single game can end only in death or survival, the repetitive generation of such games provides a binomial process. Thus, if P is the survival probability (.162) and $Q = 1 - P$ is the probability of death (.838), then the "error of the estimate" is given by

$$\sigma_P = \sqrt{\frac{PQ}{N}}$$

where N is the total number of games played. Substitution of the values for P, Q, and N gives

$$\sigma_P = \sqrt{(.162)(.838)/2500} = .0074$$

Thus, we can be virtually certain (99.7 percent confidence interval) that the "true" value of the survival probability lies in the interval

$$.162 \pm (3)(.0074) = .162 \pm .0222$$

which is, of course, so in the computations above. But, conversely, given the true value as .162, we could also have gotten other sample estimates (for other sets of 2500 games), 99.7 percent of which would lie within the interval $.162 \pm .0222$. That is, we could have gotten a *worse* estimate than we did; due to chance we could be off as much as .0222, and we should be aware of that fact. Moreover, by inspection of the formula above, we can see that we must multiply the sample size by 4 to cut the sampling variation in half, by 9 to cut it to a third, and so on, because N is under the square root sign in the formula.

In short, particularly for very complex probabilistic simulations, great precision can be costly. There is a fundamental economic tradeoff between our desire for precision and the rapidly increasing cost of getting it through simulation.

So, it pays to consider alternate methods of problem solution before turning to simulation. But if formal analytic methods fail or become excessively tedious, the use of probabilistic simulation (called the Monte Carlo method for obvious reasons), can often provide the needed solution.

Example 12 (Using Algorithms, or Numeric Methods, in a Program.)

Before a computer program can be written, a procedure for problem solution must be available. In scientific work such a step-by-step plan of action which guarantees the answer to a problem in a finite number of steps is called an algorithm. The study of numerical methods, apart from computer programming, aims at developing such computing schemes.

The following problem illustrates a powerful method (commonly known as binary search procedure) which solves equations by a series of computations, or iterations, of a guess-and-test type. The guesses, or successive new trials, are so arranged that the range of possible solution is cut in half at each new trial. In this way the search for the problem solution quickly narrows down to, or converges on, the problem solution.

For illustration, consider the equation

$$e^{-AX} + e^{-BX} = 1$$

Suppose we want to solve this equation (by finding the value of X that makes the equation balance). To do this we first examine the equation and discover that if $X = 0$ the value to the left of the equals sign is 2 (since any number raised to the 0th power is 1), e.g.,

$$Z = e^{-A(0)} + e^{-B(0)} = 1 + 1 = 2$$

On the other hand, we notice in the above equation that if $X = 5$ (and if A and B are both numbers greater than 1, so that AX and BX will be much larger than 1) the value of the terms to the left of the equality sign, which we have called Z, will be much less than 1. (Some knowledge of mathematics is required to observe these facts, and we assume you have such skills from your past experience and training.) Since the value of

$$Z = e^{-AX} + e^{-BX}$$

decreases steadily as X increases, we know that we could draw a rough plot of Z, which is a function of X, as shown in Figure 13.3.

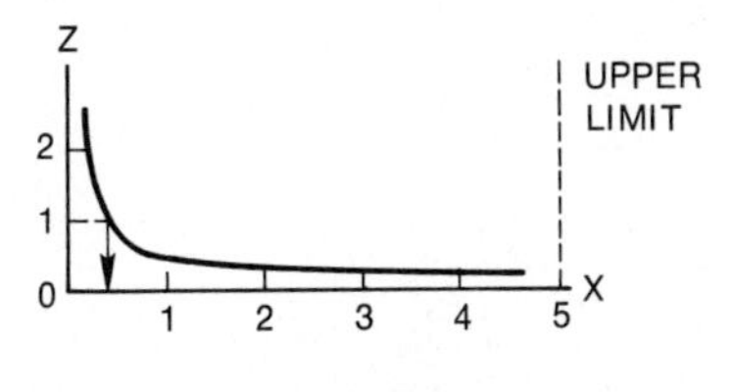

Fig. 13.3.

Our task is to find the value of X which lies between the limits $X = 0$ to $X = 5$ that will make $Z(X) = 1$ (within any given limit of error we choose).

The procedure for this, following the split-in-half argument, is

1. Having bracketed the value of X between 0 and 5, evaluate Z at the midpoint of the interval, i.e., evaluate Z(2.5).

2. Compare Z(2.5) to 1. If Z(2.5) > 1, it follows that the solution value of X must lie between 2.5 and 5; if Z(2.5) < 1, then the solution must be between 0 and 2.5. (To see this compare the previous statements to the picture of the function Z, above.)

3. Now change the limits of the search interval. If we know the answer lies in the interval 2.5–5 from the above test, we make the new *lower* limit 2.5; if it lies in the interval 0–2.5, we make the new *upper* limit 2.5.

4. Repeat steps 1 through 3, using the new interval limits successively determined in step 3, until the absolute difference (plus or minus) between Z(X) and 1 is smaller than a given acceptable error, say .01. Then stop and print the terminating value of X as the solution to the problem.

A program to implement this procedure for A = 2, B = 3, is as follows:

Solution

```
10 LET A=2
12 PRINT
15 LET B=3
17 LET L=0
19 LET U=5
20 LET W=(L+U)/2
22 LET Z=EXP(-A*W) + EXP(-B*W)
25 IF ABS(Z-1) < .01 THEN 80
30 IF Z > 1 THEN 60
35 LET U=W
40 GO TO 20
60 LET L=W
65 GO TO 20
80 PRINT W
100 END

RUN


 .283203125

  100,   NORMAL EXIT FROM PROG.

TIME:    0.118 SEC.
```

Extension We might want to extend the program to compute solutions for different values of A and B, say A = 1, 2, 3, 4, and 5, and B = 1, 2, 3, 4, and 5, for a total of 25 combinations or evaluations. Little additional work (or computing time) is required to do this, as shown in the extended program and solution set that follow. In the output shown, each *row* represents an increase in the value of A, reading down; each *column* represents an increase in the value of B, reading to the right. Thus, the solution for A = 2, B = 3, may be found at the intersection of row 2, column 3, i.e., .283203, the value previously obtained.

Solution

```
10 FOR A = 1 TO 5
12 PRINT
15 FOR B = 1 TO 5
17 LET L=0
19 LET U=5
20 LET W=(L+U)/2
22 LET Z=EXP(-A*W) + EXP(-B*W)
25 IF ABS(Z-1) < .01 THEN 80
30 IF Z > 1 THEN 60
35 LET U=W
40 GO TO 20
60 LET L=W
65 GO TO 20
80 PRINT W,
85 NEXT B
90 NEXT A
95 PRINT
100 END

RUN

 .703125        .48828125      .380859375     .322265625     .283203125
 .48828125      .3515625       .283203125     .244140625     .21484375
 .380859375     .283203125     .234375        .200195312     .17578125
 .322265625     .244140625     .200195312     .17578125      .15625
 .283203125     .21484375      .17578125      .15625         .13671875

  100,  NORMAL EXIT FROM PROG.

TIME:    0.277 SEC.
```

Comment It should be clear now that the *combination* of a good algorithm and the programming techniques already surveyed provides a major asset for the problem solver. Indeed, since a good algorithm can cut computing time by many orders of magnitude, the development of efficient algorithms with wide applications is a task of major interest in scientific work.

Example 13 (Cross-tabulation—a Data Processing Exercise.)

Suppose we have taken a survey of our employees or the citizens in our community and recorded for each: (1) race, (2) years of school, (3) salary level, (4) housing type, (5) job type, and (6) political party.

Using the coding scheme in Table 13.2, we then record this information for each case in a 6-position decimal code. For example, the code (1, 2, 3, 2, 3, 2) would represent (reading from left to right) a white high-school graduate, with a salary in the $10,000 to $20,000 range, who owns a mortgaged house, is a blue collar worker, and a Democrat. (For illustration, a set of typical data is shown in lines 100 through 130 of the program to follow.)

TABLE 13.2

Data Coding Scheme for Example 13.

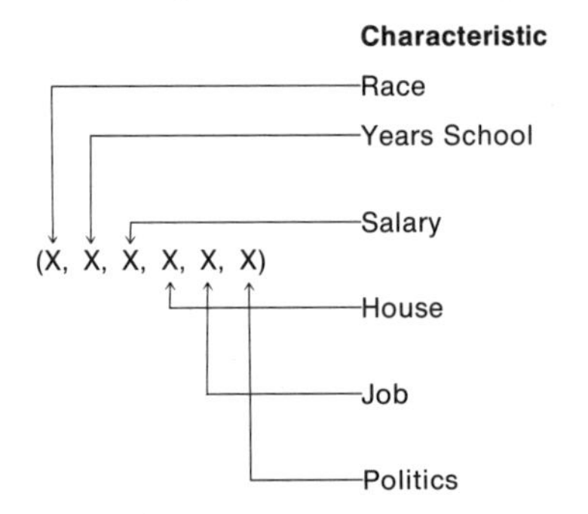

Characteristic	Level
Race	1, white; 2, negro; 3, oriental; 9, end of file.
Years School	1, grade school only; 2, high school; 3, college; 4, graduate school.
Salary	1, $5,000 or less; 2, $5,000–$10,000; 3, $10,000–$20,000; 4, over $20,000.
House	1, own completely; 2, own with existing mortgage; 3, rent; 4, other.
Job	1, management or professional; 2, white collar; 3, blue collar; 4, other or none.
Politics	1, Republican; 2, Democrat; 3, Independent; 4, other.

Notice in the coding scheme that the number of levels for each characteristic is limited to *four* possibilities (1, 2, 3, or 4). Our objective is to produce cross-tabulations of the characteristics school, salary, housing, job, and politics, given race; i.e., to generate selected 4 × 4 tables of the form in which the cell entries will show a count of the individuals of the given race who have common paired levels of the two named characteristics, such as rent-independent or housing-politics (see Table 13.3).

TABLE 13.3

Table Generated by Cross-tabulation.

Major Key: White Population **Cross-tab:** Housing vs. Politics

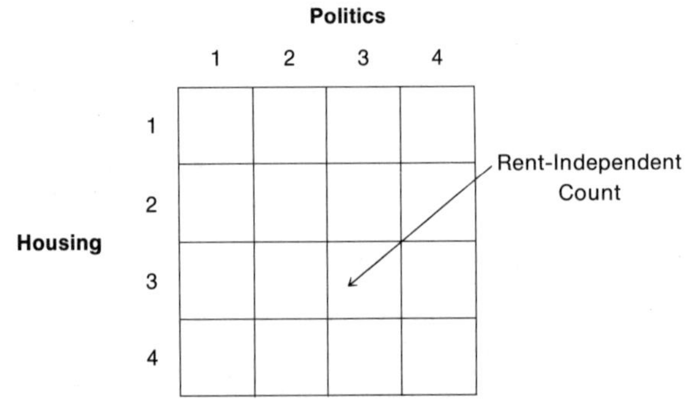

Before presenting the solution, we may wish to specify a few conventions to simplify the programming effort. (1) To denote the end of the data file, let the last record be (9, 9, 9, 9, 9, 9,), an illegal code according to our previous definition. (2) To generate the desired tables, we will use the INPUT instruction and call for a cross-tab selection at the time of execution. (3) For clarity, we want to number the rows and columns of the output table.

Solution

```
1 DIM X(4,4)
5 PRINT "WHICH POPULATION? WHITE=1, NEGRO=2, ORIENTAL=3"
10 INPUT P
15 PRINT "WHAT TWO CATEGORIES FOR CROSSTAB? SCHOOL=1, SALARY=2"
16 PRINT "HOUSING=3, JOB=4, POLITICS=5"
20 INPUT A,B
22 FOR I = 1 TO 4
24 FOR J = 1 TO 4
25 LET X(I,J)=0
27 NEXT J
29 NEXT I
30 PRINT "CROSSTAB DONE ON POPULATION" P
32 PRINT "VARIABLES USED ARE"; A;" (VERTICAL) AND"; B;" (HORIZONTAL)"
36 PRINT
38 PRINT
40 FOR I=1 TO 6
45 READ R(I)
50 NEXT I
55 IF R(1) = 9 THEN 995
60 IF R(1) <> P THEN 40
62 LET Y=R(A+1)
64 LET Z=R(B+1)
67 LET X(Y,Z)=X(Y,Z) + 1
70 GO TO 40
100 DATA 1,2,3,2,3,2
101 DATA 1,4,3,1,2,1
102 DATA 1,4,4,4,4,3
103 DATA 1,3,3,3,4,2
104 DATA 3,4,1,2,3,1
105 DATA 2,3,1,2,3,4
106 DATA 1,1,1,1,3,3
107 DATA 1,2,2,2,1,4
108 DATA 3,4,2,2,2,3
109 DATA 1,2,1,3,2,2
110 DATA 2,4,4,4,1,1
111 DATA 1,1,4,2,1,1
112 DATA 1,3,2,1,3,4
113 DATA 2,4,1,1,1,2
114 DATA 1,2,3,1,2,1
115 DATA 3,2,2,3,4,3
116 DATA 1,4,3,1,4,1
117 DATA 2,4,4,1,2,2
118 DATA 1,4,4,1,3,1
119 DATA 1,1,3,2,2,2
120 DATA 1,4,1,2,1,2
121 DATA 2,3,2,3,4,3
122 DATA 1,3,2,3,2,3
123 DATA 1,4,4,3,1,3
124 DATA 1,4,4,4,2,4
125 DATA 1,1,3,4,4,4
126 DATA 2,4,1,3,2,1
```

```
127 DATA 1,3,3,4,1,4
128 DATA 1,4,3,2,3,2
129 DATA 3,2,3,4,3,3
130 DATA 9,9,9,9,9,9
995 PRINT
996 PRINT "   ","1","2","3","4"
997 PRINT
998 PRINT
1000 FOR I=1 TO 4
1001 PRINT I,
1005 FOR J=1 TO 4
1010 PRINT X(I,J),
1015 NEXT J
1020 PRINT
1025 NEXT I
1030 PRINT
1035 PRINT
1040 PRINT "DO YOU WANT ANOTHER CROSSTAB? YES=1 NO=0"
1045 INPUT C
1046 IF C=0 THEN 9999
1047 RESTORE
1048 PRINT
1049 PRINT
1050 GO TO 5
9999 END
```

RUN

```
WHICH POPULATION? WHITE=1, NEGRO=2, ORIENTAL=3
?1
WHAT TWO CATEGORIES FOR CROSSTAB? SCHOOL=1, SALARY=2
HOUSING=3, JOB=4, POLITICS=5
?3,5
CROSSTAB DONE ON POPULATION    1
VARIABLES USED ARE 3  (VERTICAL) AND 5  (HORIZONTAL)


               1              2              3              4


 1             4              0              1              1
 2             1              4              0              1
 3             0              2              2              0
 4             0              0              1              3


DO YOU WANT ANOTHER CROSSTAB? YES=1 NO=0
?1
WHICH POPULATION? WHITE=1, NEGRO=2, ORIENTAL=3
?1
WHAT TWO CATEGORIES FOR CROSSTAB? SCHOOL=1, SALARY=2
HOUSING=3, JOB=4, POLITICS=5
?2,5
CROSSTAB DONE ON POPULATION    1
VARIABLES USED ARE 2  (VERTICAL) AND 5  (HORIZONTAL)


               1              2              3              4


 1             0              2              1              0
 2             0              0              1              2
 3             3              4              0              2
 4             2              0              2              1
```

```
DO YOU WANT ANOTHER CROSSTAB? YES=1 NO=0
?0

 9999,  NORMAL EXIT FROM PROG.

TIME:     0.685 SEC.
```

Comment The cross-tab is composed as a 4 × 4 matrix, as indicated in line 2. Lines 5 through 20 call for selection of the major key (white, negro, or oriental) and the characteristics for the crosstab. Lines 22 through 29 set all 16 cells of the cross-tab table to zero, because we want to avoid any carryover from previous computations. Lines 30 through 38 produce a title for the table. Lines 40 through 45 read a file record and test it: (a) if the record is (9, 9, 9, 9, 9, 9) the end-of-file condition is detected, and we branch to the printing steps at line 995; (b) if the record is not the last and does not possess the specified major key, we read the next record in the file. If the record passes these tests, we have a pertinent case, and lines 62 through 67 will add a count of 1 to the appropriate cell of the cross-tab table as determined by the levels of the characteristics selected for cross-tab. (These lines are a little tricky, but employ an extension of the counting method used in the poker-hand evaluation of Example 9.) We then go to the next record and repeat the process until the data is exhausted.

Lines 995 through 1035 print and space the output table. And, finally, lines 1040 through 1050 ask the user if he wants to continue with more tables. The command RESTORE in line 1047 causes the data file just scanned to be "rewound," or reset back to the beginning, so the list can be read from the top for production of the next cross-tab.

FOURTEEN

Extensions to the BASIC language

To extend your computer learning you must now confront more detail, the importance of which you may not appreciate immediately. At the same time, your intellectual understanding of a computer program's logic must be backed up with an emotional commitment, too. Computer programs come to life only by the combination of bright ideas, good logic, *and* devotion to the details of execution.

If Charles Babbage had combined attention to detail (as evidenced by his concern over poetical inaccuracy) with the vision that inspired his Analytical Engine, perhaps he would have succeeded—at least in bringing his dreams closer to realization in his time. But Babbage was a man of many, not always coordinated, parts. Frustrated by a seeming inconsistency, Babbage wrote Alfred, Lord Tennyson, about these lines: "Every minute dies a man,/Every minute one is born."

> I need hardly point out to you that this calculation would tend to keep the sum total of the world's population in a state of perpetual equipoise, whereas the total is constantly on the increase. In the next edition of your excellent poem the erroneous calculation to which I refer should be corrected as follows: "Every moment dies a man,/ And one and a sixteenth is born." The exact figures are 1.167, but something must, of course, be conceded to the laws of metre.[1]

[1] Although this anecdote has been quoted widely, the most recent citation is in *Time*, November 29, 1968, p. 14. The population growth rates Babbage cited for the 1800s are clearly less than those which obtain today in different parts of the world.

Babbage oscillated between extreme wide field and extreme tunnel vision. Perhaps that was his shortcoming and source of practical failure. He lacked the *balanced* blend. As we concentrate on the details of EXTENDED BASIC in the following sections, we must attempt to keep *our* balance.

Adult BASIC

EXTENDED BASIC offers a number of technical features we should consider: (1) matrix operations, (2) alphanumeric manipulations, (3) some additional format-handling ability, and (4) several miscellaneous commands, useful in special cases.

A note of caution before we continue, however. Except for the matrix commands described hereafter, which with one exception, are standardized, the commands in EXTENDED BASIC can and do vary slightly from one equipment installation to another. Many of these variations are only in detail, not in concept. You should have a computer manual on EXTENDED BASIC at hand as you proceed.[2]

Matrix operations

Table 14.1 lists the matrix, or MAT, commands available in EXTENDED BASIC. A short description appears next to each command. Later we describe how to use these commands.[3]

1 / MAT READ and MAT PRINT

MAT READ and MAT PRINT can be used in any program to replace the familiar nested pair of loops required to READ or PRINT a list or table. Thus, from Chapter 11, we know how to read a 3 × 4 table (see below left), where we continue our convention of always showing a DIM statement for each list or table employed in a program. On the right is the equivalent MAT READ.

```
100 DIM X(3, 4)            100 DIM X(3, 4)
110 FOR I = 1 TO 3         110 MAT READ X
```

[2] For General Electric systems see *BASIC Language Extensions*, 2d rev. ed., Publication 802207, March, 1968, GE Information Service Department, 7735 Old Georgetown Rd., Bethesda, Maryland 20014. Users of IBM's CALL/360 BASIC should have *CALL/360: BASIC Introduction*, Publication J20-0035-1, 1968, International Business Machines Corporation, Data Processing Division, Information Marketing Department, 112 East Post Road, White Plains, New York 10601. Similar manuals can be had from other suppliers or from your local computing center or time-sharing vendor.

[3] Descriptions in this section substantially follow GE's Publication 802207, cited in the previous footnote.

```
120 FOR J = 1 TO 4     - - - - - - - - -
130 READ X(I, J)
140 NEXT J
150 NEXT I
- - - - - - - - -
```

In both cases the data required would consist of 3 × 4, or 12, data elements supplied in row-column order, i.e., from X(1, 1) through X(3, 4). Notice the economy of using the MAT READ X command. Even greater economy of tabular input can be achieved by handling several tables in one MAT statement. Thus,

```
100 MAT READ X, Y, Z
```

would read in three tables, thereby replacing 15 lines of programming.

Whenever a MAT READ statement is used, you must *exactly* dimension the tables as you want them handled at read-time. So, in the three-table case just dimensioned, we would need to have

```
100 DIM X(2, 3), Y(5, 10), Z(3, 4)
```

TABLE 14.1

Matrix Operations in EXTENDED BASIC

Command[a]	**Action**
MAT READ A, B, C	Read the three matrices A, B, C which must have been previously dimensioned *exactly* as desired.
MAT PRINT A, B; C	Print three matrices with A and C in regular format, B closely packed.
MAT C = A + B	Add two matrices.
MAT C = A − B	Subtract two matrices.
MAT C = A * B	Multiply two matrices. Note this follows rules of matrix multiplication, and the dimensions of A and B as well as C must be correct.
MAT C = INV(A)	Invert matrix A. A will be a square matrix.
MAT C = TRN(A)	Transpose matrix A.
MAT C = (K) * A	Multiply all elements of matrix A by the (scalar) constant K.
MAT C = ZER	Fill out C with zeroes.
MAT C = CON	Fill out C with ones.
MAT C = IDN	Set C up as an identity matrix. The identity matrix is square with ones on the main diagonal.

[a] In both DIM and MAT statements, matrix variables must be described by *only* one letter and must have two dimension subscripts. Non-MAT dimensions and subscripted variables may start with a letter or a letter followed by a number. In all MAT operations, dimensions conformable to the operation are required, and *they must be exact.*

if we wanted to read first a 2 × 3 table, then a 5 × 10 table, and finally a 3 × 4 table. An alternate *optional* form, which places the DIM requirements in the MAT READ command is

```
110 MAT READ X(2, 3), Y(5, 10), Z(3, 4)
```

The multiple MAT READ command in either case would require the data for X first, that for Y next, and finally that for Z in successive row-column order.

The MAT PRINT command works in exactly the same way and will print out tables in row-column order. At left below is the method of Chapter 11; at right, the matrix method. We assume in both cases that the values for 6 × 8 table W, have been previously read in or computed.

```
100 DIM W(6,8)              100 DIM W(6, 8)
- - - - - - - -             - - - - - - - -
500 FOR I = 1 TO 6          500 MAT PRINT W;
510 FOR J = 1 TO 8          - - - - - - - -
520 PRINT W(I, J);
530 NEXT J
540 PRINT
545 NEXT I
- - - - - - - -
```

In both examples the ; after PRINT commands causes the output data to be packed. Omission of the ; after the MAT PRINT W would cause the output to appear in the standard five-column format. In the Chapter 11 method you must inhibit the line advance with a semicolon to get the first row on one line; the PRINT at line 540 would then advance your paper one line for the next row, I. A comma may be used for a semicolon to generate standard five-column output in either case.

Again, a number of matrices may be printed using one MAT PRINT command. For example,

```
100 DIM X(2, 3), Y(5, 10), Z(3, 4)
- - - - -
500 MAT PRINT X, Y; Z
- - - - -
```

will print out the dimensioned tables shown in the order X, Y, Z. Tables X and Z will be in standard five-column format; table Y will be packed.

Although the method of Chapter 11 is more flexible, the MAT PRINT command can save a lot of work if you wish to print tables in row-column order.

The DIM statements used with MAT operations must always have *two* subscripts, whether the dimensions are stated in a formal DIM declaration or in the MAT READ or MAT PRINT commands themselves. However, simply by defining the first subscript as 1, you may use MAT commands to handle lists (a table with one row is obviously a list). Thus, MAT READ X(1,10) will read a 10-element list as will MAT READ X, when a previous dimension statement DIM X(1,10) has been provided. Such a list may be thought of as a row. Similarly, a list read as MAT READ X(10,1) may be considered a column.[4]

Finally, as in Chapter 11, having MAT READ a list or table, you may thereafter refer to any of its elements by citing specific subscripts. To illustrate;

```
100 MAT READ X(2, 3)
110 PRINT X(1, 1), X(2, 3)
800 DATA 1, 2, 3, 4, 5, 6
999 END
```

would display the numbers 1 and 6, which are respectively the upper-left and the lower right cell contents of the 2 × 3 Table X. Computations can also be made on selected tabular cells using the LET substitution statement and the same convention above.

Although MAT READ is the most useful EXTENDED BASIC command, the remainder of the arithmetic operations shown in Table 14.1 are also very useful if you know linear algebra and want to work scientific problems. In the following description we assume that you have a knowledge of matrix manipulation from other courses (or other sources).

2 / *Matrix addition and subtraction*

The commands

```
MAT C = A + B
MAT C = A − B
```

in which the three matrices A, B, and C must be properly dimensioned, cause the corresponding cells of Tables A and B to be added or subtracted, resulting in the entries of matrix C. In order to be added or sub-

---

[4] The dimensioning rules for matrices are critical, and you should check one point of possible deviation from the above examples. The original Dartmouth specifications for BASIC *matrix* operations call for numbering tables from (0, 0), not (1, 1) as above. Most, but not all, commercial installations have revised BASIC's MAT dimension specifications to the more easily understood and consistent (1,1) starting point. Some installations give you the option of either choice. Check your manual on this detail.

tracted, two matrices must be of the *same* dimension. And, in fact, for the operation to make practical sense, the classifications used for the rows and columns of all three tables should be the same—to avoid the addition or subtraction of apples and oranges.

In general, formal *matrix* operations require a strict conformity in dimensioning all the various elements if the operation is to be performed. The fact that matrices to be added or subtracted must be of the same order, or dimension, as must the answer matrix, is one example of this requirement. Thus, for a set of arbitrary 2×2 matrices, we have

$$\begin{bmatrix} 3 & 3 \\ 3 & 3 \end{bmatrix} = \begin{bmatrix} 2 & 2 \\ 2 & 2 \end{bmatrix} + \begin{bmatrix} 1 & 1 \\ 1 & 1 \end{bmatrix} \quad \text{or} \quad \text{MAT C} = \text{A} + \text{B}$$

For the same matrices A and B, subtraction would produce matrix C:

$$\begin{bmatrix} 1 & 1 \\ 1 & 1 \end{bmatrix} = \begin{bmatrix} 2 & 2 \\ 2 & 2 \end{bmatrix} - \begin{bmatrix} 1 & 1 \\ 1 & 1 \end{bmatrix} \quad \text{or} \quad \text{MAT C} = \text{A} - \text{B}$$

In BASIC matrix operations, only one step is permitted at a time; that is,

```
MAT D = A + B + C
```

is not allowed.

3 / *Matrix multiplication*

The command

```
MAT C = A * B
```

will *matrix multiply* B times A. This operation does *not* correspond to the multiplication of the corresponding cells of matrices A and B to obtain the corresponding cells of C, an operation that must be carried out by the methods of Chapter 11, as illustrated in Program INVENTORY, page 213. Rather, matrix multiplication is a *transformation operation* and in fact, an accumulate-multiply process.

To illustrate, let matrix A represent the number of parts of kind 1 and 2 that compose production subassemblies "a" and "b." Further, let matrix B represent the number of subassemblies "a" and "b" that make a unit of the final assemblies "I" and "II." Then the product of A times B using matrix multiplication gives the number of parts, 1 and 2, used in the final assemblies "I" and "II," eliminating the intermediate classification "sub-assemblies" as follows in an arbitrary numerical example:

$$\begin{bmatrix} 12 & 13 \\ 40 & 53 \end{bmatrix} = \begin{bmatrix} 1 & 2 \\ 5 & 6 \end{bmatrix} \times \begin{bmatrix} 2 & 7 \\ 5 & 3 \end{bmatrix} \quad \text{or} \quad \text{MAT C} = \text{A} * \text{B}$$

From inspection of the above tables or from your own recall, you see that

C(1, 1) = A(1, 1) * B(1, 1) + A(1, 2) * B(2, 1) or 12 = 1 * 2 + 2 * 5

where the multiplication is simple arithmetic, *not* matrix multiplication. A similar operation, with suitable indexing, is carried out for all row-column combinations by the MAT C = A * B operation, as shown in the production parts example.

Some care must be taken in the matrix multiplication operation to make sure that matrices A and B are multiplied in the desired order (in general MAT C = A * B is *not* equal to MAT C = B * A). Further, matrices to be multiplied need not be of the same order nor square. But the number of *columns* of A must be equal to the number of *rows* of B. The resulting matrix, C in this case, will have the number of *rows* of A and the number of *columns* of B. To violate this rule produces a diagnostic message from the computer. Again notice that the column definitions, or classification names, of A should be identical to the row definition, or classification names, of B for the operation to make practical sense, as illustrated by the preceding production assembly parts example.

4 / Matrix inversion

The "inverse," or INV, of a matrix, A, is by definition a matrix, say, Q, such that if Q = INV(A), then

MAT C = Q * A = IND,

or the "identity" matrix. (An identity matrix is a square matrix which has zeroes everywhere except for the 1's on its northwest and southeast diagonals.) For this reason, inversion operations should be confined to square matrices only. In particular, if Q = INV(A) and MAT C = A * B, then MAT B = Q * C, where Q, C, A, and B are all square and of the same dimension. The inverse operation is useful in solving simultaneous linear equations, according to standard textbook methods, and you should consult those books for further reference. Conceptually, matrix inversion is a matrix un-multiplying operation, and corresponds by analogy to the arithmetic reciprocal. (Matrix division is not defined, since matrix multiplication is not *commutative*; MAT C = A * B is not equal to MAT C = B * A.)

Considerable care must be used in computing a matrix inversion, since in a number of cases the inverse will not exist in fact. This can occur because of the relationship of the numbers in a given matrix to be inverted, for example, if one row of that matrix is an exact multiple of another. Further, because of rounding errors, the inversion computed may not be particularly accurate because of the appearance of a number of very small numbers. In the latter case you will get a diagnostic message from the computer warning you of this fact.

An illustration of the matrix read, print, multiply, and inversion operations can be found in Program MATRIX.

```
LIST


10 REM PROGRAM MATRIX: ILLUSTRATES MATRIX READ
20 REM PRINT, MULTIPLY, AND INVERSION
30 DIM Q(2,2),X(2,2),Y(2,2),Z(2,2)
40 MAT READ X,Y
50 PRINT"MATRIX X"
60 MAT PRINT X
70 PRINT"MATRIX Y"
80 MAT PRINT Y
90 MAT Z=X*Y
100 PRINT"MATRIX Z"
110 MAT PRINT Z
120 MAT Q=INV(X)
130 PRINT"MATRIX Q -- INVERSE OF MATRIX X"
140 MAT PRINT Q
150 MAT Y=Q*Z
160 PRINT"CHECK MAT Y=Q*Z"
170 MAT PRINT Y
180 DATA 1,2,5,6
190 DATA 2,7,5,3
999 END

RUN

MATRIX X
 1              2
 5              6
MATRIX Y
 2              7
 5              3
```

```
MATRIX Z
 12              13
 40              53
MATRIX Q -- INVERSE OF MATRIX X
-1.49999999      .5
 1.24999999     -.25
CHECK MAT Y=Q*Z
 2               7
 4.99999999      2.99999999

  999,  NORMAL EXIT FROM PROG.

TIME:    0.152 SEC.
```

5 / *Other matrix operations*

The remaining matrix operations of Table 14.1 should be self-evident to those of you who have had a previous course in matrix algebra. One or two notes will complete our treatment.

Scalar multiplication (each element of the matrix multiplied by a constant) can be accomplished by using

MAT B = (K) * A,

where the constant, K, must be enclosed in parentheses to distinguish it from a matrix.

The "transpose," or TRN, of a matrix, which swaps its rows for its columns, can be obtained using

MAT B = TRN(A).

Alphanumeric manipulations

EXTENDED BASIC can handle alphanumeric characters (that is, alphabetic and special characters, such as punctuation and spaces) as well as the numeric manipulations of standard BASIC. This is accomplished by using a special notation that distinguishes the alphanumeric (which has been handled in the Binary Coded Decimal internal code of Chapter 2 and will not be used in computation in this chapter) and the numeric character (which will be used in computation and will be represented in binary).

Unfortunately, the special notation used varies from supplier to supplier. As a first illustration, we again refer to the General Electric conventions, which are a direct extension of the original Dartmouth BASIC specifications. You can distinguish an alphabetic or alphanumeric character by consulting the variable name. A group of alphanumeric characters, often called a *string*, will be denoted by a string variable consisting of a single letter followed by a dollar sign, $. The length that such a defined string can have varies with the installation, and can range from 6 to 60 or more characters, so again check the user manual for your particular machine.

1 / Alphanumeric READ, INPUT, and PRINT

The letter "A" may, for example, be defined as A$, and the word DOG as B$. Alphanumerics of this type may be used in READ and PRINT commands and intermixed with numeric variables, such as A and B.

To illustrate,

```
100 READ A5,A$,B$,C,D$
110 PRINT A$;B$;A5;D$;C
120 DATA 5,MONDAY, " MAY",1970,","
999 END
```

will produce the output

```
MONDAY MAY 5 , 1970
```

Note the difference between the string variables A$,B$, and C$, and the usual variables A5 and C. Also note the effect of the semicolon in the PRINT statement: (1) For string variables no space is provided; (2) for usual variables one or more spaces will be provided, depending upon the size of the number to be printed. (The string variable is treated as if it were a literal when it is printed. Recall that a statement such as 100 PRINT "M";"A";"R";"Y" will produce the output MARY.)

In the DATA statement of line 120 as well as in the READ and PRINT commands, string variables and numeric variables may be intermixed. However, should an alphanumeric string contain any characters that have special meaning or special handling in BASIC—commas, semicolons, leading spaces, etc.—that string must be enclosed in quotes in the DATA statement. For example, in line 120, " MAY" contains a *leading* space which is normally disregarded in BASIC. If you want it, as we do here, the string must be quoted. Similarly, since the comma is a special character in BASIC, it is enclosed in quotes in line 120. As we shall see in the next example, spaces within a string (embedded spaces) are not considered special in standard BASIC, so strings containing them need not be enclosed in quotes. Trailing spaces are also considered part of a string in standard BASIC. Finally, notice in line 120 that the unquoted commas serve to separate the variables and are therefore called delimiters. (In some cases, an installation may use other characters, such as an embedded space, as delimiters. This is not a standard variation, but you may see it. In such cases, strings containing embedded spaces that you want to print should be quoted.)

The same form of argument holds for the INPUT command. The command

100 INPUT A$

calls for the user to type on the Teletype (upon demand) an alphanumeric string, which must be less than or equal in length to that specified by your system.

To increase the length of an INPUT, READ, or PRINT string, we simply divide our desired string into parts. For example, if the upper limit on string length is 15 characters and we wish to handle

CHARLES BABBAGE WAS AN INVENTOR AND LADY LOVELACE WAS HIS FRIEND.

(which contains a total of 62 characters including spaces), we could READ and PRINT the entire string as follows:

```
100 READ A$,B$,C$,D$,E$
110 PRINT A$;B$;C$;E$
120 DATA CHARLES BABBAGE , WAS AN INVENTO,R AND LADY LOVE
130 DATA LACE WAS HIS FRI,END.
999 END

RUN

CHARLES BABBAGE WAS AN INVENTOR AND LADY LOVELACE WAS HIS FRIEND.
```

Note in the above example that no quotes have been used in the DATA statement, so leading spaces are ignored in the output. Also note the effect of the semicolons in the PRINT statement. Except for the leading space before WAS, it puts the sequence of strings together without intervening spaces. The trailing space after BABBAGE is retained, however, since it is considered part of the first string and occurs before the delimiting comma.

2 / *Alphanumeric substitution and comparison*

Although no numeric computations may be performed on alphanumerics, one alphanumeric may be *substituted* for another and *tested* against another.

Using the LET substitution command, you may replace one string with another, provided both are within the length constraints imposed by your system.

Thus, if A$ is JACK and B$ is MARY, LET A$ = B$ replaces JACK with MARY. After the substitution both A$ and B$ equal MARY. Similarly, if A$ is A and B$ is AMBROSIA, then LET A$ = B$ will leave both A$ and B$ equal to AMBROSIA. Finally, if A$ is THEODOSIA and B$ is SUE, then LET A$ = B$ eliminates THEODOSIA and leaves both A$ and B$ equal to SUE. In other words, one defined string will be replaced by another, even though their individual lengths vary within the maximum limit.

Another useful substitution is to introduce an alphanumeric definition within a program.

```
100 LET A$ = "GRAND TOTAL"
```

defines A$ as shown. You must always use quotes about a string literally defined in a substitution statement.

Although you should never set an alphanumeric variable equal to a numeric variable, it is possible to have numbers and special characters in your string definition. Each of the following forms is legal, under the rules described above:

```
100 LET A$ = "REPORT 23"
100 LET X$ = "23"
100 LET S$ = "$"
100 LET Q$ = "A$"
```

Because quotation marks are used for several purposes in BASIC and its extensions, it may be helpful if we summarize. Quotation marks are used to enclose

1. Literals in a PRINT statement, e.g.,

```
100 PRINT "A"
```

2. Literally defined strings in a substitution statement, e.g.,

```
100 LET M$ = "MARY"
```

3. Strings in DATA and INPUT statements that contain characters with special meaning in BASIC, e.g.,

```
800 DATA "YEA,YEA;NAY,NAY"
```

For reasons that will be clear after some thought, quotation marks must be handled with special care. In particular, quotation marks within quotation marks should be avoided, since the meaning of such a string is not clear. To illustrate,

```
100 READ A$
110 PRINT A$
800 DATA HE SAID "NO"
999 END
```

will produce the output HE SAID "NO", but to substitute for line 800

```
800 DATA "HE SAID, "NO"."
```

will cause most systems to look for a delimiter after the second quotation mark encountered. When none is found (N is not a delimiter), you will get an error message.

Using the IF/THEN statement you may compare strings using any of the six valid relations (=, >, <, >=, <=, <>). To make such comparisons, you first need to check the *collation sequence* used by your system as shown in Table 14.2. The collation sequence gives the exact order in which the computer will sequence numbers, letters, and special characters in a comparison. In the collation sequence for GE EXTENDED BASIC, shown in Table 14.2, notice that each character in the computer's character set may be given a corresponding decimal number and a corresponding Binary Coded Decimal number. In Table 14.2 the 6-bit BCD code is used. The *octal* numbers shown, which represent a count to the base 8, are a shorthand for describing the BCD code. In particular, one octal character (which may range from 0 to 7) corresponds exactly to 3 binary bits, e.g., octal 7 is equivalent to binary 111, and octal 4 is equal to 010. Looking at the 6-bit BCD as two 3-bit parts, we can describe the total 6-bit BCD code with two octal numbers, which will tell us quickly how to write the BCD detail. Thus, octal 21 corresponds to BCD 010 001, or more compactly 010001, which is also shown as the letter "A" in Table 14.2.

Since for practical purposes, the user need only know the sequence in which a computer's characters will be compared in a test, many books show only the octal numbers of Table 14.2 and the corresponding character from the computer's character set.

Returning to the collation sequence, we note that the letter A has a *smaller* number—by any of the schemes—than the letter Z; thus Z is greater than A in tests that employ the collation sequence given in Table 14.2. Similarly, J is greater than I, etc. In making comparisons of alphanumeric strings, the computer compares the BCD codes that make them up. An orderly progression of the BCD codes is thus necessary to make sequential comparisons, such as those needed when sorting, as illustrated by Program SORT of Chapter 11.

TABLE 14-2
RELATES KEYBOARD CHARACTERS TO COMPUTER BCD CODES

CHARACTER NUMBER (DECIMAL)	YOUR KEYBOARD CHARACTER	THE EQUIVALENT OCTAL	THE EQUIVALENT BCD
0	0	00	000000
1	1	01	000001
2	2	02	000010
3	3	03	000011
4	4	04	000100
5	5	05	000101
6	6	06	000110
7	7	07	000111
8	8	10	001000
9	9	11	001001
10	APOSTROPHE	12	001010
11	:	13	001011
12	(	14	001100
13	;	15	001101
14	=	16	001110
15	LEFT SLASH	17	001111
16	+	20	010000
17	A	21	010001
18	B	22	010010
19	C	23	010011
20	D	24	010100
21	E	25	010101
22	F	26	010110
23	G	27	010111
24	H	30	011000
25	I	31	011001
26	BELL	32	011010
27	.	33	011011
28	QUOTE	34	011100
29	?	35	011101
30	<	36	011110
31	RETURN	37	011111

CHARACTER NUMBER (DECIMAL)	YOUR KEYBOARD CHARACTER	THE EQUIVALENT OCTAL	THE EQUIVALENT BCD
32	-	40	100000
33	J	41	100001
34	K	42	100010
35	L	43	100011
36	M	44	100100
37	N	45	100101
38	O	46	100110
39	P	47	100111
40	Q	50	101000
41	R	51	101001
42	TAB	52	101010
43	$	53	101011
44	*	54	101100
45	END MSG.	55	101101
46	>	56	101110
47	↑	57	101111
---------	---------	----------	----------
48	SPACE	60	110000
49	/	61	110001
50	S	62	110010
51	T	63	110011
52	U	64	110100
53	V	65	110101
54	W	66	110110
55	X	67	110111
56	Y	70	111000
57	Z	71	111001
58	LINE FEED	72	111010
59	,	73	111011
60	)	74	111100
61	[	75	111101
62	]	76	111110
63	FILL	77	111111

[NOTE: SOME OF THE ABOVE CHARACTERS (COLUMN 2) MAY
NOT APPEAR ON YOUR TELETYPE KEYBOARD, OR MAY BE REPLACED
WITH ALTERNATE SYMBOLS. CHECK FOR LOCAL VARIATIONS.
ALSO SOME KEYS, SUCH AS LINE FEED, RETURN, ETC., DO
NOT PRINT. OTHER CHARACTERS, SUCH AS THE APOSTROPHE
AND THE QUOTE MARK DO NOT USUALLY PRINT IN BASIC.]

Here are some examples of string comparisons you may frequently encounter.

a. Asking a Teletype user a question and accepting his response in alphanumerics.

```
100 PRINT "DO YOU WANT ANOTHER EVALUATION: TYPE"
110 PRINT "YES OR NO"
120 INPUT A$
130 IF A$ = "NO" THEN 999
- - - - -
- - - - -
998 GO TO 100
999 END
```

At line 120 the console user will receive a "?" from the computer, and must then type either YES or NO to continue. In the example above, if the user types anything but NO, the processing will continue for another cycle. A more conservative approach would be to test for YES, and continue only when that word was received.

b. Placing words in alphabetic order. Here is a brief sorting example to illustrate string sequencing.

```
LIST




100 LET A$ = "JACK"
110 LET B$ = "MARY"
120 IF A$<B$ THEN 150
130 PRINT B$,A$
140 GO TO 999
150 PRINT A$,B$
999 END
```

The output from the program is first JACK, then MARY, because in the comparison JACK is less than MARY and line 150 applies. If two strings of different length are compared, the *shorter* string and the corresponding part of the longer string will be used. Should comparison result in an equality, the shorter string will be considered the lesser of the two (using the collation sequence of Table 14.2). By this rule, JACK is less than JACKSON.

c. Branching conditionally after an alphanumeric test.

```
100 LET M$ = "FORD"
110 IF "CHEVROLET" > M$ THEN 200
120 GO TO 300
- - - - - - - -
- - - - - - - -
```

Since CHEVROLET is not greater than FORD (it is less) in our collation sequence, program control will progress to line 300 and thereafter.

3 / *Lists of strings*

In addition to individual treatment, strings may be handled in lists. However, in most BASIC installations, strings may not be handled in tabular (or matrix) form.

To set up a list of strings we use the DIM statement *with only one subscript:*

```
DIM A$(10)
```

sets up a list to hold 10 alphanumeric strings, which may be later referenced by the subscripted string variable names A$(1) through A$(10). [DIM A$(10,10) is not permitted because of the double subscripts. Subscripted string variables must consist of a letter followed by the $, then a single subscript. A number may not be used after the first letter, e.g., A1$(10) will not be valid in most systems.]

Within these conventions, alphanumeric strings stored in or taken from lists may be handled just as single alphanumeric strings are. Thus, you can do any of the following:

```
100 LET A$(1) = B$(10)
100 IF A$(5) > C$(19) THEN 999
100 LET A$(6) = "MARCH"
```

As a practical illustration, suppose you want to have a list of the months of the year in chronological (not alphabetical) order. You may then set up a string list DIM M$(12), read in the string JANUARY through DECEMBER using the methods of Chapter 11, then at any later time produce the list of strings in monthly order by printing M$(1) through M$(12) in that order. [The most appropriate way to accomplish this is to both READ and PRINT M$(I) in a loop with the index I running from 1 through 12.]

4 / Variations in string manipulation and definition in different systems

Although the definitions and methods for alphanumeric data handling in the above paragraphs are the most widely used in EXTENDED BASIC, variations do exist. Check with your computer center or supplier for local details. Regardless of the detailed differences you may find, however, the essential procedural structure will remain the same.[5]

Tabulation and format control in EXTENDED BASIC

The TAB function, which has the form TAB(N), is available in most EXTENDED BASIC systems. TAB(N) is used with the PRINT command to move the character printer to the right under user control. The number specified by N in TAB(N) specifies how many character positions you want to move to the right *as measured from the left-hand margin.*

Recall that the only format control we have in standard BASIC is provided by the comma and the semicolon. The comma used between PRINT variables provides a standard five columns of 15 characters each; the semicolon provides spacing dependent upon the number of characters that will appear—a spacing for numbers which usually cannot be less than two characters. TAB(N) will permit you to space your output across your page under your control. Some EXTENDED BASIC systems may number the columns of the Teletype page from zero through 74, for a total of 75. If you have such a numbering system, a statement such as

```
100 PRINT TAB(14); "A"
```

will place the letter A in column 15 of your page—if you are accustomed to counting columns starting with 1 rather than zero. Other suppliers and schools have modified the TAB operation to count from the more natural column 1, so in those systems

```
100 PRINT TAB(15); "A"
```

[5] One point to check is whether your local computer center or service bureau offers *true* string-manipulation capability. The string manipulations described operate by testing, handling, and working with *each* character in a string. This form of manipulation is highly flexible and rewarding. Some computer installations of EXTENDED BASIC do not provide this character-by-character analysis, but rather offer pseudocharacter manipulation, which may seem equivalent, but is not the same. If your computing center handles alphanumerics *in groups*, you may not be able to accomplish the detailed comparisons described above. Without going into detail, group handling permits tests for equality. But, to sort letters or alphanumeric groups, in their collation sequence, or to make other comparisons you may need to employ special tricks that will depend upon your machine's construction and internal codes.

will place A in column 15 of your page. The adjustment from one system to another is easy, if you know local conventions. In the examples to follow, we assume that you will count columns starting from 1.

The only exceptions to the rules stated above are

1. You may not tab backwards. Thus if you are now at position 40, you may not TAB(10). Your statement will be ignored.

2. You must tab enough. The comma and semicolon format rules override the TAB operation, so your tabulation jump must be greater than the comma or semicolon would otherwise provide. For this reason, when using TAB always separate print segments with a semicolon, which provides the smallest possible field for printing.

3. You should not TAB beyond the end of one line, as a general rule. If you do, most systems will TAB your next output to the next line in a column position equal to your stated position *less* the largest multiple of the line width used in the system.

Consider an example (in which the columns are numbered from 1 through 75).

```
LIST


10 PRINT "THE COLUMN NUMBERS ARE:"
15 PRINT "00000000011111111112"
20 PRINT "12345678901234567890"
30 LET X=5.36
40 LET Y=-5.36
50 PRINT TAB(10);X
60 PRINT TAB(10);Y
70 PRINT TAB(10);"A"
99 END

RUN

THE COLUMN NUMBERS ARE:
00000000011111111112
12345678901234567890
           5.36
          -5.36
          A

    99,  NORMAL EXIT FROM PROG.

TIME:     0.074 SEC.
```

The above program illustrates how TAB(N) works in handling both numerics (5.36) and literals (A). Literals are tabbed exactly; numerics are tabbed to the specified column position, plus one—to allow for a possible negative sign. In the example shown above we see that the number 5.36 is spaced off to the right one more than we would otherwise expect, had we not realized that a sign might be required.

With this knowledge in mind, we may go ahead to other trials. Suppose you wanted to right-justify your BASIC output (which is left-justified under BASIC's standard conventions). What would you do?

You could begin to count characters and align your decimal points by how many integer positions there were to the left of your decimal point for any given set of numbers rounded to a given number of places. To illustrate, we present Program DEC1 that will round a set of numbers to two decimal places, then right-justify them into column 15 of your output page. (By extension, you could apply the same methods to any table or chart.)

First we show the program, then the complete output, including a detailed variable trace, and finally, the simple output, without the detail. [Variable K is the number of integer character positions for each number; N is the final factor for TAB(N), when C is the column into which you wish to right-justify. Variable C is arbitrary, and set at column 15 in the illustration.]

```
LIST


2 REM PROGRAM DEC1: PROVIDES RIGHT-JUSTIFIED
3 REM OUTPUT FORMAT IN BASIC FOR NUMBERS.
10 DIM A(1,6)
20 MAT READ A
30 PRINT
35 LET C=15
43 PRINT"THE COLUMN NUMBERS ARE:"
45 PRINT"00000000011111111112"
46 PRINT"12345678901234567890"
48 PRINT TAB(C-5);"A"
50 FOR J=1 TO 6
60 GOSUB 100
70 PRINT TAB(N);A(1,J)
80 NEXT J
85 STOP
90 REM=============ALIGNMENT SUBROUTINE=======
100 REM ROUNDS TO TWO DECIMAL PLACES
```

```
110 REM AND COMPUTES N FOR TAB(N)
120 LET A(1,J)=INT(100*A(1,J)+.5*SGN(A(1,J)))/100
130 FOR K=1 TO C
135 LET X=INT(ABS(A(1,J))/(10↑K))
140 IF X<1 THEN 160
150 NEXT K
151 REM N IS THE CORRECTION FACTOR
160 LET N=C-3-K
220 PRINT "K IS NOW ";K
255 PRINT "N IS NOW ";N
260 RETURN
800 DATA 10.23,10,1.237,1000.2569,-20.6,1000.789
999 END

RUN



THE COLUMN NUMBERS ARE:
00000000011111111112
12345678901234567890
          A
K IS NOW  2
N IS NOW  10
          10.23
K IS NOW  2
N IS NOW  10
          10
K IS NOW  1
N IS NOW  11
           1.24
K IS NOW  4
N IS NOW  8
         1000.26
K IS NOW  2
N IS NOW  10
         -20.61
K IS NOW  4
N IS NOW  8
         1000.79

    85,  NORMAL EXIT FROM PROG.
```

```
220
255

RUN


THE COLUMN NUMBERS ARE:
00000000011111111112
12345678901234567890
          A
           10.23
           10
            1.24
         1000.26
          -20.61
         1000.79

   85,  NORMAL EXIT FROM PROG.

TIME:     0.194 SEC.
```

Note in the output of DEC1 that BASIC, by convention, omits trailing zero as well as the decimal point if it is followed by zeroes.

Although we have produced an output which looks partially commercial, it still lacks the complete decimal point and zero right-justified print that more advanced languages can provide.

To provide some elegance in BASIC output, IBM's CALL/360 BASIC has provided format output control for the manager. Recently, other services have introduced a similar, if not identical, ability.

Suppose you had to find the total of interest and principal on $1000 at 5%—if the principal were invested for 5, 6, 7, 8, 9, or 10 years. We have seen similar problems before, and the loop required for the computation is familiar from Chapter 11. The PRINT command, however, is slightly different in this application. PRINT USING 60,N,A not only refers to the variables N and A, but also to the *format statement* in line 60. At line 60 each # sign indicates the position of an output character *that must be shown.* The special characters such as the dollar sign ($) and the decimal point (.) will be printed as they stand, since they are literals. The program and its associated output are given below.[6]

---

[6] From IBM Publication J20-0035-1, *op. cit.*, p. 13.

```
10 READ P, I
20 DATA 1000.00, 5
30 FOR N = 5 TO 10
40 LET A = P * (1 + I/100) ↑ N
50 PRINT USING 60, N, A
60 : IN ## YEARS, THE AMOUNT WILL BE $####.##
65 NEXT N
70 END
RUN

IN  5 YEARS, THE AMOUNT WILL BE $1276.28
IN  6 YEARS, THE AMOUNT WILL BE $1340.09
IN  7 YEARS, THE AMOUNT WILL BE $1407.09
IN  8 YEARS, THE AMOUNT WILL BE $1477.44
IN  9 YEARS, THE AMOUNT WILL BE $1551.31
IN 10 YEARS, THE AMOUNT WILL BE $1628.88
```

File capability

File capability allows you to write the results of your program, not only on paper but also in the computer's memory—as you desire. From the programmer's viewpoint, file capability in any language is essential.

When you have the output of one program in computer memory (usually disc storage), you can use it as input to your next job. This sequential process permits you to "chain" your results by feeding the output of a previous program into a secondary program or into any one that follows. Thus, you may build your reservoir of data or previous results for later exploitation.

Most EXTENDED BASIC systems offer such capability in one form or another. Yet again, the variation in detail is great. Check with your computing center or time-sharing suppliers to see if you have this provision in your system. The ability to float files from one program to the next on call is wonderfully exhilarating. To be able to do so is to be able to call on the skills and knowledge of your friends and your historical associates. That ability, like the perfection of Babbage's historical machines, can be a gift beyond compare—if you appreciate it and use it properly.

Subsidiary systems commands

As you move to EXTENDED BASIC you will look for greater system command capability. System commands, such as RUN and LIST without line numbers, were used in the previous chapters. But, there are others such as RENUMBER, which takes program line numbers and converts them to new ones under your command.

Because advanced system commands are not standardized, we will not repeat them here. In general you may merge, delete, extract, weave, and perform similar operations on program lines. Further, many advanced system applications provide "string-editing ability," which permits you to character edit, search, and modify under system control. Such capabilities are not part of BASIC or any other language, but are built into your time-sharing control system via the computer's supervisory program.

Again, check your detailed computer manual for such commands. EXTENDED BASIC and advanced system commands go together.

The merits and shortcomings of BASIC

BASIC has the virtue of simplicity and is easy to teach and learn. It is also standardized, so that what you have learned in Chapters 7 through 12 can be applied anywhere BASIC is used (which is at most time-sharing and educational installations these days). To make the language simple and to standardize its few principles, some of the things you might like to do, for example, complete format control for both data input and output, have not been included in BASIC. Many other technical features of advanced languages, such as the ability to segment data into its ultimate computer representation, the binary bit, also have been omitted.

EXTENDED BASIC tries to bridge the gap and does indeed offer one way to make the transition to greater language flexibility. The MAT operations discussed in this chapter are particularly useful if you are doing scientific work. But even the alphanumeric character-handling ability of EXTENDED BASIC, as well as its ultimate format control, the TAB function, leaves something to be desired.[7] And the details of EXTENDED BASIC have not been standardized.

What you have learned from BASIC and its extensions will be immediately useful to you in small-scale problems and conceptually useful to you in the large. For the principles are the same—only the detail differs.

But if you must learn a number of details in the extension of your knowledge it pays to devote your attention to an advanced language, such as FORTRAN—which *has* been standardized in most of the country—rather than to spend more time attempting to learn every variation and extension of BASIC. The power of BASIC as a computer language and tool should

---

[7] As noted in this chapter, IBM's CALL/360 BASIC attempts to overcome these shortcomings by providing output format control. Although CALL/360 BASIC's output format ability accommodates many small-scale jobs, it cannot achieve the flexibility provided by advanced languages. It is unfortunate that time-sharing suppliers and computer vendors have not joined to standardize BASIC extensions, but have attempted separately to specialize their own services for short-range commercial gain. Thus, they have limited the mass market standardization would provide.

not be underrated. With its few simple rules you can accomplish 90 percent of all students and simple commercial assignments. It is that final 10 percent that always breaks the user's heart. It is the very difficult business or scientific problem that demands ultimate flexibility, either because of volume production, high input/output volumes, ultimate demands upon computer capacity, or the need to use computing tricks (such as format manipulation) that BASIC cannot provide. Nobody computes a payroll using BASIC.

A Farewell to BASIC

Before we leave the BASIC language, we ask you to review the examples of Chapter 13. If you understand them, you have understood the essential principles of computer language use. Chapter 15 presents some problems that illustrate the difference between learning a computer language and its application. Then, in Chapters 16 to 18 we use the principles of BASIC to help you make the transition from BASIC to FORTRAN.

PROBLEMS

14-1 MAT READ the following DATA line, where your matrix is of order 3 × 3. Then MAT PRINT the result of your MAT READ:

800 DATA 1, 2, 3, 4, 5, 6, 7, 8, 9

14-2 A clothing store has an item in stock, classified as small, medium, and large versus red, white, and blue. The stock on hand (by size and color) is given in Table A where rows represent size and columns represent color. The price per unit is also given in the same classification scheme in Table B. How much inventory by size and color does the merchant have on hand in dollars? (Compare with Program INVENTORY in Chapter 11.)

Table A

	R	W	B
S	1	8	3
M	20	10	8
L	6	2	5

Table B

	R	W	B
S	1.00	1.25	1.30
M	1.25	1.50	1.85
L	1.35	1.65	1.92

14-3 You are given two equations of the form

$$3 * X + 4 * Y = 6$$
$$2 * X + 7 * Y = 17$$

Find the values of X and Y by any means you choose; then find the same numerical result using the BASIC inversion command.

14-4 How could you place the word PAGE on your teletypewriter page starting with "P" in column 60?

14-5 When comparing alphanumeric strings given the collation sequence of Table 14.2, why could you say that "MARY" is greater than "JOHN"?

14-6 We wish to sort a number of names and addresses in alphanumeric order to produce a management report. Why would a particular collation sequence be important to the programmer, but not the manager, in this task?

14-7 Suppose we can save the output of computation A and feed it to computation B as B's input. Then suppose the output of that operation, say, C, is fed to computation D. Why would this form of data passage via electronic media be more efficient than either manual input/output or intermediate media such as paper tape? Would it be beneficial to have a number of possible electronic input or output files to call on or write into?

14-8 Our friends at Beautiful Computer Time-Sharing Services have just lost their matrix multiplication capability, because of an unfortunate error on the part of one of their systems programmers. The system is still working, but

MAT C = A * B

fails to work. Write a program following the methods of Chapter 11 that would matrix multiply a 3×4 matrix by a 4×5 matrix, assuming your own data.

14-9 Because Beautiful Computer Time-Sharing Services could not keep up with the ascending pay scale for programmers, most of the personnel left taking many of the BCTSS-developed computer programs with them. (It is a simple matter to make an electronic copy of anything.) However, the president of BCTSS was aware of this possibility, and thought it through. So, he personally altered every stored program in his company's files by one binary bit and wrote a simple conversion routine to make the programs work. This simple conversion routine was known only to the president and one of his trusted employees—a computing machine operator. Why would one binary bit be important in this case?

14-10 If you were buying time-sharing services—or indeed any computer computational services—why would you insist upon complete standardization of your computer language implementation—whatever the language—particularly if you were trading with a number of different suppliers, all of whom might be using different electronic computing equipment?

FIFTEEN

Selected computer problems

In each of the following computer projects, the task is to formulate a method of solution, program it in BASIC, and finally test the solution method and program using suitable test data. A complete narrative, program, and test output have been provided for each problem so that you may follow the reasoning that led to the given results.

The problems illustrated here are more difficult than those shown in Chapter 13, and each requires some additional thinking beyond simple programming. In fact, the essential difference between programming and "coding" (the latter refers to writing program steps to implement a known solution method or processing procedure) is the extra thought required to formalize an unstructured problem so that its solution can be carried out in a step-by-step fashion. This chapter attempts to point out and dramatize that extra skill and to show why you need it in practice.

Computer ciphering and deciphering of secret messages

Julius Caesar devised a secret code to protect his messages. His method was crude by today's standards, but it served as a starting point for the modern science of cryptography. Caesar used a simple alphabetic offset to go from one letter to another and back again. Romans often wore special finger rings with sliding segments to provide the mechanical means for implementing this one-for-one transposition.

Suppose we write two alphabets, one above the other, with the lower offset, say, by three characters to the right. Then the letter D would align with the letter A. D could then be enciphered as A, and the reverse process used to decipher an enciphered message.[1] (The symbol = in the example below will stand for a space.)

A B C D E F G H I J K L M N O P Q R S T U V W X Y Z =
___
Y Z = A B C D E F G H I J K L M N O P Q R S T U V W X

Based on the simple table above, we could encipher the simple message "Beware the ides of March" as follows:

B E W A R E = T H E = I D E S = O F = M A R C H =
___
Z B T Y O B X Q E B X F A B P X L C X J Y O = E X

If we now number the alphabetic characters in the first line above from left to right so that A is 1 and = is 27, some thought will reveal that we can *compute* the character transposition necessary for enciphering the suggested message. Thus, for the specific alphabetic offset used in the above illustration, we have the following rules, where A(N) is the character in the Nth position of the alphabet.

1. To encipher [assuming A(N) is a character in cleartext]:
   Replace A(N) with A(N − 3) if $4 \leq N \leq 27$ (1a)
   Replace A(N) with A(N + 24) if $1 \leq N \leq 3$ (1b)
2. To decipher [assuming A(N) is a character in ciphertext]:
   Replace A(N) with A(N + 3) if $1 \leq N \leq 24$ (2a)
   Replace A(N) with A(N − 24) if $25 \leq N \leq 27$ (2b)

Once we have these rules in hand—*and their development is the secret in going from problem to computer program*—the whole process can be committed to computer execution.

Program CIPHER implements this idea. In this program, we show the original cleartext, then the ciphertext resulting from rules (1a) and (1b) (which is in agreement with our handmade solution), and finally the deciphered cleartext produced by rules (2a) and (2b). Since the process is

---

[1] In intelligence terminology, the process of substituting one character for another in a secret message is called enciphering, and the reverse process, deciphering. The words *encode* and *decode* have a slightly different technical meaning. The original message to be enciphered (cleartext) can itself be a misleading set of words, although in normal language. Thus, "Destry rides tonight" might mean, in fact, "The First Division moves at sunrise." Most secret messages are both encoded, as above, and then enciphered, providing a double screen. The enciphered message (ciphertext) is the one transmitted from sender to receiver. The process of recovering the original meaning thus involves both deciphering and decoding. In what follows, we consider the enciphering and deciphering problem only.

entirely one-for-one, or unique in each direction, we can precisely recover what was originally enciphered by using deciphering rules.[2]

In the program, lines 15 through 40 read in the alphabet to be used; lines 55 through 80 read in the number of characters in the message, the message itself, and then display the cleartext message for reference.

Lines 95 through 175 encipher the cleartext and display the ciphertext. Finally, lines 190 through 265 decipher the ciphertext and display the resulting cleartext, which, of course, must match the original cleartext message precisely—as it does in the output shown.

```
LIST

5 REM PROGRAM NAME: CIPHER -- CODES AND DECODES MESSAGES
10 DIM A(27),B(50),C(50)
15 FOR I=1 TO 27
20 READ A(I)
40 NEXT I
45 PRINT
50 PRINT "YOUR CLEARTEXT MESSAGE IS"
55 READ M
60 FOR I=1 TO M
65 READ B(I)
70 PRINT B(I):A;
80 NEXT I
85 PRINT
90 PRINT "YOUR CIPHERTEXT MESSAGE IS"
95 FOR I=1 TO M
100 FOR N=1 TO 3
110 IF A(N) <> B(I) THEN 140
120 LET C(I)=A(N+24)
130 PRINT C(I):A;
135 GO TO 175
140 NEXT N
150 FOR N=4 TO 27
155 IF A(N) <> B(I) THEN 170
```

[2] Program CIPHER deals with alphanumeric manipulation and test, and the BASIC program shown requires the application of EXTENDED BASIC for this purpose. In the present example, the method of alphanumeric handling varies slightly from that discussed in Chapter 14, so the program illustrates both this variation and the translation process. The computer used in Program CIPHER's execution was a Control Data Corporation 3600, and the conventions used for its BASIC alphanumeric handling are common to many CDC 3600 (as well as other computer) installations. In particular, an alphanumeric variable is defined at READ time by having the data in quotes. Thereafter, as in the nonequality tests, alphanumeric variables are handled just like numeric variables. However, at PRINT time, the alphanumeric variables are specified by attaching a trailing ":A" to each. In such installations, alphanumeric tests are in fact made numerically, and the function of the trailing ":A" is to output an alphanumeric character equivalent to an internal computer number. This detail in no way affects the logic of the computer program, but is a programming detail that must be considered in a specific computer application.

```
160 LET C(I) = A(N-3)
165 PRINT C(I):A;
170 NEXT N
175 NEXT I
180 PRINT
185 PRINT "THE DECODED CIPHERTEXT (ORIGINAL CLEARTEXT) IS"
190 FOR I=1 TO N
195 FOR N=1 TO 24
200 IF A(N) <> C(I) THEN 230
205 PRINT A(N+3):A;
220 GO TO 265
230 NEXT N
235 FOR N=25 TO 27
240 IF A(N) <> C(I) THEN 260
245 PRINT A(N-24):A;
260 NEXT N
265 NEXT I
270 PRINT
700 DATA "A","B","C","D","E","F","G","H","I","J"
710 DATA "K","L","M","N","O","P","Q","R","S","T"
720 DATA "U","V","W","X","Y","Z","="
790 DATA 25
800 DATA "B","E","W","A","R","E","="
810 DATA "T","H","E","="
820 DATA "I","D","E","S","="
830 DATA "O","F","="
840 DATA "M","A","R","C","H","="
999 END
```

```
RUN


YOUR CLEARTEXT MESSAGE IS
B       E       W       A       R       E       =       T
H       E       =       I       D       E       S       =
O       F       =       M       A       R       C       H
=
YOUR CIPHERTEXT MESSAGE IS
Z       B       T       Y       O       B       X       Q
E       B       X       F       A       B       P       X
L       C       X       J       Y       O       =       E
X
THE DECODED CIPHERTEXT (ORIGINAL CLEARTEXT) IS
B       E       W       A       R       E       =       T
H       E       =       I       D       E       S       =
O       F       =       M       A       R       C       H
=

  999,  NORMAL EXIT FROM PROG.

TIME:     0.549 SEC.
```

After we have written a specific program and made it work, it pays to think about how that program can be generalized to make it more useful; that is, we ask how the original program can be applied to the widest possible number of cases.

To do this we may think of the possibility of a *generalized offset* of the enciphering alphabet. Call that generalized offset Z. Then, using Z, we could with some additional thought rewrite our enciphering and deciphering rules as follows:

3. To encipher using generalized offset Z [where A(N) is a cleartext character]:

Replace A(N) with A(N − Z) if $Z + 1 \leq N \leq 27$ (3a)

Replace A(N) with A(N + 27 − Z) if $1 \leq N \leq Z$ (3b)

4. To decipher using generalized offset Z [where A(N) is a ciphertext character]:

Replace A(N) with A(N + Z) if $1 \leq N \leq 27 - Z$ (4a)

Replace A(N) with A(N − (27 − Z)) if $(27 - Z + 1) \leq N \leq 27$ (4b)

[To confirm your understanding of the generalization, let Z = 3, and check that result with rules (1a) through (2b).]

Now to bring Caesar's method up to date, you may realize that there is no reason why the offset Z has to be a constant for each character enciphered or deciphered; indeed, if Z *were* a constant any competent cryptographer could crack your cipher in short order—if you gave him enough messages to look at.[3] Theoretically, the *only* way to obscure all structural hints in the ciphertext is to let the offset, Z, be a *random variable for each character enciphered from the cleartext.* In our example Z could take on the values 1–26 at random for each enciphered character if we used a random number generation to produce it. [One experimental method is to employ the RND(X) function in BASIC to generate the character deviates 1–26 for use in the above program.][4]

The trick, of course, is that both sender and receiver, or encipherer and decipherer, must be using the same exact form of random offset in perfect

---

[3] Code breaking or, precisely, cipher breaking is based on the statistical structure all languages exhibit. In most languages vowels occur more frequently than consonants. This fact alone is a starting point in cryptanalysis. For a fascinating discussion, as well as a monumental history of the subject from Babylon to the present times, see David Kahn, *Code-Breakers* (New York: Macmillan, 1966).

[4] If Z is 1, then the ciphertext is offset by one character from the cleartext. If Z is 26, then the ciphertext is also offset by one from the cleartext, but in the opposite direction. Although the average offset (using a random Z) is numerically thirteen characters, we have an equal probability of any particular offset from 1 through 26 (in the limit). In BASIC, an appropriate programming line to generate a random number (1–26) is LET Z = INT(26 * RND(X) + 1). In general if we want random numbers chosen from the A integers of which B is the smallest we LET Z = INT(A * RND(X) + B).

synchronization! Since the RND(X) function in BASIC always produces the same sequence of numbers, *with the same starting point*, your experiments with Program CIPHER will work, so long as you both encipher and decipher on the same computing machine at the same location. In fact, you could communicate in your secret cipher (produced by the random generation of Z) with any receiver who uses *precisely* the same electronic computer with *precisely* the same BASIC compiler as you. (The *slightest difference* would garble the deciphering procedure at the receiving end.)

A complete discussion of random number generation and its control is beyond the scope of this text, and thus of this example.[5] Suffice it to say that today most military and intelligence enciphering and deciphering revolves about computer random number generation and its control. Practical and foolproof methods that provide both sender and receiver with the *exact* synchronization of random numbers required to encipher and decipher secret messages are, of course, top secret—even though the principles of this ultimate enciphering-deciphering weapon were known as early as World War I.

Try your hand at the generalization of Program CIPHER. You will have fun and will also learn much about how modern Caesars clutch their secrets to their breast.

The dating game

The computer can be used to match job prospects with employers, houses with house hunters, stock and bond buys-and-sales with available opportunities, and boys with girls for dates. Indeed, computer *data* matching is fundamental to most information processing operations. Sorting depends upon it (see Problem 11-7); so do computer tests of all kinds.

To illustrate this fact in a lighter vein, consider the computer dating problem. To obtain input data for processing, suppose we administer the highly simplified questionnaire of personal facts and opinions shown in Table 15.1. As a consequence of this administration, suppose (again for simplicity of illustration) we have *one* male and *five* female respondents to process. Our objective is to find the female in the list who would be most suitable for the single male respondent—given, of course, the suitability of the questionnaire for this matching process.[6]

---

[5] The reader interested in such topics should consult Donald E. Knuth, *The Art of Computer Programming*, vol. 2 (Reading, Mass.: Addison-Wesley Publishing Company, Inc., 1969), chapter 3. Knuth's projected encyclopedia of seven volumes, of which two are available at this writing, has already become a masterwork of computer technology.

[6] The construction of such questionnaires is a specialty in each field of endeavor, from house hunting to dating, and cannot be covered in detail here.

TABLE 15.1

Dating Questionnaire

A. Print your first name in the box marked A to the right. If your first name is longer than six characters, abbreviate it to fit the box. Start printing from the left.

1	2	3	4	5	6

box A

B. To confirm your sex as a double-check, print 1 in box U if you are male, 0 if you are female.

box U

In the following questions print the number of your answer (1–4) in the box indicated. Select one and only one choice in each instance.

C. Print your answer (1–4) in box V.
Do you prefer to
1. Listen to Bach?
2. Read *Playboy*?
3. Go for long walks?
4. Go horseback riding?

box V

D. Print your answer (1–4) in box W.
Which number best describes your height?
1. 5′0″ to 5′4″?
2. 5′4″ to 5′6″?
3. 5′6″ to 5′10″?
4. 5′10″ to 6′0″?

box W

E. Print your answer (1–4) in box X.
What do you prefer to eat?
1. Plain home cooking?
2. Pizza?
3. Grilled steak and potatoes?
4. French cooking with lots of sauce?

box X

F. Print your answer (1–4) in box Y.
How do you feel about the sexual question?
1. Only for animals in heat?
2. Only after marriage?
3. Maybe?
4. Divine experience?

box Y

G. Print your answer (1–4) in box Z.
What do you like to drink?
1. Milk?
2. Coke?
3. Beer?
4. Alcohol?

box Z

Now summarize your answers by copying them into the detailed squares below.

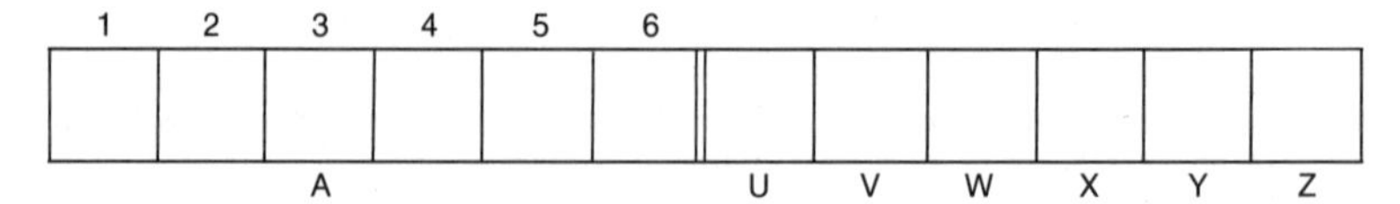

To use some arbitrary data, suppose we have the following inputs for the computer from our coded data forms:

A											
1	2	3	4	5	6	U	V	W	X	Y	Z
H	E	N	R	Y		1	4	4	4	4	4
M	A	R	Y			0	1	1	1	1	1
A	L	I	C	E		0	2	2	3	3	2
J	O	A	N			0	1	4	2	3	4
J	O	Y	C	E		0	4	1	3	2	4
Z	E	L	D	A		0	4	3	3	4	4

Given the input data as shown in coded form, we reduce it to a form suitable for a computer program in BASIC. Assuming that our data shall start at program line 800 of our forthcoming program, we have as a specific data input example:

```
800 DATA "HENRY", 1, 4, 4, 4, 4, 4
805 DATA "MARY", 0, 1, 1, 1, 1, 1
810 DATA "ALICE", 0, 2, 2, 3, 3, 2
815 DATA "JOAN", 0, 1, 4, 2, 3, 4
820 DATA "JOYCE", 0, 4, 1, 3, 2, 4
825 DATA "ZELDA", 0, 4, 3, 3, 4, 4
```

All we need now is a rule to match "HENRY" with one of the girls.

As an arbitrary rule, suppose we decide to select a girl for "HENRY" that will *minimize the sum of the squared deviations between "HENRY" questionnaire choices and those of the girls in our file*, based on the code numbers given.[7]

To simplify the matching program, let us also assume that we have pre-separated our file into boys and girls, with the boys coming first in order. We also have a count of the boys, say, B, and a count of the girls, say, G, in the total file. (The method of SORT3, Problem 11-7 could have been used to perform this preliminary arrangement, or you could incorporate SORT3 into the following program before the matching starts.) Finally, assume that we will supply our new program the B and G count at line 795 of the program as

```
795 DATA 1,5
```

---

[7] Again, the choice of such a rule is a matter of professional experience, and a discussion of how to formulate a "best" rule is beyond the scope of this simple illustration.

as a consequence of the hypothetical data proposed. With the specifications and test data before us, we can now consider Program DATE.

The input to our program is the data previously specified; the output is to be a date for "HENRY"; the method of execution is to sum the squared deviations of questionnaire code choices, boy versus girl, as previously assumed.

The careful reader will realize that our proposed matching scheme could result in a tie score for two or more girls. Which girl in that case would be reported to "HENRY"? Program DATE breaks ties by reporting to "HENRY" the *last* girl in the file with a tie score.

In the program, lines 10 through 25 provide documentation; lines 30 through 95 read in the boy-and-girl data; line 100 picks the first boy on file; lines 110 through 135 compute the girl scores for him; lines 145 through 170 scan the file and pick the last highest-score girl; lines 175 through 190 print out an appropriate message. Lines 200 through 210 ask if we have other boys to check (in this case, NO); if not we stop.

```
LIST


10 REM PROGRAM NAME: DATE -- MATCHES BOY AND GIRL
20 DIM B(20,8),G(20,8)
25 REM B IS NUMBER OF BOYS, G NUMBER OF GIRLS IN FILE
30 READ B,G
50 FOR I=1 TO B
55 FOR J= 1 TO 7
60 READ B(I,J)
65 NEXT J
70 NEXT I
75 FOR I=1 TO G
78 FOR J = 1 TO 7
80 READ G(I,J)
90 NEXT J
95 NEXT I
98 REM PICK FIRST BOY
100 LET I=1
105 REM SCAN GIRLS AND COMPUTE SCORE FOR BOY AT HAND
110 FOR Q=1 TO G
113 LET G(Q,8) = 0
115 FOR J=3 TO 7
125 LET G(Q,8)=G(Q,8)+(B(I,J)-G(Q,J))↑2
130 NEXT J
135 NEXT Q
140 REM WE NOW HAVE GIRL SCORES FOR MALE AT HAND
143 LET S=G(1,8)
144 LET D=1
145 REM PICK GIRL WITH SMALLEST SCORE
150 FOR Q=2 TO G
155 IF G(Q,8)>S THEN 170
160 LET S=G(Q,8)
```

```
165 LET D=Q
170 NEXT Q
175 REM SMALLEST GIRL SCORE NOW FOUND
180 REM PRINT RESULTS
181 PRINT
190 PRINT B(I,1):A;"  CALL     ";G(D,1):A
195 REM IF MORE BOYS GO AHEAD, OTHERWISE STOP
200 LET I=I+1
205 IF I>B THEN 999
210 GO TO 105
795 DATA 1,5
800 DATA "HENRY",1,4,4,4,4,4
805 DATA "MARY",0,1,1,1,1,1
810 DATA "ALICE",0,2,2,3,3,2
815 DATA "JOAN",0,1,4,2,3,4
820 DATA "JOYCE",0,4,1,3,2,4
825 DATA "ZELDA",0,4,3,3,4,4
999 END

RUN
```

After typing RUN at the end of Program DATE we get the following output message:

```
HENRY      CALL      ZELDA

  999,  NORMAL EXIT FROM PROG.

TIME:     0.308 SEC.
```

If we wanted to handle more than one male with the same program, all we change is the boy-girl count at line 795, and introduce the new data. This time, for illustration, call him "JOHN." The appropriate corrections and output for this new variation are as follows:

```
795 DATA 2,5
803 DATA "JOHN",1,1,2,2,1,3

RUN


HENRY      CALL      ZELDA

JOHN       CALL      MARY

  999,  NORMAL EXIT FROM PROG.

TIME:     0.341 SEC.
```

Technically, you should note we have used in this example the alphanumeric conventions used in Program CIPHER. The alphanumeric READ's and PRINT's deviate in detail, but not in concept, from the material of Chapter 14. Also note that we have not made immediate use of the male-female check obtained in box U of the questionnaire, or the 1-or-0 code used to check the first names of our respondents. We assume that such checking was performed during the separation of male and female responses which gave us the data for lines 800 through 825 of our sample program. Program DATE is a perfectly general, although highly simplified, example of practical information processing.

You will find many extensions to this simple dating problem. You could obviously expand the questionnaire or change the decision rule or print for "HENRY"—or all the other boys—not a single date, but a listing of alternate dates, with a ranked score for their computed "desirability." Similarly, you could reverse the process and report desirable dates to the girls. You could include telephone numbers, street addresses, and any other pertinent information you think your dating subscribers might like. You could even have your computer write form letters to all concerned!

Further, you should have no difficulty now in generalizing your dating program to a government or industrial setting. For example, suppose you are a police captain and want to find an officer who (1) can operate a short wave radio, (2) speak Chinese, and (3) is over 6′4″ tall. If you have a file containing this information for the men on your force, you have a dating problem on your hands: It is not boy and girl this time, but man versus job specification.

Or suppose you are an industrial scientist and want to find a material for a new product that is (1) less than $1 per pound, (2) impervious to hydrochloric acid, (3) will withstand temperatures of 300° F., and (4) can be arbitrarily colored with fluorescent dye. A dating problem, pure and simple. If you have the file to scan—and the rule to scan by—you, the scientist, could quickly obtain a list of feasible candidates.

The computer is impartial in its mating of information. If you have the files to search, you get precisely what you ask for. But to be the beneficiary of untold informational blessings could strain you. Suppose you were "HENRY" and were sent, as a consequence of a computer search, *not* one *but one hundred* "ZELDA"'s, each a tie, each with equal desirability, each to be investigated on your own time. That would be a *real* problem. You got what you asked for, but the implementation and choice remains your own. The questions put to the files were not discriminating enough.

To extend your imagination further, think of the current popularity of *management information systems* and what must be accomplished to make them work. Again, a simple dating game! The problem is not really one of electronic computation. It is a matter of choice and compromise, just as dating is. For example, if you want to create a file describing *all* the girls on your campus or in your office what in particular would you put in it? You obviously cannot include everything picked up by questionnaire or by observation. You would exceed the economic capacity of any electronic file presently known! Moreover, the more information you have in your files, the more time and money you will consume in searching for what you want. You must summarize and compromise in both your data collection and decision making to achieve timely action at reasonable cost. The moral of our dating program is about like that. The big decisions in information processing as in life turn out to be a matter of personal preference and the compromises with which you can live.

On mazes, labyrinths, and rote learning

Mazes and architectural labyrinths have intrigued mankind for centuries. Originally mazes protected or hid the valuables or remains of Egyptian and Greek royalty. Later, a maze of passageways and rooms protected Christians in the catacombs of Rome. In subsequent architectural and garden designs the construction of intricate mazes for the amusement of guests became popular. One famous example is the hedge maze at Hampton Court, England, diagrammed in Figure 15.3.

In general, there is always a direct way to run a maze and a vast number of dead-end or circular passageways to avoid. For this reason, psychologists have long used maze experiments to develop "learning curves" for animals ranging from ants and crabs to rats and dogs. Presumably, the rate at which the animal learns to eliminate unsuccessful decisions is one measure of intelligence.

Many sequential decision-making problems may also be diagrammed as a mazelike tree with many branches. From an initial decision some route (the trunk of the tree) leads to an ultimate desirable result. To find the decision sequence that leads to the desired result thus becomes a special maze problem of great practical importance in scientific and business work.

Some thought will reveal that if the most direct route through a maze has been found, it will not involve any back tracking or circular repetition of routes. For example, if each of the passageways in a maze were numbered, the successful route through them could be defined by a string of numbers containing *no* repeated values.

Two difficulties can lead to route repetition. (1) You have reached a dead end and *must* backtrack to find an alternate route. (2) You have encountered a loop and come back to a previous location, an event that is *not* allowed in a successful maze progression. Thus, you must guard against both eventualities, plan to meet them, and know how to recover if you meet that test. To know how to do this and how to implement your decision rules is the essence of Program MAZE.

First, to input the required maze data, consider the conventions summarized in the diagrams and DATA lines of Figure 15.1. The arbitrary conventions shown consist of the following. (1) Draw your proposed maze, numbering each start and end point. According to our formulation the starting point must *always* be numbered 1, as shown in the diagram. All other start and end points may then be numbered at random, as shown. (2) For each start and end point, or maze "node," record the transitions, or paths, that will lead to *larger* numbered nodes. Again, this process is illustrated in Figure 15.1. (If the prize move is to a lower numbered node, as in (d), below, record that transition as shown.) (3) Let the move that results in the prize be denoted by 999, again as shown. (4) Finally, indicate the end of the file of maze data by the arbitrary file delimiter 4E37.

Let M equal the number of nodes (exclusive of the prize number). This count must appear at line 950 of Program MAZE. Further, as a check, note that the number of data pairs used as data must exactly equal the number of connecting line segments in your maze, a number not necessarily equal to M. The pair data starts at line 970 of Program MAZE.

For example, for the four mazes shown in Figure 15.1, page 322, you should input the following data to Program MAZE:

(a) "T" Maze

```
950 DATA 4
970 DATA 1, 2, 2, 3, 2, 4, 999, 4, 5, 4E37
```

(b) Tree Maze

```
950 DATA 10
970 DATA 1, 2, 2, 3, 2, 4, 3, 5, 3, 6, 3, 7, 4, 8, 4, 9, 4, 10, 999, 10, 11, 4E37
```

(c) Circular Maze

```
950 DATA 8
970 DATA 1, 2, 2, 3, 2, 5, 3, 4, 3, 7, 4, 5, 4, 6, 5, 8, 999, 7, 9, 4E37
```

(d) Multicircular Maze

```
950 DATA 10
970 DATA 1, 6, 2, 3, 2, 6, 2, 7, 2, 11, 3, 6, 3, 7, 3, 8, 4, 8
972 DATA 6, 11, 7, 10, 7, 11, 999, 8, 5, 9, 11, 4E37
```

The multicircular maze is the most difficult one and is used for illustration in Program MAZE.

For output, we can specify one of two forms, the first showing a complete trace of the essential variables, the second showing only one successful route through the specified maze.[8] In the following program we show the complete detail and then the corrections required to eliminate the complete trace detail.

```
50 REM PROGRAM NAME: MAZE -- FINDS ONE SUCCESSFUL ROUTE THROUGH ANY
55 REM MAZE. M IS THE NUMBER OF ROWS, M+1 THE NUMBER OF
60 REM COLUMNS IN MAZE MATRIX X(M,M+1); SEE TEXT FOR DETAILS.
65 REM R(K) IS SEQUENCE RECORD. W IS A DUMMY
75 REM VARIABLE USED TO OUTPUT R(K). ENTER NUMBER OF ROWS IN MAZE
80 REM MATRIX AT LINE 950, MATRIX DETAIL AT DATA LINES 961-998.
85 REM F IS ALSO DUMMY VARIABLE USED IN LOOP ELIMINATION TEST.
90 PRINT
100 PRINT
299 REM ***********************************************************
300 REM START ROUTINE
307 DIM X(30,31),R(30)
310 READ M
312 REM READ IN MAZE CONSTRAINTS AND REWARD LOCATION.
313 PRINT "YOUR INPUT PAIRS (EXCLUDING LAST PRIZE MOVE) ARE:"
315 FOR N=1 TO 100
320 READ I
322 IF I=4E37 THEN 372
325 IF I=999 THEN 339
334 READ J
335 PRINT I;J,
336 LET X(I,J)=1
337 LET X(J,I)=1
338 GO TO 341
339 READ I,J
340 LET X(I,J)=9
341 NEXT N
372 REM ***********************************************************
375 REM RUN THROUGH MAZE STARTS
380 LET I=1
385 LET K=1
390 LET R(K)=1
392 REM ***********************************************************
500 REM ROW SEARCH ROUTINE
505 FOR J=1 TO M+1
510 REM CHECK FOR END OF GAME; IF END USE END ROUTINE.
515 IF X(I,J)=9 THEN 900
520 REM MOVE TO FIRST FEASIBLE CHOICE, USING MOVE ROUTINE.
525 IF X(I,J)=1 THEN 600
530 NEXT J
532 GOSUB 870
534 PRINT "DEAD END ENCOUNTERED"
540 GO TO 800
542 REM ***********************************************************
600 REM MOVE ROUTINE. MOVES TO FIRST AVAILABLE CHOICE IN MAZE MATRIX.
602 LET K=K+1
604 LET R(K)=J
606 LET I=J
610 GOSUB 870
612 GO TO 700
```

[8] We will not consider the problem of the shortest route through the maze, but will only guarantee that we will achieve *one* route, which may or may not be the shortest. The extension of this example to the shortest-route problem is beyond our present scope. However, interested readers may find a complete discussion in L. R. Ford, Jr. and H. S. Fulkerson, *Flows in Networks*, Princeton University Press, Princeton, N. J., 1962.

```
622 REM ***********************************************************
650 REM LOOP ELIMINATION ROUTINE. CHECKS FOR REPETITION OF ROUTE.
655 REM  IF REPETITION, PROGRAM MOVES TO ERROR ROUTINE.
700 FOR F=1 TO K-1
710 IF R(K)=R(F) THEN 716
712 NEXT F
714 GO TO 500
716 PRINT "LOOP ENCOUNTERED"
718 GO TO 800
799 REM **********************************************************
800 REM ERROR ROUTINE
802 REM BACK UP TO LAST MOVE AND DELETE UNSUCCESSFUL CHOICE
804 REM FROM MAZE MATRIX. RETURN TO SEARCH ROUTINE.
819 PRINT "K IS NOW" K
820 PRINT "R(K-1) IS NOW" R(K-1)
821 LET X(R(K-1),I)=0
822 LET I=R(K-1)
823 LET K=K-1
825 GO TO 500
862 REM **********************************************************
865 REM PRINT SUBROUTINE
870 PRINT
872 PRINT "TRIAL SEQUENCE IS:"
875 FOR W=1 TO K
876 PRINT R(W);
877 NEXT W
878 PRINT
879 RETURN
899 REM **********************************************************
900 REM END ROUTINE
905 LET K=K+1
910 LET R(K)=J
912 GOSUB 870
915 PRINT "SUCCESSFUL SEQUENCE IS LAST ABOVE"
940 STOP
942 REM **********************************************************
943 REM DATA SECTION
945 REM READ IN NUMBER OF ROWS IN MAZE MATRIX
950 DATA 10
955 REM READ IN MAZE MATRIX
970 DATA 1,6,2,3,2,6,2,7,2,11,3,6,3,7,3,8,4,8
972 DATA 6,11,7,10,7,11,999,8,5,9,11,4E37
999 END

RUN
```

After typing RUN for the above program, you will get the complete detail below. That complete trace permits you to check the progress of the proposed method.

```
YOUR INPUT PAIRS (EXCLUDING LAST PRIZE MOVE) ARE:
 1  6                   2  3                   2  6                   2  7
 2  11                  3  6                   3  7                   3  8
 4  8                   6  11                  7  10                  7  11
 9  11
TRIAL SEQUENCE IS:
 1  6
```

```
TRIAL SEQUENCE IS:
 1  6  1
LOOP ENCOUNTERED
K IS NOW          3
R(K-1) IS NOW     6

TRIAL SEQUENCE IS:
 1  6  2

TRIAL SEQUENCE IS:
 1  6  2  3

TRIAL SEQUENCE IS:
 1  6  2  3  2
LOOP ENCOUNTERED
K IS NOW          5
R(K-1) IS NOW     3

TRIAL SEQUENCE IS:
 1  6  2  3  6
LOOP ENCOUNTERED
K IS NOW          5
R(K-1) IS NOW     3

TRIAL SEQUENCE IS:
 1  6  2  3  7

TRIAL SEQUENCE IS:
 1  6  2  3  7  2
LOOP ENCOUNTERED
K IS NOW          6
R(K-1) IS NOW     7

TRIAL SEQUENCE IS:
 1  6  2  3  7  3
LOOP ENCOUNTERED
K IS NOW          6
R(K-1) IS NOW     7

TRIAL SEQUENCE IS:
 1  6  2  3  7  10

TRIAL SEQUENCE IS:
 1  6  2  3  7  10   7
LOOP ENCOUNTERED
K IS NOW          7
R(K-1) IS NOW     10

TRIAL SEQUENCE IS:
 1  6  2  3  7  10
DEAD END ENCOUNTERED
K IS NOW          6
R(K-1) IS NOW     7
```

```
TRIAL SEQUENCE IS:
 1  6  2  3  7  11

TRIAL SEQUENCE IS:
 1  6  2  3  7  11  2
LOOP ENCOUNTERED
K IS NOW          7
R(K-1) IS NOW    11

TRIAL SEQUENCE IS:
 1  6  2  3  7  11  6
LOOP ENCOUNTERED
K IS NOW          7
R(K-1) IS NOW    11

TRIAL SEQUENCE IS:
 1  6  2  3  7  11  7
LOOP ENCOUNTERED
K IS NOW          7
R(K-1) IS NOW    11

TRIAL SEQUENCE IS:
 1  6  2  3  7  11  9

TRIAL SEQUENCE IS:
 1  6  2  3  7  11  9  11
LOOP ENCOUNTERED
K IS NOW          8
R(K-1) IS NOW     9

TRIAL SEQUENCE IS:
 1  6  2  3  7  11  9
DEAD END ENCOUNTERED
K IS NOW          7
R(K-1) IS NOW    11

TRIAL SEQUENCE IS:
 1  6  2  3  7  11
DEAD END ENCOUNTERED
K IS NOW          6
R(K-1) IS NOW     7

TRIAL SEQUENCE IS:
 1  6  2  3  7
DEAD END ENCOUNTERED
K IS NOW          5
R(K-1) IS NOW     3

TRIAL SEQUENCE IS:
 1  6  2  3  8

TRIAL SEQUENCE IS:
 1  6  2  3  8  3
```

```
LOOP ENCOUNTERED
K IS NOW          6
R(K-1) IS NOW     8

TRIAL SEQUENCE IS:
 1  6  2  3  8  4

TRIAL SEQUENCE IS:
 1  6  2  3  8  4  8
LOOP ENCOUNTERED
K IS NOW          7
R(K-1) IS NOW     4

TRIAL SEQUENCE IS:
 1  6  2  3  8  4
DEAD END ENCOUNTERED
K IS NOW          6
R(K-1) IS NOW     8

TRIAL SEQUENCE IS:
 1  6  2  3  8  5
SUCCESSFUL SEQUENCE IS LAST ABOVE

  940,  NORMAL EXIT FROM PROG.

TIME:    0.969 SEC.
```

If you want to cut out the trace, eliminate lines 532, 534, 610, 716, 819, and 820 from Program MAZE. After having made that action and typing RUN again you will get

```
RUN




YOUR INPUT PAIRS (EXCLUDING LAST PRIZE MOVE) ARE:
 1  6               2  3               2  6               2
 2  11              3  6               3  7               3
 4  8               6  11              7  10              7
 9  11
TRIAL SEQUENCE IS:
 1  6  2  3  8  5
SUCCESSFUL SEQUENCE IS LAST ABOVE

  940,  NORMAL EXIT FROM PROG.

TIME:    0.546 SEC.
```

Now turn to the detail required to make the rote-learning program work. For simplicity we first consider the "T" maze of Figure 15.1. And the easiest way to explain our proposed program is to consider it line by line. Lines 300 through 341 read in the maze data, including the count, M, and the transition information, which give us the maze's structure. In the DATA lines, we only input transitions to larger-numbered points, yet we want a two-way specification to be most general in our program. Thus, lines 336 and 337 produce a symmetric matrix of possible moves for further consideration. To illustrate program lines 300 through 341 for the "T" maze, realize that at the termination of line 341 we would have stored in computer memory the matrix X(M,M + 1).

	1	2	3	4	5
1		1			
2	1		1	1	
3		1			
4		1			9

Our job now is to scan the maze data, starting from the origin, and to eliminate all unsuccessful possibilities, then remember only successful moves thereafter.

So, program lines 500 through 540 scan the maze matrix, starting from row 1, and take the first alternative available. The proposed move is printed; but before the proposed move is allowed, we check for a possible loop, program lines 650 through 718. Should a loop be encountered at any time the link leading to it is eliminated, as in line 821. Further, if a dead-end is encountered (which will be obvious in Program MAZE after the return-loop elimination), the potential dead-end is also eliminated, again using program line 821.

Of course, if at any time we have a potential move to the prize, we take it and stop the whole process, following the test at line 515.

All other details in Program MAZE are either comments (REM statements in BASIC) or output specification and control. For example, lines 865 through 879 provide a PRINT subroutine for the display of the currently proposed maze route.

The general logic of Program MAZE may be consulted in the flow chart, Figure 15.2. Now compare this general logic to the detail described in the narrative above.

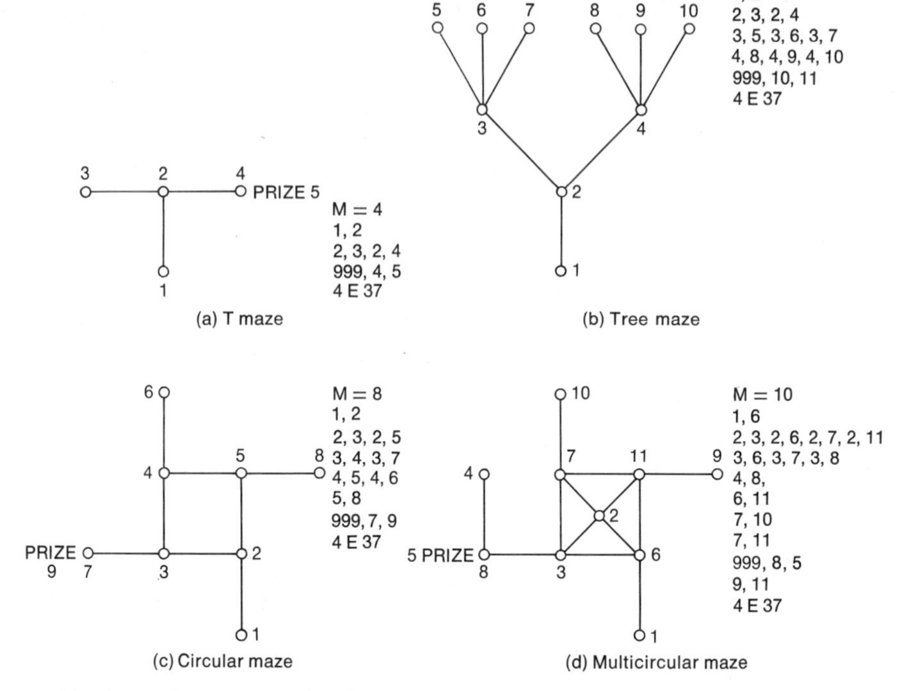

15.1. Several maze types showing numbering convention. Maze (d) is used for illustration in Program MAZE.

Run Program MAZE for the examples cited in Figure 15.1 and convince yourself that it works. (We illustrate the multicircular maze only.) Now ask yourself, How did we come to the formulation of this rote-learning program and make it work? Clearly, we had to know something more than the techniques of BASIC computer programming. We had to combine our knowledge of how rote learning might be simulated in this case with our previous knowledge of the BASIC language.[9] In fact, although some logic is required in the contruction of Program MAZE, its actual formulation is an art, rather than a science; so it is with most complex problems of practical interest. You need several skills: extraneous knowledge, intuition, and native ability, as well as language fluency and the determination to finish the job.

To further build your confidence in Program MAZE try to run the Hampton Court maze of Figure 15.3. Confidence that your programs work is

[9] Rote learning is by definition an immediate elimination of unsuccessful alternatives, and a memory retention of what is yet possible, that is, the extraneous knowledge required in this case—plus the fact that a successful maze run by our definition should have no route repetitions.

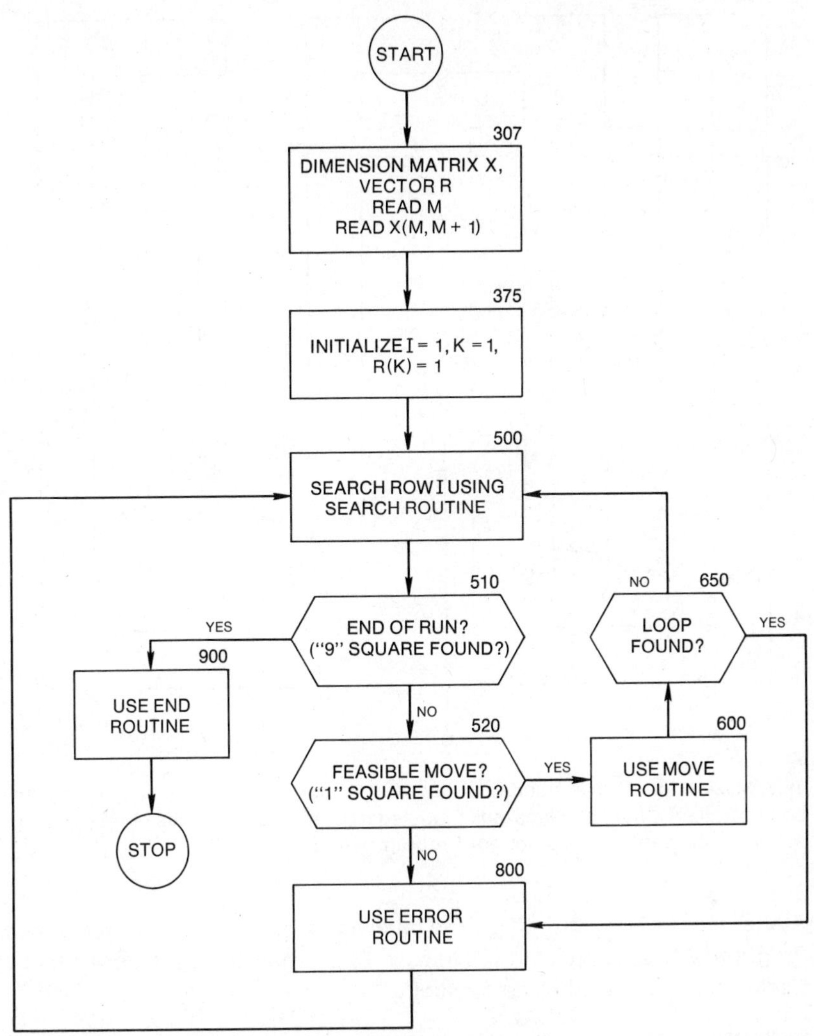

15.2. Master flow chart of Program MAZE. Output display steps, e.g., the PRINT subroutine, lines 875 through 879, are not included.

not only a matter of faith but also a matter of experience.

The input data to Program MAZE required for the Hampton Court problem is as follows:

```
942 REM ****************************************************************
943 REM DATA SECTION
945 REM READ IN NUMBER OF ROWS IN MAZE MATRIX
950 DATA 16
955 REM READ IN MAZE MATRIX
970 DATA 1,2,2,3,2,4,4,5,4,6,5,8,5,7,8,9,8,10
972 DATA 9,10,9,11,10,13,12,13,13,14,14,15,14,16,999,16,17
973 DATA 4E37
999 END
```

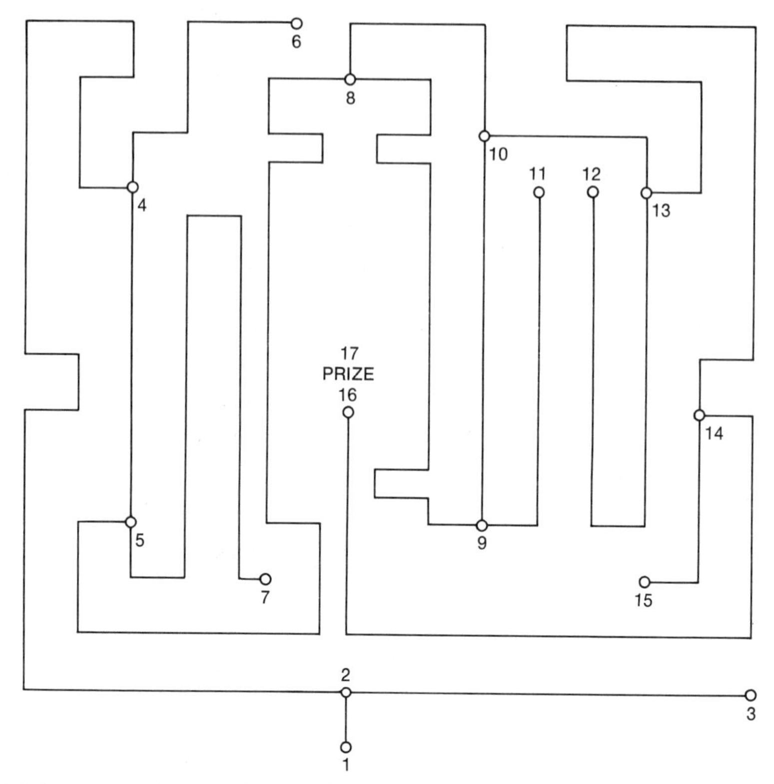

15.3. Maze in gardens at Hampton Court, England. Redrawn to rectangular dimensions for clarity, the actual maze is a twisted trapezoid. Numbers have been applied following conventions adopted for Program MAZE.

After typing RUN you will get the following results using the abbreviated Program MAZE, suggested previously. Check this against Figure 15.3 by tracing the suggested route manually.

```
YOUR INPUT PAIRS (EXCLUDING LAST PRIZE MOVE) ARE:
 1  2                2  3                2  4                4  5
 4  6                5  8                5  7                8  9
 8  10               9  10               9  11               10  13
 12  13               13  14              14  15              14  16
TRIAL SEQUENCE IS:
 1  2  4  5  8  9  10  13  14  16  17
SUCCESSFUL SEQUENCE IS LAST ABOVE

  940,  NORMAL EXIT FROM PROG.

TIME:    0.631 SEC.
```

If you have tried Program MAZE and convinced yourself that it works, you have understood something about that program's structure. But if you have thought about maze problems in general, you will realize that our present approach is hopelessly inadequate to confront the really complex problems that even simple-minded practical applications generate.

For example, in very complex decision problems, a brute-force rote-learning approach is doomed to failure, not because the search through all possible alternatives cannot theoretically be made as in our simple maze example, but because for complex problems such a search involves combinatorial possibilities far in excess of what the human mind or the computer can fathom.[10]

The way out of this combinatorial morass is to prescreen alternative possibilities with care *before* they are evaluated. This is done using the rules of experience, or *heuristics.* Reverting back to our Hampton Court maze problem, we may reveal the true key to the shortest route through the maze as the designer planned it: *Go left, then make two rights, and keep left.* Thus, we have some specific information that would lead to success without faltering. But, suppose we knew only that the designer of mazes exemplified by the Hampton Court maze generally preferred left turns in his key to right turns. Could you use that rule of thumb, or heuristic, to develop the specific key by means of a computer program? (You would still need some method of presenting maze structure to the computer in this case, but the route choice could be carried out by methods other than the numbering scheme suggested here.)

Although the search algorithms of many presently known mathematical techniques—from linear programming to the maze problems of Ford and Fulkerson, *op. cit.*—provide excellent solutions to many practical problems—even good algorithms fail in practice when the combinatorial number of alternate possibilities begins to approach the astronomical.

In really serious combinatorial maze problems, we must abandon direct logic and work with gross screening methods, of which heuristics, or the rules of thumb of experience are often our best guides. That is a mathematical fact, not a dropout from the use of logic. A typical practical example is the scheduling of job shops—perhaps the dirtiest practical task any computer programmer can encounter! Production job shops (as opposed to mass-production lines) confront us with the ultimate in mathe-

[10] Claude E. Shannon, "Programming a Computer to Play Chess," *Phil. Mag.*, Vol. 41, No. 256 (March, 1950) estimates that there are on the average 30 legal moves at each stage of a chess game and that a typical game extends for 40 rounds, where a round consists of one move by each player. This poses something like 10^{120} continuations (or sequences) to be explored ($30^{80} = 1.5 \times 10^{118}$). Assuming that one variation could be considered each micro-microsecond (10^{-12} seconds) by a computer (which is far beyond any present capability) it would take over 10^{98} years to select the first move! To put this number in perspective, the largest estimate made of the total number of atoms in the universe is on the order of 10^{76}. The Shannon figures are quoted in C. H. Davidson and E. C. Koenig, *Computers* (New York: John Wiley & Sons, Inc., 1968), p. 471, with a discussion of various learning programs.

matical variety, yet they *are* scheduled, sequenced, and controlled successfully every day by old-timers, who know their scene intimately.

Can we not learn something about the processing of variety from those hoary souls? Let us hope so, because practical experience in problems of great variety is the only maze guide possible.

Indeed, in really serious computer maze-running, we may have to use a *double* set of heuristics: (1) a heuristic (or set of them) to help us generate a feasible maze in decision-making terms, as opposed to the physical mazes used in our present examples; and (2) another heuristic, or set of them, to help us wend our way from beginning to end.

We can go no further in the space available. But the moral of this example should now be clear. In serious practice there is no substitute for well-evaluated experience.

SIXTEEN

Extending what you have learned

To become more proficient in the computer's use, we now turn our attention to present-day commercial and scientific machine applications. We must learn to control and manipulate data formats. A data format refers to and specifies how a block of information is organized, coded, and made available, and, in particular, how that block may be segmented for analysis and manipulation. As you may realize with some reflection, data format is exceedingly important in the manipulation of large-scale information files and the records they contain.

A data format example: ZIP code

To illustrate the use of data formats and record segmentation, consider the ZIP code used by the post office to facilitate mail delivery. This 5-digit number can be divided into three parts. The first digit indicates the general destination of the mail. The next two digits, when combined with the first, give the postal section, or major dispatch office through which the mail is to be routed. And, the last two digits, in combination with the first three, indicate the local post office, from which the carrier will take the mail to the addressee. Thus, ZIP code 10017, which is for the Grand Central Post Office in New York City breaks down as follows: (1) the leading 1 represents the general area that contains New York and its environs, (2) the leading 100 indicates Manhattan (as opposed, for instance, to 105 for some regions in Westchester County), (3) and finally the trailing 17 indicates the Grand Central area, within Manhattan, within the general postal area containing New York. The total code 10017 thus conveys not only a complete message (Deliver to the Grand Central Post Office) but may also be interpreted by the position and value of the data shown *at each character position.*

The importance of this record format, or code structure, may not be obvious until we begin to ask questions or interrogate a file. For example, suppose a magazine publisher wants to know how many subscribers are located in the Grand Central area of Manhattan. He would then count all subscriber addresses with the ZIP code 10017. If the publisher wanted to count subscribers in Manhattan, he would scan the file for only the first three digits and tabulate the addresses starting with the ZIP digits 100. Similarly, the most inclusive count, subscribers in the general postal area containing New York City, would be obtained by concentrating only on the first digit, 1.[1]

Another format example: product and customer codes

An extension of the ZIP code idea is the product and customer code used by commercial firms for integrated information processing.

Suppose a clothing manufacturer produces men's suits and grades them by (1) size, (2) cut, (3) basic color, (4) style, and (5) fabric. He also wishes to analyze customer sales and salesman statistics by (1) region, (2) state, (3) city, (4) store, and (5) salesman. He first proposes the following *product code*:

1. Size: 2 decimal digits showing men's sizes 30–50;
2. Cut: 1 alphabetic character, S, R, L, or X for stout, regular, long, or extra long;
3. Basic color: 1 decimal digit, appropriately defined for gray, black, brown, blue, etc.;
4. Style: 2 decimal digits, appropriately defined for Ivy, Italian, Mod, etc.;
5. Fabric: 2 decimal digits, appropriately defined for flannel, gabardine, cheviot, tropical, tweed, etc.

[1] Post office machines, specially designed to optically read ZIP codes, can sort mail at a rate of 36,000 pieces per hour—three to six times faster than by hand. Other machines under development considerably exceed these rates, current as of 1966. Historically, it is interesting to note Babbage's influence on postal delivery. He observed that the distance of delivery has little to do with delivery cost (related mostly to the number of sortings) and convinced the British government to adopt the penny post, or fixed-stamp charge, regardless of distance. Thus, we are indebted to Babbage not only for the computer but also for the ten-cent airmail stamp of 1969, which allows U.S. mail to go 100 or 6,000 miles at the same charge. American postal authorities adopted the British system of pricing, as proposed by Babbage, because Babbage was right: physical handling costs more than transportation.

The combination of these eight characters in the order shown from left to right in Figure 16.1 would be the manufacturer's product code, to which he might add an arbitrary serial digit to provide a completely unique product identification in case of possible duplication.

With such a product code, the manufacturer could analyze sales by size, cut, color, style, fabric, or any combination of these categories—if he could segment the coded record and its associated data to test the sales transaction or historical files for his selected categories of questioning. A typical question for such a file is, What is the percentage distribution of sales by size?

Similarly, the manufacturer could develop a *customer code* as follows:

1. Region: 1 decimal digit for the major geographical breakdown;
2. State: 1 decimal digit identifying the state within the region;
3. City: 2 decimal digits identifying the city in the state;
4. Store: 2 decimal digits identifying the store in the city;
5. Salesman: 1 decimal digit identifying the salesman in the region.

This 7-digit customer/salesman code could be represented by the format shown in Figure 16.2. To illustrate, 46L321143 could represent a size 46 long, blue, Ivy, flannel suit which is item 3 in that category for uniqueness. This is the product code, so a message or a record of the form 144 46L321143 would stand for 144 units of the garment described in detail above. The units could represent sales, inventory on hand, shipments, etc., depending upon the application.

A customer/salesman code such as 1031732 would stand for Eastern region, New York State, New York City, Johnny Sinclair's store, salesman Herman. If you know the format for decoding and have a simple dictionary of terms, it is easy to obtain the meaning from the code.

For statistical purposes, of course, the above customer code might be organized to conform to the ZIP code or to the statistical codes used by the Bureau of the Census, so that subsidiary statistics such as mailing lists and population statistics could be correlated directly with sales.[2]

[2] The strategy of product code development, and indeed that of most practical identifying codes, is a subject beyond the scope of our present treatment. Although general theories are available for developing "efficient" codes, applications of the type discussed above are constrained in practice by so many factors (such as the organization of corollary statistics, type of computer memory device and communication to be used, and frequency of combinatorial inquiry) that commercial code development for information retrieval and analysis is still an experimental matter. Consider the illustrations provided here as typical examples, inserted for the purpose of understanding data formatting. You will find scant literature on commercial code development due to the experimental and therefore proprietary nature of such special case studies.

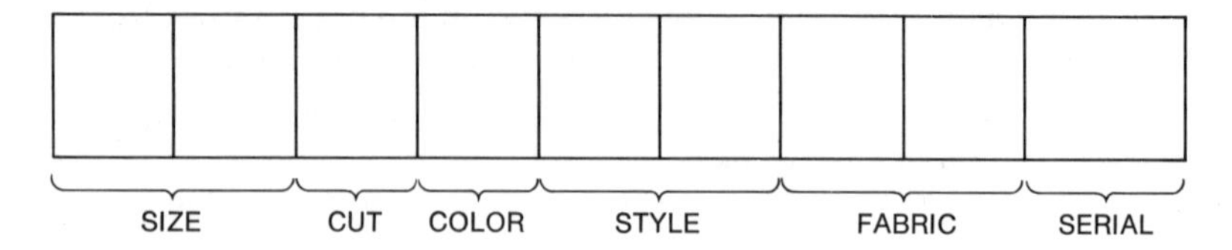

16.1. A proposed product code for a clothing manufacturer. The above 9-character code not only uniquely identifies the product but also permits easy statistical analysis. It is also partially self-interpreting, at least for the first few characters, which give size and cut directly, in familiar terms.

An integration of codes and files: format combinations

Now consider the following extension of the previous code proposals. Suppose we now create our input order record by providing a communication from the salesman to the manufacturer in the following format:

```
1031732
144 46L321143
 12 48R216612
 48 48R216612
```

The first set of numbers is the customer code for a particular store and salesman, as previously described. On the next three lines the leading numbers show the number of units ordered, and the trailing 9 digits (including the last, or serial, number) indicate the product sold, again as described previously.

The salesman might also telegraph this order to his home office as: 10317322*144-46L321143/12-48R216612/48-48R216612, where the special symbols * and / in the *alphanumeric string* are *delimiters* indicating the same break in formatting illustrated by the above listing of the same codes. (Using the interpretation shown in Figures 16.1 and 16.2, you should be aware that salesman Herman sold Johnny Sinclair's store in New York City 144 46-longs, 12 48-regulars, and 48 48-regulars.)

A set of coded transactions, such as that shown above, provides the manufacturer with essential instructions. He may now key the order to his inventory files, price files, credit files, customer shipping files, salesman commission files, and historical statistical files by product, salesman, or customer; and by subsequent manipulation to production planning files and similar files for backup operations.

In other words, given such a coded input we should be able (among other things) to (1) check price and total order value, (2) check customer credit for that amount, (3) check inventory levels for availability, (4) gen-

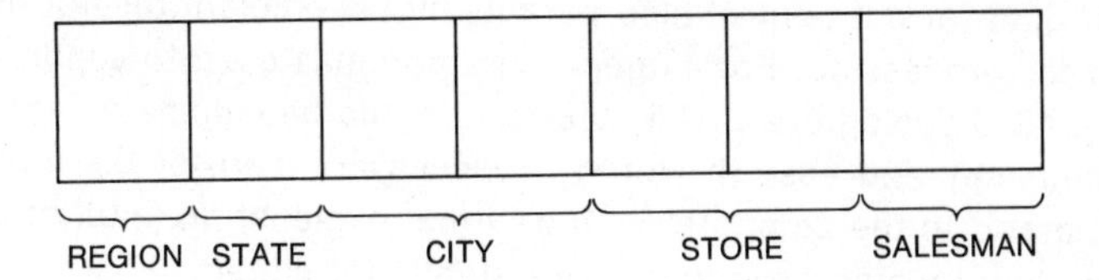

16.2. A proposed customer/salesman code for a clothing manufacturer. This code permits the indentification of the given store from which an order has been received, as well as the salesman who took it. The combination of this customer code with a set of product codes for the items ordered, when set in an appropriate format also containing the quantity of units ordered for each product, can constitute a complete order for computer processing.

erate invoices and shipping papers, (5) compute sales commissions, (6) generate historical sales records, (7) generate production orders as necessary, (8) correlate sales with other statistical market data, (9) summarize production costs by product, or sales cost by customer or salesman, and (10) study a transaction's contribution to margin! With proper planning and integration of file processing, most of the above analyses and operations can be performed *without further input of data other than the coded order received from the salesman.*

These output activities can be accomplished, however, only if we can segment and manipulate the original order data by studying its coded parts, and if the correspondingly necessary files have been maintained in a consistently coded form.

The application above illustrates the main requirement of integrated information processing: a consistent well-planned information structure.

Other format applications

In science as well as in commerce the analysis of input formats can be critical. For example, all general information retrieval problems rest upon the ability to segment and logically compare data categories; so do logical manipulations of complex experimental data, analysis of surveys, and such academically interesting applications as computer language translation, computer musical composition, and development of computer game-playing programs.

Format analysis is essential in computer communication with remote users, since sequential communication must be split up, deciphered, and stored in spatially organized memories—a format problem the computer handles internally under user programming or compiler and supervisor control.

Input data format control also permits highly efficient receipt of information for processing. For example, the commas used to separate data in the BASIC declarative DATA statement could be eliminated except for user simplicity and ease. It would be necessary then for the input data to be passed to the computer with a format explanation (and, of course, the data input would have to be consistently formatted).

Finally, all output reports—whether scientific or commercial—require some editing so that the results of a computation or a data processing effort will be comprehensible to the user. Were output not edited by some format control (whether automatic, as in BASIC, or under user control, as in FORTRAN), computer output would be an incomprehensible ensemble of continuous alphanumeric characters.

As an illustration of this point, consider the difference between the information provided in the coded input for the garment example above, and a possible output that the average person could understand.

Input: 1031732*144-46L321143/12-48R216612/48-48R216612
Edited output: In New York City, Herman today sold Johnny Sinclair a gross of 46 long code 321143, a dozen 48 regular code 216612, and four dozen regular code 2116612.

It is entirely possible to have a computer perform the deciphering and editing necessary to produce the latter statement. You can imagine which form of information the clothing manufacturer would prefer to have on his desk!

Neither the input nor the output formatting required to perform the task suggested above is available in standard BASIC. And even in EXTENDED BASIC you would find it cumbersome to carry out the format manipulations necessary to go from the string of numbers and special characters in the input to the edited output. BASIC is not designed for such use: It is a teaching language, largely confined to scientific work.

The importance of input/output formats in computer use

Although scientific work requires less stringent format control than commercial work, there are good reasons in both areas to think about the subject. In scientific work, good format control can make data input more efficient by packing data and then pulling it apart after input. Similarly there are technical advantages (described hereafter) in distinguishing between the *types* of data that must be processed in scientific as well as commercial work (e.g., integer numbers versus real numbers, that is, those with fractional parts; and numeric values versus alphabetic characters).

In commercial applications data format analysis and manipulation can become a major part of processing. It is not uncommon to find commercial data processing programs that devote (1) a third of their statement counts to data input format analysis and checking, (2) a third to processing, and (3) a third to output editing and report format manipulation. And in many commercial applications, the total input/output format control and editing operations may run to 80 or 90 percent of the total program.[3] As a consequence of the preceding examples, you should now begin to think of input and output data formatting as a serious problem.

Learning format control

The BASIC computer language was conceived to make life simple by providing a few simple format rules for both input and output.

The data input to a BASIC program is formatted by the use of commas in the DATA statement, as shown in Chapter 8 and thereafter. And a simple output format is provided in BASIC using a combination of the comma and semicolon. Using these simple input and output control symbols, we were able to produce a number of programs that did provide format control at both input and output time. (Consider, for example, the interpretation of the data inputs of the Credit and Poker Hand programs of Chapter 13, the output control exhibited by Program FORMS of Chapter 12 and CROSSTAB program of Chapter 13.)

Yet to gain more flexibility, we must now move to a more complex language. The one we have chosen for illustration is FORTRAN IV, which is widely available and standardized on most electronic computers.[4]

How FORTRAN will be illustrated

It is not our intent to explain the FORTRAN language in detail. Instead, we now proceed by example. Each of the Chapter 13 problems written in BASIC will now appear in FORTRAN IV in Chapters 17 and 18 with a detailed illustrative narrative.

In what follows, we assume you have obtained the manufacturer's FORTRAN IV manual that pertains to your computer location. Although FORTRAN IV has been standardized, these manuals vary. The variations exist

---

[3] Convince yourself of this fact by comparing by line count the output editing shown in Program FORMS of Chapter 12, as opposed to the test computations.

[4] Although we shall only mention the name of the COBOL language in this book, you might like to know that COBOL is devoted almost entirely to making formatting of both input and output easy for commercial applications in business. For that reason, COBOL at first appears exceedingly abstruse to the beginner. It is not: The reader who completes this book should also be able to read a COBOL computer manual with relative ease.

in the equipment used and its technical constraints. (For example, core memory size, the access type of memory peripherals, and input/output capability must be known in detail if you are ultimately interested in more than an academic appreciation of FORTRAN's capabilities and uses.) Consult either the manufacturer's manual or your instructor on any specific questions you may have about the detail that we now present. Manufacturers' manuals are also devoted to the ultimate detail required to apply FORTRAN on a given equipment configuration, as are special newsletters and notes from your time-sharing supplier or local computing center. Documentation of this type will now become useful to you, as you will be able to understand the terms used as well as the programming principles involved.

Essential differences between BASIC and FORTRAN

Most users agree that *three* differences exist between the simplified BASIC language and the professional computer language, FORTRAN.

1. *FORTRAN has extensive formatting capability, both for input data and output reports.*

You will find the distinctions made in this area entirely reasonable. FORTRAN specifies not only input and output data organization, but also specific data types, e.g., integer numbers, real numbers, alphanumeric characters that may be manipulated, and alphanumeric characters that will be displayed, although not otherwise used. (Alphanumeric characters are not used in any *numeric* computation in any language.)

The reasons for the character specifications in FORTRAN are several. First, it is helpful for the computer, when receiving input data for later processing, to know not only what kind of data must be manipulated but also exactly how such data is to be received; thus data may be processed most efficiently.

For example, it may be most efficient, not only in terms of computing speed but also in terms of accuracy and memory allocation, if the FORTRAN compiler can distinguish between integer numbers and numbers with fractional parts, since these different data can be handled most efficiently by different means, and should be so handled to prevent roundoff error and waste of memory space. (Integer computations require less memory space and result in greater accuracy in most cases than computations with real numbers, which have fractional parts.)

Similarly, alphanumerically processed and alphanumerically displayed characters may be handled most efficiently by yet another process of the computer. (The machine usually processes alphanumerics most efficiently in the Binary Coded Decimal code of Chapter 2, rather than in pure binary.)

The FORTRAN FORMAT statement, which is a nonexecutable statement in a program, provides the distinctions necessary to make both efficiency and flexibility of program input/output possible.

2. FORTRAN differs from BASIC in its input and output commands.

As illustrated in detail in the following chapters, FORTRAN READ and WRITE commands (which correspond to BASIC READ and PRINT commands) differ from those in BASIC.[5]

FORTRAN READ and WRITE statements are also more complicated than those used in BASIC for a good reason. They permit the user to select one or more of a number of input or output devices for use at a given time, and also reference the FORMAT control (indicated by a FORMAT statement) that will be used in each case (see the next chapter).

3. FORTRAN provides extensive stored function, user-defined function, and subroutine capability, compared to BASIC.

Advanced languages such as FORTRAN provide greater flexibility in function and subroutine application than the BASIC language does. Although you may have noted some of these extensions, through the notes in Chapter 12, you must realize that improved function and subroutine flexibility markedly improves a language's power to handle complex jobs.

FORTRAN as a language provides the most flexible subroutine capability available widely on today's computers, a feature particularly valuable for scientific work. This is one of the reasons that FORTRAN has been so widely accepted.

PROBLEMS

16-1 If you were going to read and write data in many different forms on a number of input/output devices in your computer systems, why would it be desirable to have a computer statement that would specify the exact format you would use in your READ and PRINT (or WRITE) statements?

16-2 Suppose your computing system had 50 different input/output devices which could be used in receiving data and producing reports. Suppose also that you would like to read or write on a number of these devices in different formats. Why would it be desirable to have an input READ or an output PRINT (or WRITE) statement complex enough to indicate (a) the device to be used for input or output and (b) the exact format to be used in reading or displaying the data you process?

16-3 For computer input/output format specifications, it is desirable that the user have absolute control over every input and output character position used, as well as being able to specify the exact form of data that will appear at each of these character positions. Why do you think this is so?

---

[5] Although this assertion is true in traditional card-input FORTRAN applications, many variations in remote terminal FORTRAN input/output will let one choose either strict or loose format control. You must check this capability in your FORTRAN manual or with your instructor.

16-4 In order to preserve the accuracy of a numerical computation, we usually prefer to use integers as much as possible. Why is this so? Why is it then desirable to distinguish in a format specification or in a numerical computation between integer numbers and real numbers?

16-5 In BASIC, the number of nonsubscripted variable names is limited to 286, e.g., A1–A26, plus A through Z. And these symbols are not directly related to the name of a variable as it might be used in English. Why might it be useful to permit a computer language to use more alphabetic (and/or numeric) characters in the specification of variable names?

16-6 Recall the discussion in Chapter 12 about subroutines. Why might it be desirable for a computer language to employ subroutines that took their input variables as *arguments*, as the stored and user-defined functions in BASIC do? For example, if a number of people are writing subroutines for common use, what are the comparative advantages of the approach used in BASIC and the argument approach suggested here?

16-7 In BASIC the output from a program is left-justified in the fields defined, either by the comma or the semicolon. What would be the advantages of providing sufficient format information to the output routines of a computer program so that the printed output could be right-justified, that is, pushed to the right of the field instead of the left?

16-8 Why might an output format specification be more complex and demanding than an input format specification in any program for a computer?

16-9 What would you expect should happen in a computer language if an integer number, such as 2, is added to a real number, such as 3.14? Why would you want to make a distinction between the two if you could during computation?

16-10 In general, would you like to have more flexibility in a computer language than you have observed in BASIC, even though the language might be a little harder to learn? For example, would you like to have more stored functions available? Or the ability to READ or WRITE a table or list in one line of programming? Would you like to omit the repetitive word DATA from your input information specifications in BASIC?

SEVENTEEN

Thirteen FORTRAN translations (Part I)

You must master grammatical rules before you can follow any new language. Thus, in each of the following problems—which are direct translations from BASIC to FORTRAN using the same examples (in the same order) presented in Chapter 13—we point out each change that you must know to understand the FORTRAN example.

Although Example 1 is short, it demonstrates many of the differences between BASIC and FORTRAN. Thus, the discussion that accompanies this first illustration is of necessity the longest in the chapter. To progress successfully, do not move to later examples until you understand each point. Consult your FORTRAN computer manual for more detail as needed. See Appendix D for a list of appropriate manuals by computer type. For your reference, Appendix A provides a side-by-side comparison of BASIC and FORTRAN commands and notes.

Example 1 (How to compute and write in FORTRAN.)

This example performs an arithmetic computation with numeric literals and prints the answer. In particular, it illustrates the following technical points that must be followed in FORTRAN programs:

1. Statement number versus sequence, or line, number;
2. Comments and how to use them in your program;
3. Variable definition in FORTRAN;
4. Types of variables used in FORTRAN;
5. Arithmetic operations in FORTRAN;
6. The mixed mode problem in FORTRAN;

7. FORTRAN WRITE commands;
8. FORTRAN FORMAT statements;
9. The FORTRAN END statement.

As in Example 1 of Chapter 13, the objective is to find the numeric value of $(3.1416)^2$. Here is the equivalent program in FORTRAN, so that you may compare the two examples. (A complete explanation of the three program variations shown below appears following the third illustration.)

```
      PROGRAM ANYNAME
C     BASIC TO FORTRAN,NO.1
      ANS=(3.1416)**2
      WRITE(6,1) ANS
1     FORMAT(1X,F15.5)
      END

         9.86965
```

At first glance, the FORTRAN program may seem very different from the BASIC one. However, the structure is the same, only the detail differs.

First, what you see above is the punched-card version of FORTRAN (we show the teletype version momentarily). In this form, line numbers are not used; only statements referenced by *other* statements need be numbered, e.g., note the number 1 for the FORMAT statement, next to the last line. In this form, the required logical sequence is provided by the *physical* sequence of cards fed to the computer; the order is from top to bottom as before. Statement numbers are arbitrary; they are "tags" only, not for line sequence control. If a statement is a comment, the letter C is used in place of a statement number. The remainder of the program text will commence in the seventh card-column position. To illustrate, Figure 17.1 is a picture of the actual cards used to produce the above result.[1]

If you are using a teletype or other remote terminal, most systems permit you to use a line number for a statement number, as in BASIC, or to use *both* a line number and a statement number, so that you may automatically convert your remote terminal program to a card program. The remote terminal program equivalent to the card program for Example 1, assuming line numbers for statement numbers, is as follows:

---

[1] We shall omit the details of the card-punching process. Consult the manual for the key punch or other input unit you may use. In most of the translated programs that follow, the first line shown is the word PROGRAM followed by a name. Most computer installations do not permit this identification without the leading C for comment. Others, such as the CDC 3600 require it. Check your local manual for details.

```
100*       BASIC TO FORTRAN NO.1
110        ANS=(3.1416)**2
120        WRITE(61,130) ANS
130        FORMAT(1X,F15.5)
999        END
RUN
          9.86965

TIME:      0.078 SEC.
```

Here is the same problem shown in remote terminal FORTRAN, with *both* line numbers and a statement number. The upward arrow in this installation indicates that the statement number following should be used for reference, rather than the line number. (In terminal FORTRAN, the line numbers perform exactly the same function as in BASIC; statements will be sorted in line number order when you type RUN, and all the other system editing features will be made available to you.)

```
100*       BASIC TO FORTRAN NO.1
110'       ANS=(3.1416)**2
120        WRITE(61,1) ANS
130↑     1 FORMAT(1X,F15.5)
999        END
RUN
          9.86965

TIME:      0.077 SEC.
```

Now that you have seen the range of possibilities for this simple program, we can make some additional observations. This time, we consider the program line by line, from top to bottom.

The first line indicates the program name. In any FORTRAN installation, you may introduce a comment, indicated by a C in column one or, in some installations, by the alternative option * before the remark. The comment corresponds to the BASIC statement REM.

The second line is the substitution, or "replacement," statement familiar as the LET command in BASIC. In FORTRAN, the word LET is not used, but is assumed when an equals sign appears in a statement without a command word. The rules are the same as in BASIC: Only one variable name may appear to the left of the equals sign, but a mixture of variables, constants, and arithmetic operations may appear to the right. The arithmetic operation rules are the same in FORTRAN as in BASIC, except that

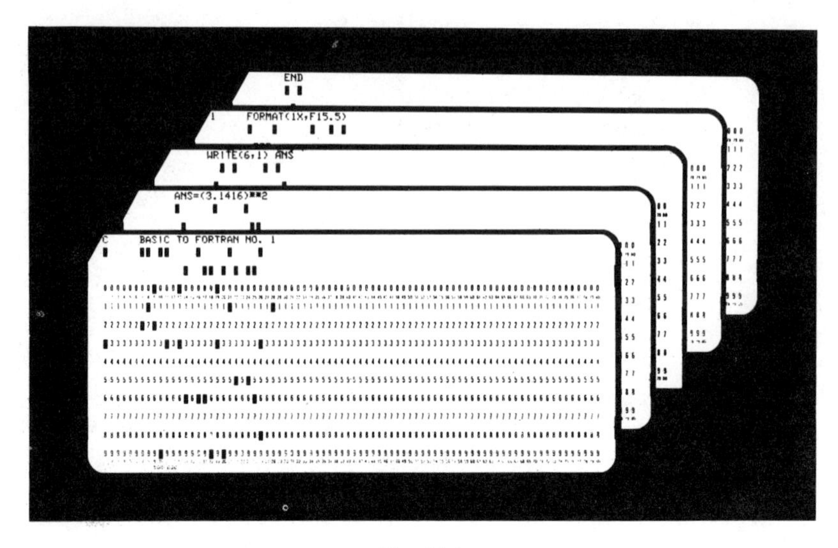

Fig. 17.1.

you usually use the double asterisk, **, for exponentiation, instead of the upward arrow, ↑. The use of parentheses and the order of evaluation are the same as before.

One or two essential differences between the languages now appear. The variable names used in BASIC and the way numbers are expressed form a fundamental difference we must now consider.

In FORTRAN numbers may be expressed in at least three format forms: the integer, fixed-point, and floating-point forms previously used in BASIC. Other modes of expression may also be used.[2] In FORTRAN, the mode in which a number is expressed becomes important (remember in BASIC you could express a number in any form within an expression).

There is a twofold reason for the distinction in FORTRAN. First, in order to provide complete format control for input and output, we want to make the distinction, so we may, for example, control the number of decimal places in a fixed-point number or whether a number with a fractional part will appear as a fixed-point number or in the exponential form. Further, we may wish to assure that our computations with integers will be performed in integer arithmetic, which is not only much faster than other forms but also assures the ultimate in precision within the size of the number permitted at a given installation. Integer arithmetic assures us, for example, that when we multiply 2 by 2 we will get precisely 4; we can never encounter the roundoff problem in the conversion into binary of

[2] Advanced applications of FORTRAN may employ logical and complex variables as well as double-precision modes. You must consult your vendor's manual for these advanced capabilities, which may or may not be available at your location.

decimal numbers with fractional parts that were mentioned in Chapter 2 —unless, of course, we create a result in a computation that is larger than the maximum number size permitted in the system.

For these reasons, several points are intertwined in the construction and use of FORTRAN. These are (1) the definition of variable names; (2) the construction of a FORMAT statement for both input and output operations; and (3) additional constraints upon the mixture of number types (e.g., integer, fixed-point, and floating-point) within an expression.

In FORTRAN, a variable name may be one alphabetic character, or one letter, followed by one or more alphabetics, A–Z, or the digits, 0–9. However, the first letter used indicates whether the number in question is an integer (a starting letter of I, J, K, L, M, N), or a real number, which has a fractional part (fixed- or floating-point) and will start with any of the *other* alphabetics. Thus, ANS, shown in Example 1, is a variable name indicating that the result of evaluating the expression to the right in line 3 may have a fractional part and in any case will show a decimal point. The length of a variable name varies with the FORTRAN installation, but four characters will always be accepted, and a usual limit is six to eight characters.

In the expression leading to a result, as determined by the set of constants, variables, and operations to the right of the equals sign in a substitution statement, you must *not* mix modes. For example, you should not add numbers of different mode. The expression 2 + 2.0 is not allowed, because we do not know whether the result should be an integer or a number with a fractional part, nor precisely how to handle the addition. Either 2 + 2 or 2.0 + 2.0 would be correct. Our first illustration provides the exception to the rule: a number with a fractional part may be raised to an integer power. Usually other mixed-mode combinations in an expression are not legal.

Check your supplier to see if the mixed-mode problem has been eliminated or reduced. One common variation is to permit mixed modes across an equality sign; e.g., KAT = 2.0 + 2.0 would result in the integer result 4, and KAT = 2.05 + 3.1 would result in 5. In such installations when a real-number result is converted to an integer, in the final substitution the fractional part is simply dropped, or truncated. The reverse may also be available; e.g., CAT = 2 + 2 may produce a result with a decimal point (i.e., 4.). In general, however, it pays to observe absolute consistency in your FORTRAN expressions and substitution statements.

Now, consider the WRITE statement. This is the first time we come to the manipulation of a FORTRAN output format. The parentheses following WRITE in line 4 contain two numbers. The first number is a numeric code indicating the output unit upon which you wish to produce the answer to the problem, or the results of the WRITE. In this case, code 6 is the usual convention for a high-speed line printer when using card FORTRAN, or the Teletype itself when using terminal FORTRAN. Some variations exist.[3] The second number in the WRITE parentheses shows the FORMAT statement number associated with that WRITE, that is, it specifies how the answer shall be printed. Following the WRITE parentheses, we have a *list*, here one variable name, of the results to be printed.

Although most FORTRAN installations offer a wide range of input and output formats, here we consider only a few of the more frequently used forms (see Table 17.1). Necessary variations will appear as required by later examples.

TABLE 17.1

Output Format Rules in FORTRAN[a]

General Form	*Example*	*Meaning*
Iw	I5	A 5-position integer field. Count must allow for possible sign.
Fw.d	F15.5	A fixed-point number that has a field width of 15 places, of which 5 are to the right of the decimal point. The field count for a WRITE must include a position for the decimal point and one for a possible sign. The output will be rounded to d places.
wX	5X	Five spaces.
Aw	A6	A field for 6 alphanumeric characters.
wH	12H	The following 12 characters should be shown as they stand; they are literals, or Hollerith characters.
Ew.d	E10.3	The output field for this floating-point form is w characters wide and must include a count for sign, decimal point, the letter E, the sign of the exponent, and a 2-digit exponent. Usually, a leading space and a zero are also assumed, so $w \geq d + 7$. Output will be a fraction plus exponent; e.g., −0.932E+03, so decimal points can be aligned. The example shown is in E10.3 output format. Some local variations may exist.

[a] See text and footnote 6 for variations in format for input data versus output.

In the table the lowercase w indicates the width of the field provided by the format specification. Recall that a field is the number of characters reserved for printing. The lowercase d in the Fw.d specification tells us the number of decimal places to be shown and sets the precision of the number in question. (The integer value d is always less than or equal to w minus 2.) The H format specification is used to designate titles (and

[3] For example, Control Data Corporation's 3600 FORTRAN employs codes 60 and 61, respectively, for standard input and output units. Many systems may also have alternate input and output capabilities; e.g., tape or disc, and special codes, often defined locally, are used with them. Code 61 is shown in the Teletype examples of p. 339, because 61 was the device code used for output on the Teletype at the author's computing center.

thus corresponds to the quotation marks used in BASIC). In many FORTRAN installations, the quotation marks may be used just as they were in BASIC. An alternative option for some systems is use of the asterisk in place of the quotation mark. The meaning of w and d in the Ew.d output specification is the same as in Fw.d, except for the extra characters that w must contain.

With this information in mind, turn to line 5 of Example 1. It is a FORMAT statement. In FORTRAN, each WRITE statement, and usually each READ statement, has its associated FORMAT statement, as specified by the second parenthetical number in these input/output commands.

When we WRITE the numeric result of a variable, we must specify the format desired in the FORMAT statement associated with a WRITE statement, and the format specified must agree in mode from left to right with the list of variables to be written. Thus, if a real variable name is specified in a WRITE statement, an F-type or E-type format must correspondingly appear in the associated FORMAT statement. In FORTRAN the FORMAT statement is a declaration, providing information for the executable command WRITE. In the FORMAT statement of Example 1, we show the list of formats to be printed within parentheses.

The first character of the first format specification within the parentheses is a *line-spacing control*, so that we can single-space, skip lines, or otherwise move down the printed page. The blank indicated by the 1X is (by standard convention) the symbol for a single space.[4] Then, we show the exact way in which we want the numeric value of ANS printed. Here

---

[4] The description given above is the popular explanation of the carriage control character, but a more detailed analysis is required for later understanding. The FORMAT 1X indicates that a blank should be written, just as 15X indicates that 15 blanks should be written. On the line printer, however, actual printing starts with the second specified character position and proceeds to all successive characters to the right until an end-of-record signal is encountered, usually provided by the closing parenthesis of the FORMAT statement but sometimes by an earlier slash as illustrated in Example 3. In some systems, the carriage then advances (after printing) one or more spaces as determined by the carriage control character. Other systems take carriage control action based upon the first nonprinting *before* printing the subsequent text. The latter case is more frequent, but check locally for this detail. In either case, if the carriage control character is a blank, the paper advances one space; if a zero, two spaces; if one, the paper skips to the top of the next page. At advanced installations, other control characters are available, e.g., half a page may be skipped. Take care that the first character of the first specified format is what you want, and remember that it will *not* be printed. A leading 1X, or 1Hb, where b stands for a space gives a single space; 1H0 a double space, and 1H1 a skip to the next page. You may inadvertently generate these control symbols by other means, e.g., suppose with an output FORMAT(I2) you tried to print the number 12. Not only would you fail to print the leading 1, but that number would actuate a page skip after (or before) 2 has been printed (depending upon your local before or after convention). In most installations control characters other than decimal digits will cause a single space, although the first character will still not be printed. For this reason titles, for example, should always be preceded by one or more blanks.

The conventions cited above apply *only* to line-printing devices. For example, for punched-card output, the first record character is punched like any other and serves no control purpose.

the format F15.5 means: The result of the computation will appear right-justified in a 15-column field. Five digits will be shown to the right of a decimal point, which will also be shown. (The first character of the first format specification associated with a WRITE command is for carriage control only, so it does not affect spacing across a line.) In our present case, note that the terminal 5 in the result 9.86965 appears right-justified in column 15. That answer appears just below the program. To verify this, count characters from left to right in the printed output. (It may help in this verification if you remember that the E in the END command starts at column 7.) Note that when we have FORMAT detail, the computer can easily right-justify its results. In BASIC, left-justification was the rule, since no format was available in the standard BASIC language. In the Teletype versions of Example 1 the command RUN appears, as it might have in BASIC. That system command is not shown in the first illustration, that of card FORTRAN. Check your local computing center for the control commands needed to execute your card FORTRAN programs, since these commands vary from one installation to another.

In FORTRAN, as opposed to BASIC, you must leave *enough* room to WRITE your answers. That is, you must either anticipate the number of digits that will appear in your final results or resort to the same expedient used in BASIC, namely, move to the exponential form if you expect to generate very large or very small numeric results. For example, if you provide for an F15.5 fixed-point output format and your result is actually as wide as 20 digits (including sign and decimal point) you would *not* get the numeric result you want. (Most good installations produce an error message in this case; less desirable installations simply give you the wrong numeric result.) Protect yourself and leave plenty of room for printing your output numbers. An alternative is to print answers that may have a wide range of variation (often typical in scientific work) in the E-type format. For example, to specify that a real number be printed in E16.8 format will give you a result containing a field width of 16 positions with 8 positions to the right of the decimal point. The associated output exponent will show you where to move the decimal point and the numbers printed will have their decimal points aligned. (BASIC shifts to this alternate format automatically for very large or small numbers.) To illustrate, here is a version of Example 1, using the E-type output format in FORTRAN.

```
100*      BASIC TO FORTRAN NO.1
110       ANS=(3.1416)**2
120       WRITE(61,1) ANS
130↑    1 FORMAT(1X,E15.6)
999       END
```

```
RUN
     .986965E+01

TIME:      0.077 SEC.
```

You have now encountered many of the details which cause beginning students difficulty in FORTRAN: the problems of FORMAT and mixed mode. Before continuing, you should practice a few variations on Example 1, so that you will have a feeling for the new details. As a suggestion, try doing the same program over again with an integer computation, say, KAT = 2 ↑ 2, then with alternate output formats. You might even try to mix modes at your installation or to provide mismatching format specifications (say, an integer result and a fixed-point output specification) to see what will happen.

With what you have now learned, you may move ahead more rapidly.

Example 2 (A more complex expression.)

Nothing new appears in this example except the use of parentheses in an arithmetic expression, as in BASIC, to make sure the order of evaluation is what you want.

```
      PROGRAM PRINTOUT
C     BASIC TO FORTRAN. NO. 2
      ANS=(12.963*42.312)**2/(3.753-1.212)**3
      WRITE(6,1) ANS
1     FORMAT(1X,F15.1)
      END

        18336.8
```

Note, as in the previous example, that no mixed-mode arithmetic appears in the expression of line 3 except for raising a real number to an integer power, which is allowed. All other lines of this program are similar to Example 1.

Example 3 (Evaluate several expressions in one program.)

Example 3 shows how to evaluate more than one expression at a time and also introduces a new format idea: the use of the slash, /, to indicate the end of a record and provide a line advance when writing results.

```
      PROGRAM NEWLINE
C     BASIC TO FORTRAN, NO. 3
      ANS1=(2.42)*(3.17)**2+(4.73)*(1.96)**.5
      ANS2=(1.73)*(1.93)/(7.42)-(1.96)**.33333
      ANS3=(1.73)*(1.93)/((7.42)-(1.96)**.33333)
      WRITE(6,1) ANS1,ANS2,ANS3
1     FORMAT(1X,F15.4,/,1X,F15.6,/,1X,F15.6)
      END

        30.9403
      -0.801476
       0.541279
```

Note that we now have three real, or noninteger, values to compute, denoted by the variable names ANS1, ANS2, and ANS3. In the WRITE command, we want to print each of these results, as evaluated in the previous substitution statements, so that the variable names, separated by commas, are listed in the WRITE line.

The FORMAT statement, identified by number 1, is more complex than previous statements. Scanning across the FORMAT line, we see three F-type formats, which will be used to specify how we want to print the three numeric answers. Note that ANS1 is shown with four places to the right of the decimal point, whereas ANS2 and ANS3 are shown with six, as called for by their corresponding Fw.d specifications.

The new variation here is the slash, /, seen between the F-type specifications. Like the closing parenthesis,), of the FORMAT statement, it signals the end of a record, so the paper advances one line and starts printing anew. The meaning of the repeated 1X is the same as before (see footnote 4), and we obtain the three answers, *one below the other*, as shown. Had we omitted the slash and its associated comma, we would have printed the three answers *across* the page; the second and third 1X specifications would then have provided one space between each of the 15-character fields into which ANS1, ANS2, and ANS3 would be printed.

For practice, try to produce the same output as shown above using *three* WRITE statements and *three* associated FORMAT statements. Example 3 accomplishes the same result with two lines of programming, rather than the six that would be required for the complete set of WRITE and FORMAT statements.

As a technical point, the commas following the X format specification as well as those following the slash are usually optional, so an equivalent form for the FORMAT statement shown would be

1 FORMAT(1XF15.4/1XF15.6/1XF15.6).

Commas are usually employed for programming clarity, even though they are not required.

We have illustrated the use of the slash *within* the FORMAT statement to indicate the end of a record. However we may also repeat the slash mark within the FORMAT statement or use it to initiate or terminate the format specifications, that is, use slashes just after the opening parenthesis or just before the closing parenthesis. The effect of the slash differs slightly in the two instances. First two adjacent slashes, //, within the format specification generate an automatic 1X, and lead to a line skip. Thus, for most systems n adjacent slash marks within the specification will produce n−1 blank lines. When the slash appears at the *beginning* or the *end* of the format specification, it is often taken to mean skip a line, not to end the record, so n slashes at the beginning or end of the specification will result in n skipped lines. (Again some FORTRAN installations vary from this rule, so check your vendor's manual.) Following the rules just cited, the statement

```
1  FORMAT(1XF15.4//1XF15.6//1XF15.6)
```

would double space the results of Example 3. Similarly a format of the form

```
FORMAT(1X,F15.6///)
```

would skip three lines after printing the number specified as F15.6.

Example 4 (Print a table using a loop.)

This example introduces

1. The H-type format specification;
2. The FORTRAN DO loop and its associated CONTINUE statement, which correspond to the FOR/NEXT pair of statements in BASIC;
3. Stored functions in FORTRAN.

The purpose of the program is to produce a 5-column table showing X, X^2, LOG(X), EXP(X), and the square root of X, or X**.5, for values of X from .5 through 5 in steps of .5.

```
      PROGRAM DOLOOP
C     BASIC TO FORTRAN, NO. 4
      WRITE(6,3)
3     FORMAT(15X,1HX,11X,4HX**2,9X,6HLOG(X),9X,6HEXP(X),10X,5HX**.5)
      X=0.5
      DO 5 I=1,10,1
      XSQR=X**2
      ALOGX=ALOG(X)
      SQRTX=SQRT(X)
      EXPX=EXP(X)
```

```
      WRITE(6,2) X,XSQR,ALOGX,EXPX,SQRTX
2     FORMAT(1X,F15.1,F15.2,F15.6,F15.5,F15.6)
      X=X+0.5
5     CONTINUE
      END
```

X	X**2	LOG(X)	EXP(X)	X**
0.5	0.25	-0.693147	1.64872	0.7071
1.0	1.00	0.000000	2.71828	1.0000
1.5	2.25	0.405465	4.48169	1.2247
2.0	4.00	0.693147	7.38906	1.4142
2.5	6.25	0.916291	12.18249	1.5811
3.0	9.00	1.098612	20.08554	1.7320
3.5	12.25	1.252763	33.11545	1.8708
4.0	16.00	1.386294	54.59815	2.0000
4.5	20.25	1.504077	90.01713	2.1213
5.0	25.00	1.609438	148.41316	2.2360

Again working from the top, we notice in line 2 that the WRITE command has no list of the variables to be printed, although it does reference statement 3. This list omission is acceptable, since the output is to be a series of titles which do not involve the numeric value of any variable. In such a case, the text to be printed will be shown in the FORMAT statement, with format specifications provided by X and H. The first specification in FORMAT statement number 3, 15X, provides 15 spaces, the first of which will be our carriage control; the net printed result is 14 spaces. Then, the specification 1HX calls for the literal X to be printed. It will occur in the next character position, or column 15 of the output page.[5] Continuing, we now want to print X**2. To conform to the BASIC program, let the second column to be printed terminate in column 30. To make the second column heading right-justified above its column, we skip 11 spaces (11X), then show 4HX**2. (Note that the 4H of 4HX**2 is *not* printed and

[5] You should not confuse the output character count established by the BASIC command TAB(N), discussed in Chapter 14, and the FORMAT specifications in FORTRAN, as described in this chapter. In BASIC, the value N in TAB(N) specifies the output character position which *begins* a new field, *as counted from the left-hand page margin.* In FORTRAN, no such standard left-hand reference is shown in a field specification. Instead, the field widths specified in FORTRAN are accumulated left to right. The total number of characters specified in a FORMAT statement for one output line should therefore not exceed the maximum width of the line in a given print media. (For the Teletype, the maximum number of characters per line is usually 75; for a high-speed printer, 120 or 132, depending upon the installation.) To determine the total character count in a FORMAT statement, add up all the w specification numbers. By the same token, to determine in which position a given variable will appear, add up the w count to the *left of and including* the field in question. To illustrate, the output line printer format specification

```
FORMAT(1X,F10.2,I6)
```

uses up 16 character positions from left to right on the page. Similarly, if we have

```
   WRITE(6, 2) A, B, C, K
2  FORMAT(1X, F10.2, F6.3, F4.1, I6)
```

the integer value K will appear on the printed line right-justified into a field terminating (at the right) at character position 26, e.g., 10 + 6 + 4 + 6. In both cases, the 1X carriage control character does not add to the count.

does not enter the count; X appears in column 15 + 11, or column 27.) This procedure continues until the desired title has been completely specified. By carefully counting spaces and title length, you have complete control over the spacing of the output text.

The line X = .5 sets the initial value of the real variable X. Then we encounter a new command

```
DO 5 I = 1, 10, 1
```

the counterpart of FOR/NEXT. This statement has the same meaning as in BASIC. The first part of the instruction, DO 1, says, Continue repeating the program lines from this point through statement number 1, which is CONTINUE, until an upper limit is reached. The limit is set by the second part of the DO statement, I = 1, 10, 1. Variable I is an arbitrary index. Its first value is 1, its terminal value 10, and the progression is in steps of 1, as shown by the three numbers, respectively, from left to right in the statement. In FORTRAN the DO index, the limit, and the increment *must* be integer variables. (BASIC does not have this requirement.) The integer constraint prevents problems that might occur in decimal-to-binary conversion. Noninteger variable increments are handled within the loop, as indicated here. Compare with BASIC Example 4. Note that the CONTINUE statement need not reference its associated DO index; the corresponding statement number in the DO and CONTINUE statement lines take care of this. Often CONTINUE may be omitted, as described later.

Within the loop defined by the DO statement, that is, up to statement number 5, computations are made for the various values of X from the initial .5 through the final 5.0. Since we will progress in steps of .5, there will be 10 lines of output, and the DO loop counts those lines. Note that the statement numbers in Example 4 are not in sequential order, since sequential order is not necessary when statement numbers, instead of line numbers, are used for reference.

We come now to the next new point: FORTRAN stored, or library, functions. Within the DO loop we have four substitution statements before the WRITE. The first of these is a normal arithmetic operation. The remaining substitutions, however, employ stored functions, e.g., SQRT(X). The operation of these stored functions is just as in BASIC. To avoid excess detail here, Appendix B provides a listing of the usual FORTRAN stored functions. Note that some of the functions are common to both BASIC and FORTRAN, but that the FORTRAN functions have variable length names followed by the argument in parentheses, whereas BASIC uses *three* letter names. In FORTRAN take care not to select as a variable name the name of a stored function. Thus, recalling the subscripted variables in BASIC, which will also appear with the same form of subscripting in later FORTRAN examples, you could guess that SQRT(X) might cause some confusion if you try to use it as a variable name. It will be considered a stored function. (In BASIC such an error is not possible, because of the constraint on variable name construction.) You may use FORTRAN stored functions as you do those in BASIC. FORTRAN provides a much wider range for your use, as indicated by the list in Appendix B. Also note that ALOGX, SQRX, and EXPX are variable names, not functions, because no parentheses appear.

The remainder of Example 4 contains nothing new; the output is printed using the specified format, the value of X is increased, or incremented, by .5, and the process is continued until the tenth line is printed. As in BASIC, the DO loop tests for a value of the index *greater* than the upper limit before terminating. When that event occurs, control passes to the statement following the specified terminal statement (here statement 1). In the present example, the next statement is END, so the program stops.

Although in subsequent examples we illustrate variations in DO-loop application, the fundamental one is shown here. Note in the output table that the decimal points are lined up, the specified precision is shown, and all the numbers are right-justified in the columns. In FORTRAN as in BASIC a number without a plus sign is assumed positive; minus signs are shown only for negative numbers.

Example 5 (READ and implied loops.)

This example introduces

1. The implied DO loop;
2. The READ command;
3. The DIMENSION statement.

This example differs slightly from BASIC Example 5 to illustrate the above points.

```
      PROGRAM IMPLIED
C     BASIC TO FORTRAN, NO. 5
      DIMENSION X(10),Y(10)
      WRITE(6,1)
1     FORMAT(8X,8HCASE NO.,14X,1HX,14X,1HY)
      READ(5,2) (X(I),I=1,10)
2     FORMAT(10F5)
      DO 20 I=1,10
      Y(I)=1.+3.*X(I)**2+4.*X(I)**3
20    WRITE(6,4) I,X(I),Y(I)
4     FORMAT(1X,I15,F15.2,F15.4)
      END
```

```
2.75 3.43 4.56 1.23 8.74 7.92 9.98 8.70 4.73 8.21

       CASE NO.                    X                 Y
              1                 2.75          106.8750
              2                 3.43          197.7091
              3                 4.56          442.6561
              4                 1.23           12.9822
              5                 8.74         2900.6733
              6                 7.92         2176.3516
              7                 9.98         4275.8492
              8                 8.70         2862.0820
              9                 4.73          491.4140
             10                 8.21         2416.7629
```

Following BASIC Example 5, we want to READ 10 data values that will be different values of X and compute corresponding values of Y. As in BASIC Example 5, we choose to identify the 10 values of X as X(1) through X(10) employing the subscripted variable notation for illustration. (In FORTRAN you handle the subscripts just as in BASIC.)

In FORTRAN (unlike BASIC in which a DIM declaration was optional for dimensions less than 10) a list or table, if used, must *always* be declared at the outset using the DIMENSION statement. (The word must be spelled out in FORTRAN.) The second line of Example 5 illustrates the dimensioning of two 10-element lists:

DIMENSION X(10), Y(10).

The first list is for the data input values, the second for computed output values. As in BASIC Example 5, list use is not necessary to get the results shown; they are used for illustration of the implied DO.

The next two lines of Example 5 write the headings desired following the FORTRAN rules given previously.

Now we come to the READ statement, which has two parts. READ(5,1) tells the computer to read from the input device code 5, according to FORMAT statement number 1, certain values to be specified. The second part of the command, to the right, lists the values to be read.

For example, we could have used

READ(5,1) X(1), X(2), X(3), . . . , X(10)

to read the values shown just below END. (In FORTRAN you need no DATA declaration, and the data values are provided after, not before, the END statement.)

An alternate and more compact form of list identification appears in Example 5: (X(I), I = 1, 10). The symbols shown illustrate an *implied* DO operation. The meaning is that the list to be read shall consist of the values X(I), where the index I shall start at 1 and range to 10. A step of one is assumed, since no step specification appears. The result is identical to the detailed list of the previous paragraph.

Before continuing to the next program line, note that READ (5,2) referenced FORMAT statement number 2, which is FORMAT(10F5). The meaning of 10F5 is that the data will appear in 10 successive fields of 5 positions each. The 10 before F5 is a shorthand way of indicating specification repetition and is equivalent to 10 F5's separated by commas. From our previous experience with the F specification, we expect the data to be read, with a fractional part. No d specification is shown, because we will let the data provide its own decimal point within the specified field. When the various X(I) values are read, the specified decimal point in the data will be taken as it stands, a procedure which avoids one form of data input error that could occur due to minor column misalignment in data preparation.[6]

With the data now in hand, Example 5 proceeds to compute and print the 10 desired results. This is done by the DO loop containing the substitution and WRITE statements, terminating at statement 20, the final

---

[6] Input format rules differ slightly from output format rules. In this note we consider the F, I, and E formats.

The F format, of form Fw.d, may be used for fixed-point input data for which the decimal point is shown in the data, or for which it is omitted, but assumed by the F specification. In any case the count for w must include all the digits shown *plus* the decimal point and sign positions if shown. (A number with no sign is assumed positive.) If *no* decimal point is shown in F-type data, the d specification places an assumed decimal point d places from the *right* side of the specified field, w. If a decimal point is shown in the data, that decimal point will *override* the format specification. Thus, if the data contains a decimal point, the d specification is superfluous, and an Fw specification is sufficient. To be safe, always use the decimal point in your data. To see why, suppose you specified a F5.2 number and proposed data with an assumed decimal point. Let b stand for space. Then, if your data were bb123 the computer would take the number b1.23, assuming a decimal point. However, if you were off one column in the field, e.g., b123b, the computer would take that as 12.30, treating trailing blank spaces as zeroes. But, if you specify a decimal point in F-type data, there is less chance of error, e.g., 1.23b and b1.23 are both taken as 1.23. When a decimal point is shown, only the field width w, is critical; your data may *not* stray outside of that specification. Out-of-field digits will be lost from the specified field and may create major errors in adjacent data fields. To be safe with F-type data, use very wide fields (make a large w) and show all decimal points in the data.

With integer or I-type data, you must always be absolutely precise in your alignment of data into specified fields if your system requires formatted input. (Some remote terminal systems permit *unformatted* data input as in BASIC; most card installations require input formatting.) Suppose you specify a I5-data format and the number in question is 12. The computer will take bbb12 as 12, bb12b as 120, and b12bb as 1200! One column off, and your data is off by a factor of 10. So take care with integer input data.

The E-type format can be even more hazardous for input data (even though it is the safest form of output format). With an E-type input, whether a decimal point is shown or not to be off by one column is to effect the *exponent*, which drastically changes the desired result, as the following example in E8.2 input format indicates.

WRITE. A nonimplied "DO-loop" may terminate with any statement that does not initiate any form of branching operation, as illustrated here. Many starting programmers prefer to use the CONTINUE termination of Example 4 to avoid inadvertent difficulty. CONTINUE has no function other than that of a reference.

The other statements of Example 5 are forms we have seen before. Note, however, that READ and WRITE FORMAT statements may be placed as you desire in a program. Most programmers prefer to cluster all FORMAT statements at the beginning or the end of their programs for easy reference.

Example 6 (Two vectors or lists.)

This example differs from Example 5 only in that two variables X and Y are used to compute Z. Ten values of each variable are to be evaluated and to be read in as lists before evaluation. Finally, the 10 values of Z are to be computed and stored in a list; the respective values will be printed immediately after computation.

```
      PROGRAM VECTOR
C     BASIC TO FORTRAN, NO. 6
      DIMENSION X(10),Y(10),Z(10)
      READ(5,101) X
101   FORMAT(10F6)
      READ(5,101) Y
      WRITE(6,102)
102   FORMAT(8X,8HCASE NO.,14X,1HX,14X,1HY,14X,1HZ)
      DO 7 I=1,10
7     Z(I)=1.0+3.0*X(I)**2+4.0*Y(I)**3
      WRITE(6,103) (I,X(I),Y(I),Z(I),I=1,10)
103   FORMAT(1X,I15,F15.2,F15.2,F15.3)
      END

12.0  24.0  46.0  3.0   72.0  12.43 9.72  9.0   2.0   46.0
24.0  2.0   5.0   7.0   63.0  7.36  2.16  3.0   7.0   46.0
```

Appearance of number in field	Value understood by Computer to be
b+2032E3	20.32×10^3
+2032E3b	20.32×10^{30}
+2.032E3	2.032×10^3
2.032E3b	2.032×10^{30}

As in the F-type specification the input decimal point overrides the E specification of d, and a plus sign is assumed if not shown. But note that trailing blanks in the exponent are taken as zeroes. Since the difference between 10^3 and 10^{30} is more than substantial, yet only one keystroke off base, it is a prudent policy to avoid E-type inputs whenever possible.

CASE NO.	X	Y	Z
1	12.00	24.00	55729.000
2	24.00	2.00	1761.000
3	46.00	5.00	6849.000
4	3.00	7.00	1400.000
5	72.00	63.00	1015741.000
6	12.43	7.36	2059.268
7	9.72	2.16	324.746
8	9.00	3.00	352.000
9	2.00	7.00	1385.000
10	46.00	46.00	395693.000

The DIMENSION statement provides for the three upcoming lists. The first and second READ commands read the values of X and Y as two lists (the list for X, then the list for Y) using the implied DO operation of Example 5. Note that both READ commands reference the *same* FORMAT statement. This is possible because we used the same format specifications for both input variables. Similarly, the same output format specification is used for each printed line, because we want column alignment in the output table.

We then write the heading according to line 102's FORMAT specification. The DO 7 I = 1, 10 in this illustration computes the 10 values of Z(I) via the substitution statement number 7. (CONTINUE is not used here.) Although it would have been possible (and more efficient) to WRITE our results as they were computed, we perform that operation separately to illustrate an implied DO when employed with a WRITE command. When program sequence comes to the final WRITE and the associated statement 103 FORMAT, 10 values of X, Y, and Z are available for reference. The implied DO of the WRITE command

(I, X(I), Y(I), Z(I), I = 1,10)

indicates that the variables shown are to be printed *across* a line following 103 FORMAT, and that 10 lines should be printed with I moving from 1 to 10. The 103 FORMAT is the same for each repeated line. Given the possibility of extensive lists and tables in storage, the implied DO in a WRITE command is a powerful tool.

As in BASIC Example 6, we note again the advantage of separating data variable values in rows rather than alternating their values in sequence. This design permits us to change the values of X without changing Y, and vice versa.

Example 7 (Use of tables.)

This example illustrates how you can handle the data of Example 6 as a two-row, 10-column table instead of two individual lists. The computation and output desired is the same as Example 6, only the method of achieving the results differs.

```
      PROGRAM ARRAY
C     BASIC TO FORTRAN• NO• 7
      DIMENSION A(2•10)•Z(10)
      READ(5•11) ((A(I•J)•J=1•10)•I=1•2)
      WRITE(6•12)
      DO 2 J=1•10
      Z(J)=1•0+3•0*A(1•J)**2+4•0*A(2•J)**3
2     WRITE(6•13) J•A(1•J)•A(2•J)•Z(J)
11    FORMAT(10F6•/•10F6)
12    FORMAT(8X•8HCASE NO••14X•1HX•14X•1HY•14X•1HZ)
13    FORMAT(1X•I15•2F15•2•F15•3)
      END
```

```
12•0  24•0  46•0  3•0   72•0  12•43 9•72  9•0   2•0   46•0
24•0  2•0   5•0   7•0   63•0  7•36  2•16  3•0   7•0   46•0
```

```
        CASE NO•              X              Y              Z
               1          12•00          24•00      55729•000
               2          24•00           2•00       1761•000
               3          46•00           5•00       6849•000
               4           3•00           7•00       1400•000
               5          72•00          63•00    1015741•000
               6          12•43           7•36       2059•268
               7           9•72           2•16        324•746
               8           9•00           3•00        352•000
               9           2•00           7•00       1385•000
              10          46•00          46•00     395693•000
```

DIMENSION A(2, 10), Z(10) declares a data table of size 2 × 10 and a list of 10 elements for the computational results.

The more complex READ command again uses the implied DO operation to read in the table of data. The specification shown initially sets index I to 1, then varies J from 1 to 10 in steps of 1. Then I becomes 2, and the J range repeats. Both loop limits are thereby satisfied, and the READ is complete. The "nesting" is from left-to-right in the implied DO shown. Note the use of parentheses in this detail.

FORMAT statement 11 controls the data input. Again for reasons discussed in footnote 6 we use the explicit decimal point. The / in the input format specification indicates, as it did in an output format specification, end of record, so one input format statement can be used for more than one line of data. A shorter alternative

11 FORMAT (10F6)

is equivalent because the repetition of the J range in the implied READ DO loop references statement 11 again if the) end-of-record indicator has been encountered, terminating the format declaration.

At this point we have table A (I,J) available and may refer to any of its items by the index coordinate pair (I, J). A (2, 9), for example, contains the number 7.0, the ninth value of Y.

The computation and printout now proceeds via the DO loop to statement number 2. Note that in this example, unlike the just previous one, there is no necessity to subscript the output variable, since it is printed as computed. However, in the subscripted form shown we have retained all the answers and could add to the existing programs, using the stored results for other purposes. Such extensions would not be possible if the answers were printed, but not simultaneously stored in an output list. As in BASIC Example 7, note the ease of program modification when the data appears in tabular form.

Example 8 (Conditional branches in FORTRAN.)

This example illustrates

1. Integer Computation;
2. Arithmetic IF tests in FORTRAN;
3. Conversion from integer to real numbers, or vice versa.

This is the first program in both FORTRAN and the BASIC set that takes alternative action depending upon the input data values tested by the program.

Recall that this example seeks a credit evaluation based upon an applicant's salary, years of employment, years of current residence, and ratio of monthly rent (or mortgage) to salary. Credit is approved if salary ⩾ \$7500 *and* monthly rent ⩽ salary/52 *and* either ⩾ 3 years can be established for continuous employment *or* residence. The details of converting this prose to a program was previously illustrated in BASIC. Here they are in FORTRAN.

```
      PROGRAM BRANCH
C     BASIC TO FORTRAN, NO. 8
1     READ(5,5)ISAL,IEMP,IRES,IRENT,IDENT
5     FORMAT(I5,2I3,I4,I5)
      IF(IDENT) 15,6,7
7     IF(ISAL-7500) 800,2,2
2     IF(ISAL/52-IRENT) 800,3,3
3     IF(IEMP-3) 4,900,900
4     IF(IRES-3) 800,900,900
800   WRITE(6,805) IDENT
805   FORMAT(1X,8HCASE NO.,I5,5X,15HCREDIT REJECTED)
      GO TO 1
900   WRITE(6,905) IDENT
907   FORMAT(1X,8HCASE NO.,I5,5X,15HCREDIT APPROVED)
      GO TO 1
15    WRITE(6,500)
500   FORMAT(1X,43HERROR ON INPUT. IDENT IS A NEGATIVE NUMBER.)
6     END
```

```
 8600  2 10 200 1728
 7400  3  7 200 0619
 6200  6  5 150 1032
 4800 10 20 125 8004
15000  3  3 285 5596
    0  0  0   0    0

CASE NO. 1728        CREDIT REJECTED
CASE NO.  619        CREDIT REJECTED
CASE NO. 1032        CREDIT REJECTED
CASE NO. 8004        CREDIT REJECTED
CASE NO. 5596        CREDIT APPROVED
```

This example contains data for five test cases, each considered a record. The five fields (from left to right) are (1) annual salary, (2) years at present employment, (3) years at present residence, (4) monthly rent (or mortgage), and (5) an identification code. For illustrative purposes each of the numbers in each record has been rounded and is shown as an integer (no fractional part or decimal point). Moreover, in this example, as opposed to BASIC Example 8, arbitrary identification numbers have been shown.

To make the variable names remind us of what they mean (a desirable possibility under the more flexible variable name rules of FORTRAN) we use SAL to indicate "salary," etc. But because these data are all to be integers, we arbitrarily prefix each variable name with the letter I so the machine will know we want integer arithmetic. The salary variable is thus ISAL. The other integer variables are handled identically. (The use of the leading I to denote mnemonic, or memory-assisting, integer names is common practice when such names would otherwise result in real variables.)

The program proceeds to read the first record of five integer fields, as formatted in statement number 5. (With this integer input format, field column alignment must be perfect, otherwise you will get data input errors, as indicated in footnote 6).

With this data in hand, you may refer to Figure 13.1, the logical flow chart of BASIC Example 8, to see what happens next. The implementation in this FORTRAN example is identical, except that the BASIC IF/THEN test is replaced here by the FORTRAN ARITHMETIC IF.

At statement 7, for example, we note

```
IF(ISAL–7500) 800,2,2
```

which means: If the arithmetic result of the expression within the parentheses – here (ISAL–7500) – is negative, i.e., *less than* zero, proceed to statement number 800; if the result is *equal* to zero, then statement 2; and if positive, i.e., *greater than* zero, then statement 2.

The FORTRAN ARITHMETIC IF provides a *three-way* branch (for –, 0, +, as shown by the statement numbers left to right following the arithmetic test in parentheses). In this example, the three-way possibility has been reduced to two by repetition of statement numbers in the branching possibility triad. For example, if (ISAL − 7500) is negative, we immediately reject the applicant by branching to statement 800; otherwise we proceed to statement number 2, which in this example happens to be the next line. (In general, this adjacency need not hold; the three-way split from a FORTRAN ARITHMETIC IF can take you to any of the three specified statement numbers). This FORTRAN feature is potentially much more flexible than the BASIC IF/THEN (which offered only a two-way branch), although to make the examples conform to BASIC Example 8 our present program does not exercise these capabilities.

Program statement 2 above

```
IF(ISAL/52 − IRENT) 800, 3, 3
```

demands special consideration. The result of integer division (ISAL/52) is also an integer with any remainder discarded.

In this example, using integer arithmetic and data, the truncation resulting from integer division in statement 2 does *not* cause decision error. For example in the first case, reported salary is $8600 and integer division of 8600/52, actually $165.38 as a *real* number to two places, gives the integer result $165 with no decimal point. If the reported rent (or mortgage) is $165 or less, the testing progresses; if $166 or more, credit is rejected at once (via statements 800 and 805).

Would the situation differ with noninteger, remainder-keeping division in this case? Technically, no; practically, maybe.

Since both ISAL and IRENT are expressed as integers in the data of this example, truncation error will not affect the test as opposed to the alternative real test evaluation, which gives the same numerical data in real form, i.e., SAL = 8600.00, RENT = 200.00 and

```
IF(SAL/52. − RENT) 800, 3, 3
```

in which the numeric literal, 52., is also a real number.

To check this out, note that the number within the parentheses is (165.38 − 200.00) or negative. Credit is rejected. Now, consider the critical rents $165.00 and $166.00, reported as whole numbers, but in the real mode. Using the real test again, $165.00 would be acceptable, $166.00 would not, just as with integer arithmetic.

But, if we presented real input data (*with* fractional parts), e.g., RENT = 165.39, the precision of the data becomes important and a monthly rent of $165.39 would reject credit, while $165.38 would not.

Thus, in practice, how we round off numerical data to get integers, or how many decimal places we keep when reporting and handling real numbers can affect close decisions. It is a small point, but nobody wants his credit rejected for a one-cent comparison error. Similarly, you might wonder in the integer arithmetic of this example how the reported input data were rounded (or otherwise converted) from their original values, if they had fractional parts. In close cases, such conversion rules can make the difference between pass and fail. What, for instance, do you do with an applicant who passes the salary and rent tests, who has just taken a new job, but who has resided at his present address for only two years and eleven months? Depending upon how you rounded or truncated the residence data to an integer value, the program above would accept or reject the applicant. That is, the applicant may become the victim or the beneficiary of a clerical input decision over which neither he nor the loan officer have any control and perhaps any knowledge unless the data input is traced from its inception to its computer result.

These are some of the questions raised by computer testing. In particular, since the computer will make its tests precisely as you specify them, it makes sense to evaluate carefully the practical consequences of a given test, or decision rule, before it is implemented.

Following this first illustrative division, all other tests are for integers, and the program logically proceeds until the applicant's credit is either rejected or accepted (there is no intermediate alternative). The above remarks about real versus integer tests apply to all the other tests of this example.

After each final decision, the program sequence returns to statement number 1, another READ. When the five data records have been processed, the next READ of all-zero data automatically halts the program in following the test after statement 5,

```
IF(IDENT) 15, 6, 7
```

IF IDENT (an expression containing a single variable) is itself zero, the program terminates; if less than zero, we print an error message via statements 15 and 500, then stop; and if greater than zero, we continue with the evaluation. This detail is not shown in BASIC Example 8, where the program terminated when we ran out of data. The extension shown here is desirable, since it provides a controlled program halt.

The unconditional branch GO TO 1, shown twice above, is the FORTRAN counterpart of GO TO in BASIC, and operates identically. Trace through this example and determine to your own satisfaction, *under the input and computational assumptions made*, why only applicant 0005 had his credit approved.

One technical point is worth noting in this example with regard to the ARITHMETIC IF test. When you make the test (shown within the parentheses following IF), the subtraction indicated (or alternate expressions within the parentheses in other problems) *must* involve numbers, or variables, which have *identical* modes. Thus, IF (ISAL − 7500.00) 800,2,2 is *not* legal—because the comparison is between the *integer* variable ISAL and the *real* literal 7500.00. You will discover that this is an easy error to make in FORTRAN, so guard against it.

Before you continue with a further study of the BASIC to FORTRAN translations make sure you understand the FORTRAN format, mode, and computational rules illustrated thus far. In the next chapter we consider advanced tests, tabular manipulations, and subroutines in FORTRAN, using as illustrations the previous BASIC Examples 9 through 13.

PROJECT

If your location permits Teletype FORTRAN programs to be run, rewrite each of the translated FORTRAN programs shown in this chapter for execution on a Teletype. Use line numbers instead of statement numbers. Note that when you do this you must adjust all statement number references shown in this chapter to the corresponding *sequential* line numbers you must necessarily employ in remote terminal FORTRAN. The diagnostic messages you receive at a time-sharing installation will aid in detecting minor errors in FORTRAN as they did in BASIC.

EIGHTEEN

Thirteen FORTRAN translations (Part II)

We continue our BASIC to FORTRAN translations, following the numbered examples of Chapter 13. The examples that follow are slightly more difficult than those of Chapter 17, but since you have already seen their logic in Chapter 13, we are mostly concerned now with the details of the FORTRAN language. Although you may write a variety of FORTRAN programs based only upon the rules discussed in Chapter 17, the details contained in this chapter will increase your ability to produce FORTRAN programs of wider use.

Example 9 (The logical IF.)

The objective of the poker-hand example is to read the values in a hand of five cards, then have the computer determine what kind of a hand has just come up.

In the following program,

```
DIMENSION K(13),M(5)
```

provides for two lists; the first the counting list for card values, the second the list containing the data for a given hand. List K(J) is first initialized to zero, as are the counters N2 (pair) and N3 (three of a kind). (As we mention later no count is made here for four of a kind.) Then the data for the first hand are read using the implied DO of Chapter 17 in the 5I3 format of statement number 24.

The next line is our first encounter with the FORTRAN logical IF statement, which is an alternate to the arithmetic IF of Chapter 17. The general form of the logical IF command is

IF (logical comparison) command to execute if comparison is true

Instead of an arithmetic comparison, which, remember resulted in a +, 0, − result and a three-way branch for the arithmetic IF, we now use the following symbols to indicate our comparisons. Compare the table below to that shown for BASIC in Chapter 10, and note that the meaning is identical to what has come before regarding the BASIC IF/THEN command.

FORTRAN notation	*Equivalent BASIC*	*Meaning*
.EQ.	=	Equal to
.NE.	<>	Not equal to
.LT.	<	Less than
.GT.	>	Greater than
.LE.	<=	Less than or equal to
.GE.	>=	Greater than or equal to

Comparisons using the FORTRAN abbreviations (which must show the period before and after, exactly as above) will result in a "true" or "false" condition, as in the BASIC IF/THEN command. If the comparison is true, then the command indicated to the right of the comparison is executed; if not, control passes to the next statement succeeding the test. Thus, in this program, the command

```
IF(M(1) .EQ. 0) GO TO 25
```

checks the first element of the data list. If a zero is present, control passes to statement number 25 END, and the program halts. (We use 0 here as an end-of-file indicator, since no card may have that value; only the values 1 through 13 are permissible.) The remaining logical IFs in this program work in the same way.

The executable statement following the logical comparison may be any other FORTRAN command except another IF or a DO. In some instances, execution of such a command will not divert sequential control, and the statement following the logical IF will be executed next. To illustrate,

```
IF( K .LT. 10) K = K + 1
```

is a legal logical IF command. In this case, the substitution to the right causes K to be increased by 1 if the previous value of K was less than 10: However, whether or not K is altered, the next statement encountered by the program would be the one following the comparison. Note how flexible the FORTRAN logical IF is because of the wide range of commands that may follow its comparison.

With the detail of the logical IF in mind, the program below follows BASIC Example 9, using the FORTRAN details of Chapter 17. There is only one logical variation. In BASIC Example 9, for clarity we introduced a counter for four of a kind, which could take on the values 0 and 1. But this counter is not really needed. Since four of a kind can occur only once in a five-card hand, we may immediately terminate any further search of the card count if we encounter that combination. This direct approach is taken care of by the test

IF(K(J) .EQ. 4) GO TO 22

which appears within the DO 8 J = 1, 13 loop following statement number 3.

A word of caution. As with the arithmetic IF you should take extreme care when making an .EQ. test on *real* numbers because of the possible roundoff vagaries, which we have already mentioned repeatedly. To be safe, use integer values *only*, as shown in this program, when the strict equality demanded by the .EQ. condition is necessary.

```
      PROGRAM POKER
C     BASIC TO FORTRAN, NO. 9
      DIMENSION K(13), M(5)
1     DO 2 J=1,13
2     K(J)=0
      N2=0
      N3=0
      READ(5,24) (M(J),J=1,5)
24    FORMAT(5I3)
      IF(M(1).EQ.0) GO TO 25
      DO 3 J=1,5
3     K(M(J))=K(M(J))+1
      DO 8 J=1,13
      IF(K(J).EQ.2) GO TO 6
      IF(K(J).EQ.3) GO TO 7
      IF(K(J).EQ.4) GO TO 22
      GO TO 8
6     N2=N2+1
      GO TO 8
7     N3=N3+1
8     CONTINUE
      IF(N3.EQ.1) GO TO 11
```

```
      IF(N2.EQ.2) GO TO 16
      IF(N2.EQ.1) GO TO 14
12    WRITE(6,13)
13    FORMAT(1X,7HNO PAIR)
      GO TO 1
11    IF(N2.EQ.1) GO TO 20
      WRITE(6,19)
19    FORMAT(1X,15HTHREE OF A KIND
      GO TO 1
14    WRITE(6,15)
15    FORMAT(1X,8HONE PAIR)
      GO TO 1
16    WRITE(6,17)
17    FORMAT(1X,8HTWO PAIR)
      GO TO 1
20    WRITE(6,21)
21    FORMAT(1X,10HFULL HOUSE)
      GO TO 1
22    WRITE(6,23)
23    FORMAT(1X,14HFOUR OF A KIND)
      GO TO 1
25    END
```

```
  1  2  3  4  5
  7  7  7  7  8
  2  3  4  3  2
 13 13 13 11 11
 11 13 12  1  2
  2  4  2  4  4
  3  6  6  6  6
  5 12  5  5 12
  1  2  8 12 12
  4  4  9  9  9
  4  5  6 12  4
  2  7 12  2  2
  2  7  4  6  2
  7  8  8 12  8
  0  0  0  0  0
```

```
NO PAIR
FOUR OF A KIND
TWO PAIR
FULL HOUSE
```

```
NO PAIR
FULL HOUSE
FOUR OF A KIND
FULL HOUSE
ONE PAIR
FULL HOUSE
ONE PAIR
THREE OF A KIND
ONE PAIR
THREE OF A KIND
```

Although we do not illustrate the following point in the above program, the logical IF may be extended to *compound* logical forms on many FORTRAN systems. To create a compound logical IF you may use, in addition to the six comparisons given in the above table, the three logical operations .AND., .OR., and .NOT., again with the periods before and after, exactly as shown. Thus, in effect, you may make several tests in one program line. As an illustration, the following are also legal logical IF commands

```
IF(X .LT. B .OR. D .GE. C) GO TO 50
IF(K .EQ. ITEM .AND. J .LT. 5) A = B + C
IF( .NOT. (C .GT. 0.)) GO TO 10
```

The first illustration states that if *either* X is less than B, *or* D is greater than or equal to C, the result will be true and we should progress to statement number 50. Similarly, the next IF indicates that the stated substitution should be made if K is greater than ITEM *and* J is *also* less than 5. Note that as always mixed-mode comparisons are not allowed. Finally, the effect of the .NOT. in the last line is to negate the following logical comparison. So, if (C .GT. 0.) is "true" .NOT.(C .GT. 0.) is "false," and the test result is reversed. When using .NOT. with variables having a numeric value, you must enclose in parentheses the logical phrase to be negated.[1]

Example 10 (The subroutine.)

We now weave cloth again, but still on the computer's line printer instead of the loom. This is the same deterministic simulation we presented in Example 10, Chapter 13, but here we introduce one of the major differences between BASIC and FORTRAN, the use of the advanced subroutine.

---

[1] In this text we do not discuss the possibility of employing logical variables in FORTRAN, i.e., those which have not a numeric value but a logical value, "true" or "false." Such variables may be used in some FORTRAN systems, and are useful for performing Boolean algebra or the analysis of complex true/false expressions on the computer. For such extensions, consult your vendor's manual. With logical variables, .NOT. may be handled without the parentheses shown above.

It is important that you understand the difference between the subroutine in BASIC and its application in FORTRAN because there is a major variation not only in form but also in capability. FORTRAN subroutines are substantially more powerful than those we have previously discussed in Chapter 12 for BASIC.

In FORTRAN, the subroutine is handled by the computer as a *separate* program, distinct from the main, or "calling," program. That is, you write a main program, then separately write one or more subroutine subprograms to be used by the former. The subroutine subprograms, as shown in Example 10, are appended after the main program and are called by it as needed.

To use a subroutine subprogram you proceed as follows. First, you construct one or more subroutines, each of which is given a name with associated arguments, if needed. The number of arguments defined by the subprogram may range from zero to the maximum set by your FORTRAN compiler. For example, the Control Data Corporation 3600 computer will handle up to 63 distinct arguments in a subroutine. The arguments in a subroutine are *dummy* arguments, as were the arguments of BASIC functions (see Chapter 9). Indeed, since the subroutine in FORTRAN is considered an entirely separate program from the main program, the arguments used in the subroutine may either duplicate or differ from those in the main program, as we shall shortly illustrate. This flexibility means that FORTRAN subroutines may be written in a general form and used without alteration in many programs. Each FORTRAN subroutine must terminate with its own END statement and contain one or more RETURN statements. The general form is

SUBROUTINE <u>name</u> (a_1, a_2, a_3, . . . , a_n)
– – – – – – – –
– – – – – – – –
RETURN
END

Each subroutine must commence with the word SUBROUTINE followed by the name, which follows the variable name rules for FORTRAN. No mode, however, is presupposed by the subroutine name chosen. The arguments in parentheses must contain a list of all the values which will be passed to the subroutine by the main program and all those which will be passed back to the main program by the subroutine. The requirements are flexible. There may be *no* arguments in some subroutines, e.g., a subroutine to print a page heading. In others variables may be passed to the subroutine, but none may be returned to the main program. In general, however, some variables are passed to the subroutine and some are returned to the main program. In processing the subroutine, control reverts to the main program whenever a RETURN statement in a subroutine is encountered. As illustrated in this example, subroutines may be combined with looping and other conditional testing techniques to increase their versatility.

The main program reaches a FORTRAN subroutine by use of the CALL statement, which has the general form:

CALL name $(a_1, a_2, a_3, \ldots, a_n)$

The name cited in the CALL statement must be the exact name of the desired subroutine. The arguments following the subroutine name must agree precisely in order, number, and mode with the list of arguments specified in the corresponding SUBROUTINE. That is, reading from left to right in the parenthesized list you must have the same correspondence of intended variables, the same length of list in both cases, and the same format mode (real, integer, etc.). However, the *names* of the arguments need not be the same in both cases: the arguments of the CALL statement will automatically be substituted for the arguments listed in the named SUBROUTINE. Most computer manuals for this reason refer to the arguments of the CALL statement as *actual* arguments and those of the SUBROUTINE as *dummy* arguments. The distinction is important. In BASIC, the variables passed to a subroutine are the actual variables of the main program, and the subroutine in BASIC must be written in terms of these same specific variables. Moreover, in BASIC all manipulations upon the subroutine variables will affect the corresponding identical variables in the main program, and vice versa. In FORTRAN this is not the case. The subroutine is an entirely separate program; and variables, statement numbers, and other internal subroutine details are independent of other subroutines as well as the main program. The link which ties the whole together is the relation between the CALL argument list and the SUBROUTINE argument list. In fact, FORTRAN subroutines are actually compiled separately from the main program, and the link between the CALLs and the SUBROUTINEs of a given program occur at the time of execution.

We belabor this point before giving our new Example 10 because, as indicated in Chapter 16, the FORTRAN subroutine and its flexibility is one of the language's strong points. In contrast to BASIC, in which each subroutine in a given program must conform in its variables to the main program, thereby being totally interdependent with it, FORTRAN breaks this chain of complexity by means of the argument approach noted above. Thus, in FORTRAN you may create extensive libraries of useful subroutines and paste them into your programs at will, observing only the correspondence between the CALL and SUBROUTINE argument lists—even though the names of the variables are not the same in both. In this way you may greatly multiply your programming power, whereas in BASIC you must generally treat each program as an entity unless you plan carefully in advance.

Most of what we have just said will be clearer once you look at the details of Example 10. In this example we show the simplest FORTRAN subroutine, one with only *one* argument. However, the essential points can be made clearly, and then we may extend the discussion to more difficult cases. Example 10 follows:

```
      PROGRAM JACQUARD
C     BASIC TO FORTRAN, NO. 10
C     JACQUARD LOOM PROBLEM - PRINTS SELECTED PATTERNS
      M=0
5     M=M+1
      READ(5,10) I1,I2,I3
10    FORMAT(  3I4  )
      IF(I1.EQ.-1) GO TO 2
      WRITE(6,15) M
15    FORMAT(///,1X,17HFABRIC DESIGN NO.,I2,/)
      DO 20 I=1,2
      CALL PAT1(I1)
      CALL PAT3(I3)
      CALL PAT2(I2)
20    CALL PAT3(I3)
      GO TO 5
2     END

      SUBROUTINE PAT1(J)
      DO 2 I=1,J
2     WRITE(6,15)
15    FORMAT(1X,25HXXXXX     XXXXX     XXXXX)
      RETURN
      END

      SUBROUTINE PAT2(J)
      DO 2 I=1,J
2     WRITE(6,15)
15    FORMAT(1X,25H     XXXXX     XXXXX     )
      RETURN
      END

      SUBROUTINE PAT3(J)
      DO 2 I=1,J
2     WRITE(6,15)
15    FORMAT(1X,25HXXXXXXXXXXXXXXXXXXXXXXXXX)
      RETURN
      END

   2   2   0
   2   0   2
   1   1   1
  -1  -1  -1
```

```
FABRIC DESIGN NO. 1

XXXXX     XXXXX     XXXXX
XXXXX     XXXXX     XXXXX
     XXXXX     XXXXX
     XXXXX     XXXXX
XXXXX     XXXXX     XXXXX
XXXXX     XXXXX     XXXXX
     XXXXX     XXXXX
     XXXXX     XXXXX
```

```
FABRIC DESIGN NO. 2

XXXXX     XXXXX     XXXXX
XXXXX     XXXXX     XXXXX
XXXXXXXXXXXXXXXXXXXXXXXXX
XXXXXXXXXXXXXXXXXXXXXXXXX
XXXXXXXXXXXXXXXXXXXXXXXXX
XXXXXXXXXXXXXXXXXXXXXXXXX
XXXXX     XXXXX     XXXXX
XXXXX     XXXXX     XXXXX
XXXXXXXXXXXXXXXXXXXXXXXXX
XXXXXXXXXXXXXXXXXXXXXXXXX
XXXXXXXXXXXXXXXXXXXXXXXXX
XXXXXXXXXXXXXXXXXXXXXXXXX
```

```
FABRIC DESIGN NO. 3

XXXXX     XXXXX     XXXXX
XXXXXXXXXXXXXXXXXXXXXXXXX
     XXXXX     XXXXX
XXXXXXXXXXXXXXXXXXXXXXXXX
XXXXX     XXXXX     XXXXX
XXXXXXXXXXXXXXXXXXXXXXXXX
     XXXXX     XXXXX
XXXXXXXXXXXXXXXXXXXXXXXXX
```

Again from the top, we have severai comments: note the initialization of the design number, M, and a READ of the parameters for a given case. Here we READ the design specifications, instead of using the BASIC INPUT statement of Chapter 13, to conform to standard card FORTRAN.[2] In the program listing above, take care to distinguish between the letter I and

[2] Most time-saving applications of FORTRAN also permit you to use an INPUT command comparable to BASIC. However, the program shown will work on both batch and remote-terminal time-sharing systems. Check your local dealer for use of the FORTRAN INPUT command, if available.

the number 1 which on most computer printers appear very similar. Thus, I1, I2, and I3 in the READ (5, 10) statement are integer numbers from the data set, representing the repetitions of the patterns to be illustrated in the Jacquard loom printout.

The statement

```
IF(I1 .EQ. -1) GO TO 2
```

is an end-of-file test, and terminates the program if I1 is −1. Program statement 15 and its associated WRITE produces the title for each case. The slash symbols /// and / in FORMAT statement 15 provide, respectively, three spaces between each case and one space between the title and the printed design.

Now we come to the subroutines. The

```
DO 20 I = 1,2
```

statement repeats twice the pattern generated by the following CALLs. Each CALL represents one pattern line, which is to be repeated in the design the number of times indicated by its associated argument. The subroutine names PAT1, PAT2, and PAT3 generate the patterns to be displayed in the order of the CALLs in the main program, which terminates with statement 2 END.

Note that each of the three designated subroutines, shown following the main program, contains its name following the word SUBROUTINE, an associated argument (J in each case), a RETURN, and an END. Note also that in the listed subroutines the statement numbers (e.g., 2 and 15) have been duplicated, a practice permissible in FORTRAN, since the subroutines are independent not only of each other but also of the main program (note also statement numbers 2 and 15 in the main program).

What happens when the main program is executed? As in the BASIC function, we have a transfer of variables, the actual for the dummy. The values I1, I2, and I3, respectively, are substituted for J in PAT1, PAT2, and PAT3. Each of the subroutines is then sequenced by the CALL statement naming it, and the program continues to completion after two repetitions of the PAT sequence shown in the main program. The output illustrates this for the three cases required by the input data.

Before continuing to our next example, we pause to consider some extensions of the subroutine, first, the case of more than one argument.

Suppose that a program had the CALL statement

```
CALL JACK(A,B,I,B(3),XRAY)
```

consisting of five numeric values at the time of the CALL. Suppose also that an associated subroutine, named JACK, had the following five dummy arguments:

SUBROUTINE JACK(X,Y,K,C,Z)

Suppose further that the first four variables were to be passed to the subroutine and that the last was to be returned to the main program, i.e., the subroutine computes Z based upon the values it receives for X, Y, K, and C and returns that value to the main program under the name XRAY. Obviously, in this case we must have some statement in SUBROUTINE JACK which evaluates Z. Similarly, note the left-to-right correspondence in the CALL and SUBROUTINE arguments lists between the "input" and "output" variables, e.g., the value of X in the subroutine is set equal to the numeric value of A from the main program, etc. Note also that any of the variables mentioned in the CALL and in the main program could also appear in the detail of SUBROUTINE JACK, i.e., variables A, B, I, B(3), and even XRAY could appear in SUBROUTINE JACK without effect upon the main program. However, note that the two lists agree in order, length, and mode, i.e., argument I in the CALL agrees with argument K in the SUBROUTINE, both of which are the third variable in both lists, and both of which are integer variables in both lists.

In general, most systems will not permit subscripted variables in the SUBROUTINE argument list, i.e., C above may *not* be replaced with, say, X(1). Moreover, you should not use the name of any subroutine you intend to call in any main program as a variable name or as any other form of a main program declaration. The latter is a reasonable request to avoid confusion. Also, if you intend to use lists or tables in a subroutine, the subroutine must usually provide for them with a DIMENSION statement. These and other details are best checked by reference to your local vendor's manual for FORTRAN.[3]

Finally, we may note several special cases in which transfer of variables from the main program to a subroutine and vice versa does not require a complete input/output sequence. In general, a FORTRAN subroutine may accept from zero to many arguments and may return to the main program from zero to many results. For example, a subroutine may be used for an application such as forms control (see Chapter 12 for the BASIC equivalent), in which *no* variables need be passed to the subrou-

[3] We shall not consider the FORTRAN declarations COMMON and EQUIVALENCE, nor many of the other details of the language as they apply to subroutines, but you may wish to do so as you progress with the language. Consult your manual's index for such special statements under Subroutines.

tine. Instead, each time the subroutine is called, it generates new page headings, numbers, and other detail on its own; so a main program such as CALL FORMS (without any argument in the called SUBROUTINE) would be legal. Similarly, a subroutine may receive many variable values, but return nothing to the main program. A typical example is a subroutine that prints a diagnostic statement only under certain conditions. Consider the following proposal in which SUBROUTINE ERROR is supposed to display a line of explanation when the sum of I, J, and K in the main program reaches the integer total 100.

```
      CALL ERROR (I, J, K)
      - - - - -
      SUBROUTINE ERROR (L, M, N)
       IF (L + M + N .EQ. 100) GO TO 800
      RETURN
800   WRITE (6, 900)
900   FORMAT(1X, 120H- - -TOTAL EXACTLY 100- - -)
      RETURN
      END
```

Although we do get some output as a consequence of the subroutine when the sum equals 100, nothing is returned to the main program under any circumstance.

As mentioned in Chapter 12 for the BASIC subroutine, FORTRAN subroutines may not be called recursively. One subroutine may call one or more others, but if A calls B, B may not call A, nor may A call itself.

Example 11 (Functions and statement continuation.)

This example differs only slightly from BASIC Example 11 and only in three details: (1) statement continuation, (2) the use of a function often supplied in different forms by different computer centers, and (3) a standard library function that converts an integer to a real number. This example, you may recall, simulates the game of Russian roulette, which we described in detail in Chapter 13. The objective of the program is to compute the estimated percentage of persons who would survive 10 trials at this game or the probability of one man's survival under the stated conditions. The variable NGAMES and NDEAD are integer numbers representing respectively the number of experiments conducted, and the current count of those "killed" in the computer simulation. We note again that simulating such results on a computer is a much less deadly, messy, and costly procedure than conducting an actual experiment, or performing a historical analysis.

First, we write a title, according to FORMAT statement number 5. Since this format specification is long it is continued onto the next program statement line, a process which is legal in FORTRAN, but not in BASIC. To indicate a continuation, we enter a nonblank character in column six of the program card. Usually such a character is a number (1 through 9) or a letter (A through I) to indicate a successive continuation, which in most systems may continue for nine lines.[4]

```
      PROGRAM ROULETTE
C     BASIC TO FORTRAN, NO. 11
      NDEAD=0
      NGAMES=0
      WRITE(6,5)
5     FORMAT(4X,12HNO. OF ITERS,5X,10HSIM PR SUR,5X,10HACT PR SUR,10X,5H
     AERROR)
      ACTU=(5.0/6.0)**10
      DO 70 I=1,10
      DO 60 J=1,250
      DO 40 K=1,10
      W=RANF(-1)
      IF(W.LE.0.166667) GO TO 50
40    CONTINUE
      GO TO 60
50    NDEAD=NDEAD+1
60    CONTINUE
      NGAMES=NGAMES+250
      SIMU=FLOAT(NGAMES-NDEAD)/FLOAT(NGAMES)
      ERROR=SIMU-ACTU
70    WRITE(6,80) NGAMES,SIMU,ACTU,ERROR
80    FORMAT(/,1X,I15,3F15.6)
      END
```

NO. OF ITERS	SIM PR SUR	ACT PR SUR	ERROR
250	0.160000	0.161506	-0.001506
500	0.166000	0.161506	0.004494
750	0.173333	0.161506	0.011828
1000	0.173000	0.161506	0.011494
1250	0.171200	0.161506	0.009694
1500	0.166667	0.161506	0.005161
1750	0.171429	0.161506	0.009923
2000	0.170000	0.161506	0.008494
2250	0.167111	0.161506	0.005606
2500	0.163600	0.161506	0.002094

[4] In most time-sharing systems where column alignment is sometimes difficult, another symbol, or symbols, may be used as a continuation indicator, e.g., the ampersand, &. Check locally for your own conventions. When such a special symbol begins a program statement line, the line so indicated is considered a continuation of the previous statement regardless of column alignment.

We next compute the theoretical probability of survival for this game, ACTU, in which the survival probability for one trial is 5/6, and the survival probability for 10 successive trials is (5/6)**10. (Check Example 11 in Chapter 13 for the details of this result.)

Thereafter, we simulate 2,500 experimental trials, each one of which consists of 10 "trigger-pulls." The total number of individual trials (25,000) may be determined by the multiplication of the upper limits (10, 250, and 10) of the three successive DO statement (DO 70 I = 1, 10), (DO 60 J = 1, 250), and (DO 40 K = 1, 10).

Each individual trial generates a random number, using the substitution W = RANF(−1) of the next line. In FORTRAN the random number generator function is *not* standard and is usually supplied in a special form at each computer center. (Remember that in BASIC RND(X) is a standard library function.)

In the particular case at hand, which was executed on a Control Data Corporation Model 3600 computer, the function RANF(K) is supplied by that computer compiler as a standard item, and the argument (−1) indicates that the random number generated should be in the real mode. The generated result will be a number between 0 and 1, to the degree of precision offered by the computer. Here we choose to use six significant digits for our subsequent tests, to conform to BASIC Example 11. If the random number generated in an individual trial is less than .166667, we increase the NDEAD count at line 50; if it is not, we continue to generate new trials. Note that the three DO loop statements summarize 10 trials for each experiment, print an accumulative result for each 250 experiments, and cause the program to continue for 2,500 experiments, as shown in the output for this program.

The detail following statement number 60 provides a display of cumulative results after each 250 experiments, as was the case in BASIC Example 11. Note, however, the somewhat complex statement

```
SIMU = FLOAT(NGAMES − NDEAD)/FLOAT(NGAMES)
```

which employs the FLOAT function to convert integer to real division to avoid truncation error. The library function FLOAT causes the integer values preceeded by the letter "N" to be converted to numbers with a decimal point, and the division indicated keeps any remainder resulting from the division. (In BASIC this precaution was not needed, because the arithmetic there was always carried out in the real mode.)

The statement

```
ERROR = SIMU − ACTU
```

is a real substitution and results in a number with a fractional part, as shown in the output. The simulated results as well as the error values shown do not agree with the BASIC Example 11 in absolute detail because of the different random number generator used in each case.[5]

The remaining lines of this example are not new. They simply display the results showing the accumulated detail after each 250 experiments, as in BASIC Example 11. The leading / in 80 FORMAT causes the results to be double-spaced. In this example, as well as in BASIC Example 11, the technical statistical comments of Chapter 13 apply.

Example 12 (A standard translation.)

This program hardly differs from BASIC Example 12. To make a difference, we add one refinement: the error resulting from a less-than test is displayed with the solution to the problem, a detail that we did not formerly show.

Example 12 in BASIC used the binary search approach to solve an equation which otherwise might have presented some problems.

```
        PROGRAM SEARCH
C       BASIC TO FORTRAN, NO. 12
        A=2.0
        B=3.0
        AL=0.0
        UP=5.0
20      W=(AL+UP)/2.0
        ERROR=EXP(-A*W)+EXP(-B*W)-1.0
        Y=ABS(ERROR)
        IF(Y.LE.0.01) GO TO 80
        IF(ERROR.GT.0.0) GO TO 50
        UP=W
        GO TO 20
50      AL=W
        GO TO 20
80      WRITE(6,100) W,ERROR
100     FORMAT(1X,3HW =,F10.6,10X,7HERROR =,F10.6)
        END

W =   0.283203                ERROR = -0.004857
```

[5] The details of random number generation are beyond the scope of this text. However, we may note that the way random numbers are generated by a computer depends upon its internal electronic construction, and so the method and the numeric results obtained are likely to differ slightly from machine to machine. Over a large number of experiments, however, the variations in equipment become less important, as may be observed by a comparison of BASIC and FORTRAN Examples 11.

This corresponding FORTRAN program uses the same method as before: dividing the difference from the old and new trials in an iterative process, interchanging upper and lower trial limits as needed (see statement 20 for the compromise). The statements UP = W and AL = W make the swaps as needed, and as determined by the test IF(ERROR .GT. 0.0) GO TO 50 and its sequel statements.

The latter statements of the program, that is, 80 and 100, display the results of the computation when the critical test terminates the program. Compare the results of this program to BASIC Example 12, and note that the difference between ERROR and .0 which terminated the program is −.004857, a number clearly less than the specified .01 level of necessary precision.

Note in particular, that the function ABS (ERROR) in this program is identical to the same function in BASIC with the exception that the variable name within parentheses follows the rules for FORTRAN variable names as opposed to those in BASIC (see Appendices A and B).

Example 12A (An extension with variations—the TYPE declaration.)

This extension of Example 12 illustrates how you may deviate from the rigid variable-name rules of standard FORTRAN and use variable names without regard to their implicit mode if you are willing to declare a mode *type* at the beginning of your program. To show this point clearly, we now shift the variable names used in Example 12, although we follow precisely the same method of problem solution, computation, and program construction.

As in the extended version of BASIC Example 12, we also show a complete table of output results for parameters A and B, each ranging from 1 to 5. If you recall that we were attempting to solve the equation

$$e^{-AX} + e^{-BX} = 1$$

by determining the value of X which balances the equation, you may also realize that we should get a different value for X for each change, or variation, in the pair of parameters, A and B. In BASIC Example 12A the variations to be computed were handled by a pair of FOR/NEXT loops. In this FORTRAN program we use only one loop, but generate a 5-element list, or row, for each line of output to be printed (which corresponds to the five successive values of A from 1 to 5 as rows and the five successive values of B as columns in the output table.)

In a FORTRAN program you may obviate the usual variable mode assumptions, as indicated by the first letter of your variable names, by a TYPE declaration at the start of your program. Thus, to say TYPE REAL (list), or simply REAL (list) before those variables are used in your program operations, will cause the variable names to be taken as you specify (real, integer, or otherwise), regardless of what you call them. In this example only one variable is declared to be different from what it would be assumed to be by the usual conventions; i.e., the statement REAL LOWER, which is the second line of the above program, indicates that the variable LOWER, which would normally be an integer variable, should now be considered as a real variable, i.e., one with a decimal point and possibly a fractional part. Note that the variable name UPPER, used later in the program, is by normal convention also a real variable. Thus, both variables may be used in a given expression, since both now have the same mode, because of the use of the initial TYPE declaration or its abbreviated equivalent. (The process works vice versa, so that we may also declare at the outset

```
INTEGER CAT, XRAY, Z, A, B
```

a statement that converts normally real variables to the *integer* mode.) The virtue of this particular practice is that you may create variable names that remind you of what they stand for without regard to the mode problem. Thus, in this example, the variables UPPER and LOWER stand for what they mean; the upper and lower limits of the computation as they exist in the progression of adjustment and testing.

Only a few other details of this program deserve attention. Note that the results of parameter B's variation are temporarily stored in the list originally DIMENSIONED STORE(5), and displayed, as necessary by statement 130, using the implied DO and the statement 135 FORMAT for output control. The statement

```
DO 130 I = 1,5
```

produces the 5-line repetition (for the variations of A) that completes the output results.

As a final observation, we may observe that some of the program statements in this example appear to employ illegal mixed-mode arithmetic, e.g., W = (LOWER + UPPER)/2.0. But, as we have noted, that illegality is removed by the appropriate TYPE declaration REAL LOWER at the outset of the program. Although the TYPE declaration at the start of your FORTRAN programs may alter the rules of the game, it is a beneficial device in helping you document your programs or make them self-documenting. That is, if you may call things by their usually acceptable names, you can make your logic and your processing clearer to others who may have to understand and use your work.[6]

[6] But please check your vendor's computer manual for the order in which declarations such as DIMENSION and TYPE should appear in your programs. In general, the DIMENSION declaration must follow TYPE declarations in FORTRAN programs, as shown in Example 12A.

```
      PROGRAM TYPE
C     BASIC TO FORTRAN, NO. 12 (EXTENDED)
      REAL LOWER
      DIMENSION STORE(5)
      DO 130 I=1,5
      A=I
      DO 80 J=1,5
      B=J
      LOWER=0.0
      UPPER=5.0
20    W=(LOWER+UPPER)/2.0
      ERROR=EXP(-A*W)+EXP(-B*W)-1.0
      Y=ABS(ERROR)
      IF(Y.LE.0.01) GO TO 80
      IF(ERROR.GT.0.0) GO TO 50
      UPPER=W
      GO TO 20
50    LOWER= W
      GO TO 20
80    STORE(J)=W
130   WRITE(6,135)  (STORE(J),J=1,5)
137   FORMAT(1X,5F15.6)
      END

       0.703125       0.488281       0.380859       0.322266       0.2832
       0.488281       0.351563       0.283203       0.244141       0.2148
       0.380859       0.283203       0.234375       0.200195       0.1757
       0.322266       0.244141       0.200195       0.175781       0.1562
       0.283203       0.214844       0.175781       0.156250       0.1367
```

Example 13 (The alphabetic mode and a computed GO TO.)

This is a cross-tabulation problem, which corresponds to BASIC Example 13. In this example all of the input data is in the integer mode and consists of the category numbers and levels of description obtained from an interview questionnaire, as detailed in Example 13, Chapter 13. Since the variable names used in this FORTRAN translation are relatively numerous and differ from those of the BASIC example, we summarize them in Table 18.1.

TABLE 18.1

Summary of Variable Names in FORTRAN Example 13

1. IDATA — The input interview data. A maximum of 400 records, each containing six elements, or fields, as defined in BASIC Example 13. The first record containing 9 as its first element indicates the end of file.
2. ISTD — A list of six, 4-character alpha ("A") elements representing the first four letters of the cross-tab specification words.
3. MAJCAT — A word of 8 characters or less, from the set of six indicated by the 4-character abbreviations of ISTD; specifies major category for cross-tabulation.
4. MAJLVL — A 1-digit integer indicating the subclassification of MAJCAT chosen for cross-tabulation; may be 1 to 4 except for RACE, 1 to 3; if 9, it indicates the end of job.

5.	ICAT1	A word from the allowable set (see MAJCAT) indicating the first cross-tab category. The levels are shown as rows of the output table.
6.	ICAT2	A word from the allowable set (see MAJCAT) indicating second cross-tab category. The levels are shown as columns of the output table.
7.	IARRAY	The cross-tabulation result table to be printed after IDATA record summary.
8.	I	The row index for IARRAY operations.
9.	J	The column index for IARRAY operations.
10.	MAJOR	The decoded number of the major extraction category.
11.	ICROSS1	The decoded number of the row cross-tab category.
12.	ICROSS2	The decoded number of the column cross-tab category.

This example introduces, as a final FORTRAN variation, the use of alphabetic characters as a variable; that is, we illustrate here the alpha, or A, variable mode, first mentioned in Table 17.1 but not illustrated until now in any example. We also illustrate the FORTRAN computed GO TO, which corresponds to the BASIC computed GO TO first mentioned in Chapter 10, p. 167.

The following program also differs slightly from its BASIC equivalent in that the INPUT statement is not used, and the desired variations in cross-tabulation appear in the data as alphabetic requests. (Note the detail at the end of the numeric data input.) Instead of using the BASIC command RESTORE, as in the previous BASIC Example 13, this program also uses a *table* of data, which is read in until an end-of-file indicator, consisting of the first record element (9 in this case) is encountered.[7]

The general procedure for this program's processing is first to read in all the interview data (which terminates when an end of file is encountered), then read in the cross-tabulation specifications. These cross-tab specifications will be accepted by the program in the alpha, or "A," mode, and will be deciphered by the program (as described hereafter) so that the desired cross-tabulation categories may be generated from your specifications of common English words, e.g., RACE, SCHOOL, SALARY, HOUSING, JOB, or POLITICS. The program terminates when the specification for any given cross-tabulation contains the number 9 in its MAJLVL category (which is located by 19 FORMAT in the program to follow as the second data element in the specification record). The general logic of the following program appears in Figure 18.1.

[7] The command in FORTRAN which corresponds to the BASIC command RESTORE is REWIND, which in most applications implies a rewind of a magnetic tape, or the corresponding reset to origin of a direct access file. Check your vendor's manual for details.

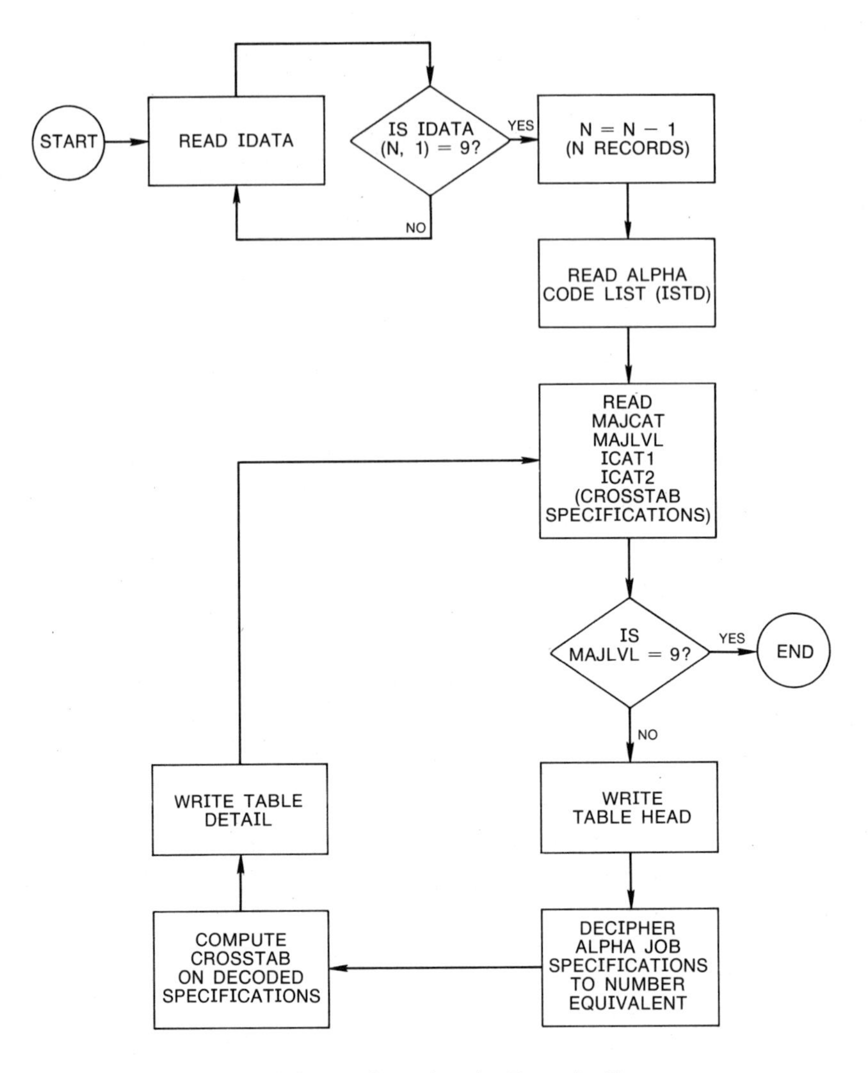

18.1. Master flow chart for Example 13.

Before presenting the FORTRAN program in detail, note that an essential step in the procedure, after reading in the interview data as a table, is to receive the cross-tabulation specifications as English words, then decode them on the basis of their alphabetic input characters. To do this, the program first receives a set of data (the first following the interview data) which provides the first four or less alphabetic characters of the key words that may be later used to call for cross-tabulation decoding.

This operation occurs according to the command

READ(5,101) (ISTD(J) = 1, 6)

which is associated with

101 FORMAT(6(A4,1X)

the latter implying that we will receive six 4-character alpha, or "A" format, inputs, separated by one space. (See the first line of the following program's data after the numeric interview data, noting that a blank, or space, is considered as an alpha character in FORTRAN.)[8]

```
      PROGRAM CROSSTAB
C     BASIC TO FORTRAN, NO. 13, WITH MODIFICATIONS
C     INTRODUCTION TO A FORMAT.
      DIMENSION IDATA(400,6),IARRAY(4,4),ISTD(6)
      DIMENSION MAJCAT(2),ICAT1(2),ICAT2(2)
      DO 1 N=1,400
      READ(5,100) (IDATA(N,J),J=1,6)
100   FORMAT( 6(I1,1X) )
      IF(IDATA(N,1).EQ.9 ) GO TO 3
1     CONTINUE
3     N=N-1
C     N=NUMBER OF DATA CARDS STORED IN TABLE NAMED IDATA.
      READ(5,101) (ISTD(J),J=1,6)
101   FORMAT( 6(A4,1X) )
C     FIRST 4 LETTERS OF ALL 6 CATEGORIES ARE STORED IN LIST NAMED ISTD.
19    READ(5,102) MAJCAT,MAJLVL,ICAT1,ICAT2
102   FORMAT(2A4,1X,I1,1X,2A4,1X,2A4)
      IF(MAJLVL.EQ.9) GO TO 46
      WRITE(6,103) MAJCAT,MAJLVL,ICAT2,(I,I=1,4),ICAT1
103   FORMAT(//,1X,18HMAJOR CATEGORY IS ,2A4,7H LEVEL ,I1,//,25X,2A4,/,
     A 1X,I12,3I10,/,1X,2A4)
C     TABLE, ROW AND COLUMN HEADINGS HAVE BEEN PRINTED.
      NAME=MAJCAT(1)
      DO 7 I=1,3
      DO 8 J=1,6
      IF(NAME.EQ.ISTD(J)) GO TO 9
8     CONTINUE
7     CONTINUE
9     GO TO (5,10,15) I
5     MAJOR=J
      NAME=ICAT1(1)
      GO TO 7
10    ICROS1=J
      NAME=ICAT2(1)
      GO TO 7
15    ICROS2=J
C     MAJOR AND TWO CROSSTAB CATEGORIES HAVE BEEN DECODED.
      DO 2 I=1,4
      DO 2 J=1,4
```

[8] The Aw format of Table 17.1, includes the complete character set available at a given computer installation, including special characters as well as pure alpha characters. The more appropriate term is "A" for alphanumeric, since the "A" format also includes numbers and special characters. Thus, A12$ is a legal A4 input, although that variation is not used in the example at hand. The variable name for an alpha variable may usually be any legal FORTRAN variable name, e.g., real or integer; however, most systems prefer integer-type names for efficient processing. An integer-type name is used in this example.

```
2       IARRAY(I,J)=0
        DO 50 I=1,N
        IF(IDATA(I,MAJOR).NE.MAJLVL) GO TO 50
        IX=IDATA(I,ICROS1)
        IY=IDATA(I,ICROS2)
        IARRAY(IX,IY)=IARRAY(IX,IY)+1
50      CONTINUE
        DO 60 I=1,4
60      WRITE(6,104) I,(IARRAY(I,J),J=1,4)
104     FORMAT(1X,I8,I4,3I10)
        GO TO 19
46      END
```

```
1,2,3,2,3,2
1,4,3,1,2,1
1,4,4,4,4,3
1,3,3,3,4,2
3,4,1,2,3,1
2,3,1,2,3,4
1,1,1,1,3,3
1,2,2,2,1,4
3,4,2,2,2,3
1,2,1,3,2,2
2,4,4,4,1,1
1,1,4,2,1,1
1,3,2,1,3,4
2,4,1,1,1,2
1,2,3,1,2,1
3,2,2,3,4,3
1,4,3,1,4,1
2,4,4,1,2,2
1,4,4,1,3,1
1,1,3,2,2,2
1,4,1,2,1,2
2,3,2,3,4,3
1,3,2,3,2,3
1,4,4,3,1,3
1,4,4,4,2,4
1,1,3,4,4,4
2,4,1,3,2,1
1,3,3,4,1,4
1,4,3,2,3,2
3,2,3,4,3,3
9,9,9,9,9,9
RACE SCHO SALA HOUS JOB  POLI
RACE       1 HOUSING   POLITICS
RACE       1 SALARY    POLITICS
END  OF   9  FILE CARD.


MAJOR CATEGORY IS RACE       LEVEL 1

                                POLITICS
              1          2          3          4
HOUSING
         1    4          0          1          1
         2    1          4          0          1
         3    0          2          2          0
         4    0          0          1          3

MAJOR CATEGORY IS RACE       LEVEL 1

                                POLITICS
              1          2          3          4
```

```
SALARY
            1     0          2          1          0
            2     0          0          1          2
            3     3          4          0          2
            4     2          0          2          1
```

To explain this program's progression we again move from the top line of the program downward in the following discussion.

First, all tables and lists to be used are provided for by DIMENSION declarations at the outset. IDATA is the complete set of interview records, each consisting of six fields. (We may have less than 400 interview records—we have less in the data for this program—but not more without alteration of the associated IDATA "DIMENSION" declaration.) IARRAY is the table to be printed, and ISTD is a list of decoding terms that will convert user requests in English to their numeric tabular equivalents. MAJCAT, ICAT1, and ICAT2, are the job specifications for a given case. (Hereafter refer to Table 18.1 for a glossary of this program's variable names, should you forget them.)

In this example, you must watch some details carefully, one of which is the alpha specification for the input values of MAJCAT, ICAT1, and ICAT2. In the input job specifications, each of these data fields is alphanumeric, following the 102 FORMAT specification. To allow us to test only the first four characters of the English words represented by MAJCAT, ICAT1 and ICAT2, we have chosen to FORMAT each as a maximum of eight alphanumeric characters, divided into two blocks of four characters each. With this 2A4 format, using the DIMENSION declarations shown, the words may be split, and the first four characters may be referenced as the first element of each specified list, dimensioned into two elements by

```
DIMENSION MAJCAT(2), ICAT1(2), ICAT2(2)
```

Note that since MAJLVL is simply a one-integer digit in 102 FORMAT, its variable need not be declared in a DIMENSION statement nor must we decode it.

Statement

```
19 READ(5, 102) MAJCAT, ICAT1, ICAT2
```

operates as did the READ statements of FORTRAN Example 6, Chapter 17; that is, the READ for MAJCAT reads in the total list of characters (8 in this case) previously dimensioned for that variable. A DO loop is implied even though not stated, because the READ variables were previously dimensioned correctly; the same observation holds for ICAT1 and ICAT2.

We next WRITE the table heading for the first case, following 103 FORMAT. The title displayed will be spaced according to the FORMAT statement. The effect of the / symbols may be compared to the output table.

Note that the 103 FORMAT statement continues to the following line, using the continuation symbol "A" in column six. In the WRITE(6,103) command, the column table levels are provided by the implied DO shown as (I, I = 1,4). As noted in the subsequent COMMENT statement, the program to this point has now displayed the first three printed lines of the first table, with line skips as determined by the slashes in 103 FORMAT.

Our next step is to examine the job specifications for the first case, then decode their English names into numeric values for table manipulation. This is accomplished in the next block of statements down to statement number 15. We proceed in three substeps. First, MAJCAT is decoded, then ICAT1, and finally ICAT2. Thus, we first set NAME=MAJLVL(1), which picks up the first four alpha characters of the MAJLVL word specification. (In the cases illustrated here NAME will be set equal to RACE.) This is the first test (of three) generated by DO 7 I = 1,3. We then scan the decode list ISTD from the first to the sixth element (using DO 8 J = 1,6) until we find a match for MAJCAT(1). When such a match is found, we proceed to statement number 9, which is a FORTRAN computed GO TO. This statement causes transfer to one of the listed statement numbers within the GO TO parentheses, depending upon the value of the integer index, I (if I is 1, we go to 5; if 2, to 19; if 3, to 15). The index, I, is the number of the word to be decoded, e.g., 1 for MAJCAT, 2 for ICAT1, and 3 for ICAT2; thus, in the first instance, we attempt to decode MAJCAT, I = 1. Similarly, the index J is the position in the decoding list ISTD in which a match was found. Again, in the first illustrative case J=1 for MAJLVL, since RACE is in the first formatted-element position. As a consequence, transfer of control goes to statement number 5, and MAJOR, a variable used to control record selection, is set to the current value of J, or the integer 1.

Having decoded the first job specification word, we set NAME to ICAT(1) and GO TO 7, the CONTINUE statement which ties the operation back into the original searching loops, the DO 7 and DO 8 pair.[9] The search proceeds as before to find a match for ICAT1(1), and when it is found, ICROSS1 is set to J, using the computed GO TO as before. The same process continues to decode ICAT2(1), which becomes ICROSS2. When the three decodings are complete, as noted in the program COMMENT statement following this procedure module, we have in hand three numbers to be used in the cross-tabulation. (Compare this final result with the numeric input required for BASIC Example 13. We have gone to some

---

[9] Note that the IF(NAME .EQ. ISTD(J)) GO TO 9 statement causes a jump out of the nested loops to the statement 9 computed GO TO and that we later have a return to 7 CONTINUE which brings the program sequence back into the nested loop operation. This is a dangerous procedure, which may not work on some systems. However, branching out of and back into a DO loop sequence will work on most systems if you take care not to disturb the DO indices in your "patch" or similar program diversion before returning.

trouble and complexity in this program to permit the user to enter English words rather than numeric symbols, which he may have difficulty remembering or find unnatural to use. Thus, we have put an additional burden upon the program to avoid the program's user difficulty, a general principle which will gain additional favor as computer time relative to human time decreases in value.)

The remainder of this program follows the identical logic of BASIC Example 13. We can scan the entire file and pick up only the records that agree with the current MAJOR and MAJLVL specification. As acceptable cases are found, they are accumulated in the 4 by 4 table IARRAY until all N records of the file IDATA have been processed. This cross-tabulation module extends from DO 2 I=1,4 to 50 CONTINUE.

Finally, we write out the cross-tab values, together with a row-level number, following statement 60 WRITE and its associated 104 FORMAT. The whole process repeats itself from the top of the program to the END, until the last job specification has been processed as indicated by the number 9 in the MAJLVL position of the job specification (see the last line of data before the tabular output results).

If you can follow this last example, you have—as a consequence of your progress to this point—the most frequently used manipulation rules for the FORTRAN language and may safely move ahead on your own.

Final comments

In both Chapter 13, as well as Chapters 17 and 18, we have purposely neglected to illustrate the user-defined functions in BASIC and in FORTRAN. One reason for this omission is that you may accomplish anything with a subroutine subprogram form that you can with a function, because the subroutine is the most general approach to modular program construction. However, a few words are in order with regard to FORTRAN user-defined functions.

In FORTRAN, you may have two forms of user-defined functions: (1) the statement function and (2) the function subprogram, which is not to be confused with the subroutine subprogram, or most general case illustrated in Example 10. One difference between either of the function forms and the subroutine subprogram is that a function operation must result in one, and only one, numeric result which will necessarily be returned to the main program after evaluation. In FORTRAN, however, as opposed to BASIC, functions may have one or more independent variables, the upper limit depending upon the computer used. (For example, the Control Data Corporation 3600 Computer permits a maximum of 63 independent variables, or function arguments.) Obviously, the FORTRAN function capability, because of the large number of independent variables or arguments that may be used, is considerably greater than that of the BASIC user-defined function, which allowed only one independent variable.

The FUNCTION statement in FORTRAN has the general form

<u>name</u> (a_1, a_2, a_3, . . . , a_n) = <u>expression</u>

an example of which is

```
FUNCA(A,B) = 3. * A + B ** 2. + X + Y + Z
```

The name follows the usual rules of FORTRAN variable names. Thus, the function above is a real function and provides a real result. The variables A and B shown in the parentheses are dummy variables, and assume the values specified by the variables named when the function is used in an expression, as is the case in BASIC. The only difference in FORTRAN is that more than one argument is permitted. As in BASIC, a statement function must be defined in the main program before it is used.

The FUNCTION subprogram in FORTRAN, unlike the statement FUNCTION which is defined in the main program, is a separate subprogram of its own, like the subroutine subprogram. The general form is

FUNCTION <u>name</u> (a_1, a_2, a_3, . . . , a_n)
— — — — —
— — — — —
RETURN
— — — — —
END

The dashed lines represent FORTRAN statements which will generate the desired result: a single numeric value. To use a FUNCTION subprogram, you need not employ a CALL statement, as required for a SUBROUTINE subprogram. You need only mention the function's name, as the following example illustrates:

<u>Main Program</u>	<u>FUNCTION Subprogram</u>
— — — — —	FUNCTION DIVZ(X,Y)
— — — — —	DIVZ = X / Y
X = DIVZ(B,C)	RETURN
— — — — —	END
— — — — —	

The defined function will in statement sequence follow the main program, which as always has its own END statement. Note the dummy arguments of the FUNCTION definition, and that the defined function has at least one RETURN and its own END statement. Finally note that a FUNCTION subprogram must have at least one substitution statement that defines the numeric value of its name, here DIVZ, since a numeric value by that name will be returned to the main program. (For a further discussion of functions in FORTRAN, please consult your vendor's manual.)

In concluding this final chapter, you should look back at the general principles illustrated by BASIC and FORTRAN both as computer languages and as tools for the implementation of problem solution and data processing.

If you think about it, you will note the essential elements of computer language use are few, as indicated in Chapter 6. Moreover, you should now be familiar with most of the usual programming methods using BASIC and be able to appreciate why FORTRAN is useful and interesting in many cases for which we need greater flexibility, as indicated in Chapter 16, and by the examples of the last two chapters.

PROJECT

As you did at the end of Chapter 17, try to rewrite each of the FORTRAN examples in strict Teletype FORTRAN. Remember that the only major change required is to change the statement numbers used here to line numbers with a corresponding change of statement number references to their respective line number references.

Appendix A
A comparison of BASIC and FORTRAN

BASIC	FORTRAN
1. Line numbers and statements	
Each BASIC statement requires a line number.	In remote terminal FORTRAN each statement will usually require a line number. When card FORTRAN is used, statement numbers are required only for statements referenced by other statements.
2. Numbers	
May appear as integers (123), real values (123.123) with a decimal point, or as floating point values (1.23.123E-8). In BASIC no distinction is made between these forms; all computations assume real numbers. Most BASIC installations permit 9 input digits for a number; and at output time will produce from 6 to 9 digits. Check locally.	Same three forms as in BASIC except the language makes a distinction between integer and real numbers. Distinction indicated in FORMAT statement, see below. Integer arithmetic usually completed in pure binary; real arithmetic usually executed in floating point form to preserve decimal point alignment. Integer and real numbers may not be mixed in FORTRAN expressions.
3. Variables and their names	
BASIC makes no distinction between integer and real numbers in the construction of variable names. Simple variables may be A–Z or one of the letters followed	FORTRAN makes a *critical* distinction between integer and real numbers, as well as their variable names, as indicated in paragraph above. Simple variables may be

by one of the 10 decimal digits, e.g., A0–Z9. Subscripted variables may be one letter followed by one or two subscripts, enclosed in parentheses. The subscripts are assumed to be integers, or a number without a fractional part. Otherwise, truncation results. A(I), X(I,J) are legal. For alternate legal and illegal forms, see Chapter 11. Some forms of Extended BASIC permit alphanumeric variables to be used, yet the definition of such variable names varies widely with installation. Most common is a single letter followed by a dollar sign, e.g., A$. See Chapter 14 for details.

one letter followed by a mixture of letters and numbers. Should the first letter of the variable name be I,J,K,L,M, or N, the variable is assumed integer; all other starting letters indicate a real number for the variable. Subscripted variables follow the same rules as in BASIC, with the constraint above. The constraint may be avoided by use of the specification REAL or INTEGER, which see hereafter. Some FORTRAN installations permit more than two subscripts to be used. Note that FORMAT specifications, as indicated below, tell the computer the form of number intended. As in BASIC, FORTRAN permits alphanumeric variables, when FORMAT specifications so indicate. Variable names in FORTRAN may be from 4 to 8 characters in length; see local details.

4. Statements

END

STOP

PRINT *list*

Where in BASIC a previous line number is required, and where the word list indicated the sequence of literals or variables to be shown. Evaluation of expressions allowed in PRINT list. No format specifications permitted in standard installations.

READ *list*

Where in BASIC each PRINT must be associated

END Same as in BASIC

STOP Same as in BASIC

WRITE (i,n) *list*

Where i stands for the output unit type upon which writing should occur; n for the numbered FORMAT statement required to edit output.

READ (i,n) *list*

Where, as above, i stands for the input unit type upon

with one or more declarative DATA statements which will contain the values to be read. No format specifications permitted in most installations for input.

which reading should occur; n for the numbered FORMAT statement required to edit input.

DATA

Required in BASIC when READ is used. One or more DATA statements will be needed for each READ. Data pickup is sequential for each variable mentioned.

Not used in FORTRAN. Usually data values follow the end statement. Usually one record read for each READ. Note variations.

Not Used.

statement number FORMAT (*list*)

Used to specify the exact format of a READ or WRITE statement. The statement number is that indicated by the corresponding READ or WRITE, and the list, within parentheses, must agree in order and in mode with the variable names mentioned in the referencing statement. For details of FORMAT rules, see Chapter 17. Note slight differences between input and output FORMAT requirements. In outline, major distinction is made between integers, real numbers—which may in turn be shown with a fixed decimal point or in the exponential form, and alphanumeric characters. Respectively, these are known as I, F, E, and A formats. In addition, other format symbols are used to indicate spaces (X), literal, or "Hollerith" characters to be used for titles (H), etc.

GO TO *line number*

Causes immediate diversion of program sequence from GO TO to specified line number.

GO TO *statement number*

A statement number may be used for a line number in card FORTRAN. Same as BASIC otherwise.

ON i GO TO (n_1, n_2, n_3, . . .)

Upon specification of variable name i, sequence goes to stated line number, e.g., if i is 2, then sequence diverts to line number n_2.

GO TO (n_1, n_2, n_3, . . .), I

Same as BASIC, only form differs.

IF/THEN (Arithmetic IF)

If expression mentioned after IF is *true* THEN diversion of program will occur to line number mentioned after THEN. The modifier STEP may be used in this expression; see text. Should comparison be false progression of sequence goes to nest following line number.

IF(a) n_1,n_2,n_3

Corresponds in part to statement at left. If arithmetic expression shown as (a) above is negative, diversion of program sequence goes to n_1; if 0 to n_2, if positive to n_3. Available at almost all FORTRAN installations. Provides a three-way branch, as opposed to BASIC two-way branch.

(Logical IF)

In FORTRAN, as available on most machines, you may substitute the letters shown as FORTRAN relations below for arithmetic symbols, as used in BASIC. Note that IBM/360 Level D and E FORTRAN does not permit this option, but requires use of the arithmetic IF only.

(Relations)

In BASIC the following six relations available for use in IF/THEN statements:

In FORTRAN the equivalent relations must be shown in "logical" IFs (see above) as:

BASIC		FORTRAN	
=	Equal to	.EQ.	Equal to
<>	Not equal to	.NE.	Not equal to
<	Less than	.LT.	Less than
>	Greater than	.GT.	Greater than
<=	Less than or equal to	.LE.	Less than or equal to
>=	Greater than or equal to	.GE.	Greater than or equal to

FOR/NEXT

A typical FOR/NEXT statement in BASIC is FOR I = 1 TO 10 STEP 2. This statement would be associated with a later NEXT I, since FORs in BASIC are always followed by one or more NEXTs, having reference to the originally cited variable, in this case, I. The modifier STEP is optional and assumed equal to "1" unless otherwise specified. The FOR/NEXT statements may be nested according to the rules of Chapter 11. The same rules apply in FORTRAN. The limits shown in this BASIC statement must be numbers without a decimal remainder, or else the language will convert real numbers to their integer equivalent by truncation.

DO n i = m_1, m_2, m_3
(and CONTINUE)

The meaning of the above is about the same as the BASIC statement to the left. The symbol "i" is an index; the symbols m_1, m_2, and m_3 indicate respectively, the start of the range of computation, the end of the range, and the value of the increment, which if omitted—as at left—is assumed to be the number "1." In FORTRAN all the limit values *must* be integers, or integer variable names. (In BASIC these values are converted to "equivalent integers," or numbers without a decimal point, before execution, but in FORTRAN use integers only.) The reference stated by n may refer to any statement in FORTRAN that does not generate another branch. We suggest you always use a terminating CONTINUE (corresponding to NEXT in BASIC). Please see text. The "implied" DO, not shown above, may be used as part of a READ or WRITE statement in FORTRAN. See Chapter 17.

GOSUB/RETURN

The command GOSUB causes sequential transfer to the line number thereafter stated. Then, at the first RETURN encountered, control goes back to the line number first following the GOSUB "call." All variable values at "call-time" will be transferred to the variables in the subroutine. Then, when the subroutine in BASIC is completed, the result of its evaluation—including the variables mentioned in the "main" program—will be passed back. So, be careful here to adjust your subroutine variables to those in the main program. This is similar to FORTRAN, but lacks the argument advantage which permits change of variable names when you ask for a subroutine. This is a *major difference* between BASIC and FORTRAN, since FORTRAN permits much greater flexibility in use of subroutines.

CALL/RETURN

In FORTRAN, a subroutine is initiated by a statement of the form CALL NAME ($a_1,a_2,a_3, \ldots$) which will be also associated, as in BASIC, with the final associated statement RETURN. The CALL arguments (shown in parentheses) must agree in order and mode with the definition of the subroutine in FORTRAN, which is of the form SUBROUTINE NAME ($a_1, a_2,a_3 \ldots$), where the "NAME" in both cases must correspond. The variable values from the main program CALL will be associated with the variable names in the SUBROUTINE definition. After the evaluation of the variables passed to the subroutine, you will get back to your main program that result, but defined by the name, and in the order of the variables mentioned in the original "CALL." This may seem to be a subtle difference—but it is a major one. FORTRAN subroutines—unlike those in BASIC—can be made completely independent of the main program.

INPUT *list*

In BASIC in the time-share mode, this is a very useful command. The effect is to produce a pause in program execution and ask

INPUT *list*

In FORTRAN, this command is not always available; but usually so in terminal FORTRAN. The comments to the left apply you for an input of data (see READ and DATA). This is the command that makes BASIC conversational to the user, in terms of getting data to the machine after seeing previous results.

exactly, except in FORTRAN you may have some format control.

DIM *list*

In BASIC you must DIM lists over 10 elements long, and tables over 10 x 10 in size. The form is DIM X(23), Y(23,46). You *must* use unsigned integer values to specify those dimensions in BASIC as well as in FORTRAN. Suggest you always use a DIM statement for lists and tables on general principles.

DIMENSION *list*

Be sure to spell the word completely here. The use is the same as in BASIC, except for the complete spelling. *All* lists and tables *must* be dimensioned in FORTRAN, whereas BASIC will automatically assume a 10-element list or a 10 x 10 table if no DIM declaration is made.

REM

A remark, or comment. Any line starting with this three-letter declaration will be printed as shown in the program, but will not be executed. Use profusely in all your programs to document your work.

C (or its equivalent)

In remote terminal programming, this symbol is just like REM in BASIC. Please see your local conventions for local variations.

Matrix Operations

BASIC offers an extensive matrix manipulation repertoire. Please consult Chapter 14.

(Equivalent forms)

FORTRAN in its standard forms does not offer matrix operations unless you program them. The nearest equivalent is the implied "DO" in FORTRAN. Please see your supplier's manual or Chapters 17–18 for the necessary details.

RESTORE

Causes DATA list to be reset to the start.

REWIND

Similar to the left, but causes (in general) a mag-

BASIC	FORTRAN
	netic tape to be rewound to the start, so data can be used more than once.
——	REAL
——	INTEGER Neither of above available in BASIC, since BASIC does not distinguish between REAL and INTEGER numbers. These declarations may be used at the start of a FORTRAN program to modify the implicit definition of variable names. (See Variable Names and FORMAT, below.)
——	COMMON Not used in BASIC. A FORTRAN declaration which will reserve common memory space for your main program and your subroutine. Useful if you are tight for space. Consult your supplier's manual for details at your location.
——	EQUIVALENCE Not used in BASIC. Sets variables with different names equal to one another. Useful in putting together your program statements with those of others. Please consult your supplier's manual for details at your location.

Note: Most BASIC and FORTRAN installations will offer you many other optional forms and commands. Here, you find only those which are standard. Please check with your local supplier or computer center for the variations.

Appendix B
Selected functions in the FORTRAN language

The following is a selected list of functions, normally called stored or library functions in FORTRAN. The list shown is by no means complete, and you should consult your computer center's manual for the extended list available at most FORTRAN locations. Please compare this short list to the complete list of BASIC stored functions given in Table 9.1. Note that the BASIC function RND(X) is not usually provided as a standard FORTRAN function, but that it is usually available as a local library function at most computer centers. You must check locally for the details of its use in FORTRAN. In addition to the list shown here, about 30 other stored functions are standard in FORTRAN IV, and many more may be available at your location, as a result of your local supplier's efforts to provide the most commonly needed functions. In the functions listed below, as in BASIC, only one argument is allowed. Please note the distinction between real and integer numbers, which is required in FORTRAN, but not in BASIC.

COS(X) Same as in BASIC. The argument must be a real number, the result will be a real number.

SIN(X) Same as in BASIC. The argument must be a real number, the result will be a real number.

EXP(X) Same as in BASIC. Provides the natural logarithm of the argument, X. Both the argument and the result will be real numbers. Provides antilog of natural logarithm.

SQRT(X)	Same as SQR(X) in BASIC. Both argument and result will be real numbers in this application.
ABS(X)	Same as in BASIC. Provides the absolute value of a real number by discarding its sign.
IABS(K)	Not available in BASIC. Provides the absolute value of an integer number, shown here as K, by discarding its sign.
INT(X)	Same as in BASIC. Provides the integer value of the real number X by truncating all values to the right of the decimal point. Same as FORTRAN's IFIX(X).
FLOAT(K)	Not available in BASIC. Converts an integer number in FORTRAN to a real number.
IFIX(X)	Not available in BASIC. Converts a real number in FORTRAN into an integer number. Equivalent to INT(X).

Appendix C
Use of Teletypes not directly connected to telephone lines

1 / For directly connected input/output communications terminals

Please consult your local conventions. However, in general, the direct wired terminal unit may initiate contact with the computer by depression of the "HERE IS" button of the Teletype machine—if you are using that device or its equivalent. Thereafter, proceed as noted in the text in the chapter entitled "Getting the computer to work."

2 / For audio couplers attached to your remote terminal machine

Again, you should consult your local supplier for the absolute details, but, in general, here is how to use your unit of this class.

Turn your terminal "ON." In the case of the Teletype made for audio coupling service, the "ON-OFF-LINE" switch is located on the lower right front panel of your console. Turn this switch to "LINE" to connect to the computer. Thereafter, the output of your terminal will be required to match the needs of the telephone line and your computer. Normally, the device known as your acoustic coupler will take care of the necessary conversions between your typed characters and the computer's needs.

With most devices, you must place the telephone handset in a specified pair of holes—to match up the send/receive components of your telephone—a placement that should be obvious. Take care to have the line cord of your telephone match the stated requirements of your coupler, which will be shown clearly on the unit. Thereafter, all operations usually conform to the rules of this text.

Appendix D
Selected FORTRAN reference manuals

Chapters 17 and 18 presuppose you have available a manufacturer's or supplier's FORTRAN IV manual for reference, in particular that for the computer you will use. The following list provides a selected set of references. You may obtain one of the necessary manuals by contacting your computer center, your manufacturer's representative, or time-sales vendor. The cost is nominal. Ask for the latest edition of the manuals cited; they are revised constantly to correct errors and reflect latest practice.

The references cited are for card FORTRAN IV or its local variant; ask also for supplementary (or summary) time-sharing FORTRAN manuals if you have access to time-share FORTRAN. Generally, the latter manuals represent a subset of commands from the former and will vary with supplier to some extent.

1. IBM System/360
   - FORTRAN IV, Form C28-6504 (Level D, or essential commands)
   - FORTRAN IV, Form C28-6513 (Level E, more commands for larger computers)
   - FORTRAN IV, Form C28-6515 (Level H, complete FORTRAN set available only on the largest computers)

2. Burroughs B5500
   - FORTRAN IV for Burroughs B5500

3. General Electric GE-635
   - GE-635 FORTRAN IV Reference Manual

4. Honeywell Series 200
   Honeywell Series 200 FORTRAN, Compiler D Reference Manual
5. Univac 1107
   Univac 1107 FORTRAN, Programmer's Reference Manual U-3569
6. Control Data 3600
   CDC 3600 FORTRAN, Programmer's Reference Manual

Glossary

The following glossary of terms includes not only those which you may wish to reference as a consequence of your reading here, but also selected terms which appear in popular computing literature.

The listing appears in a natural order, e.g., Digital Computer, rather than Computer, Digital.

For more extensive listings, you may wish to consult one of the following:

American Standard Vocabulary for Information Processing, U.S.A. Standard X3.12-1966 (American National Standards Institute, 1430 Broadway, New York, N.Y.)

U.S. Bureau of the Budget, *Glossary of Automatic Data Processing*, December 1962, Government Printing Office, Washington, D.C.

Datamation's Glossary of Information Processing Terms (*Datamation Magazine* 35 Mason Street, Greenwich, Conn., 06830, $1.00 each, $0.75 10–49, $0.50 50 or more copies.)

The latter glossary contains over 700 listings and is most easily available. Like most widely distributed glossaries of computer terms, the *Datamation Glossary* is derived from the Bureau of the Budget work.

Absolute Address The specific physical location in a computer memory device at which a given number, set of characters, or other information may be stored. The absolute address layout for a given memory device is determined by the manufacturer, and is a permanent hardware feature. Usually associated with machine-language programming.

Access Time The time required to reach a given memory location and retrieve its contents. See Cycle Time. In general the time required to retrieve a given item of information from a file.

Accumulate To create a total, especially one which increases over time, as to accumulate a grand total. The arithmetic operation "add" is an accumulation in its simplest form.

Accuracy In conformity with the truth, i.e., the quality of being correct. As opposed to precision (which see), accuracy implies that a numeric result, although perhaps containing few significant figures, is nevertheless near to and not biased from the "correct" value. It is possible to compute precisely the wrong answer; the desired condition is to be both accurate and precise.

Address A general term referring to a memory storage location. Because there are many ways of refering to a desired address, either directly in using absolute addresses or symbolically in using translation and compilers to provide the transition from a user-oriented to a machine-oriented language, the term must be qualified in a specific application.

ADP Abbreviation for Automatic Data Processing. The term implies processing with little or no human intervention, as, for example, processing by means of electronic computers.

Algorithm A step-by-step procedure for solving a problem. Named after the Ninth-Century Arabian mathematician *al-Khuwarizmi*, who wrote books on arithmetic procedures. Designers of algorithms seek to produce guaranteed results in the smallest number of steps.

Alphameric See Alphanumeric.

Alphanumeric Characters that are either the digits 0–9 or the letters A–Z. Many alphanumeric character sets also include many special characters, such as $, ?, and *.

Analog A term implying continuous measurement rather than counting (digital) as a method of computation.

Analog Computer A computing device that performs analog manipulations. The inputs and outputs from such a device are continuous in character, and a number of results may be obtained simultaneously through the measurement of voltages, currents, angular positions of shafts, etc. Limited in precision by the measurement process, analog computers are often used for engineering work where only a few significant digits are required in an answer. Since they must be rewired for each new application and usually do not permit symbolic programs to be executed, analog computers usually have specialized, rather than general application. A slide rule is a familiar form of a non-electrical analog computer.

Analog-Digital Conversion The process of converting a continuous measurement into a set of numeric values, often by quantifying numerically the value of a continuously varying quantity at discrete and usually closely spaced periods of time. The result of the process is a series of numbers, in effect a sample from the continuous signal, which may be processed by the digital computer.

Argument A variable and its numeric value used to evaluate a function or, which, by extension, either explicitly or implicitly provides the input for a subroutine. For example, X is the argument of the BASIC language stored function SQR(X). (An argument may consist of more than one variable.) In mathematics, one of the variables upon which the value of a function depends.

Array A general term used in mathematics and computer programming to denote an orderly set of information to be referenced in a given manner. A one-dimensional array is also known as a list or a vector; a two-dimensional array as a table or a matrix. See Vector and Matrix. Arrays of more than two dimensions may be specified in some languages by special variable subscripting rules, or as in BASIC by other programming expedients.

Assembly Process The translation step that reduces a symbolic language to a machine language. The process converts symbolic addresses to absolute addresses, converts symbolic operation codes to machine instruction codes, and often provides other translation features.

Assignment Statement See Substitution Statement.

Base With regard to a number system, the numeric value which shall be taken to an increasing power as one moves from right to left in positional notation. See Number System, Binary, Octal, Decimal. Synonym for Radix.

BASIC Abbreviation for Beginners All-purpose Symbolic Instruction Code. BASIC is a high-level, user-oriented language.

Batch Processing That form of processing which involves the grouping of jobs before any of them is individually executed in order to exploit the economies of mass processing. As opposed to individual job processing, conversational processing, or the usual form of remote-terminal processing. See also Remote Batch Processing.

BCD See Binary Coded Decimal.

Binary The base two. In the binary system of computation, the allowable numbers are zero and one. Most computers do their arithmetic and processing with some form of binary manipulation.

Binary Coded Decimal (BCD) A form of coded character representation often used when alphanumeric data must be processed. Usually employs six binary bits per individual character of text. The typical character set provided by the scheme contains 64 or less characters. Extended BCD uses eight bits.

Bistable Device An electronic component, such as a switch, which may assume either one of two conditions or states. Transistors or their equivalent, as well as magnetic recording devices, can perform this function in the electronic computer. The use of bistable devices for speed and reliability suggests the use of binary manipulations, which also require only two states, 0 and 1, for arithmetic and other data-handling chores.

Bit A binary digit or position in a binary number. An abbreviation for binary digit.

Branch See Unconditional Branch and Conditional Branch.

Bug An error, in either computer hardware or software (programs). See Debug.

Byte A group of bits. A typical byte is defined as eight bits. A general method for rating the size of a memory device; e.g., a machine with a memory of 50,000, 8-bit bytes can store 400,000 bits. Byte sizes other than eight bits may be used in some machines or may be specified by the user in some installations. Alternate byte definitions may always be reduced to an equivalent number of binary bits for comparison. The use of the term byte, however, provides small numbers for comparison or discussion.

Carriage Control The control of the paper feed at a line printing device to single space, double space, eject a page, inhibit line feed, etc.

Cathode Ray Tube (CRT) The image-creating electronic component familiar in the home television set, which is also used in computer input/output terminals and similar devices for display purposes. The CRT may be used to display alphanumeric characters, charts, graphs, drawings, and other art forms, in either black and white or color and is a major component in the newer input/output devices.

Central Processing Unit (CPU) That computer hardware module which usually contains the arithmetic and control functions and sometimes the main high-speed memory of the computing system. Opposed to peripheral units such as auxiliary memory devices and input/output units.

Character One of a set of symbols acceptable to a given computing system for processing. One or more characters create a data field, or data element. Although each computer or communications device has its own acceptable character set, the character set for many devices is uniform so that they may be interconnected. Characters are usually numeric, alphabetic, or of a special type, such as a dollar sign.

Character Set Those numeric, alphabetic, and special characters acceptable to a given computer, or in particular, to a given programming language used in conjunction with a given computer.

COBOL Abbreviation for Common Business-Oriented Language. A form of high-level, user-oriented language, especially designed for file processing and special report generation, COBOL was fostered by the U.S. Department of Defense to gain some uniformity in government installations and to provide machine independence, i.e., to enable a given program to be run on the machines of several manufacturers. Now widely used in industry, the language is written in stylized English and is therefore to a large extent self-documenting, or understandable to non-programmers.

Coder Specifically, one who takes the logic or procedure of a given application or task and reduces it to the grammatical requirements of a programming language, thereby creating the specific program statements required. A coder is frequently not involved in the development of the logic or procedures he codes, but rather receives the required specifications from a systems analyst or programmer.

Collating Sequence A term usually associated with binary coded decimal character representation, or its equivalent. Since BCD codes have an equivalent numeric value, that number may be used to arrange or sort characters in a given order. That detailed order, which may vary from one machine to another, is the collation sequence for the particular installation.

Command See Executable Statement.

Compiler A specialized program which converts a user-oriented computer language through one or more steps into a machine language. The compiler often acts like an encyclopedia to generate many detailed instructions as the result of one user instruction. A different compiler is required for each computer language that may be used on a given machine. The purpose of each compiler is to match the user language to that machine language required by the given hardware—as well as to provide the user greater ease in program creation. The compiler makes a language machine independent, since it can convert a language, standardized at the user level, into the various detailed instructions required by different machines. BASIC, FORTRAN, and COBOL are compiler languages that are acceptable on many computers.

Computer Language One of several forms of user communication with the computer. Each computer language, such as BASIC, FORTRAN, or COBOL, has its own rules of grammar, conventions, commands, and detailed restrictions. Nevertheless, most computer languages have many common functional features, as for example, do English, German, and French. Thus, knowledge of one language usually aids greatly in mastering the details of another. See Machine Language, Compiler, Assembly Process.

Conditional Branch A program command which will alter the serial progression of program statement execution only when stated conditions are true. The conditional word "IF" is most frequently used to introduce such conditional branch statements, which may have one or more forms in a given language.

CPU See Central Processing Unit.

CRT See Cathode Ray Tube.

Cycle Time The time required to access a given memory location, read its contents, and to restore its contents, should the reading process be destructive (which is usually the case with magnetic core memories).

Data Those characters to be processed by a computer program. See Character, Item, Data Element, Field, File, Database.

Database A group of files from which specific desired categories of data may be drawn for processing. The term implies that the group of files is heavily cross-referenced, so that they are interrelated as a whole. Thus, a wide variety of information categories may be employed in extracting, manipulating, and reorganizing the data as desired. Sometimes called Databank.

Data Element One or more characters of data to be taken as an item or unit, e.g., the value of a variable provided by a data input. Sometimes called a field. Several data elements make up a record.

Data Error Mistaken input information which may be caused by erroneous specified values, communication malfunctions, or more likely by human transcription or input difficulties. Input editing of data, under program control, is frequently used to detect data errors. Obviously, a correct program can still produce erroneous results if its input data is erroneous.

Debug To find and correct logical errors in a program. In general, to remove mistakes.

Declarative Statement One which informs the computer's compilation programs of certain facts necessary to the compilation and translation process, especially facts concerning data input and output formats, the size of lists and tables that will appear in a computation, and similar details. A Declaration, or Declarative Statement, is not executed when the program itself is run. The opposite of an executed statement, often called a Command.

Define To provide a numeric value for a variable name. May be accomplished by reading data, by a substitution statement, by an input statement, or may be assumed; e.g., In some BASIC installations a variable is assumed, and therefore defined, to have the value zero unless otherwise stated. An undefined variable may not be processed, since its value would be unknown.

Delimiter A special character, often a comma or space, used to separate variable names or other items in a list, or to separate one string of characters from another, as in the separation of data elements. The semi-colon and quotation mark can also be used as delimiters in some cases.

Diagnostic Message A computer generated output as a consequence of the compilation process which informs the user that he has made one or more grammatical errors in program construction. Usually provided by most compilers that implement a given computer language. Since the diagnostics provided refer to language, not problem details, they cannot detect logical errors in a program's construction unless such errors are also of a grammatical type.

Digital In general, the term refers to computation which is discrete and proceeds by counting as opposed to measurement. See Analog. In particular, unless otherwise noted, digital refers to the number system with base 10, and the digits 0–9. A binary digit, or bit, refers to base two, or the binary number system, in which the allowable digits are 0 and 1.

Digital-Analog Conversion The opposite of Analog-Digital Conversion. The process by which a series of numbers is converted into a continuous signal or measurement, usually through some method of averaging, smoothing, or extrapolation. A necessary step when the output of a digital computer is to be used for the control of continuous processes, the generation of output graphics, etc.

Digital Computer The digital computer employs an internally stored program to sequence computational or processing steps without human intervention. Such internally stored programs make the digital computer a general purpose, rather than a specialized, machine. It is the program that specializes the general machine to the particular application. The digital computer operates by counting, rather than by measurement (analog computer).

Direct Access See Random Access.

Document As a verb, the act of detailing the assumptions, logic, and method by which a computer program was constructed, as well as its final form. Complete documentation of a program is desirable if it is widely used, or if it is to be used over a period of time. As a noun, an original or official paper used as the basis, proof, or support of anything else, especially original input or output entering or leaving a computer system in paper, or hard-copy, form.

EDP Abbreviation for Electronic Data Processing. Implies that an electronic computer is used in processing, and that there is no human intervention during processing. Same as ADP.

Electromechanical A term indicating that both electrical and mechanical components are used in combination in a given device. Usually implies that electronic devices are not employed. A telephone relay is an electromechanical device.

Errors One of many mistakes, difficulties, or malfunctions that may occur in the preparation of a computer program and its execution, including those involving data, hardware, or communications facilities. See Grammatical Error, Logical Error, Data Error, Machine Error, Round-Off Error, etc.

Executable Statement One which demands immediate action on the part of the computer when a program is run, e.g., READ. As opposed to a Declaration, or Declarative Statement, which provides information for compilation.

Family Concept A machine design philosophy which provides consistent connections between computer devices so that a variety of computing systems can be made by plug-in attachment of standardized equipment modules.

Field A subdivision of a record consisting of one or more characters. A data element.

File A collection of records, usually referring to a common subject, e.g., an employee file or an inventory file.

Fixed Record Length One of the characteristics of a set of records each of which has the same size, in particular the same number of characters in total, or to say the same thing, the same total field width including all the record's data elements. Records of this type are useful in financial, accounting, scientific, and similar applications where tabular input/output of limited numeric range is common.

Fixed Word Length Machine A computer designed so that the main memory, usually magnetic core, is laid out in fixed areas, or words, each containing a given set of binary bit positions. Each word may be referenced by its absolute address or by other address forms. See Absolute Address and Symbolic Address. Typically, the number of bits per word will be some power of 2, e.g., 16, or are divisible by a power of 2, e.g., 48 which is divisible by 8.

Floating Point Number A number which may have a fractional part, but which is expressed in exponential form, i.e., as a fixed-point number which gives the significant digits desired and a number indicating the position of the decimal (or radix) point. For example, 1.23E+3 is a floating point number taken to be 1230; the E+3 indicates the decimal point should be located, or floated, three places to the right, just as E–3 would have indicated a decimal point three places to the left. Equivalent to the form 1.23×10^3. Floating point representation permits a wide range of numbers to be expressed with a given number of significant places, a desirable feature in many scientific applications. A useful representation when the numeric value of a calculation's output is not known in advance, or cannot be estimated easily.

Flowchart A diagram which describes, at a given level of detail, the logical structure and processing sequence of a computer program. The flowchart focuses upon procedural tests and their conditional branching from the normal serial flow of action. A detailed flowchart will show the progression of each program statement; a summary flowchart may group statements into blocks or modules for ease of overall understanding. The latter may be known as a system flowchart, or an executive flowchart. Standardized symbols (circles, rectangles, diamonds, etc.) are employed to indicate the operations intended.

Format A specification of form, especially a detailed specification of character type, e.g., alphabetic or numeric, and a character count for the width of a record field. A record format contains the specifications for the fields within that record. Some computer languages, such as BASIC, provide an automatic format, using prespecified, or assumed, conventions, whereas other languages, such as FORTRAN, permit and require the user to specify input/output formats in complete detail. In general, the form of a publication and its style. Thus, the term may be applied also to the overall design of a report or other document. In the latter sense the specifying of a detailed format leads to the overall result.

FORTRAN Abbreviation for FORmula TRANslator. A user-oriented language especially designed for processing algebraic and scientific computations; in some cases used for business applications as well.

Generation (of computers) A term usually applied to the progression of electronic computers from those using vacuum tubes (first generation), to those using transistors (second generation), to those using integrated circuits (third generation), and to those using large scale monolithic circuits (fourth generation).

Grammatical Error A violation of the rules of use of a given computer language. Often such errors will be detected by the compiler as it converts the user's program statements into machine language. Diagnostic messages will then direct the user to his errors.

Hard Copy The output of a communication or computer device that appears on paper or similar permanent form, as opposed to temporary output such as that which might appear upon the face of a cathode ray tube terminal.

Hardware Physical components of a computing system.

Heuristic (From the Greek *heuriskein*, to discover) In computer terms, a method or procedure which is likely, but not guaranteed, to lead to a problem's solution. Often, heuristic programs rely upon a guided trial-and-error approach to problem solution—using rules of experience, rather than those of mathematical logic—to achieve a result.

High-Level Language Term generally applies to user-oriented computer languages which must be translated through several steps into the computer's own machine language before processing. As opposed to low-level, or machine, language.

Hybrid Mixed, of one or more forms. A computer composed of both analog and digital parts is a hybrid computer. A computer component constructed using more than one technology is a hybrid component, etc.

Input Device A unit which receives data and program steps from the user and converts the characters received to appropriate communication or computer codes for transmission, storage, and processing.

I/O Device An Input/Output Device I/O is a general abbreviation for input/output.

Instruction Repertoire The set of operations permitted by a given language, including input/output, arithmetic, data manipulation, and tests. Strictly speaking a machine's instruction repertoire refers to its machine, or hardware, instruction capabilities.

Integer Number A number without a fractional part; a whole number.

Interface That point in a system's design at which one unit or component connects to another, usually for the transfer of information, for example, the human–machine interface, hardware module interconnections, and the logical interconnection of program modules.

Item An arbitrary quantity of data treated as a unit; a data field, or data element. A general term, usually qualified for clarity, e.g., record item.

Jump See Conditional Branch and Unconditional Branch.

Justify See Right-Justify and Left-Justify.

Key With particular reference to the process of sorting records and extracting certain desired records from a file, the term *key* implies the specification of the characteristics which will describe the item desired, or the precedence of their desirability. In particular, a "search" or "sort" key provides a computer program with the detail required, by data field within a record, to select or compare the standard against the data available and implies one or more conditional tests or branches within the program using the key.

Key Punch A keyboard electromechanical device which prepares punched tabulating cards.

Left-Justify To cause a string of printed characters to be moved to the extreme left of a given field with any blanks appearing to the right. May also apply to descriptions of memory storage and internal computational operations.

Light Pen A device associated with cathode ray tube input/output units which permits graphical input to the computer by "drawing" upon the face of the tube.

Line Number An integer serial number which precedes each program statement in most time-sharing applications of a computer language. The line number is used both for sequencing program statements in proper order before compilation and execution, and for reference in non-serial program operations resulting from logical branches and their equivalent. See Statement Number.

Line Printer Usually a high-speed output device which prints one line at a time, rather than one character at a time, thereby greatly increasing potential computer output on paper. Sometimes used loosely to indicate any device which will print a line of output by any means.

Logical Error As opposed to a grammatical or a data error, a mistake in the problem-solving sequence stated in a computer program. In general, most computer languages and their associated compilers cannot protect the user against other than grammatical errors. The user may, however, use screening tests and experiments with test data to check for logical errors in a given program.

Low-Level Language A computer language which requires few, if any, translation steps before direct machine processing. A language similar to machine language, and therefore not usually user-oriented, nor machine independent.

Machine Error Those possible, although relatively infrequent, mistakes in a computer program's results which may be attributed to hardware difficulties originating within the computer, its memory devices, its peripheral devices, or its associated communication and remote terminal links. Sometimes communications errors may be separated from other forms of hardware errors.

Machine Independence The ability to run a program on the computers made by different manufacturers, or upon the various machines made by the same manufacturer. This often desired characteristic is usually provided by a compiler, which makes the appropriate translations from a standardized user language into the detailed machine instructions required for a given piece of equipment. In some cases machine independence leads to some inefficiency in a given machine's utilization, since many of its special hardware features may not be exploited by the general, higher level language the user employs. For this reason, in highly repetitive applications, or in those which must exploit every machine feature, lower level languages are sometimes used by experienced programmers.

Machine Language That form of symbolic communication with the machine which may be processed directly without compilation or translation. The lowest level language. Machine languages are typically specific to a particular class or type of computer and frequently are entirely numeric, thus difficult for a human to understand.

Machine Operator A person who handles the physical manipulations required to maintain operation of the central processing unit and the associated peripheral units at its location. At most installations, the machine operator is mainly concerned with mounting magnetic tapes, switching memory devices as needed, and restoring the system to operation in case of failures other than hardware malfunctions.

Machine-Oriented Language One that a machine can accept directly with little intermediate translation for processing.

Macro-Instruction A term which technically indicates a program statement at a higher level which generates more than one subsequent detailed program step for a single user statement. Although the term is restricted usually to a final language translation from symbolic to machine language, in reality most user-oriented languages may be thought of as dealing almost exclusively with macro-instructions.

Magnetic Card A form of magnetic memory, of the semirandom access type, in which plastic cards with a magnetic coating temporarily act as the coating for a small magnetic drum. In most devices of this kind, individual magnetic cards may be retrieved at random, but the information desired must thereafter be located by sequential search over the card's area. Very large data volumes may be handled inexpensively by such units.

Magnetic Character Reader An input device which can accept stylized characters, printed in special magnetic ink. The most familiar application is in the processing of bank checks, which have such characters printed across the lower edge. By extension, an input device that may also accept other forms of magnetically inscribed or recorded information, e.g., credit cards.

Magnetic Core A direct access memory device made up of many minute donuts of magnetic material. Each individual core may be used to store one binary bit. Usually the main working memory of most present computer designs. In the future, integrated circuit and similar alternate designs may displace the core memories now in use.

Magnetic Disk A semirandom access memory, similar to a record player, made from one or more rotating nonferrous plates each coated with a magnetic recording material. Usually, one or more movable reading and recording heads move about to locate desired information on the disks. In more expensive designs, fixed heads eliminate the mechanical search.

Magnetic Drum A semirandom access memory device consisting of a rotating nonferrous drum coated with magnetic material. READ/WRITE heads arrayed along the drum's axis handle information in selected tracks as the drum moves. In some designs the heads may be moved to access a wider area. Faster and more expensive than the magnetic disk, yet slower and less expensive than magnetic core memory.

Magnetic Recording and Reading Heads Small electrical components, similar to those found in the home tape recorder, but of greater precision and designed to handle greater recording densities, computer READ/WRITE heads are employed in most magnetic memories that have moving parts (tape units, card units, disks, drums, etc.).

Magnetic Tape A form of serial access memory media used to store large volumes of information inexpensively. The least expensive memory media.

Matrix Another name for an ordered table, or two-dimensional array. Implies the use of subscripted variables with two indices, the first representing the desired row, the second the desired column, of a table, e.g., in general has the form X(I,J).

Memory Device One of many devices, usually constructed to exploit the recording properties of magnetic materials, which store information for computer processing. See Magnetic Core, Magnetic Disk, Magnetic Card, Magnetic Drum, Magnetic Tape, etc.

Micro-Circuit A minute electronic device produced by bringing together in a single unit a number of transistors and other electronic components on one module or chip. Sometimes called an integrated circuit.

Micro-Programming A form of advanced program capability based upon the use of one small fast computer to control the operations of a larger somewhat slower one. Through a dual programming process, programs written for the small control computer can be used to set the machine language instruction repertoire of the larger machine unit. In this way, a given micro-programmed machine may be easily adjusted to duplicate the characteristics of another machine, so that programs written in machine language for other computers can be handled without reprogramming. Similarly, the same ability permits the user to, in effect, design his own machine for specialized purposes. The approach frees the user from inherent hardware constraints.

Microsecond One millionth of a second. Often abbreviated μs.

Millisecond One thousandth of a second. Abbreviated ms.

Mixed Mode A condition which exists when numbers of two different types, integer and real, are combined in an expression. Beginning languages, such as BASIC, permit mixed mode expressions; advanced languages, such as FORTRAN, often do not. By avoiding mixed mode expressions, greater machine efficiency and roundoff error control can be obtained; the user is burdened, however, with added programming constraints to maintain mode consistency.

Monolithic Circuit Another name for a large scale integrated circuit, or micro-circuit, containing many components. The term implies that a large number of components are manufactured as a whole unit, by advanced technology, as a single piece of material.

Multi-Processing A term which indicates that a computing system may be composed of several central processing units, each of which may be assigned a different function, or which may share functions. The objective of this approach is to better organize the computer system as a whole by utilizing a hierarchy of operations and control. In addition to greater system reliability, multi-processing permits portions of tasks to be carried out on different processors each most suited to the particular task. Multi-programming and micro-programming may be combined with Multi-processing in advanced systems. See Multi-Programming and Micro-Programming.

Multi-Programming A term which indicates that a computing machine may process several jobs concurrently. The objective of this approach is to utilize more effectively the computer's main memory device.

Nanosecond One billionth of a second. Abbreviated nsec.

Number System A specific method of counting used in a given case. For example, the decimal system uses the base 10 and represents numbers as powers of that base, or radix. Thus, the decimal number 123 is taken to mean $1 \times 10^2 + 2 \times 10^1 + 3 \times 10^0$. The number of available digits is the base less one, e.g., the digits 0–9 for the decimal system.

Octal A number system to the base, or radix, eight. The available numbers per character position are 0–7. One octal number is exactly equal to three binary bits, since 2^3 is 8.

Operation Specifically, one of the arithmetic operations permitted in a given computer language, e.g., add, subtract, multiply, divide, and exponentiate. In general, the term may apply to other arithmetic or data handling manipulations available in a given computer language.

Optical Reader A form of input device that will accept information from a typed, printed, or hand-written document for conversion into machine symbols and codes without manual keyboard operation. Optical readers use one of several photoelectric conversion devices to provide this direct reading ability.

Output Device A unit which displays or otherwise produces the results of computer processing for human understanding, direct control of subsequent processing operations, or provides intermediate storage of results for later use.

Overflow A technical term indicating that a number or result, usually as a consequence of a computation, is too large for a computer to handle in a given storage or memory location. Usually terminates the computation unless provision has been made in advance for handling this form of error.

Paper Tape An intermediate memory media often used in communication systems, especially in association with the Teletype, to permit a record to be made of keyboard input, either for security, for later transmission at high speed over the communication line, or to reproduce in machine readable form a computer's output. A relatively slow but inexpensive form of media. The mechanical limitations of punching holes in paper may be overcome in various ways, particularly when paper tapes are read by photoelectric rather than by mechanical means.

Parity Check A method that provides an additional binary bit position in a character's binary code structure (see BCD) so that checks of even or odd counts of "1's" within the character's representation may be used to confirm "equality" with that intended. Used to pick up electrical and mechanical malfunctions in the communication and computing system. A check may be made for an even number of "1's" (even parity), or for an odd number of "1's" (odd parity). The user is seldom concerned with such checks, since they are automatic features of most communication and computer equipment.

Picosecond One-thousandth of a nanosecond, i.e., 10^{-12} seconds. Abbreviated psec.

Precision In computer terms, the number of significant figures expressed in a given number, either in input, output, or during a computation; the exactness with which a quantity is stated. Two decimal digits 00–99 provide the discrimination between 100 items, whereas three decimal digits 000–999 provide the discrimination between 1000. The latter is a more precise discrimination. Precision should not be confused with accuracy, which is the quality of being correct. Computers produce results which have high precision and give the illusion of accuracy; only user confirmation of results in a given case can assure both.

Program A sequence of steps to be performed by the computer, written in one of several possible computer languages. See Routine.

Programmer One who converts the details of a problem's solution into a particular computer language, or computer program. Distinction is often made in practice between individuals who produce the logic required for problem solution and those who then convert that logic into the grammar of the given language. The latter step in programming is sometimes known as coding; the individual who performs the last detailed step, a coder.

Radix See Base.

Random Access The ability to go directly to a specific memory location which may be specified at random. Opposite of Serial Access.

Random Number A statistical term referring to a set of numbers, each of which is unrelated by any test which can be applied to its set members. In particular, many computer languages (or their local implementation) provide for functions to generate such a series of numbers, the most prevalent form of which produces a sequence of numbers lying in the 0–1 range with equal probability, i.e., a uniform distribution. Technically, since the computer must generate random numbers by a known method, the numbers produced are often called pseudo-random numbers. The numbers so generated are not in fact random, but will serve that purpose for most applications.

Read-Only Memory A memory device containing permanent reference information which may not be altered during processing. Memory of this type may be wired into the hardware, provided by optical media, or consist of a segment of core or other magnetic memory which is not altered.

Real Number A number which may have a fractional part and a decimal point, or its equivalent. As opposed to an integer.

Record A group of information detail consisting of one or more fields, usually descriptive of a given item, e.g., an employer, a product, a customer. One or more characters create a field; one or more fields a record; one or more records a file; and one or more files a database.

Relation In a computer language, a relation refers to the various test conditions, e.g., those associated with a "IF-type" statement, which are allowed. For example, the six relations permitted in the BASIC language are: equal to, not equal to, greater than or equal to, less than or equal to, less than, and greater than, which symbolically are expressed as =, <>, >=, <=, <, and >, respectively.

Remote Batch Processing As the term implies, the user may save up several jobs or many data values and execute all of this work at once, or in a batch, from a location remote from the central processor. Usually special terminals are provided for high-speed input/output when remote batching is used. The user does not expect instantaneous response by this method but must usually wait several minutes or hours for his answers. The objective of this approach is to utilize communication and computing facilities to a greater extent than is usually possible in real-time processing, which requires computational time for sharing user demands, as well as extra memory space for more complex supervisory control routines.

Remote Terminal A computer device which may be located some distance from the main computing facility. Usually employed for input/output operations either by a human user or for automatic data collection and output control. However, a remote terminal may itself be a computer which pre-processes information going to the main machine, or post-processes information coming from it. A hierarchy of remote terminal organization is possible and in current use.

Right-Justify To cause a string of printed characters to be moved to the extreme right of a given field, with any blanks appearing to the left. May also apply to descriptions of memory storage and internal computational operations. As opposed to Left-Justify.

Round The process of converting a real number to one of a lower precision according to a fixed rule which takes account of the discarded remainder. Usually the rule is to increase the least significant digit of the final answer by one if the remainder starts with a digit five or greater, and not otherwise. By this rule 1.234 is 1.23, whereas 1.235 is taken as 1.24 to two decimal places. Other rules may also be used.

Round-Off Error That error introduced in the conversion of numbers with fractional parts from one number system to another, or by the necessity for limiting the number of places to the right of a decimal point (or its equivalent), or when a large integer number must be reduced to floating point form with a limited number of significant digits.

Routine A perfected computer program, in which all the statements are in order for the processing of a particular job. Sometimes used synonymously for program, but more precise, implying a working program.

Semi-Random Access The method of locating information in memory which combines in the search for the desired item some form of direct access, usually followed by a limited sequential search. See Magnetic Drum, Magnetic Disc, Magnetic Card.

Serial (or Sequential) Access That method of memory access which requires search through a number of records to find the one desired. Magnetic tape is a memory media which requires serial access. Compare searching for information on a scroll (Serial Access) to searching for information in a card file (Random Access). Does not require physical addressing for location, uses comparisons instead. Use of serial, e.g., tape, media usually requires presorting, or ordering of records for all files used in a given application to avoid lengthy delays required for random search through a serial file. As opposed to Random Access.

Significant Figure The number of places in a number which may be relied upon. A distinction should be made between the apparent number of significant positions in a number, and those which are meaningful. Assuming that the numbers shown are correct, or accurate, each of the following contains three significant figures: 123, 1.23, .123, 1.23E+3, 1.23E–3, the latter two forms being examples of floating point or exponential representation in computer language.

Simulation Technically, a form of computer program which seeks to produce results which model a process or activity, and which may therefore be used for predictive purposes. Several specialized computer languages have been designed to handle this form of application.

Software Often used as a collective term, to indicate a group of programs, including a computer's supervisory routines, required to operate a given installation. The term refers to those logical rules of operation provided by symbolic structure and contained in one or more computer programs.

Sort To put items of like kind together. In popular use, the term generally refers to categories ordered by a fixed rule, e.g., according to alphabetic sequence from A–Z, or in numeric sequence 0–9, etc., in which case sorting provides ordering.

Statement A program line which states one logical step in a computer program. A general term, which may be more specific by qualified reference. See Executable Statement, Declarative Statement, Command.

Statement Number A number prefixed to a program statement so that it may be referenced by one or more program statements. In most languages, statement numbers need not be shown for non-referenced statements, especially when punched card input is employed. See Line Number.

Stored Function Sometimes called a library function. One of several arithmetic operations specified for a given computer language which will produce a single result given one or more numeric values as arguments, or dependent variable values. Provided by the computer language's compiler, and not created by the user. See User-Defined Function.

Stored Program A term indicating that the computer internally stores the user's program in one of its memory devices before execution. The stored program concept distinguishes an electronic computer from a calculator, which does not employ stored programs.

String A set of characters which constitutes a field, or a logical set of data. In a continuous series of characters, one intended string is differentiated from another by a delimiting character. See Delimiter. A typical string is a group of data characters supplied to a computer program for later manipulation.

Substitution Statement A program command which substitutes the numeric value of an expression for the value of a stated variable. Such statements, of the form LET C = A + B, may contain only one variable to the left of the "=" symbol. If the same variable appears on both sides of the "=" symbol, as in LET N = N + 1, the numeric value of the variable named on the right is considered the "old" value, that on the left the "new" value. Substitution is not to be confused with an equation; it is a memory updating operation. Some texts show a substitution in flowcharts by the symbol "←" to avoid the equality confusion, e.g., N ← N + 1.

Supervisory Software Those specialized control programs which usually reside permanently in a computer's main memory device to control the flow and processing of different jobs, or applications programs. Various synonyms, such as system software, supervisory routines, etc., exist.

Symbolic Address A symbolic reference to a given memory location which is translated into an absolute address by the computer using an internally constructed dictionary during the compile-assembly sequence of translation from a user's language into machine language.

Symbolic Language A term generally applied to that form of user programming intermediate between a compiler, or user-oriented language, and machine language. A symbolic translation can be obtained as an intermediate output upon user's request in the compiler to machine language sequence (at most installations). Unlike the higher level compiler languages, a symbolic language usually corresponds step-by-step to the actual machine processing detail. Thus, symbolic languages are usually machine dependent. They provide for the experienced user a check on the translation process, and may also be used for program construction in highly repetitive jobs to exploit the features of particular hardware configurations. See Assembly Process.

System Command A user's instruction, not part of any programming language, which calls for control action by the computer's resident supervising programs, or system. In most time-sharing installations using on-line terminals, a system command is not preceded by a line number, thereby distinguishing it from a program statement, which requires a preceding line number.

Systems Analyst An individual who devotes his time to problem formulation or the diagnosis and improvement of present operations. The specifications developed by such analysts are then given to a programmer for detailed implementation.

Test Data Data especially created to test the operation of a given program. Often selected to test extreme cases, complex test action, and input/output accuracy. Usually, one or more hand-computer results, or otherwise known results, will be associated with test data so the program under test may be validated.

Time-Sharing The mutual and simultaneous use by many persons of a single computing facility so the high speed capacity of a computer can be matched to the slower input/output capabilities of the uses. Often results in "conversational" interaction of user and computer because of speed, and permits the costs of computer operation to be spread over a number of users.

Trace To follow the changing numeric values of one or more variables in a computer program so that the program's detailed action may be followed in detail. See Debug.

Unconditional Branch A program command which always alters the serial execution of program statements by jumping the sequence of execution either forward or backward in the order of progression. The imperative "GO TO" is most frequently associated with such statements.

Unit Record A record which may be handled as an individual unit for processing. For example, the information contained on one punched card.

User-Defined Function As opposed to a stored, or library, function, one which is specified by a user in his program. After it has been specified, a user-defined function may be used by reference to its name, often following the same rules in most languages as for a stored function. The exact rules of specification follow the rules of a given computer language.

User-Oriented Language One that permits a user to employ terms and grammar often in the vocabulary of his own job or specialty in program construction.

Variable Record Length Implies a set of records, all of which are not of the same length, or of the same character count, or of the same field format specification. Typical of business application, e.g., a file of names and addresses, in which each name or address may be of differing length. Another common form of variable record is one in which a variable number of field repetitions may occur, e.g., the number of item lines included in a customer order will depend upon the number of distinct items ordered, etc.

Variable Word Length Machine A computer with a main memory layout usually in character modules so that words of varying length may be stored efficiently without wasting memory space.

Vector Another name for an ordered list, or single-dimensional array. Implies the use of subscripted variables with one index, e.g., X(I).

Voice Output A form of audible computer output usually consisting of numbers, phrases, or tone sounds put together from a limited vocabulary or list by computer sequencing of recorded possibilities. Such devices permit the computer to deliver answers by the spoken word. Used for credit checks, stock quotes, file inquiry, etc. Makes any telephone or similar device a computer output unit.

Index

(Page numbers in italic type refer to illustrations.)

F G H I J